Liquor and the Liberal State

Liquor and the Liberal State

Drink and Order before Prohibition

DAN MALLECK

© UBC Press 2022

All rights reserved. No part of this publication may be reproduced, stored in a retrieval system, or transmitted, in any form or by any means, without prior written permission of the publisher, or, in Canada, in the case of photocopying or other reprographic copying, a licence from Access Copyright, www.accesscopyright.ca.

30 29 28 27 26 25 24 23 22   5 4 3 2 1

Printed in Canada on FSC-certified ancient-forest-free paper (100% post-consumer recycled) that is processed chlorine- and acid-free.

Library and Archives Canada Cataloguing in Publication

Title: Liquor and the liberal state : drink and order before prohibition / Dan Malleck.
Names: Malleck, Dan, author.
Description: Includes bibliographical references and index.
Identifiers: Canadiana (print) 20220132747 | Canadiana (ebook) 20220134588 |
    ISBN 9780774867160 (hardcover) | 9780774867177 (softcover) |
    ISBN 9780774867184 (PDF) | ISBN 9780774867191 (EPUB)
Subjects: LCSH: Drinking of alcoholic beverages – Government policy –
    Canada – History. | LCSH: Drinking of alcoholic beverages – Government
    policy – Ontario – History. | LCSH: Liquor laws – Canada – History. |
    LCSH: Liquor laws – Ontario – History. | LCSH: License system –
    Canada – History. | LCSH: License system – Ontario – History. |
    LCSH: Prohibition – Canada – History. | LCSH: Prohibition –
    Ontario – History. | LCSH: Liberalism – Canada – History. |
    LCSH: Liberalism – Ontario – History.
Classification: LCC HV5087.C3 M35 2022 | DDC 364.1/730971—dc23

Canada

UBC Press gratefully acknowledges the financial support for our publishing program of the Government of Canada (through the Canada Book Fund), the Canada Council for the Arts, and the British Columbia Arts Council.

This book has been published with the help of a grant from the Canadian Federation for the Humanities and Social Sciences, through the Awards to Scholarly Publications Program, using funds provided by the Social Sciences and Humanities Research Council of Canada.

UBC Press
The University of British Columbia
2029 West Mall
Vancouver, BC V6T 1Z2
www.ubcpress.ca

This book is dedicated to my friend, erstwhile editor, and occasional drinking buddy Melissa Pitts.

Contents

List of Tables and Figures / ix

Preface and Acknowledgments / xi

Introduction: Arguing over Liquor and Liberalism / 3

Part 1: Managing the Province's Liquor Problem

1 The Place of the Government in the Drinks of the People / 21

2 Centralization, I: The Crooks Act / 46

3 Power and Influence in the New System / 64

4 Politics, Law, and the License Branch / 96

Part 2: The Complications of Liquor in a Federal Liberal State

5 How Drinking Affects the Constitution, 1864–83 / 117

6 McCarthy and Crooks Enter a Tavern, 1883–85 / 141

7 Attempting to Water Down the Scott Act, 1884–92 / 158

8 Plebiscites as Tools for Change? 1883–94 / 172

9 Talking and Blocking National Prohibition, 1891–99 / 197

10 Dodging Decisions at the End of the Liberals' Era, 1894–1905 / 234

11 Drinking in Whitney's Conservative Liberal State, 1905–07 / 257

12 Centralization, II: Beyond the Crooks Act, 1907–16 / 295

Conclusion: Liquor, Liberalism, and the Legacy of the Crooks Act / 309

Appendix 1: Questions Sent by the Select Committee / 321

Appendix 2: Liquor-Related Laws in Force in Ontario / 325

Notes / 327

Index / 375

Tables and Figures

TABLES

1.1 "Class" of correspondents contacted by the Select Committee / 35
3.1 Licenses granted and refused after passage of the Crooks Act / 80
5.1 Crooks Act and McCarthy Act compared / 136
9.1 Results of the dominion prohibition plebiscite, 1898 / 222
11.1 Minimum license fees for taverns (categorized by population) / 273
11.2 Local option votes, 1904–14 / 282

FIGURES

3.1 "Off with his head! 'Richard III' as played by Mr. Crooks throughout the province," *Grip*, 6 May 1876 / 79
6.1 "The smart boy takes a tumble," *Grip*, 2 May 1885 / 144
7.1 The Scott Act in Ontario (map) / 160
9.1 Licenses issued and liquor consumed throughout the Scott Act period, 1873–90 / 206
11.1 "Welcome to Whitney," *Telegram*, 8 February 1905 / 259

11.2 "There's no place like home," *Telegram*, 16 February 1905 / 260
11.3 Increase in local option areas, 1905–14 / 282
13.1 Change in liquor consumption in Ontario, 1868–1914 / 310

Preface and Acknowledgments

I hadn't intended to write this book. All I wanted to know was whether the spectre of the saloon that haunted post-prohibition liquor regulation was mythical or actual. Yet the further I dug, the deeper the story became. My first attempt to understand the liquor landscape was following the increasingly restrictive liquor licensing laws, a project that resulted in a presentation in Bristol, England, at a conference on the Victorian pub organized by the inestimable Pam Lock. The group must have wondered why a Canadian talking about taverns in such a (literally) provincial context was in their midst, and I thank Pam and the attendees for their patience, camaraderie, and feedback. The Drinking Studies Network and other booze historians in the United Kingdom are inspirational and welcoming, and I look forward to seeing them again after this pandemic has ended. James Kneale, James Nicholls, David Beckingham, Deb Toner, Annemarie McAllister (who will not like what I say about temperance here), and so many others: we shall yet have those pints together.

Laws are not formed in a vacuum, so as I learned about the legal framework I needed to understand what drove it. Clearly, it wasn't just about temperance, because by the 1880s the temperance movement advocated prohibition, yet liquor licensing laws were not prohibition. So understanding the richer and more complex context in which the licensing process expanded led me on a much longer and more intricate adventure. It also allowed me to present more of my work to colleagues in the United Kingdom and beyond. And when I realized, halfway through writing this book, that there was a bigger story, one about the liberal state,

I introduced it to a number of audiences who must have wondered why this guy was talking about the liberal order framework as if he had just discovered it. I had. I'm not a "Canadianist"; I'm a historian of alcohol and drugs whose material is from Canada. Familiarizing myself with the Canadian liberal state/liberal order literature required entering a whole new historical landscape; if I have altered it at all, I hope I have done so well.

As an accidental project, the research was unfunded and incremental, and I was surprised at how long it took and how far it went. Few records exist from the pre-prohibition License Branch, so I absorbed them and kept going. As the project proceeded, I found other bits of evidence in unexpected places. I thank the archivists at the Archives of Ontario for respecting my rambling inquiries and for the interesting conversations about the spottiness of preservation in Ontario's early political history; most especially thanks to Serge Paquet, who fielded many of my requests. Any new scholar who reads this book should be reminded that the archivist is your best friend, and you should not be shy about asking weird questions about sources. Archivists know their stuff and like it when you want to use it.

My thanks to research assistants and inspiring students Melissa LePine and Kaitlyn Carter. Melissa worked through many hundreds of newspaper articles and assorted archival records, a process that led her to pursue a degree in library and information sciences. Her research assistance was experiential work that led to a promising career. Kaitlyn had the unappealing but essential task of assembling import, export, and excise records that helped me to track alcohol consumption over the period in question. I don't want to think that this project led her to pursue a master's degree in history that had as little connection to tables, graphs, and Excel files as possible, but it is entirely likely.

The map in this book was kindly designed by Sharon Janzen at Brock University's map library. I thank her for her expert navigation of my awkward data and the quick turnaround. What we have now is far superior to the map I have been using at conferences: it's professional, scalable, and accurate. The two cartoons from the *Toronto Telegram* were accessed in the midst of the third wave of the pandemic through the efforts of Beau Levitt at the Toronto Reference Library. That sentence does not capture how many administration and library access issues he had to deal with before getting those two images to me.

I also thank the often unsung heroes of modern historical research, the digitizers and microfilmers. I imagine copying and digitizing as monotonous and thankless work, so I thank you. All I know about you can be gleaned from images of your hands holding down the pages of the documents you copied. Know that those years of work and the probable repetitive strain injuries continue to help us uncover the past.

This book covers a long period and a broad geography, but I have to acknowledge what it does not cover and nod to the limits that could and should be part of a separate project. This book is mostly about "Old Ontario," the southern swath that was the earlier location of European settlement. "New Ontario," what we might now call northern and northwestern Ontario, opened up during the period under examination, but the licensing arrangements were much more obscure and tempered by corporate interests (mining and logging camps had specific rules about drinking) and prejudice about Indigenous people and alcohol. Adding that complex layer to this project probably would have increased it by fifty percent, and I don't think my editors would have liked that. (It would be a great research project for someone.) I also do not discuss the operation of hotels that received "beer and wine" licenses. These licenses were created soon after the Crooks Act passed, allowing hotels to sell what were often considered less problematic alcoholic beverages rather than spirits, but few establishments took such licenses. Thus there was little discussion of these types of licensees in the material I consulted.

It is important to add a brief word on language. In the period under examination, most members of what we call "the temperance movement" had begun to adopt the argument that only the total suppression of the liquor trade would solve the problems they saw with drink. They were therefore prohibitionists, and for the most part, I use the terms "temperance supporter" and "advocate" interchangeably with the term "prohibitionist." For both I use the term "Drys," which captures the idea of people who were opposed to drink. In a similar way, people who were members of the liquor industry, from manufacturing on down to tavern keepers, were "Wets." Those who criticized temperance ideas but were not self-identified as engaged in the liquor industry were neither Wets nor Drys, but rather moderates, or simply citizens who were making interesting arguments. Labelling gets tricky in this period, and indeed some Drys might characterize all their opponents as "the liquor men" even if they had nothing to do with the trade (or were not men). To add to the confusion, some moderates positioned themselves as advocates of "true temperance" but distanced themselves from what they saw was an overly restrictive temperance-cum-prohibition movement. It gets complicated.

Although this project proceeded without financial support, it was facilitated by personal assistance. Members of the Beer Club (Terry, Val, Karen, Adam, Becca, Will, and Deb), a motley collection of health scholars dedicated to the development of innovative ideas and the consumption of inebriating beverages, provided much needed moral support through some tough moments. They also approved of the socialization represented in the cover image. The various UBC Press staff who have worked with me have consistently and cheerfully supported the ebbs and flows of this project. Thank you Darcy Cullen, James MacNevin, Karen Green, Megan Dyer, Katrina Petrik, and Carmen Tiampo. With so many different overlapping aspects, I found this book especially difficult to bring to fruition. Their guidance and input has been fundamental to helping me make this expansive story coherent, and look good, too.

Even more essential was the support of Bonnie Tompkins. She endured many of my angst-ridden complaints about the absence of sources and then complaints about reading so many damned newspapers. Our serene canine companion Honey, now departed, often sat silently waiting for the next walk, or lay beside me as I dozed and pondered next steps. Recent addition Penny the pandemic puppy has had little patience for such musings but certainly has added much needed distraction, as puppies tend to do. Zeeba the cat has had no productive effect on this book whatsoever, unless physically inserting herself between me and what I was reading can be considered productive.

This book is dedicated to Melissa Pitts, my former editor, current press director, and friend. The dedication is not just a symbolic nod to our decade-long friendship but also an acknowledgment that in some ways this project was inspired by her enthusiasm for my work. Often when uncovering some funny story or fascinating anecdote, I would think, "wait until Melissa hears this," and if occasionally I wrote something I thought especially clever I'd think, "Melissa is going to love that." And later she reminded me how a good editor can be a value-added friend, because she ripped apart chapters I thought were decent while telling me something I thought was horrible wasn't so bad. So this book has been encouraged by her and dedicated to her approving nod. I'm sure many of her authors have been similarly inspired.

As always, any mistakes are mine alone, but maybe they were intentional. That will keep you guessing.

Liquor and the Liberal State

Introduction:
Arguing over Liquor and Liberalism

Liquor complicates liberalism. Poised on the pillars of freedom, equality, and property, the liberal state has confronted few challenges so intractable as those presented by the pursuit of distraction through intoxication. The individual's right to self-determination is fundamental to liberalism, as is the role of the state in removing impediments to achieve that freedom. But when some people see it as their right to pursue alcohol-induced recreation, and others view that distraction as an impediment to their ability to realize true freedom, how should the state respond? What does a government do with an industry that allows individuals freely to indulge in ethereal amusements that may drain the family resources and lead to drunkenness and disorder? And even if you accept as legitimate the state's role of regulating such an industry, what about regulating the activities of the people? How do we balance the rights of the individual against the rights of the overall population? Is it appropriate to constrain an industry because some of its customers might overuse its product? Is it appropriate for a liberal state to impose something so illiberal as prohibition of an industry on people who want to consume that industry's products? Is outright prohibition even possible? What, then, is the role of the liberal state in managing the activities, recreation, and pleasures of the individual?

As in many places in the last half of the nineteenth century, the residents of the province of Ontario wrestled with these questions either indirectly or directly, repeatedly, and sometimes with passionate intensity. Some of the discussions were local, parochial, and limited in their impacts on the broader society, whereas others were fundamental, reaching into the heart of what kind of society would emerge from the framework of the British North America (BNA) Act. More than just affecting the drinking behaviours or consumer choices of everyday people, the liquor issue helped to shape fundamentally the role of governments in the newly formed country. It was central to key arguments about the powers deployed at different levels of government, from municipal councils whose neighbourhoods experienced the direct impacts of looser or tighter licensing restrictions to the provincial and dominion governments that were charged, within their constitutionally defined realms of authority, with overseeing different elements of the liquor trade. Many of these arguments also reached to more profound considerations of the nature of democracy in the new country, the degree of intervention a government (or governments) should be allowed to have in the lives of individual residents, and what such involvement in people's lives said about the form of liberal democracy being developed in this Dominion of Canada. In both subtle and overt ways, liquor had a tremendous impact on the development of the country.

Some of this impact was constitutional.[1] The BNA Act assigned specific authorities to provinces and others to the dominion (federal) government. These authorities often overlapped. For example, section 92(9) of the Constitution specifically granted provinces the right to license taverns for revenue purposes, but section 91(2) assigned the authority over trade and commerce to the dominion government. This was one of several areas of jurisdictional fuzziness that often required judicial interpretation. Indeed, the first case heard by the Supreme Court of Canada, legislated into existence just under a decade after the country was formed, involved the rights of the provinces to require breweries to hold a provincial license.[2] Subsequent cases sought to define provincial and federal jurisdictions relating to the licensing, manufacture, and sale of liquor. The precedents set by such decisions, sometimes confirmed and sometimes overturned by the final court of appeal, the Judicial Committee of the Privy Council, at the jurisprudential heart of the empire, resonated well beyond the seemingly narrow confines of section 92(9). As John Saywell has argued, decisions related to liquor made by the Judicial Committee, a group of lords (ideally) with legal expertise and several judges, ultimately limited the extensive federal authority that the authors of the Constitution had intended.[3] These limits joined other changes at the end of the century to complicate dominion-provincial jurisdictions.[4]

More of the impact of liquor on the operations of the state was local, cultural, and philosophical. From the beginning of the 1870s into the second decade of the twentieth century, municipal governments, businesspeople, temperance advocates, ministers, politicians, and everyday residents debated whether, how, and to what extent the state should interfere with the lives of the people. Part of this debate emerged from an absence in the British North America Act itself: prior to Confederation, municipalities had the right to issue licenses to sell liquor to taverns, saloons, and shops.[5] But the BNA Act did not designate powers to municipalities: it conferred no rights or authorities on any political unit smaller than a province or territory. It did specify, however, that laws in force at the time of Confederation would remain in effect until a legislature chose to change them, and this included laws governing municipalities. As a result, until the government of Ontario decided to look at the system of liquor distribution across the province, municipal councils had the authority to issue licenses, collect fees, and enforce the provisions of the Act Respecting Tavern and Shop Licenses. Local licensing soon became problematic, and in the 1870s the provincial government, urged by concerned citizens to do something about what many saw as rampant drunkenness, decided to change how liquor licenses were distributed, thus taking more direct control over the administration of the law. This single act of oversight engaged the provincial government in an ongoing and increasingly complex regulatory project. Its effects are still felt today.

This book traces those changes. The original question driving this research was a simple one: How different was the liquor licensing system before Ontario's experiment with prohibition (1916–27) from the one that replaced prohibition and created the Liquor Control Board of Ontario? It emerged from my work on post-prohibition liquor control and admits a blind spot in the history of liquor licensing.[6] Historians often divide the liquor system in North America into three separate periods: pre-prohibition, post-prohibition, and (of course) prohibition. The latter period has received the bulk of attention, driven no doubt by the salacious stories of rum running, gangsters, violence, and subversive partying, along with a general incredulity that an entire society would ever ban liquor.[7] Reproduced in popular culture, mass media, and casual conversations, this perception usually appears as characterizations of the period either as some kind of collective madness or as policy decisions driven by a retrograde evangelical temperance movement that somehow got its hands on the levers of power. The story, of course, is much more complicated, and such generalizations do no justice and give no credit to the people and the period under investigation. Although the reasons that prohibition became law are addressed only briefly at the end of this book, the long period of licensing, increasing regulations on liquor, constraints on where it could be sold and consumed, discussions of different ways to manage the liquor traffic, and indeed questions about the role of the state in the lives of the people, illustrate how prohibition was not the result of episodic madness but simply one of several options for how best to deal with the complications of liquor.

Although recognizing that the impetus for prohibition was more complicated, nuanced, and socially popular than some might appreciate, this book is decidedly not an apology for the temperance movement. It is true that the vocal and passionate advocates of temperance (the "Drys") were progressives who saw the elimination of the liquor traffic as a major step toward creating a utopia, or a Kingdom of God on Earth. They saw their efforts as benign attempts to elevate the downtrodden and represent the wishes (so they thought) of the disadvantaged. But theirs was not necessarily a hegemonic vision. Many people, often a majority of residents, disagreed with, or at least did not fall in lockstep behind, the Drys. One thing often overlooked in the historical record of the temperance movement is that its adherents were often more idealistic than pragmatic. Faced with the challenges of implementing prohibition, and repeated arguments that it would be difficult to enforce any law that constrained an activity that many people enjoyed and that would result in a tremendous loss of government revenue, many temperance leaders simply shrugged and said that the government would figure it out. Once prohibition was enacted, they reasoned, all would be better. Faced with examples of various experiments with prohibition that had not worked, they simply argued that it had not yet been given enough of a chance or that it was not a well-conceived version of the ideal form: the *total suppression* of the liquor traffic. Faced with the argument that many people who did not support complete prohibition were also not rapacious representatives of the drink industry or slobbering drunks, prohibitionists doubled down on righteousness; because they saw the world through the binary of "you're either with us or against us." If you were not a teetotaller, you were part of the problem. And, faced with persistent and unequivocal examples of alternative and enforceable ways to mitigate the damage done by an unfettered liquor industry (in effect by fettering that industry), prohibitionists simply said that there could be no compromise with liquor, which would be tantamount to compromise with the devil. Reading the many letters, articles, and testimonials of temperance adherents who pushed for nothing less than the total suppression of the liquor traffic, I realized that these adherents clung to a vision of the role of the state guided by the ideal of a moral society rather than the reality of practical policy making, a bloody-mindedness that made them both righteous and unrealistic.[8] Opponents could, and did, characterize (and caricature) them as irrational individuals dismissive of the messiness of governing in a pluralistic liberal state.[9]

More profoundly, the arguments for and against prohibition revealed an aspect of the liquor question that altered the direction of my research: everyone seemed to be articulating different views of the role of government in the liberal state. Prohibitionists wanted to destroy the liquor traffic because it interfered with the idea of individual freedom. Thereby they would liberate people from the bondage of liquor and allow them to be truly free to pursue a moral life. Opponents of prohibition, many of whom were either moderate drinkers or even abstainers, countered with their own vision of liberty, one in which the state played as little a role as possible in the lives and industriousness of the people and in which the individual was free to pursue his or her own enjoyment and make his or her own mistakes. They rejected the images of the predatory liquor dealer and an unwitting victim, preferring to see the debate to be about constraints upon a legitimate industry that could flourish and enrich the nation, and restrictions on the autonomous individual who could choose whether or not to consume its products. The discussions about liberalism were also discussions about the appropriate constraints on the use of individual property. Ideally, the government would place as little restriction as possible on the activities of industries, but by the end of the nineteenth century, governments were taking a more active role regulating problematic businesses.[10] The state was expanding, but to what degree it would interfere in the lives of individuals and industries remained the topic of intense discussion.

Prohibitionists, many of whom professed evangelical Christian beliefs, claimed to have God on their side; opponents of prohibition drew from other ideals. John Stuart Mill was no god, but he was certainly the patron saint of liberalism. In *On Liberty,* he criticized arguments about liquor prohibition in the United States and the push for overly restrictive liquor laws in Great Britain. Mill contended that private consumption of fermented beverages was an individual act and not within the purview of the state. Moreover, he noted that even though the state did have the authority to regulate "social acts" (such as selling liquor), such regulation encroached on a private, individual act (drinking that liquor) and was therefore contrary to liberalism.[11] Mill also argued that few people would want their recreational activities to be regulated by the "religious and moral sentiments of the stricter Calvinists and Methodists."[12] Indeed,

Mill viewed the tendency of some reformers to zero in on the activities of others as incredibly dangerous to the liberal state. He argued that the idea that "every other individual shall act in every respect exactly as they ought, that whosoever fails thereof in the smallest particular ... violates my social right," was "far more dangerous than any single interference with liberty; there is no violation of liberty which it would not justify."[13] Clearly troubled by the tendency among zealous religious types to push their views on others, he asked whether people whose liberty was interfered with in that way would not "desire these intrusively pious members of society to mind their own business."[14] Such arguments, whether directly or indirectly linked to his words, were at the heart of resistance to the "intrusively pious" temperance movement, a resistance that saw such zealousness to be antithetical to the rational individual on whom the liberal state depended to operate effectively.[15]

Liberalism and the liberal state in Canada have been topics of considerable investigation in the past few decades. Spurred especially by Ian McKay's contribution to a *Canadian Historical Review* forum on "The Liberal Order Framework," historians have interrogated the various ways that liberalism has been debated and implemented or rejected in the long history of the northern part of North America. McKay argued that "the category 'Canada' should ... denote a historically specific project of rule" and that, rather than defining Canada as a single entity, historians would be better advised to consider it as the "implantation and expansion ... of a certain political-economic logic ... liberalism."[16] How liberalism functioned and how it was shaped within a Canadian context are important factors when interrogating this project of rule. Subsequent works have sought to engage with McKay's manifesto, either critiquing or expanding its stated mission for historians. The liberal order framework provides this book with a strong conceptual tool. It is especially useful in two ways: first because McKay's call to action is about the idea of Canada as a manifestation of liberalism; second because the "framework" is about order. The liberal order was interested in an orderly society within a country whose government's key role was "peace, order and good government." Concern about disorder was the impetus for the Ontario government to take a more active role in liquor regulation. Debates about the role of the liberal state in a context shadowed by very real concerns about constructing an orderly society are important ways to understand the liberal order. Indeed, many of the constitutional debates that wrestled with the authority of dominion or provincial governments to legislate liquor engaged with the complexity of liberalism itself.

Seizing on the liberal order framework, many historians have offered nuances, modifications, contradictions, and comparisons that help us to see the various forms of liberalism and the different ways in which the liberal state might operate. For example, some historians, following McKay, have emphasized the role of the state in protecting property and facilitating capitalist accumulation.[17] Others have focused on the "liberty" part of liberalism, exploring in some depth how that liberty was contested, confirmed, and protected.[18] As Philip Girard puts it, "this renewed interest in liberal*ism* in Canada's past did not give rise to much discussion of liber*ty*."[19] Liberty was central to the idea of Canada, but, as Michel Ducharme has indicated, it was a specific type of liberty. In his pathbreaking study on the idea of liberty in Canada between the American Revolution and the Rebellions of 1837–38, Ducharme explores two versions of liberty at play. Liberal revolutionaries articulated a "republican" liberty centred on the sovereignty of the legislature and captured in the catchphrase "liberty, equality, fraternity (community)." This idea of liberty was set against a "modern" liberty that emphasized the sovereignty of the individual along with liberty, property, and security.[20] Ducharme argues that the modern idea of liberty prevailed in Canada, creating the type of liberalism upon which Canada was founded. Modern liberty begat the liberal state, mandated by the people to facilitate the individual's liberty to pursue his (gendered pronoun intentional) chosen future. Many people in English Canada who engaged in the debates about liquor emphasized the elements of this modern liberty. Government, to them, was supposed to support the freedom and property of the individual; defining what that freedom looked like and indicating how it was to be protected comprised a central tension of the liquor question.

Several authors have illustrated how values of liberty and property were interconnected. Girard notes that the form of tenancy implemented in Prince Edward Island, in which a proprietor elite controlled most of the land, was contested by residents who saw such systems as contrary to principles of liberty.[21] Similarly, the issue of property and traditional rights in the operation of the seigneurial system created points of tension between tenants and landlords in Quebec.[22] In her study of tenancy in Ontario, Catharine Anne Wilson argues that the idea of freedom was so essential to immigrants who sought land in the province that the tenantry system was rarely mentioned in literature that encouraged immigration. Tenantry was anathema to liberalism because a tenant was in a state of dependence.[23] Bruce Curtis has noted that the framers of the Constitutional Act of 1791 had "hoped for the creation of a Canadian aristocracy through the distribution of colonial lands," but that did not come to fruition, and the "exceptionally liberal" legislation in 1791 created a freehold franchise and an executive branch not based upon hereditary title, all elements of a nascent liberal state.[24] In these cases, we see ideas of property rights intertwined with ideas of liberty along with a rejection of the traditional systems of elitism in favour of some kind of representative democracy.

How the liberal state operates to protect those values has also been a matter of debate. Critiquing McKay's liberal order framework as based upon a too-narrow understanding of liberalism, Robert Macdonald notes that, in the liberal state, those three pillars of liberalism (liberty, equality, property) were joined by "rationality, a belief in rational change, a commitment to legality and constitutionality, and a concern for the general good."[25] These elements appear in different forms of liberalism, and the difference in jargon becomes confusing. By the late-Victorian and early Edwardian periods, the "classical liberalism" of the middle class (a version of Ducharme's "modern" liberalism) – supporting individualism, property rights, lower taxes, and limited government – was counterposed with a "radical" liberalism that rejected monopoly and resisted elites and a "new liberalism" that was "far more deliberately collectivist." This latter form of liberalism argued for more active state intervention in the lives of the people in order to correct extreme social disparity. Macdonald reminds us that Mill himself said that individual liberty had meaning "only within the collective identity provided by local self-governing units."[26] These additional concepts – including the standardized governance of municipalities, the tension between individual and collective rights, and the emphasis on rationality, legality, and constitutionality – were manifested, deliberated, and persistently critiqued in debates about liquor. They were also intimately interconnected. Discussions of property rights included things such as limited economic intervention, an element of trade freedom. Those of equality included issues such as fairness and justice, equal treatment under the law, and common civic responsibilities. Liberty was embedded in all of these things.

The protection of liberty and property and the implementation of a legal system based upon equality were not just ideas, for they needed a state apparatus to operate. Thus, numerous authors have examined the implementation of the liberal order throughout society. They have emphasized that self-government was a crucial component of liberalism but that, in order to function effectively, provincial governments sought to rationalize how municipal governments operated.[27] Michèle Dagenais observes that provincial governments sought to standardize the structure and function of municipal governments, removing subjectivity and in effect turning municipal governments "into abstractions," rational models of government that could be understood without understanding specific, subjective local contexts.[28] This was necessary, she argues, to ensure that a government "founded upon the principle of liberty" could ensure "the orderly and proper functioning of society" rather than "resulting in chaos."[29] Similarly interested in the connection between the central government and the activities of individuals at the local level, Bruce Curtis has argued that, even though one of the key elements of liberalism is individualism, the liberal state had to develop a collective affinity for the operation of government in order to function effectively. He points to the development of various provincial bureaucracies, notably the public education system, as part of a process of standardizing how the liberal state operated to shape the individual and strengthen the relationship between the individual and that state.[30] The rational individual raised, educated, and shaped by the apparatus of the liberal state would then, ideally, actively protect the values of the state.[31] Similarly, the process of developing a centralized liquor licensing system engaged the citizenry in a constant interplay with provincial governments, permitting some form of local autonomy under the dispensation and observation of a central license office. By the end of the period under study, that connection was both pervasive and generally accepted as standard, despite persistent complaints about its dysfunction.

As a philosophy centred on the individual, liberalism hinged on the type of individual nurtured by and involved in the operation of the state. This ideal citizen, who would both enjoy the benefits of the liberal state and mould its form, was the "rational actor." As McKay and others have argued, the strength of liberalism hinged on the ability of rational individuals to engage in the sort of debate that shaped the structure of the state. Curtis notes that liberty was "antithetical to dissolute personal habits, to irregular sexual unions, to religious idolatry, to sloth and disease."[32] His work has been especially useful in describing the way that the education bureaucracy was developed to inculcate and reproduce this idealized individual.[33] Yet liquor upended this expectation in two ways. First, and most obviously, a person under the influence of liquor, especially one habitually drunk, could not be considered to be acting rationally (notwithstanding rumours of Sir John A. Macdonald's drinking tendencies). Drunks, therefore, represented a danger to the liberal state in their wilful tendency to do something that corrupted their rational faculties. In his study of smoking in Montreal, Jarret Rudy shows how assumptions about the rational actor in liberalism shaped ideas of who was able to use tobacco appropriately: white men could exercise self-restraint, whereas women and ethnic outgroups were too irrational to act appropriately.[34] With respect to liquor, prohibitionists saw these sorts of illiberal tendencies as endangering the future of the state. Yet prohibitionists did not get off scot-free. Their passion represented a second complication for liberalism: the tendency for rational discourse to be replaced by (irrational) histrionics. Repeatedly, prohibitionists were referred to as "cranks" or "fanatics," or similar terms denoting excessive, irresponsible passion. Why would you listen to such crazies when shaping rational policy? So both the consumption of alcohol to excess and the excesses of the campaign against alcohol represented irrational threats to the liberal order, with an emphasis yet again on order.

The intersection of liberalism and liquor was not unique to Ontario, let alone Canada. Researchers of the British liquor traffic in the nineteenth century have been especially vigorous in exploring the connections between government and the liquor trade. In the United Kingdom it was a much more assertively political and overtly divisive issue. This research has also investigated the range of options open to regulators as tensions built between temperance supporters (less consistently evangelical in origins than their North American colleagues) and the "drinks industry" (far larger and much more established than that in Canada). John Greenaway has considered the broad process of liquor policy formation as a tension between different views of the place of the state in the lives of the people. He notes that even classical liberals such as Mill were not entirely against constraints on the liquor trade, but that policy had to follow public opinion, not be in advance of it.[35] James Nicholls observes that the temperance movement revealed "deep divisions within political and cultural liberalism" between those who "located freedom in individual liberty (including the liberty to drink)" and those who thought that freedom was to be achieved "by progressive legislation ... however much that progress may involve the restriction of personal liberties."[36] Unlike in Ontario, in Britain the "drink question" became wrapped in partisan interests, with the Conservatives allying with the alcohol industry and the Liberals with the temperance movement.[37] This might explain why, as Greenaway notes, by the beginning of the twentieth century, discussions of liberties in the issue of drinking had been replaced primarily by discussions of property rights (mostly those of brewers) and revenues since these issues typified the differences between Liberals and Conservatives.[38]

The British literature varies significantly from the sizable research undertaken on Canada's closest neighbour. Studies of liquor and governance in the United States have looked, for the most part, at the growth and development of the temperance movement with an eye on prohibition. It is not an insignificant issue, for temperance developed relatively spontaneously in the United Kingdom, United States, and Canada near the beginning of the 1800s, and both Canada and the United States experienced different forms of national prohibition a century later.[39] Nevertheless, the debates in the United States tended to be about the legal implementation of different forms of control and the intersection of the ideal of freedom in the American republic with the notion that liquor was a threat to that ideal. Such discussions connected to the broader liberal project, and there was considerable cross-pollination across the Atlantic and beyond. Indeed, Canadians arguing for or against strict controls on liquor, or even its prohibition, drew inspiration from both the United States and the United Kingdom. To be sure, temperance organizers moved easily across the land border. Nevertheless, as I will explore in this book, the liberalism to which most Canadian commentators referred was a distinctly British form. Even though it appeared in the collectivist arguments of evangelical Drys and the laissez-faire arguments of the Wets, Americans' republican liberalism was often decried as contrary to the ideals that Canadians emulated and to which they aspired.

Throughout the English-speaking world, then, the principles of liberalism had been found to be potentially dangerous when applied, well, liberally, to the drink issue. As both David Beckingham and James Nicholls have demonstrated, the idea of freedom in trade was taken to an extreme under the Beer Act of the 1830s. This legislation, designed by a Conservative government as an attack on both the "long-established monopoly power of brewers" and the "seemingly arbitrary and certainly unaccountable authority of licensing magistrates," created a relatively cheap "beer house" license issued by excise officers. The move was intended as a liberal reaction against the powers of elites, specifically magistrates, and the tendencies toward monopoly implied in the power of the brewers.[40] Magistrates' decisions had seemed to be subjective and arbitrary, based upon a cluster of considerations, including the "needs" of a neighbourhood and the character of a licensee.[41] The Beer Act backfired spectacularly, and the number of public drinking establishments exploded.[42] The city of Liverpool, for example, with a population of 165,175 in 1831, added 800 licensed premises in three weeks, increasing the proportion of pubs to one for every twenty-nine families.[43] Across the country, over 24,000 new beer shops opened in the first year, many in poor neighbourhoods. The Beer Act certainly constrained the magistrates but did little to weaken brewers, whose economic power allowed them to keep their houses in operation by undercutting the new competition.[44] The law was restrained by legislation in 1834 and 1840, but the system of licensing by excise officers remained in place until 1869.[45] Along with demonstrating the dangers of overly liberal liquor licensing, the Beer Act added another institution to the range of public drinking spaces in the United Kingdom: to inns (places of food, drink, and lodgings) and alehouses (with long histories as places to procure ale made on the premises) were added beer houses, generally lower-status establishments for drinking beer, whether or not it was brewed on the premises. Such institutions were reproduced in pre-Confederation liquor laws but modified in post-Confederation Ontario.

As in Britain, in Canada before Confederation, liquor was generally a municipal responsibility. As noted above, pre-Confederation laws granted municipal councils authority over licensing and over determining how licenses would be granted and how laws would be enforced.[46] With few constraints, municipal councils could increase the number of licenses in order to generate more revenue. But they were often reluctant to annoy tavern keepers, who – having a captive audience of collegial drinkers, selecting the politically biased newspapers to keep on hand, and willing to host meetings for like-minded politicians – were politically powerful in many small communities.[47] This arrangement created the volatile mix of liquor and politics, and using liquor licensing to boost municipal revenue could be especially attractive during the depression of the 1870s.[48] Combined with the power of basic market forces, it meant that more taverns were being licensed and had to sell more liquor to recoup the cost of the license. From there, the fundamentals of supply and demand economics kicked in. More taverns meant a greater supply of liquor, which meant that tavern keepers, who needed booze revenue to survive (and to pay the licensing fee), had to drop their prices to encourage sales. Lower-priced liquor meant more drinking; more drinking could lead to more drunkenness. At the same time, the low licensing fee and easy turnover in liquor created a disincentive for tavern keepers, many of whom were expected to have sleeping accommodations for travellers, to do anything other than sell booze. The Liberal government of Oliver Mowat found such a system to be untenable, productive of both disorder and persistent complaints from concerned citizens and the worst examples of a nearly free market, and took action to address it.

To investigate the long process of change in Ontario's licensing system, I follow the modifications to liquor regulations from Confederation to the First World War. These dates are not just the convenient historical benchmarks. Confederation was the moment when, constitutionally, municipalities disappeared and provinces could take control over whichever aspects of municipal life they believed needed more centralized guidance. At the same time, the Constitution created a situation in which provincial and dominion rights had to be established through a legal forum. The First World War spurred the advent of provincial prohibition. In 1915, the provincial government created a centralized Board of License Commissioners, sweeping away the changes that had begun in the 1870s and establishing a licensing system designed to reduce many of the administrative challenges of the previous forty years. The next year, facing calls for the elimination of the alcohol traffic that were grounded in concerns about the future of the nation framed by mobilization for total war, Ontario followed other provinces into that undiscovered country of prohibition. One should not assume, however, that prohibition was inevitable. It came about as a result of war, and the arguments about the freedom of the individual and of business were secondary to the arguments about the freedom of the nation in the face of a seemingly illiberal enemy. Indeed, if we wanted to engage in metahistorical speculation, it seemed that, immediately before the war, prohibitionist arguments were losing steam. The long period of change – tweaking the prices of licenses, adjusting where and when people could buy and consume liquor, and establishing increasingly bureaucratic processes to oversee and control the actions of the people with respect to alcoholic beverages – shaped the cultures of drink and the assumptions about the appropriate location, time, and manner in which someone could consume alcohol. These cultures of drink persisted throughout prohibition and influenced the structure of legal drinking under liquor control after 1927.[49]

The book proceeds generally chronologically in two sections. The first section looks at the process of creating and implementing a significantly revised liquor licensing system in 1876. After several investigations of the operation of municipal licensing in the mid-1870s, the government of Oliver Mowat passed a heavily revised Act to Amend and Consolidate the Law for the Sale of Fermented or Spirituous Liquors, credited to Treasurer Adam Crooks and commonly called the Crooks Act. This law removed the direct role of licensing from the hands of municipalities, required all inspectors to be employees of the province, divided the province into license districts, and appointed an unpaid, three-person Board of License Commissioners for each district. It thus expanded the bureaucracy of liquor licensing and centralized its administration in a "License Branch," variously attached to the provincial secretary or treasurer. The first four chapters address how that system emerged and operated. The chapters in Part 2 trace the politics of drink at all levels of government in Canada across the period, from the 1870s to the enactment of prohibition in Ontario in 1916. It is not a positivistic narrative of improvement and "evolution," but rather it traces the different paths down which the liquor question could lead policy makers and shows which routes they took.

There are parallel tracks here. While the province was managing and modifying the licensing system, politicians at provincial and dominion levels, as well as the advocates of prohibition and the liquor interests, were wrestling with various attempts at local prohibition, known as local option. Under local option, electors in municipalities could vote their communities dry. This initiative related initially to a pre-Confederation local option act called the Dunkin Act, which applied only to Quebec and Ontario. In 1878, the dominion government of Liberal Prime Minister Alexander Mackenzie passed the Canada Temperance Act, championed by Senator Richard Scott and called the Scott Act, which updated the local option provisions and extended the local option system to the entire country. The relationship between the dominion and the provinces with respect to liquor continued to be debated as Sir John A. Macdonald's Conservative government attempted, unsuccessfully, to take over liquor licensing in the early part of the 1880s and as the provinces attempted, with more success, to gain the authority to implement province-wide prohibition in the 1890s. As these changes unfolded at the national level, the government of Ontario continued to wrestle with the issue of how best to constrain but permit drinking. At the political level, leaders were reluctant to upset either the temperance advocates or the liquor interests until Conservative Premier James Whitney ended the thirty-four-year reign of the Liberals, brushed off the demands of the temperance movement, and rejected prohibition entirely. Ten years later prohibition was the law of the land under a different Tory premier in significantly different geopolitical conditions. That is the structure of the narrative, but this analysis will require us to jump around, between the 1870s and the 1890s, between Ottawa and Toronto, between the municipal affairs and the national context, in order to understand how liberalism was squeezed and prodded to deal with the complicated, intractable liquor question.

The regulation, control, and potential for prohibition of intoxicating and recreational substances remain major issues of discussion and probably will for some time to come. Not only cannabis legalization but also tobacco restriction, vaping, gambling, prostitution, and other stars in what John Burnham called the "vice constellation" remain significant and important areas of concern for policy makers, social commentators, and activists.[50] Although alcohol and other substances of recreation and intoxication vary in myriad ways, the systems of thought behind them and the justifications for regulation and restriction, and especially for prohibition, need to be scrutinized constantly and assessed against a backdrop of the pragmatism of enforcement, the implementation of harm reduction, and the fundamental values of our society. The imposition of government in our lives can be salubrious or sinister, and this book offers an investigation of a process that, depending on who you read, might be both.

Part 1
Managing the Province's Liquor Problem

I
The Place of the Government in the Drinks of the People

Whether or not an adult male resident of Canada West celebrated his instant transformation, on 1 July 1867, into an Ontarian, he might well have learned about this change over a drink in a tavern. In many parts of Upper Canada/Canada West/Ontario, the tavern was an active centre of the community. As historian Julia Roberts has demonstrated, the tavern was a place of socialization, accommodation, repast, and repose.[1] Taverns formed the backbone of the transportation network across the colony as settlers moved into newly surveyed tracts of land and as various entrepreneurs set up shop. The first resident of London, Ontario, is believed to have been Peter McGregor, who built a log cabin and put a jug of whiskey on a tree stump, calling his home a tavern.[2] More familiar to many Ontarians, Montgomery's Tavern is steeped in the lore of the province, being where the Upper Canada Rebellion ended, thus allowing many students to wonder if the whole thing was a drunken escapade. It was not. Taverns were multipurpose public meeting places, serving variously as centres of political activity, formal and informal debates, social support, and job opportunities.[3] Our newly minted Ontarian would have heard or read of the creation of Canada from a partisan paper stocked by the tavern keeper, possibly over a locally brewed ale or whiskey distilled from regional grain, and then debated the merits of the new country and its founders. Although, as Roberts demonstrates, the tavern was not exclusively a male environment, the tavern's drinking space was generally more sex specific. As a result, this new Ontarian would have debated the creation of Canada with like-minded male colleagues in a familiar, accommodating barroom.

By the time of Confederation, the drinking space was a legally structured business, held to specific criteria, and shaped by customs, locations, and community expectations. All taverns outside cities and towns were required to have at least four bedrooms available for patrons' use (that is, beyond the rooms used by the families of the owners). They also needed to have accommodations, both stables and sheds, for at least six horses and accompanying wagons.[4] These were legal requirements and commercial necessities, since in many communities the tavern and its accommodations for humans and teams were essential for new settlers en route to their allotted lands, local farmers bringing products to market, and commercial travellers plying their wares.[5] Pre-Confederation laws allowed city and town councils to exempt a few taverns from the requirement for sleeping accommodations, and such places were informally (not statutorily) known as saloons. The law also identified different types of drinking spaces rooted in British tradition – notably, inns, ale houses, and beer houses – although it did not describe the differences among these establishments. The variety of drinking places disappeared in post-Confederation law as the standard term "tavern," with or without accommodations, became the only legal public place (private clubs being exempt from much scrutiny) in which to sit and have a drink.

Legislation in pre-Confederation Canada West assigned the main licensing authority to municipalities. Town, village, or township councils, or boards of police commissioners in cities, determined how many licenses to distribute, their cost, and who would receive them. The provincial legislature enacted only general restrictions for the sake of public order and revenue. For example, in 1858 it set out provincial duties to be charged for each license for the enrichment of the provincial coffers, and in 1860 it permitted no more than one tavern to be licensed for every 250 people in the community, but otherwise councils had the power to define the lay of the liquor landscape in their communities. Councils were also responsible for enforcement of the law, keeping an eye on the activities in the taverns and, in theory at least, shutting down transgressors of local norms and morals. This arrangement, which in effect politicized the tavern, was ripe for corruption and manipulation.

The general local autonomy granted in liquor licensing represented a quintessential liberal concern with how to balance rights and responsibilities. In pre-Confederation Canada, as in the United Kingdom, the government decided that determining the balance should be left to municipalities. Historical geographer David Beckingham explains that "the historical framework of licensing took its purpose and philosophy from the locales and cultures in which it was embedded and ... responded to the priorities and principles of local politics."[6] Michèle Dagenais argues that in Canada autonomy was a principle of liberalism represented in a degree of municipal independence.[7] Yet the ideal of local autonomy was hitting its limit in Canada West before Confederation. The 1860 law that set the population ratio for taverns (1:250), required four bedrooms for customers, mandated that a petition of thirty electors was needed for a council to grant a new tavern license, and created the bedroom exemption for a few saloons in cities and towns was entitled An Act to Diminish the Number of Licenses Issued for the Sale of Intoxicating Liquors by Retail. Its preamble stated that "the number of Tavern Licenses is larger than the necessities of the community require," and its restrictions demonstrate that even before Confederation municipal autonomy was not viewed as necessarily the best way to manage liquor sales.[8] However, since the law was enforced by municipal staff beholden to their political masters, little changed.

The importance of local conditions and the value of local autonomy to determine how many taverns could be licensed and who would run them persisted into the post-Confederation period. Since the British North America Act did not assign specific powers to municipalities, provincial governments determined when and if municipal powers would expand or contract. When Ontario's first provincial government, under Premier John Sandfield Macdonald, amended the licensing law in 1869, it affirmed the central role of the municipality in issuing licenses and enforcing the law. It set a minimum license fee, increased the duty that the province would receive, allowed a few more taverns in cities and towns to operate without bedrooms, and set out more penalties for disobedience, but it did not alter the centrality of the municipality in shaping the license landscape and enforcing the rules.[9] Such an arrangement, respecting the liberal value that a central government generally would spend little time meddling with the operations of municipalities, was soon found to be problematic.

The legislation set out the types of drinking spaces allowed, but in a geographically dispersed province, and in the diverse communities across the province, such spaces overlapped and merged, often in violation of the law. Many licensed taverns were reported to operate merely as saloons, without the necessary sleeping accommodations. Proprietors might create four slapdash bedrooms that people rarely used, claim that beds used by family members were actually for patrons, or adopt both strategies. Shop licenses were available to general merchants, and shop owners could violate the law by serving alcohol by the glass or mixing it with other beverages. People reported that some shopkeepers provided free liquor that would loosen the wallets of their patrons. Some shops were reported to have the paraphernalia of a barroom – including decanters, glasses, and beer pumps – in full view and thus functioned as unlicensed saloons. Such attempts to skirt the law had much to do with the integrity, activity, and indeed availability of a municipal license inspector. Where municipalities employed them, most inspectors worked part time (often also as the license-issuing clerks) and were usually political appointees. They would thus be encouraged, either actively or through an understanding with their political masters, to ignore the transgressions by partisan confreres. In a political culture that functioned on such a deeply rooted clientelist basis, such relationships were intricate parts of the warp and woof of the social fabric.[10]

Indeed, the political place of tavern keepers should not be underestimated: they had social authority and political clout. A tavern keeper could encourage patrons to vote in certain ways, stock partisan newspapers, and – in the time before secret ballots enabled electors to keep their voting preferences private – urge or pressure clients to vote for preferred candidates. On top of this, the license to sell liquor was remarkably lucrative, so people vying for this legal authority had an additional incentive to use their influence and money in ways that some people might see as unsavoury if not actually illegal. Taverns and saloons were often the sites of political campaigns: liquor sellers made good money and spread it around to influence both those who made the laws and those who elected them to office. Brewers and distillers were often leading members of their communities, and across the province names such as O'Keefe, Carling, Cosgrove, Labatt, Walker, Gooderham, and Taylor implied political clout. Indeed, John Carling was part of Sandfield Macdonald's first provincial cabinet, and Eugene O'Keefe was a persistent, chummy correspondent with Sir John A. Macdonald.[11] Municipal councillors were thus reluctant to attract the ire of the tavern keeper and the captains of the liquor industry. Moreover, the liquor license was a source of municipal revenue, so increasing the number of licenses could build both a support base for local politicians and a revenue base for the community. Consequently, in many communities across the province, drinking places abounded where councils were not populated by temperance-oriented councillors, since the 1:250 tavern-to-population limit of the 1860 law was replaced in 1869 with a clause allowing councils to pass bylaws setting their own limits.[12] The temptation could increase during times of depression, such as the one in which the province languished in the 1870s, when more money from license fees could boost a municipal budget. With an increase in drinking spaces but a limited number of drinkers, some tavern keepers were tempted to drop the price of liquor in order to sell more and make up the cost of doing business. Here market economics drove drunkenness; it was not as bad as the situation in the United Kingdom after the passage of the Beer Act, but to some observers it was still disgraceful. In some communities, such an arrangement could lead to reports of excessive drunkenness unimpeded by a loosely enforced municipal licensing system.

Not surprisingly, such situations spurred protests by temperance organizations across Ontario. In the early 1870s, there was nothing that could be described as a single "temperance movement" in the province. Rather, organizations of varying sizes lobbied for social and legal changes to limit access to alcoholic beverages, often in coordinated campaigns. The push for temperance had begun earlier in the century and initially advocated moderation in liquor consumption rather than prohibition.[13] Nevertheless, by Confederation most temperance groups had replaced calls for moderation with demands for personal abstinence and legal prohibition of the liquor traffic. Many vocal temperance members were motivated by their evangelical beliefs and focused on spreading the gospel and inculcating morals that they saw as a necessary precursor to the return of Christ and the establishment of a Kingdom of God on Earth.[14] The immorality that they saw in taverns – drunkenness, gambling, swearing, prostitution, indeed all of the stars in the "vice constellation" – was at least hindering the realization of this goal if not actually driving society in the opposite direction.[15] Drys saw excessive drinking by their fellow residents as a cause of much distress, poverty, social disorder, and illness in the community. Combine this view with the stories of good middle-class families destroyed by the influence of the tavern, reproduced ad nauseam by the temperance press in North America and Great Britain, and representative of the status anxiety that made many middle-class temperance adherents afraid that their families could follow similar downward paths, and the opposition to the public drinking space could be virulent.[16] Temperance advocates had succeeded, prior to Confederation, in seeing legislation passed that enabled electors in individual municipalities to vote to prohibit the sale of liquor in their communities, a system known as "Local Option." The Canada Temperance Act, 1864, popularly known as the Dunkin Act after legislator Christopher Dunkin, who had championed it, remained in place after

Confederation, allowing municipalities in Ontario and Quebec (where the Dunkin Act had been in force before 1867) to follow its increasingly outdated mechanisms to vote themselves dry.[17]

Ontario's temperance advocates were buoyed, then, in 1871 by the election of the political party known as Reform (the Grits), the political precursor to the Liberals and the political rival of the Conservatives (the Tories). Reformers tended to be sympathetic to the temperance cause, rooted as both were in progressive ideals and often evangelical Protestantism. The Reform leader Edward Blake resigned a year later to stand for the Dominion Liberal Party and was replaced by Oliver Mowat. Lawyer, magistrate, and former member of the pre-Confederation Legislative Assembly of the Province of Canada, Mowat had trained under John A. Macdonald in Kingston, although they do not appear to have been friendly by the 1870s. Mowat was a Methodist who did not drink, but he was not strictly aligned with temperance; he was too politically astute to throw his weight behind one social movement, no matter how loud and persistent its adherents' voices. He did, however, pay it plenty of lip service. Such equivocality was born of political necessity. Unlike in the United Kingdom, where by the 1860s liquor interests aligned with Conservatives and temperance adherents with Liberals, in Ontario, and indeed throughout Canada, there were Drys and Wets on both sides of the political divide.[18]

For a member sitting in the newly elected Legislative Assembly of 1871–72, the liquor question would have been hard to ignore. In the first few years of Mowat's premiership, issues related to liquor and drunkenness were notable features of legislative activity. The legislature received many petitions demanding that the government do something about the rampant consumption of liquor. Indeed, far more petitions on the effects of intoxicating liquor were read in the legislature each year than on any other single issue. Whereas the legislature of the year before received seven petitions related to the licensing law, the first session of the new legislature received dozens.[19] Most requested amendments to the licensing law that Sandfield Macdonald's government had passed in 1869, and at least one petition demanded that liquor be "forbidden." The legislature also received eighty-nine petitions asking for an inebriate asylum in the province. Many of the petitions for the asylum were probably circulated by the people who were urging changes to the liquor laws and who sat beside each other in church pews and association meetings, and at general store counters. This uptick in petitions related to liquor has several likely explanations. First, as noted earlier, this was the first government headed by Reform, and temperance advocates likely saw it as important to remind the new government whose votes (so they imagined) had handed the party its victory. Second, many of the petitions were submitted by church-based groups, which suggests a coordinated campaign. This likelihood is strengthened by the concentration of petitions in the middle of February. From 20 to 24 February, the legislature received fifty-nine petitions on changes to the licensing law and sixty-two petitions on the inebriate asylum. Yet, despite these excited expressions of temperance, the government did little to address the concerns of the petitioners in the legislative session of 1871–72.

In the session of 1873, however, the liquor issue returned with a vengeance. In the speech from the throne, Mowat's government announced its plan to create a "hospital for habitual drunkards" (a term frequently interchanged with "inebriate asylum" in debates and popular discussions). Moreover, the legislature received a remarkable 461 petitions related to the intoxicating effects of liquor (the next most popular topic for petitioners was the School Act, which inspired eighty-three petitions). Members of the Legislative Assembly (MLAs) discussed four private members' bills related to liquor and drunkenness: one to prohibit liquor sales,[20] two to amend the licensing law,[21] and one to take control of property out of the hands of habitual drunkards.[22] Along with these private members' bills, the government presented two bills, one by Treasurer Adam Crooks to consolidate and address some weaknesses in the tavern and shop licensing laws, the other to create and fund the asylum for inebriates. Finally, to investigate the extent of the problem of drunkenness across the province, prompted by the hundreds of petitions and driven by the Drys in both parties, the legislature struck a twenty-four-person select committee "to inquire into the working of the Tavern and Shop License Act of 1868."[23] These legislative activities began to shift how the government dealt with liquor in the province.

The Inebriate Asylum and the Limits of the Liberal State

The bill to fund a hospital for habitual drunkards had extensive debate in the legislature, and in these discussions many of the complicated aspects of the drink question appeared. Many members expressed, implicitly or explicitly, conflicted and contradictory perceptions of the solution to excessive drinking and the role of the government in this work. Was government intervention in the lives of drunks necessary? Did this mean that moral suasion, a key feature of temperance action, was a failure? Did an institutional solution to drunkenness indicate that the state would never support prohibition, legislation that, many argued, would render an asylum unnecessary? Many members retained strong laissez-faire economic principles and rejected any additional cost that would burden the people in order to treat a small cohort of problematic cases. This reluctance was intensified by the general disagreement about the nature of inebriety, whether it was a medical or moral issue, and thus whether drunks needed or deserved special treatment, let alone formal internment, by the state.

In these debates, most members agreed that drunkenness could be a problem but disagreed on how to solve it. The very nature of liberal government as limited and non-interventionist was challenged by the fact that, before debating the asylum bill itself, the house was presented with a request to allocate $100,000 to build it. Some opposition members balked at both the rationale and the predicted expense. Matthew Cameron, leader of the opposition, argued that, instead of erecting a new building (the price for which, he argued, was excessive), the government should first fund an experiment to determine if an inebriety cure even worked. Even more virulent was Edmund Burke Wood, a Conservative from Brant South who warned members that funding such an institution would see the new province "fast gliding into the European system of despotism in these matters, which dried up all feelings of enterprise in private benevolence," and undermine the liberal emphasis on individualism and entrepreneurialism to solve social problems.[24] Wood might have had in mind the New York State Inebriate Asylum founded a decade earlier by a group of reformers who received little financial support from the state government.[25] Contradicting his party's leader, Wood predicted that the cost of $100,000 was far below the mark and used the estimates for other types of asylums in Brantford, Belleville, and London to show how expenses could balloon. Worst of all, in his estimation, was the fact that such expenses would help the wrong people, allowing staff and physicians to "fatten and enrich themselves" even "if it did not help the poor drunkards."[26] Also opposed to this government bill, Conservative Abraham Lauder goaded supporters of prohibition by contending that an asylum was tantamount to "a declaration that the liquor traffic was to continue." Alluding to an upcoming debate on a prohibition bill, Lauder argued that "the gentlemen who were urging ... the passage of a Prohibitory Law must strenuously oppose the scheme at present under discussion." The champion of that prohibition bill, physician and Norfolk North Reform MLA John Clarke defended an asylum as an effective way of treating inebriety. His fellow Dry from across the aisle, John Grange, disagreed, contending that prohibition would render an asylum (and its $100,000 expense) unnecessary because "there would be an asylum then extending from one end of the Province to the other."[27]

As the exchange between Clarke and Grange indicates, in this debate the Drys were divided by partisan politics. Vocal and ardent temperance Reformers, notably Abraham Farewell and Clarke, defended the government's asylum bill, whereas Tories, both Dry and Wet, criticized the plan, focusing on the finances and practicality of such an institution. Some argued that the books were balanced and that there was no need to go back into debt. Others took a harder line on drunkenness, viewing drunks as criminals rather than sick people. Lincoln Tory John C. Rykert made the case bluntly: "If the government would make men found drunk on the streets or deserting their families go through hard labour as a punishment, instead of sending them on to a hundred acre farm and allowing them to play the gentleman, they would strike a blow directly at the evil."[28] Some noted the irony that the government received about $75,000 annually from alcohol industry revenue and that it probably would be a better approach to save money by eliminating that industry through prohibition. Premier Mowat countered that argument by noting that the members seemed happy to receive $75,000 in excise and tax revenues from the liquor industry, so they should not have a problem with spending an additional $25,000 to deal with its worst effects. He noted that, even if prohibition were enacted immediately, it would take years to eliminate the damage caused by inebriety. Perhaps, he said, with an optimistic flourish, some day when drink was eliminated entirely and the asylum was no longer necessary, citizens of the province would look at the now useless building as a memorial of the good work done to eliminate the liquor traffic.[29] It was certainly an odd justification for such an investment of public funds. Despite several further attempts to alter the shape of the bill, the asylum legislation passed.

The partisanship that divided the Drys when discussing the asylum legislation, a government bill, eroded when it came to debating John Clarke's prohibition bill. Although Clarke was a Grit, his Act to Prohibit the Sale of Intoxicating Liquors as a Beverage in Ontario was a private member's bill, and so government members were not "whipped" to support it, and opposition members were not compelled to criticize.[30] Clarke used his medical training to support his temperance perspective. He argued in the legislature that alcohol was a poison and that "it would be well for persons who argued [that alcohol did not cause disease] to refer to authorities who had thoroughly established the fact that drunkenness was a most prolific cause of disease." He proceeded to list several medical authors who linked alcohol to a range of physical problems, from general fatality to the production of weak offspring.[31] Even though Clarke's scientific certainty masked what remained a highly debatable issue among physicians, he held up his medical expertise as both a shield and a weapon.[32] For him, there was no disconnect between advocating treatment of inebriety and advocating prohibition of the liquor trade. The latter was a preventative measure for the former.

Clarke's bill seemed to have broad bipartisan support, but even if a majority of members supported prohibition (and it is not clear that they did), they would not have been enough to see it become law. The bill was halted in its journey through the legislature because of what was to be an ongoing issue of constitutional jurisdiction. After an extended debate during the bill's second reading, Rykert, the Conservative member for Lincoln, raised a point of order, asking that the speaker of the house rule on whether the bill was even within the purview of the province. Speaker James G. Currie ruled that the bill was ultra vires the province: that is, constitutionally beyond the authority of the provincial government. He reasoned that regulating trade and commerce was a dominion responsibility, and since the prohibition of liquor was clearly a restriction on trade, it was beyond the authority of provincial governments. What the provinces could do with respect to liquor, as clearly outlined in the British North America Act, was to license taverns for the sake of raising revenue. Currie's ruling had a long-lasting impact on provincial efforts to constrain drink. Immediately after this decision, and arguing that his bill contained principles "substantially the same" as those in Clarke's bill, Abraham Farewell withdrew his bill to amend the licensing law despite urgings from Dry members of the house to "stick to his colours as a temperance man."[33] For the time being, the Ontario legislature's attention on drink would focus on addressing more discrete concerns about the operation of licensing laws, clearly intra vires the provincial government. It did not contemplate prohibitory measures again until the 1890s.

The License Amendment Act, 1873

With the issue of prohibition set aside for the time being, the government could move to address deficiencies in the licensing act. In his bill, Treasurer Adam Crooks sought to fix loopholes in the existing law that had allowed cagey barristers to help their clients avoid prosecution. For example, judicial interpretations of the 1869 licensing law determined that a conviction for illegal selling of liquor required someone to witness the sale; merely finding people sitting drinking liquor in an unlicensed space or during a time when sales were illegal (such as on Sunday) was insufficient evidence for prosecution. Also, in the case of a charge of selling liquor without a license, the law required the prosecution to prove that the accused was in fact unlicensed, which could be difficult if an issuer of licenses did not keep good records or chose not to provide a copy of the license. Finally, the information used by the prosecution was gathered by independent informers, who would receive a portion of the fine levied in the event of a conviction. Reportedly, many accused proprietors found it more efficient simply to pay off the informants rather than face the more significant costs of going to court.

Crooks's bill addressed these loopholes in several ways. First, the presence of alcohol-dispensing and -serving equipment such as "beer engines" (for pumping beer from casks), glasses, and so on, would be considered prima facie evidence that an individual was selling liquor; a sale did not need to be witnessed. Second, those accused of selling liquor without a license would be required to prove that they were licensed to sell liquor. Third, the reliance upon unofficial informants would be replaced with an inspector paid by the municipality to enforce the law. In contrast to earlier legislation, which merely permitted municipalities to hire an inspector, the 1873 legislation required them to do so. Moreover, the legislation empowered the provincial government to hire two inspectors of its own, allowing a second level of investigation and enforcement across the province separate from local politics. Fourth, the amendment also made owners of buildings responsible for the behaviour of their tenants or employees. They could be charged under the law even if they had (or claimed that they had) nothing to do with the illegality taking place in their premises. And fifth, a change that Crooks admitted he was not sure he liked, was clause 9, which would reduce the minimum amount of liquor that a shop owner was permitted to sell. The previous minimum had been three half-pints, equivalent to roughly one quart, a volume based upon traditional wine measurements and a standard size for liquor bottles. Crooks noted that in several cities in Quebec, a similar change had resulted in a reduction in the number of taverns in a community, because instead of going to a tavern to have a drink, people with lower incomes could afford to buy small amounts of liquor at a shop and take them home rather than having to buy a larger amount.[34]

Legislators on both sides of the house, and from both Dry and Wet camps, approved most of these changes, but many Dry members wanted the legislation to go further. Several argued that shop licenses were a major problem since shopkeepers were tempted to sell or give away small amounts of liquor to encourage people to patronize their stores or, as some contended, to get customers drunk so that they would spend more money. These MLAs argued that, if liquor sales continued in general stores, then they should be entirely separate from the sale of other products. Stormont Grit James Bethune suggested that wholesale liquor vendors' stocks be inspected to deal with the apparent problem of liquor adulterated with "poisonous materials," which was, he argued, a major cause of harm.[35] He also thought that something should be done about places called "concert saloons" that he saw on King Street in Toronto, which he claimed that the police described as "half-way houses to vice and immorality."[36] John Clarke wanted even stricter control over taverns. He thought that essentially all activities except drinking should be forbidden in public drinking spaces, urging Crooks to add a clause "prohibiting billiard tables or any games of amusement in the vicinity of bars; not even to allow newspapers there or anything that would attract people thither."[37] Many commentators harshly criticized clause 9, which would allow shopkeepers to sell booze in smaller volumes. Grey East Tory Abraham Lauder said that it was "an insult to every well-regulated tavern" to allow shopkeepers to sell smaller amounts, "and drunkenness certainly would increase." Others said they failed to see how such a clause would reduce drinking, for liquor sales in shops seemed to be one root of the drunkenness problem. As Leeds Tory H.S. Macdonald observed, if clause 9 were to pass, "there would be an additional inebriate asylum needed."[38]

What might have been the most significant innovation in the legislation, the introduction of a government inspection system, faced relatively little opposition. Lennox Conservative John Grange agreed that "general inspection of the licensing business should be directly under Government control." Alfred Boultbee, a Conservative from North York, concurred, saying that "the prostitution of the liquor traffic could only be repressed by the Government appointing officials to look after these unlicensed shops ... [I]f [the unlicensed traffic] could be repressed, a great deal of good would be done to the temperance cause." In contrast, fellow Conservative John Rykert "disapproved of increasing the patronage of the Government by the appointment of inspectors"; whether or not he agreed with the principle of government inspectors was unclear.[39] With such limited opposition, the licensing amendment passed relatively quickly into law, the only notable changes being the deletion of clause 9 (which Crooks claimed he had introduced merely for the sake of discussion) and the removal of the specification of the number of inspectors the province could hire.[40]

The many petitions, failed private members' bills, and modifications to the licensing legislation were evidence of concern about the perceived increase in drunkenness, but they also illustrated vastly different impressions of the scope of the liquor problem. Many inside and outside the government agreed that further information about the liquor trade was necessary in order to understand how best to manage the perceived problem of overconsumption of alcohol in the province. With the expanded inspectorate permitted by the amendments to the license act, Mowat's government hired five inspectors to travel the rail lines that radiated out from Toronto and investigate how councils were managing the drinking spaces in their municipalities. Detailed reports of these investigations were presented to the legislature the following year (and are examined in detail below). Before this work was undertaken, in February 1873, Abraham Farewell, a Grit temperance member, proposed that the government form a select committee on the liquor traffic. Farewell framed the motion to create this committee as allowing the legislature "to take the matter into consideration for the purpose of ascertaining if something could not be done to place the liquor traffic on a better basis, so that the terrible results flowing therefrom might be stayed." After extensive debate in the legislature, Mowat offered his half-hearted, painfully equivocal support for the committee. Understanding that the committee would be investigating the advisability of prohibition and knowing that the legislature "might or might not have the constitutional right to pass a law of this description," he noted that even "if they had that constitutional right this method of suppressing intemperance might or might not be the best." Nevertheless, he agreed that it was important to have the facts. And so the Committee to Investigate the Workings of the Tavern and Shops Act, usually referred to as the Select Committee on Liquor Traffic, began its work.[41]

Far from investigating various strategies for alleviating the worst problems of drinking, the committee's work from the outset was to gather evidence to convince legislators that the only way to deal with the drink problem was through prohibition. The very motion to form the committee indicated the direction that the committee would take, giving it the mandate to "inquire into the working of the Tavern and Shop License Act of 1868, with reference to its influence upon the spread and baneful effects of intemperance; also, into the extent and general effects upon the morals of the community of the liquor traffic of the Province."[42] The committee selected Farewell as its chair and included Dr. Clarke and other notable Drys as well as a few not known for their temperance sympathies. Its twenty-four members included fifteen Reformers and nine Conservatives. Few of them actually attended the meetings. Normally, the same six people attended, evenly split between Tories and Grits, mostly known temperance supporters.[43] Indeed, the attendance was so poor that after the first meeting the committee asked the legislature to allow it to reduce its quorum to five. Although empowered to hold hearings and call witnesses, the committee's main activities were drafting and sending questionnaires to various cohorts of community members, gathering data on the number of petitions on liquor issues sent to the legislature (including the number of names on the petitions), and using this material to inform the legislature about how liquor consumption should be managed in the province. The committee sat until the end of the session and was revivified in 1874 to complete its work and present its report, which included detailed responses to targeted questions and reiterated a need for prohibition.

This outcome – to reinforce the call for prohibition – was doubtless Farewell's purpose in forming the committee. To achieve its goal, Farewell and company adopted a clever, and typical, policy-making approach. When considering a new policy direction, legislators and other policy makers can control the type of information they use to inform their decisions by strategically selecting sources of information to favour a specific policy outcome. It is a process that political scientists call setting the "field of conflict."[44] Policy makers can bias the understanding of an issue depending on the opinions that they choose to hear, and committees such as the Select Committee on the Liquor Traffic had the power to hear the perspectives of only those whose opinions were solicited. In open hearings, evidence can be invited from proponents or opponents of an issue; in written submissions, which are not public utterances, information might be gathered from diverse sources, but final reports can draw only from the submissions and testimonies that support the intended outcome. In such cases, the chair has tremendous authority to shape the conclusions to satisfy his or her interests. The Select Committee on the Liquor Traffic, then, is best understood as a prohibitionist effort to build knowledge based upon the idea that liquor is an imminent threat to the community and the province. It generated, or reiterated, a perspective that persisted into the twentieth century.

In both the questions that it posed and the individuals to whom it posed them, the committee sought proof of the damning effects of liquor on the province. It sent questionnaires to occupational groups that, although containing many respectable members of the community, were also those most likely to have encountered problems resulting from overdrinking (see Table 1.1). Ministers, judges, coroners, insurance agents, physicians, and industrialists were among those contacted. The committee discussed but rejected the idea of reaching out to members of municipal councils. Given that many municipal councils were known to favour the liquor trade, this decision further suggests the confirmation bias inherent in the committee's work. The committee did send questionnaires to brewers and distillers but only to seek information about the costs, revenues, and productivity of the businesses. (All questions are listed in Appendix 1.)

Table 1.1 "Class" of correspondents contacted by the Select Committee

Class	Type of occupation
I	Medical practitioners
II	Clergy
III	Sheriffs, county attorneys, magistrates, and chief constables
IV	Judges, police and stipendiary magistrates, and justices of the peace
V	Coroners
VI	Superintendents and inspectors of lunatic asylums, hospitals, and poor houses, wardens of penitentiaries, inspectors of gaols and reformatories, gaol surgeons, and overseers of houses of refuge
VII	Brewers and distillers
VIII	Manufacturers, merchants, and contractors
IX	Railway managers, owners, and masters of vessels
X	Insurance companies

Source: "Report of the Select Committee on the Liquor Traffic," *Journals of the Legislative Assembly of the Province of Ontario,* 1874, Appendix 2.

The language and imagery of temperance appeared in and directed the focus of the questions. Apart from the brewers and distillers, all of the other "classes" of correspondents were asked to address how intemperance negatively affected their communities, their businesses, or both. The phrasing here is important because it encouraged the respondent to address only the dangers of intoxication. For example, manufacturers were asked this question: "In what respect do you consider the use of intoxicating liquor as a beverage in these [labouring] classes productive of injury?" The understanding here is that intoxicating liquor is only injurious. Class VIII (manufacturers, etc.) and Class IX (railway managers, etc.) were asked about the "proportion of accidents" and the "percentage of property destroyed annually" as a result of intoxication. Although this question was about proportions and percentages, it also framed intoxicants as productive only of problems. The question was paired with only one other, asking if abstainers were preferable to workers who drank liquor, and the respondent was asked to "rate their comparative efficiency and trustworthiness." Again, this line of questioning was prejudicial, embedded with the idea of liquor as a problem. It did not ask, for example, whether liquor consumption built camaraderie or loyalty among employees, or whether it was used to get through onerous workdays, or whether people tended to drink heavily or lightly. Unlike investigations elsewhere, notably in Great Britain, where public drinking was seen by many as an essential component of socialization, in this committee's questions alcohol could be considered only problematic.[45]

Along with implying only one way to view intoxicants, the questions often presented a false dichotomy between total abstainers and hopeless, dissolute drunkards (the sort of people who would be candidates for the newly funded inebriate asylum), thereby permitting little opportunity to argue for a middle ground. Several physicians took issue with this assumption, but many of the other respondents voiced no such qualms. Questions such as "do you consider licensing the sale of intoxicating drinks as a beverage, productive of crime" (asked to judges, police, stipendiary magistrates, and justices of the peace and asked in a different way to sheriffs, county attorneys, magistrates, and chief constables) do not allow for equivocality. Intemperance might have meant excess, but "intoxicating drinks" could be consumed in moderation. So to say that any degree of crime was the result of "intoxicating drinks" was to imply that the consumption of any amount of such drinks could lead to crime, when that might not have been the case. This was a trope of the temperance movement that always included drunken law breaking, violence, and destroyed families.⁴⁶ A few correspondents attempted to correct this insinuation, but most of them merely provided some brief off-the-cuff estimates of the number of cases related to drinking alcohol.⁴⁷

Many physicians were critical of the direction of the question. Consider "does the use of intoxicating liquors, as a beverage, predispose to mental and physical disease or otherwise?" Some physicians responded uncategorically: "Most decidedly it does";⁴⁸ "most assuredly it does";⁴⁹ "it is beyond doubt."⁵⁰ Yet others were not so pleased about the direction implied by the question. E. Hickman of Bolton argued that "this question is so put as to permit only an affirmative answer."⁵¹ Others offered balance. M. Barrett, a lecturer on physiology at the Toronto School of Medicine, noted that the "use of intoxicating liquors does not predispose" one to disease; however, "the immoderate use, or in other words, the abuse of intoxicating liquors does." William Morton of Wellesley reminded the committee that "moderation and excess are but comparative terms."⁵² Hamnet Hill of Ottawa was similarly concerned about the language of the question, noting that "the '*abuse*' and not the use of such beverages, no doubt predisposes to both mental and physical infirmities, ... but with persons who regularly make use of beer or wine with their meals, *without ever committing any excess,* I see no difference."⁵³

Whereas physicians provided some attempt at balance, such was rare in the responses from ministers. Indeed, one might wonder why ministers were consulted at all, for they would have been unlikely to provide anything but intense arguments against the deleterious moral effects of liquor consumption. Then again, that was the point of this knowledge-creation exercise. The testimony of ministers, with few exceptions, channelled the histrionics of the temperance movement, and indeed the questions seemed to encourage it. Most of these questions met Dr. Hickman's classification of pointing the respondent in a certain direction. As well as asking the ministers more concrete information about the number of taverns and whether the community had attempted to pass the Dunkin Act (which seemed more appropriate to municipal officials), the questions pointed the ministers in one clear direction: "1. State the extent of the evils of drunkenness"; "2. Probable cause thereof"; "3. Results of intemperance."

The clergy filled the pages with standard temperance rhetoric. "You have not given me enough space for this," wrote A. Beamer, who identified himself as an "M. E. Minister" in an unspecified town of about 1,800 (which he claimed had thirty-three places where liquor was sold). "The answer [to the first question] is the general one: crime, pauperism, tears and death."⁵⁴ Others were not so moderate in their rhetoric. William Burgess of East Tilbury barfed temperance all over the page:

> [The evils of intemperance] extend not only to the temporal and eternal ruin of the inebriate himself, but to the impoverishing of wife and child, to broken-hearted parents when their children are its victims; it destroys the peace of society, the morality of youth, the purity of women (for both sexes are its prey); the respect for and observance of law, and the prosperity of a country; neutralizing the philanthropic labours of divines and legislatures; it is the fount of nine-tenths of existing crime; destroying individual, social, and national happiness; and transmitting hereditary disease to future generations.⁵⁵

The ministers were generally in agreement about the fourth question, which asked for the best way to deal with the problems: "total prohibition"; "prohibition"; "the total suppression of the liquor traffic"; "even drunkards say put it out of our reach"; "*Prohibition! Prohibition!!*" ⁵⁶

A few dissenting opinions came from not surprising places. P. Eugene Funcken, a minister in St. Agatha, in Waterloo County, contended that the Dunkin Act would never succeed in that location given the large population of Germans there. He advocated a more nuanced, market-based solution than simple prohibition: "encourage the fabrication and sale of small beer, (German Lager), importation of French and German wines, and its Catawba [a wine made from a native North American grape], etc. free of duty, but increase duty and taxes on brandy, whiskey, gin, etc."⁵⁷ Both the curate and the rector of St. George's Anglican Church in St. Catharines offered a six-point solution that was remarkably prescient. Since the Anglican Church resisted calls for prohibition, the sophisticated response is indicative of a more measured assessment of the problem: abolition of bars except in hotels; restricting locations for off-site sales; shifting the license-granting powers to non-elected local officials and placing inspections under the auspices of the provincial government; enacting heavy fines for violators of the rules; and creating a system of guardianship of and treatment for confirmed drunkards.⁵⁸ Such complex suggestions were rare in a document filled with temperance rhetoric and prohibitionist solutions. The responses that demonstrated a more sophisticated and localized approach to the problem of the excesses of liquor consumption, and especially the problem of enforcing prohibition, do not appear to have informed the committee's conclusions, although many did manifest themselves in future liquor laws.

The evidence sought from coroners, judges, and other jurists; sheriffs and chief constables; manufacturers and contractors; and brewers and distillers was similarly skewed. Coroners informed the committee that liquor was a significant cause of death; judges saw a high proportion of crimes as the result of drunkenness; industrialists preferred abstainers, finding drunks to be unreliable and even dangerous. In his final report, Farewell described the evidence from brewers and distillers as "too incomplete to be of any service, and therefore none are printed."[59] Given that, in the dominion Royal Commission on the Liquor Traffic held two decades later, evidence of the positive impacts of distilling and brewing on local economies was used to argue that prohibition would seriously damage the economies of many communities, perhaps the evidence from brewers and distillers – however "incomplete" – did not support the prohibitionist aims of the committee. Contrast this decision not to print information from them with Farewell's decision to print a selection from the submissions from superintendents of asylums. They were also "not numerous" and yet Farewell thought it prudent to "annex a few as a fair index to the whole."[60] How "fair" a representation is impossible to know, since the original responses seem not to have survived. The asylum superintendents' answers were generally brief and told, for the most part, of a high proportion of admissions to asylums and jails as being linked to intemperance.

The committee's recommendations circumvented the sophistication of the dozens of pages of evidence printed and the thousands of responses to the questions that Farewell claimed to have received. Recognizing that "nothing short of entire prohibition can afford that relief and security from the evils of the traffic which society demands" but that the province was constitutionally unable to pass a prohibitory law, the committee concluded that the first order of business was to seek "such a modification of the constitution as will place the retail liquor business of the province entirely under the control of the provincial authorities."[61] In the meantime, Farewell argued, the government should put the authority to grant a license into the hands of the local population by publishing the names of all license applicants and requiring a majority of ratepayers to agree to the granting of licenses. Also, to deal with the numerous abuses that it had heard about in the vending system, the committee recommended that the province abolish the sale of liquor in saloons and separate the sale of liquor in shops from the sale of other goods, such as provisions and groceries. These were mere stopgap measures, the committee argued, until prohibition could be secured.[62]

The work of the Select Committee is a good example of the type of knowledge creation that Foucault describes as a "power-knowledge" nexus. In this understanding, those in positions of power create a certain type of knowledge, and that knowledge serves to reiterate their power. Yet it is difficult to assess whether this was a successful power-knowledge project. Despite the lengthy report, and extracts from responses that offered more equivocal insights into the liquor-selling system, the committee retained its emphasis on prohibition, having confirmed, through the skewed data-gathering process, that access to intoxicating liquor was unquestionably a problem. The report might have been the inspiration for the single action related to liquor during the legislature's 1875 session: it sent a formal request (authored by John Clarke) to the lieutenant governor asking the dominion government either to pass a federal prohibition law or to change the Constitution to allow provinces to do so. However, for nearly two decades, no further attempt was made to seize for the provinces the power to institute prohibition. Legislation to separate liquor sales from the sales of other provisions in shops and to abolish saloons was already being discussed in the legislature. The contention that the community should have a more direct say in the licensing process gained some currency over the next few decades, following the examples provided not only in the Select Committee's reports but also in other provinces.

Provincial Investigation of Municipal Licensing

While the Select Committee sent questionnaires to confirm the view that prohibition was the only solution to the liquor question, Crooks's office sent inspectors to gather more detailed information. The provisions of the licensing law amendment of 1873 empowered the government to hire provincial officers "to enforce the observance of the provisions of this act."[63] The task was soon found to be too big for one person, so Crooks's office hired four additional inspectors.[64] Inspector William Smith was joined by E.P. Watson, Robert Peters, Russel Hardy, and William Martin with the mandate to travel the main rail lines of the province in order to investigate licensed and unlicensed premises and to provide an assessment of the situation in each community that they visited. They also scrutinized the work of municipal officials empowered to enforce the law, from council members to the issuer of licenses and the license inspector. Although the rail-based travel meant that the inspectors could not visit every community in the province, their reports provide valuable insights into the nature of drinking and the challenges of licensing across the province. These inspectors provided a cross-section of attitudes toward licensing legislation and underscored the difficulties of exerting control over a system traditionally managed and manipulated at the local level. Their reports also illustrated excesses of the violations of liquor licensing in the province.[65]

The provincial inspectors observed that the newly tweaked law appeared to have had positive effects, but they also identified a number of challenges to its implementation resulting from the legacy of variable municipal oversight. A major problem that the inspectors identified was the limited effectiveness of local inspectors, many of whom were described as nothing short of incompetent. The inspector in Seaforth "exercises but little zeal in the discharge of his duties," two inspectors appointed in St. Mary's "are not efficient," and the inspector in Oshawa "does not understand his duties." Colborne's inspector was described as "a pedler [sic] and absent from his home the greater part of the time," indicating the limited interest of municipal authorities in hiring someone who could do the job. Of particular concern was the inspector in Dunnville, who "does his duty only in so far as he is called upon to report favourably of every applicant for a License, and to grant a certificate thereto; whether such applicant has the proper qualifications or not."[66] Even when inspectors appeared to be competent, they could be hindered by either disregard or ignorance of the law. In Clinton, the provincial inspector noted that the parameters of the law "so far as they are known are generally observed" but that "ignorance of the law is prevalent."[67] In Belleville, the inspector "endeavour[ed] to perform his duty" but was hindered by municipal officials "charged with ignorance of the law and apathy."[68] Notably, many councils were either unaware of or did not care that the 1873 amendment required each municipality to appoint an inspector. In his report, William Smith observed that "when the requirements of the law are more fully known, and competent men are appointed as inspectors, its success will be very much greater."[69] On top of that requirement, the 1868 act permitted, but did not require, a municipal council to pass a bylaw setting the maximum number of tavern, saloon, and shop licenses permitted in the community.[70] Russel Hardy noted that, as far as he could tell, few of the municipalities had "taken advantage of the act to limit by by-law the number of licenses to be issued." He recommended that the limit "should be fixed by legislative enactment as Municipal Councils are too much dependent upon the support of the classes dealing in liquors to act with entire independence in such matters," suggesting, therefore, the re-imposition of some central control over the number of taverns in a community which had been implemented in 1860 and removed in 1869.[71] Yet this did not always mean that the licensing situation in the community was problematic. In Petrolia, although no limiting bylaw had been passed, the council permitted "no saloons," the local inspector was deemed efficient, and the law "on the whole ... is fairly carried out," with only two people found selling liquor without a license.[72]

Ignorance and lack of interest were not the worst problems that the provincial inspectors found, for many municipal councils appear to have been working actively against enforcement of the law. E.P. Watson reported that even a zealous inspector could be thwarted by local power: "I find that where an Inspector has been found fault with, and his case has been brought before the Council, there is always considerable conniving among his friends to clear him; and so long as he imagines that his friends are in the ascendance in the Council he does as he pleases."[73] In Kingston, where William Martin described many taverns as "but low grog-holes," the local inspector had endeavoured "to make the law respected but is almost powerless to control many of the places ... owing to the objectionable character of the premises, and of those who control them."[74] Here "control" might have referred to something more than ownership of the establishment. Martin, whose travels took him to the communities along the rail line that ran from Toronto through Kingston (John A. Macdonald's riding) to Ottawa, noted that the "immense influence wielded by tavern and saloon keepers in Dominion, Provincial, and Municipal elections, causes them to be courted by those whose especial duty it is to enforce the law."[75] Martin's exposure to political influence might have been greater than that of those who rode the rails toward Fort Erie, Sarnia, or Waterloo, but officials at all levels of government throughout the province were not immune to using the influence of the tavern.

Along with the operation of the legislation, inspectors reiterated and gave some vivid descriptions of the problem of illegal sales in licensed shops. Russel Hardy noted that the problem was not unlicensed shopkeepers selling liquor but licensed ones "who sell by the pint or glass."[76] This was a frequent observation and caused considerable consternation in the communities. In Sarnia, "drinking in shops is done to an alarming extent."[77] Tavern keepers in Paris complained that people were getting "drunk at the shops especially on Saturdays, and then going to the taverns where there was a difficulty in getting them out at seven o'clock," the statutory Saturday closing time.[78] In some shops in London, "a bar and counter with all appliances or necessaries for selling by the glass are in full view," an observation repeated in Hamilton, with many shops that "have all the appliances or necessaries, and openly and conspicuously sell by the glass and small measure."[79] Smith found in many shops "beer pumps, decanters, and glasses and all the appliances necessary for drinking in full view."[80] He also noted that some shopkeepers who were selling alcohol by the glass claimed that they were not violating the law since they also had a tavern license for an adjoining property.[81] Hardy reported that he did not see any shops selling liquor by the glass, but "from the frequency of the complaints made I am persuaded that they are well founded."[82] Inspector Peters noted that this was also a complaint made about druggists.[83]

In their reports, the five provincial inspectors offered a range of observations aimed at improving operation of the licensing law. Watson suggested that the government should appoint local inspectors who "would then be free to act without reference to, or being influenced by, the local authorities."[84] Smith noted that the law itself was sound, but many of the problems that he found would not have occurred "had the municipal inspector performed his duty." He recommended that the municipal inspector be "compelled under a penalty to faithfully discharge his duties."[85] The location of licensed establishments was also a concern. Martin noted that, although liquor was no longer being sold at Grand Trunk Railway saloons, any advantages "are almost wholly counteracted by the easy access to the other saloons and taverns immediately adjoining the grounds of the company." He recommended that no licensed premises be permitted within "forty rods of a railway."[86] Watson decried saloons, those taverns without sleeping accommodations permitted in some communities; he described them as "the greatest source of complaint" and argued that they should be abolished.[87] This was also the inspectors' assessment of licensed shops. Martin argued that a shop license should be separated from all other forms of business since "in nine cases out of ten, where general traders take out a shop license, the liquor therein sold is used as a decoy to lead customers on to purchase goods. Treating [i.e., giving liquor for free to] the customer and his family is the first preliminary to purchases."[88]

The inspectors' reports included a special assessment of the situation in Toronto penned by Clerk of the Treasury Department Henry Totten. It rattled the community. Totten's analysis compared the situation in Toronto to what was going on elsewhere in the province. Even though cities such as Ottawa and Kingston were described as having an excess of drinking places and many shops that functioned essentially as saloons, Toronto, as Totten described it, was far worse. Indeed, many of the problems listed by the other inspectors as occurring intermittently and to varying degrees in other communities were all found in Toronto. Nearly half of the 249 licensed taverns did not have the requisite accommodations for travellers. Many shops operated, Totten said, as open bars, with "all of the appliances for selling by the glass such as beer pumps, decanters, glasses &c."[89] There was a "grey market" in licenses, with license holders selling their licenses to people who then opened their own businesses without being inspected. The inspector, seventy-year-old Ogle R. Gowan, was a long-time Conservative partisan and Orangeman openly hostile to temperance.[90] *Grip* satirized his work as an inspector by calling him a "thorough going prohibitionist in his way of making it an invariable rule not to permit the opening of more drinking dens than an average of one to every three houses on a street."[91] Gowan was accused of creating some kind of shifty license exchange system in order to pocket the transfer fee but not distribute more licenses. His actions were credited with increasing the number of taverns in the city. Even though the Board of Police Commissioners, empowered to oversee the licensing situation in the city, had declared that no more licenses would be issued after 12 May 1873, somehow over a dozen more taverns received licenses.

Although Totten laid most of the blame on Gowan, he noted that the law itself allowed the type of abuse at which Gowan seemed to be especially adept. This was the result of the relationship between the issuer of licenses and the inspector. The provincial legislation allowed the inspector of licenses to receive 6 percent of the license fee as remuneration (it had been 10 percent until 1869). Totten outlined the main problem:

> In the city the issuer of licenses is also the Municipal Inspector. As such Inspector, he is required by by-law ... to receive and keep a registry of all applications for certificates of Licenses or transfers, to ascertain that the petitions [for a license] are correct and true, and to make an inspection of the premises and see if they have all the conveniences and accommodations required by law, and to report thereon, to ascertain by inspection and enquiry from time to time whether the persons receiving certificates for Licenses continue to comply with the provisions of the law.

Yet, since the issuer of licenses received a 6 percent commission for all licenses issued, "from the nature of the duties required of him, he has a direct pecuniary interest in reporting favourably of all applicants."[92] The situation in Toronto might have been excessive, but as the inspectors' reports illustrate, violations in the liquor laws and the resulting potential for social disorder were certainly not unique to larger centres.

***

Before the end of the first decade of Canada's existence, the legislature of Ontario had begun to investigate the problems caused by municipal control of retail liquor sales and to consider how to address them. In these efforts, the legislature was influenced by a vocal and growing temperance movement, and a general reluctance to impose overly stringent and illiberal restrictions on the trade. It was also limited by constitutional boundaries in terms of its authority. Government involvement in the lives of individuals, such as in the building of an inebriate asylum, might have been justified as government interest in the welfare of people who were victims of their own weaknesses or the predations of the liquor trade. Yet such an institution did not interfere with the laissez-faire economic ideas of the liberal state. Indeed, the utility of state-run asylums had long been accepted as a reasonable measure to help unfortunate citizens, but intervening in trade, commerce, and the commercial activities or personal pastimes of the people was a far greater imposition on freedoms. Nevertheless, the investigations into the licensing situation across the province initiated a process by which the provincial government, faced with increased pressure to do something about drunkenness and evidence that the liberty afforded to municipalities to manage their own affairs was a major cause of the problem, began to consider taking over the whole system itself. The problem was how to do so without violating the principles of equality, liberty, and individual autonomy so fundamental to the operation of the liberal state.

2

Centralization, I:
The Crooks Act

The evidence provided by the Select Committee on the Liquor Traffic and the investigations of the government's inspectors illustrated the need for changes to the licensing regime in Ontario. The transformation was incremental, spread over two legislative sessions, and showed a reluctance for Oliver Mowat and Adam Crooks to overturn the autonomy that municipal councils had enjoyed in managing the liquor system according to local characteristics. Such limited government involvement was essential to the ideal liberal state. As a result, Mowat's government attempted to deal with the most significant problems identified in the inspectors' reports while allowing municipalities to retain control of the system. It was not until these adjustments to the licensing system were found to be inadequate that Crooks introduced a sweeping change to licensing in the province in which the government limited municipal authority while still retaining elements of local, or at least regional, individuality.

On 3 February 1874, Crooks presented a "bill for the consolidation and amendment of the liquor laws." By bringing together the various amendments made over the past few years, the bill aimed to eliminate the ignorance of the law that the inspectors found in many municipalities and to reduce the potential for opportunistic manipulation of the licensing system at the local level. The municipal inspector was now expressly separate from that of the issuer of licenses, a change that would have caused consternation to party heelers like Ogle Gowan. To deal with situations in which municipal inspectors were not "as zealous as they ought [to be]," the bill gave county judges the authority to remove inspectors; it also specifically required police officers to assist in enforcing the law.[1] Previously, municipalities were permitted, but not required, to pass bylaws setting limits on the number of licenses to be issued in their communities. Under the new legislation, licenses would not be issued until such a bylaw was passed.[2] This law made it the "duty" of a council to pass bylaws outlining the conditions that needed to be met before a license could be issued.[3] Although it remained legal for licensed shops to sell other products besides liquor, shopkeepers were specifically forbidden to allow customers to drink liquor in any part of the building.[4] The amendment, designed to address what the *Globe* called "injury and demoralization," seemed to cut to the heart of problematic drinking. "A fine of twenty dollars for each case ... will help to stop such baneful liberality."[5] Finally, the legislation set a minimum amount that a municipality could charge for a liquor license.

In the legislature, the bill received general approval, although some members thought that it might trample on individual rights. Several speakers were troubled that the bill removed a plaintiff's right to appeal a conviction, an issue especially problematic because police magistrates often were not considered to have the same depth of knowledge of the law as county judges. Without the right to appeal, the argument went, many improper convictions could result, and so the right to appeal was restored during the committee process. Other members were concerned about the constitutionality of the bill. Opposition leader Matthew Cameron argued that, although the BNA Act allowed provinces to license taverns for revenue purposes, it did not specifically allow them to issue licenses for any other purpose, such as for public safety or health. Crooks countered that "so long as the legislature did not assume to prohibit entirely this traffic, it had a right to protect the health and interests of the Province by any regulations considered expedient."[6] Several members thought that the new minimum fee structure would be too high, so some minimum fees were reduced. Finally, and not surprisingly, some temperance MLAs argued that the changes were not sufficient. Temperance stalwart John Clarke argued that "Inspectors of Licenses should be responsible to the Government for the proper discharge of their duties, and not to [municipal] officials dependent upon the people for their positions."[7] Norfolk South Grit Simpson McCall went even further, concluding that the government should "take the whole management of this matter into its own hands."[8]

Outside the legislature, the bill was generally well received. Mowat had noted that both licensed victuallers and temperance supporters had been consulted in the creation of the legislation, and in the press support came from all sides. Editor and legendary Reformer George Brown of the Toronto *Globe*, who not surprisingly supported the measure from the outset, noted that Crooks "has not gone unduly ahead of public opinion" despite some passages about which "some may grumble." It predicted an easy passage.[9] The Conservative Toronto *Daily Mail* was also supportive, expressing its approval based upon the principles of temperance and support for respectable licensed victuallers while cautioning readers about those on both sides who had dubious intentions. Recognizing that intemperance "utterly destroys untold thousands of human beings every year," the *Mail*'s editor Thomas C. Patteson, gave faint praise to "men in authority" doing "what in reason can be done to check intemperance by imposing severe restrictions upon the trade in intoxicating liquors." Yet Patteson cautioned against overly zealous restrictions as fundamentally contrary to liberal ideals: "What must be the result of subjecting [the liquor trade] to what they consider unjust and vexatious prosecutions, unless to array them with all the powerful influence which they possess against any and every reform?" Meanwhile, having reminded readers of the power of the liquor industry, the editor cautioned temperance advocates against the main threat: "The real and substantial opposition to the [temperance] movement arises from the injudicious action of some who wish to be thought its best friends, but who are in reality not properly to be so classed." He referred specifically to Clarke, who, he argued, was using temperance "for mere political purposes." The danger, Patteson noted, was that such politically motivated extremism would drive the liquor industry to use its "powerful influence" to destroy any progress made by the temperance movement. It was an adept rhetorical exercise, simultaneously supporting the temperance movement and the liquor industry while criticizing the government, which itself claimed to be listening to both sides and seeking a middle ground.[10]

Hope that the legislation of 1874 would address problems with municipal licensing was quickly found to have been misplaced. In an editorial two months after the amendment received royal assent, the *Globe* railed against the ongoing problems and abuses of the liquor system. Brown noted that the provision in the law making the presence of various types of drink-selling apparatus (decanters, glasses, casks, etc.) prima facie evidence that drinks were being sold was thwarted when "the occupier of the house and his wife swear that there was no liquor sold." Moreover, the shop license – what Brown called "the union of groceries and groggeries" – also remained problematic: "More harm is done to morals and sobriety by the tippling in grocers' stores, and the sale in them of quantities of liquors 'for the use of families' and 'not to be consumed on the premises' than in any number of taverns, though even of the most questionable order of respectability."[11] Brown was no prohibitionist, but his frustration was shared by temperance supporters who continued to petition for prohibition at both provincial and dominion levels. A correspondent to the *Daily Mail* signing his name "A Son of Temperance" argued that, whereas a well-run licensing system might be a solution, "if the country cannot have this ... there is only one other remedy, and that is the executioner, Prohibition."[12] This refrain was repeated in temperance meetings throughout the province. For instance, in December 1874, a meeting under the auspices of the Toronto Temperance Reform Society resolved that too many licenses were still being issued. At the conclusion of the meeting, the group sent a message to the Board of Police Commissioners, which had the authority to issue licenses in the city, asking that the number of licenses be capped at 100 (the board did not heed this request). Nevertheless, many speakers at the meeting, including Clarke, reiterated that prohibition was far preferable.[13]

Not everybody was convinced. In March 1875, Brown, concerned more about the fortunes of Mowat's government (which had just won the election and increased its majority) than about the success of temperance, argued repeatedly against prohibition. His reasoning was simple: the public was not (yet) ready for prohibition, and it would be worse for such a measure to be passed and to fail than for it not to be passed at all. Moreover, he argued, there was already a prohibition act on the books, but it was not being used to its fullest extent. The Dunkin Act not only prohibited the sale of liquor in the municipalities in which it was in force but also contained a number of provisions for prosecuting those who sold liquor to people subsequently found drunk or injured because of drunkenness. The *Globe* editor's disdain for the argument that only national prohibition would solve the problems of the "drink question" hinged on the inaction of temperance advocates themselves:

> Now why are all those provisions of the Dunkin Act a dead letter? Is it said that their enforcement would take trouble? Of course it would, but surely moral reformers, if in earnest, are prepared for that. They don't wish us to believe that they merely think of a great splurge and then over with it; of a flaming speech at a public meeting, and no more ... It would be something to be able to say: "We have honestly and to the best of our ability carried out the law we have and now we wish one more stringent [law] ... " But surely it is not the most logical way of going to work to say

"We have allowed the measure of prohibition we have to be unemployed and useless; and we with [wish?] something stronger, which will work of itself, and save us the necessity of putting forth any effort or exercising any amount of vigilance."[14]

Brown insisted that the zealous members of the temperance movement had a lot of work to do to enforce the existing laws before being in a position to argue convincingly, if ever, that prohibition was the solution to this seemingly intractable problem.

Reactions from prohibitionists, as expected, were immediate and passionate and followed the common arguments against local option. What was the point of local option, they argued, when people could simply head across the town line to buy alcohol in another community? Without prohibition across the province (or, better yet, the nation or even the world), the liquor trade would continue unabated. Moreover, as *Globe* correspondent "Temperance" noted, the Dunkin Act did not go far enough to prohibit liquor since vendors could still sell it in larger quantities of small bottles (at least a "dozen bottles of three half pints") and physicians could still prescribe it for medical use. With these aspects of the law, "you will cease to be surprised that temperance men *with brains* are not enthusiastic over the Dunkin Bill."[15] Others argued that the problem was the inaction not of Drys but of local authorities, especially, as Rev. James Gray of Milton noted, in small communities where "administrators of law who are in sympathy with the license system can embarrass and defeat the [Dunkin Act], and render it inoperative. It is a mere patch-work affair at best."[16] J.B. Aylsworth of Collingwood, meanwhile, contended that prohibition was necessary but supported the *Globe*'s argument that the prohibitionists needed to do more work by placing the onus on churches to motivate their members to "undertake to secure and enforce the Dunkin Bill." This, rather than outright national prohibition, Aylsworth argued, was a necessary first step.[17] Similarly, J.A. McClung explained that temperance supporters had not seen the success that they wanted because of "a want of a thorough canvass" of communities to have petitions signed to trigger a local option vote.[18]

Those involved in the liquor traffic did not remain silent, but they used different tactics. Whereas temperance adherents relied upon a mass movement of active concerned citizens, leaders of the liquor industry sought more subtle legislative and legal approaches to defending their livelihoods. One tactic was to use the courts. When, in 1874 the Ontario government attempted to require brewers to hold a provincial license, the brewers took the government to court. Since manufacturers already were required to be licensed by the dominion government, the brewers argued that it was beyond the constitutional authority of the province to require a further license to sell the manufactured products. As noted earlier, the brewers' licensing case was the first appeal heard by the Supreme Court of Canada after it was created in 1875, and the brewers won.[19] Retroactive legal action was one approach for the Wets, but it was better to address legislation before it came into force rather than in courts afterward. So, whereas the temperance forces held many public meetings and gathered petitions through their churches and other associations, the brewers, distillers, and vendors of liquor generally took to direct lobbying, often through the action of "licensed victuallers" associations. Based upon similar organizations gaining influence in the United Kingdom, these groups offered a respectable, market-oriented, liberal, and mildly progressive face on an industry that the temperance movement characterized as unapologetically evil.[20] Use of the term "victuallers" was undoubtedly a rhetorical tactic to distance themselves from the liquor selling that they had in common, and to connect themselves with the positive idea of providers of sustenance and hospitality. Traditionally, a victualler was a supplier of food and drink associated with the classic taverns or inns characterized as resting places for travellers.[21] Many of the prominent members of Ontario's licensed victuallers associations were businesspeople – mostly grocers, brewers, and distillers – who had clear financial stakes in the freedom of grocers and tavern and saloon keepers to sell booze. The first president of the Licensed Victuallers Association of Ontario was Senator Frank Smith, an industrialist who made part of his fortune in the grocery business; Patrick G. Close, one of the vice-presidents, was also a grocer. First Vice-President Eugene O'Keefe was a prominent brewer; Secretary George D. Dawson was the owner of the Bodega Wine Company; Treasurer William Copeland was a Toronto brewer.[22] In contrast to the massive temperance machine with its substantial local organization, paid speakers, and expansive publishing system, the influence of licensed victuallers is less easy to trace in Canadian history because much of the work was through direct appeal to the government rather than in spectacular, emotionally charged meetings. Their influence, however, was considerable.

In early January 1876, members of the Licensed Victuallers Association of Ontario, including President Smith and Secretary Dawson, met with members of Mowat's cabinet, including the premier and Crooks, to offer their solution to the problem of intemperance.[23] In contrast to the implication from the temperance crowd that the liquor interest was going to destroy the country, Smith and Dawson observed that they and their members had "as deep an interest in the prosperity and well-being of the Province at large as any other class or any other traders in the community." They reminded Mowat that they were "a large and by no means an uninfluential body in the country ... engaged in legitimate, and in very many instances, long established businesses," heavily invested in employing many citizens, and therefore had "a large stake in the country." Having established their loyalty, respectability, and contributions to the nation, they proceeded to offer a counternarrative to the temperance argument against the liquor trade. Their argument was multi-pronged. They noted that they also deplored "the evils resulting from intemperance" and were "anxious to lend our assistance to any practical scheme to mitigate the sad consequences which result from it." They argued that something more than "mere conversation" or "simple attempts at legislation" was necessary "to meet and remedy this great social evil." They then laid out a list of actions which, in their view, would mitigate the greatest harms caused by intemperance:

- Enforce the license laws.
- Increase penalties for those found guilty of breaking the laws.
- Eliminate the grocers' license to sell liquor (or at least stringently enforce the rules related to shop sales).
- Change the Saturday closing law to 9 p.m. from 7 p.m. to accommodate workers who finish work after 7 p.m.
- Appoint government inspectors to enforce the rules, especially against groggeries and gambling joints, leaving the police to "the discharge of other duties."
- Impose fines on drinkers found breaking the law in unlicensed spaces.

They concluded by arguing that all citizens should be engaged in the process of enforcing the law "by giving their active aid to the authorities in the suppression of illicit traffic."[24]

During an extensive discussion after reading their address, the members of the association expanded the reasoning for their suggestions. O'Keefe stated that he knew that in Toronto, "1,000 houses ... sold liquor without licenses," a statement that apparently astonished Mowat. Smith explained that even the request that taverns be permitted to stay open until 9 p.m. on Saturdays was to encourage temperance. Labourers "went out with their wives on Saturday night to do the marketing and they wanted a glass of beer, but as they could not get it [later], many of them got drunk before they went home, whereas if they knew they could get a glass afterwards, they would go home satisfied." Moreover, young men living in rooming houses who had no place to socialize would go to unlicensed taverns or send for a bottle "and take it to their rooms." The association was also concerned about the existence of "sham hotels" across the province. Mowat asked whether the association was made up of all the tavern keepers, and Smith described its membership as "respectable licensed men in that trade." When the premier asked, somewhat incredulously, "do I understand that the Association approves of discrimination in the issue of licenses and a diminution in the number?" several members replied "decidedly."[25] It was a powerful display of an alternative perspective to the excesses of temperance rhetoric, couched in the familiar liberal language of freedom, fairness, and protection of property rights.

The licensed victuallers offered a contrasting approach to the management of liquor sales, one that either predicted or heavily influenced the subsequent direction that the province took. By insisting that they were legitimate businesspeople interested in the welfare of their fellow citizens, they undercut the temperance movement's perspective that the liquor industry was run by immoral, rapacious, and greedy men whose profligacy would destroy the nation. By agreeing that they were concerned about intemperance and illegality, they placed themselves on the side of moderation and law and order, countering the argument that liquor vendors encouraged social chaos and illegality. They doubled down on their respectability by agreeing that grocers should not be allowed to sell liquor, seeing stand-alone liquor stores as better able to protect more vulnerable residents. They expressed concern that women and children were routinely exposed "to many evils resulting from the sale and too frequently the drinking of liquors" in licensed groceries, whereas they would have little reason to frequent single-purpose liquor shops and thus be protected.[26] Moreover, by arguing for stricter enforcement of the regulations and the appointment of government inspectors, they offered a solution that would disconnect, or at least distance, the corrupting issue of liquor from municipal politics and centralize the authority over liquor in the hands of the provincial government. Finally, by surprising Mowat with the assertion that the association wanted stricter controls and more "discrimination" and insisting that its members were "respectable hotel keepers," the victuallers reinforced their image as decent, law-abiding, and productive members of society whose roles within the liberal state were simultaneously to drive the economy and defend individual liberty. It is not clear whether these plans were already in the works, or whether the licensed victuallers deputation influenced the government's legislation, but several of these suggestions became central features of the Liquor License Act, 1876.

The Crooks Act

The years 1873–75 might be seen, in retrospect, as a period of legislative experimentation and investigation, a nascent form of policy learning.[27] The amendments to the licensing act passed in 1873 and 1874 allowed the government to introduce tweaks to the licensing system while gathering important information about the perceived problems of liquor regulation across the province. The information gathered by the government inspectors in 1873 and 1874 provided an important picture of the challenges presented by a municipally based and politically charged system of inspection and enforcement. The municipal oversight of liquor no longer seemed to be either efficient or expedient. The vivid reports of Toronto's licensing regime, characterized as deeply corrupt and out of control, although possibly exceptional compared with other communities, confirmed the worst fears of temperance advocates and tweaked the concerns of moderates who otherwise would have had little to do with temperance associations. If police commissioners with the resources of the provincial capital could not keep a lid on excessive drinking, then perhaps it was time to take that authority out of local hands.

This was the rationale behind the extensive changes that Crooks introduced in the Liquor License Act, 1876: to eliminate the potential for corruption at the local level by depoliticizing the granting of licenses and the inspection of licensed premises. The Crooks Act, as it soon became known, removed the authority to select inspectors from the hands of municipal governments, thereby decoupling the inspector's livelihood from local politics. This allowed inspectors, in theory, to act independently of municipal politics, in which, as one legislator noted, tavern owners "were on nearly every Council" (if true, it was a violation of the Municipal Act).[28] Further distancing licensing from municipal authority, the legislation created a three-person Board of License Commissioners in "license districts" roughly matching the political ridings of the province. Board members were appointed by the government and unpaid. The commissioners were thus to be prominent members of the community who would do the work as a public service. Finally, the legislation imposed a new population-based maximum number of licenses that could be issued in a community. It granted municipal councils the authority to reduce the maximum number (but not increase it) as long as the number remained above zero (which, in effect, would institute prohibition, still considered ultra vires the provincial government). The law also established minimum fees for licenses, allowing councils to increase those fees to a set maximum. The system was more complex than previous licensing regimes, and the legislature spent several sittings going through the legislation in detail.

Although both the reduction in numbers of licenses and the removal of municipal authority over licensure were generally seen as good ideas, opponents jumped on many of the elements of the law as indicative of political overreach and illiberal extension of government power. Opponents insisted that the law would not reduce drinking, it would create a monopoly, it violated individual property rights, and it was simply an opportunity for the government to gain power by creating a massive patronage machine. By reducing the number of licenses, opponents argued, the Liquor License Act would simply concentrate the number of drinkers and increase illegality rather than reduce the amount of drinking. A correspondent to the *Daily Mail* argued that restriction would actually increase disorder: "If you unduly restrict and hamper the legitimate calling, the effect will be ... a great increase of smuggling, ... unlicensed hotels would multiply on every hand, and the present evils [would] increase tenfold."[29] Such sentiments lay at the heart of the argument presented by the licensed victuallers during their deputation to the government a few months earlier. As one correspondent told the *Globe,* granting too few licenses would create a virtual monopoly and cause more problems that the law was intended to solve, since it would "throw the way open to the greater evils of low and unlicensed groggeries ... [resulting in] more drinking and disturbance."[30] Another writer worked out how many drinks it would take for a tavern keeper to pay for his license, concluding that a restriction would increase the concentration of drinkers because the licensee would need to sell more drinks: "A tavern keeper on a country road ... is compelled to sell 2400 glasses of liquor to pay for his license before he makes any profit for himself. If there are thirty taverns in a township, they must sell 72,000 glasses a year to pay the license fees only." He suggested that a tavern keeper be licensed like "a pilot, a surgeon, [or] a school teacher, ... and once licensed you allow them to continue [being] licensed unless through gross misconduct ... Give a license to the right man without a fee, and thus take off the inducement he now has to sell liquor to every man, drunk or sober."[31] During debates in the legislature, opposition leader Matthew Cameron, a professed teetotaller though not a prohibitionist, asserted that reducing the number of licenses would simply increase both the illicit traffic and the profit earned by the small group of tavern keepers who kept their licenses. Cameron rejected excessive government interference in the market, preferring to take a law-and-order approach. He wanted to lock up the drunks for the sake of the future: "The man who drank to excess should be punished as if for a crime. This ... would be the only means of training the young to avoid excessive drinking."[32]

Proponents of the legislation fought this form of supply-and-demand economics with their own calculations. In reaction to Cameron's assertion that the demand for drink would increase when the supply of licenses went down, Provincial Secretary S.C. Wood presented an alternative calculus. He argued that an increased supply of licensed taverns would lead to fewer customers per tavern. To survive, tavern owners would have to sell more booze to more people. Under the new system, Boards of License Commissioners would ensure that licenses would be held by respectable tavern owners, who would not be driven to sell "all the liquors they could – to take the purchaser's last dollar sometime – in order to make their living."[33] Indeed, when introducing his legislation, Adam Crooks had included evidence from the system of "free licensing" introduced in Liverpool, England. There the traffic was not limited, "but the results had been so appalling in two years that the magistrates were induced to introduce a stringent licensing system."[34] In the *Globe*, Brown characterized Cameron's argument as a "somewhat stale idea, which ought by this time scarcely to be dignified with the name of argument." Liquor, Brown argued, was not a normal commodity and not subject to "the principle of supply and demand."

> Universal experience shows that as far as the sale of intoxicating liquors is concerned, another principle comes into operation, and another standard of judgement has to be applied. The appetite for strong drink is an artificial one, and grows according to the facilities afforded for its indulgence. It is absurd to talk of just so much liquor going to be consumed, when every dealer in this article does his best to encourage the consumption and makes it continually more.

The *Globe* ended with a call for common sense: "It is simply insulting ordinary intelligence, and setting at naught ordinary experience, to tell us that the number of drinking places has nothing to do with the increase of drunkenness."[35]

Supply-and-demand principles of economics might not have been viable, but a stronger argument (at least to liberal-minded individuals) was concern about creating monopolies. Patteson of the *Daily Mail* argued that, although drunkenness was a problem, permitting monopolies and enriching the few might be greater sins:

> The privilege of selling liquor – one of no little monetary value as things are – would, under restriction, become of much greater value – would become in fact one of the most valuable franchises that the State has to bestow. Liquor selling would be the immensely profitable monopoly of a few, and to grant a man a license would be equivalent to voting him a fortune.[36]

In a separate editorial, the newspaper reminded its readers that the question was addressed before. Citing a report of the Legislative Council of Upper Canada from 1856, the *Daily Mail* offered sage advice from the past on how to deal with intoxicating drinks: "regulate as best [as possible] their sale; define the extent and manner in which [a] licensing system may be carried out, … but not to such an extent as to make the business of liquor selling a monopoly."[37] These were powerful arguments because a monopoly was anathema to the liberal marketplace. Indeed, the legislation based its allotment of licenses in a community upon the population size, thereby suggesting that an individual seller would have access to a specified number of residents. Although no individual would hold complete control of alcohol distribution in the province, in some scantily populated areas significant reductions in the number of licenses could mean that only one person would hold a license in a sizable geographic region. Predictions that the legislation would create something tantamount to a monopoly, therefore, were not without some foundation.

Many saw the law to be an imposition on one of the key pillars of liberalism: individual rights, especially property rights. In 1873, when debating the bill to restrict the property of habitual drunkards, several opponents balked at such an affront to individual rights, no matter how sodden the individual.[38] Similarly, arguments about the rights of businesspeople to have viable opportunities were at the heart of opposition to the Crooks Act. This was the main basis upon which members of the Licensed Victuallers Association built their argument when they met with the cabinet in early January 1876. A member informed the government ministers in attendance that the victuallers were concerned about its rights, quoting Article 3 of its bylaws, which described the association as "a social compact for the purpose of protecting their rights, resisting any arbitrary measures intended to injure their business or calling."[39] Later that month, as the debates became increasingly heated, a licensed victualler who had been part of the deputation published an open (though anonymous) letter to the government arguing that the abrupt reduction in the number of licenses would "certainly be regarded as an unjustifiable disregard of the rights of property and as a measure fraught with positive injury, if not ruinous consequences, to numerous individuals." Losing a license would leave a business owner in possession of "useless and unsaleable stock, in the shape of pumps, bedding, furniture, and fixtures."[40] A few days later John Cosgrave, Toronto brewer and chairman of the Executive Committee of the association, penned an open letter to Crooks, also published in the *Daily Mail*, accusing the government of hypocrisy in its view of the vested rights of businesses. In a previous debate on lumber licenses, the government had concluded that "if [it] withdrew the license now held by lumber men that they [the government] would be interfering with vested rights … Now, sir, I am at a loss to know why the rights of the one should be respected and those of the other ignored."[41] Cosgrave argued that such contraventions of rights should at least be met with compensation, making a link between licensed liquor vendors and unlicensed, but duly compensated, slave owners:

> Has not the trade in liquors been licensed and recognized for years and years? Men engaged therein, while adhering to reasonable restrictive laws have always felt that if at any time a Government laboring under the hallucination that in the interests of temperance it were desirable to undertake to make a reduction they would at least place the trade upon an equal footing with the slaveowners of the West Indies by granting indemnification for the loss sustained.[42]

Arguments about rights and infringements of economic liberty might have had some power but were not always convincing. The satirical magazine *Grip*, edited by prohibitionist John W. Bengough, who had little sympathy for either side of the licensing argument, ridiculed claims by tavern keepers that higher license fees would kill their businesses, so they should receive significant compensation. It was risible because tavern keepers also argued that their businesses were so precarious that they could barely afford the increased fees: "Men who were not known to possess anything had thousands of dollars in sofas, tables, beds, and beer-jugs. If remuneration for outlay were duly granted, we should soon learn that some unsuspected millionaires had been living with us in a very out-at-elbows state ... [W]hat a business they were doing."[43] Clearly, to Bengough, the heavy financial investment supposedly poured into furnishing these "low groggeries" was illusory.

Whereas economic, pragmatic, and philosophical arguments against Crooks's bill dealt with its details, the main criticism focused on its major change, and arguably its greatest strength, the centralization of liquor licensing. After several amendments to the licensing acts that had attempted to reduce the corruption and misuse of the liquor license at the municipal level, the Crooks Act removed that power altogether. When introducing the bill in late January 1876, Crooks explained why he was prepared to break with the long tradition of municipal control of licensing. Previous efforts to reduce abuses had failed, he said, because

> these efforts had been made hitherto by means of the local municipal bodies, those bodies by which under our system of local self-government, we have been accustomed to regulate all matters of this kind affecting the welfare of the community. The effect had not been satisfactory, for it had been found that these bodies had failed when called upon to exercise for the benefit of the community those powers with which they had been clothed.[44]

The change, he argued, would have several positive results. Tavern owners could no longer rely on friends in local councils to urge the issuer of licenses to look the other way; tavern keepers would no longer be seen as lucrative, influential allies in municipal elections; inspectors would no longer be tempted, threatened, or bribed to ignore transgressions of licensees out of fear of losing their jobs. With the provincial government in charge of these matters, and an impartial, unpaid Board of License Commissioners overseeing each municipality's liquor system, so the argument went, such abuses would be a thing of the past.

To be sure, the centralization of liquor control was neither a new nor an unpopular idea. Brown told the *Globe*'s readers that nobody seemed to oppose the idea of taking the power of licensing out of the hands of municipalities: "The abuses arising from that arrangement have been so many and varied, that the all but universal feeling has been that almost any change would be for the better."[45] During debates in 1873 on the licensing law amendments, Conservative member for Lennox, John T. Grange, argued that "general inspection of the licensing business should be directly under government control," and as noted earlier Simpson

McCall made a similar argument during the debates in 1874.[46] At the meeting between licensed victuallers and Mowat's cabinet earlier in January, when Christopher Fraser, the commissioner for public works, asked the deputation for its opinion on taking licensing out of municipal councils' hands, the response was generally positive. Several victuallers noted that "this system was in vogue in Montreal, and worked very satisfactorily," and Frank Smith argued that the only "difficulty would be in getting men of sufficient judgement to act fairly towards all."[47] A few days after Crooks introduced the legislation, the *Globe* voiced its support for centralization. Explaining to confused readers that it was in favour of "the general advantages arising from the local management of local affairs," Brown argued that this time things were different:

> The appointment of certain officials is taken from those who, in the peculiar circumstances in which they are placed, might be inclined, and often are, to favour certain interests and to wink at abuses ... [L]ocal interests and personal partialities come continually into play, so as to secure a license for a locality where none is needed, and for an individual whose character and standing are none of the best.[48]

In the legislature, Provincial Secretary S.C. Wood echoed this sentiment, saying that licensing "was not safe in the hands of the Municipal Councils ... [whose members] were to a great extent in the cities and towns elected by the vote[s] of the tavern, saloon, and shop-keepers. If a man were elected by the influence of a certain class, it was natural that he should look kindly upon its interests."[49] Remove this interest, and you remove the abuses of the licensing system. The editor of *Canadian Monthly Review* concurred, setting aside the argument about tavern keepers influencing municipal governments and making it about the economics of the business influencing decisions at the municipal level: "The temptation to excess keeps pace with increases in the number of licensed houses, and hence the obvious conclusion that they should not be multiplied *ad libitum*. If municipal officers abuse their powers – and we think they do – they ought to be deprived of them."[50]

The opposition saw one flaw in the logic of releasing licensing from the nefarious hold of municipal politics: putting the licensing power in the hands of provincial appointees would not eliminate the temptations, threats, and opportunities but simply transfer them from municipal to provincial politicians. Such a move would add a tremendous amount of patronage to the Mowat government's impressive and growing patronage network. Not only would the law create over one hundred new paid inspectorships, but partisan commissioners would also favour Grit-oriented tavern keepers, all to the disadvantage of Tory licensees, however respectable. The *Daily Mail* stated "in plain words" that the government "proposes to put the trade under the surveillance of the politics; for as politics go now, the commissioners and inspectors appointed to regulate the traffic will, without doubt, be political partisans of local might and celebrity, and skilled in the low arts of electioneering and ward chicanery."[51] The *Canadian Monthly Review,* otherwise supportive of the legislation, noted that "centralization, unnecessarily monopolizing, and a profuse multiplication of offices, are new 'Planks' in the Reform 'Platform' devised since the party secured office."[52] The Conservative Toronto *Leader* was unimpressed from the outset, rejecting the idea that municipalities should lose what it called the "undoubted privilege" of appointing their own officers, crying foul about the general tendency of Mowat's government toward arbitrariness and centralization, and recognizing that Mowat's party "has shown a degree of shrewdness in advancing its interests ... [T]hey have got, as it were, to the leeward of the temperance folks, and are fighting a battle for themselves" in proposing a measure that, ostensibly to deal with the impoverishing damage of drink, instead enriched the party with more patronage opportunities.[53]

Beyond economical, practical, and philosophical considerations, such political concerns drove discussions in the legislature. During debate on the first reading of the bill, Simcoe South MLA George MacDougall complained that, although there was a need for improvement to the licensing situation, the bill was simply "a grand scheme to secure the political support of tavern-keepers," a patronage system that he likened to an earlier bill that gave the government the power to appoint marriage license granting authority.[54] Even Conservative members who otherwise supported the spirit of the legislation were uncomfortable with the patronage that it permitted. Abraham Lauder, the Conservative from Grey East, "was afraid the government would use the patronage conferred by this bill in their own interests ... so as to get the liquor interests to sustain them at the elections."[55] Tory leader Matthew Cameron outlined what he saw as the Grits' game plan: "If some licenses had to be cancelled, the opponents of the government were nearly sure to suffer."[56] Even professed supporters of the government, such as brewer John Cosgrave, voiced his concern not only about patronage but also about the potential for that power "at any time [to] be exercised arbitrarily and corruptly," a power that would "in any case at least unduly influence the trade in favour of the government of the day."[57] He was not arguing that this power would benefit only Reformers; rather, it would allow any government to exercise its patronage to boost its fortunes at the polls. This was a perspective that the *Daily Mail,* a decidedly partisan newspaper, also suggested should make even Grits think twice about the legislation. "It is a 'reform' junta to-day; it may be a Conservative junta to-morrow."[58]

In both the legislature and the newspapers, supporters of the government insisted both that the cries of patronage were overdone and that in any case centralization was the best way to deal with the challenge of municipal corruption in licensing. Responding to comments made during the first reading, Mowat noted that "the feature [of centralization] ... was the most important one in the Bill – the very one upon which the voice of the public, including the licensed victuallers themselves, was most unanimous." In a statement that would be a common refrain of the government, Mowat noted that the responsibility of taking over the selection of licensing authorities "was a most distasteful one to the government, but which had been neglected by the municipal bodies, on whose shoulders it had rested in the past." Nevertheless, he did not entirely reject the idea that the government would dole out favours based upon partisan considerations. "Everything else being equal, no Administration was in the habit of preferring their opponents to their friends in making appointments." He added, however, that "the Government honestly endeavoured in appointing their officers to secure efficient men."[59] In subsequent debates, other members supported this perspective. Crooks argued that "this was not a measure which ... any government would be likely to use as a political engine."[60] Welland Liberal James G. Currie "didn't believe any government could strengthen itself by such patronage."[61] A few weeks after the bill received royal assent on 10 February, the *Globe* observed that the government's actions were reinforcing this professed non-partisan spirit. It reported that Crooks was sending blank forms to "good men of both political parties" asking for "the names of those thought to be best suited for the discharge of the different duties involved."[62] It was yet to be seen whether the information provided, however bipartisan, would be acted on in a similar manner.

For its part, the Tory *Daily Mail* balanced itself between angrily denouncing and lightheartedly mocking the actions of the government. The newspaper included a regular satirical column ostensibly written by a fictitious Grit partisan named Jimuel Briggs (a pseudonym of Thomas Phillips Thompson).[63] After the Crooks Act was passed, and while many partisans were clamouring for appointments as inspectors, the fictional

Centralization, I: The Crooks Act

Briggs detailed his exploits as a newly appointed license inspector for the town of Yorkville. After reminding Mowat that he had been promised the inspectorship, and despite Mowat's claim that the government would be better off appointing a Tory in order to make a Conservative ally, Briggs got the job. He was then sent off to prepare an initial report on the state of things in the taverns of Yorkville. The subsequent account presented a typically satirical take on the assessments of factors such as the character of the applicant and the suitability of the location:

JOHN MCGRINDLE –Tavern – Knowing him to be a staunch adherent of the cause didn't think any further inspection necessary. His liquors are up to the mark. He headed the subscription list with $100.

SAM SWINTON –Tavern – This establishment appears deficient in accommodation. Asked landlord to "accommodate" me with a loan ... and he refused.

J. MOODLE –Saloon – Grumbled a good deal at having to subscribe but finally put down his name for $25. Says he don't take much interest in politics. Noticed some pernicious literature in his bar, such as *the Mail, Leader,* &c. to which I drew his attention. He promised to substitute the *Globe* in future.

MICHAEL MULVANY – Tavern called the "Shamrock House." Ordered him to change the name of his place to the "thistle" or the "bow Park House" as being more indicative of true Grit principles. A fair article of whiskey. I recommend that he be continued.

H. SANKEY – Tavern – Tory of flexible principles – says he has always voted for Tory candidates, but that his views have lately undergone some modification ... Observed pernicious literature in his sitting room, and ordered him to suppress it. Also noticed some cartoons from *Grip* in his bar, which I had removed on the spot. *Grip* hits the Tories pretty hard sometimes, but it don't spare us either ... He can be utilized and should be kept on.[64]

The account by Briggs satirically underscored the argument made in the *Daily Mail* a month earlier that, rather than fixing the problem of politics in the licensing system, the legislation was nothing more than "a vast inquisitorial machinery for working [the government's] own purposes under the guise of moral reform."[65] The accuracy of these predictions would be tested in the next few months.

3
Power and Influence in the New System

By establishing provincial oversight of Ontario's liquor licensing system, the Crooks Act necessitated the creation of a new bureaucracy and the deployment of a certain administrative logic to achieve its goals. These efforts would test the ability of the liberal state to deal with liquor. To effect order and structure in an often disorderly and poorly structured liquor landscape required a rational administration run by competent officials. To be effective, such state institutions were not exclusively top-down operations. Reflecting on the role of municipalities in the development of the liberal state, Michèle Dagenais argues that a better way to think about the connection between municipal and central governments is "in terms of interconnections, of encounters, of relationships ... between two 'entities' whose parameters were neither fixed nor definite."[1] Such an approach was embedded in the Crooks Act, which connected a central administration that oversaw the implementation of the legislation with license commissioners and inspectors who had considerable autonomy to enforce the new law at the local level. Moreover, finding people to fill the hundreds of new positions required Oliver Mowat's government to seek recommendations from local party committees and members of the legislature to find the best men for the job. Such networks were fundamental to the character of provincial politics at the time, still deeply embedded within a clientelist system based upon networks of obligation and reward. So, when examining the implementation of the new licensing system created by the Crooks Act, it is important to consider the interplay between different levels of government and how their competing priorities and understandings of how an effective licensing system should operate affected the implementation of the legislation.

A major consideration in constructing the new administration involved imagining the ideal character of the officers whose job would be to make the system work. What were the characteristics of an ideal license inspector, an ideal liquor commissioner, and indeed an ideal liquor licensing system? Such questions addressed deeply seated assumptions about the efficient operation of the state; to get it wrong would be to cast disrepute on the entire licensing arrangement and even the government. Mowat argued that appointees would be "efficient men"; George Brown of the *Globe* went further, editorializing that it would require "the best and most impartial officers" and that inspectors needed to be "men of nerve and courage, as well as of the strictest integrity and honour."[2] These ideals notwithstanding, there remained more practical characteristics to consider, especially given the political nature of the drink question. Were commissioners and inspectors to be temperance advocates who sought to dry their communities as much as possible? Would they be friends of the liquor traffic who could cajole vendors to encourage moderation? What about partisan politics? Was it necessary to appoint strong party workers to defend the government's interests (and thereby raise the "I told you so" ire of the opposition)? Or, as the fictitious and satirical conversation between Jimuel Briggs and Mowat suggested, was it important to bring Tories onside by granting them some of the fringe benefits of the new system? Certainly, letters to the newly created License Branch from Ontarians who sought appointments for themselves, family members, or friends manifested most of these possibilities. The ideal license official was dry or wet; a good Reformer, a respectable Tory, or non-partisan; a friend of the liquor trade, a good "temperance man," or a moderate; a young man with energy and ambition or a retiree who had the gravitas of age and experience. Crooks and the officials at the License Branch had to work through scores of recommendations in which every possible configuration of potential license official was argued as ideal.

Underpinning the process, and infiltrating every aspect of its operation, was the long history of patronage in Ontario. S.J.R. Noel has described the province's political system, and indeed much of its social order, as "clientelist," based upon relationships between patrons, people with power and authority, and clients, people to whom they could provide some service, favour, or resource. Noel describes such relationships as "diffuse, whole person, and face to face rather than impersonal or explicitly professional in nature."[3] Such a system created two-way dependency. A client might need the services or resources of the patron, but the patron relied on the work, support, or backing of the client in certain situations. Noel argues that the clientelist system, which had undergirded much of the early settlement of Upper Canada, had begun to change by the time Mowat came to power. Under his government, simple and regional patron-client relationships were evolving – or devolving – into a system in which partisan loyalty was built by deploying the resources of government and in effect transforming and strengthening the party system. Mowat became an undisputed master at using the distribution of patronage positions (and indeed building more of them) to strengthen his party's power. Nevertheless, the expectation and provision of partisan rewards reiterated the two-way nature of clientelism: those who sought favours could argue that without their work the party might not have succeeded and imply that if the party did not reward its loyal workers, then its future was in jeopardy.[4] It was not an empty threat given the long history of short lived pre-Confederation administrations and the fact that Mowat's government, although sitting with a comfortable majority of seats, barely gained a majority of votes over the Tories in the elections of 1872 and 1875.[5] The trick in building the new licensing regime, then, was to balance the demand for patronage against the need for a system to alleviate many of the problems that even those who were not temperance advocates recognized to be rife in communities across the province.

Several historians have observed that the Crooks Act provided a remarkable opportunity to build party loyalty and reward partisan workers while undermining the support of the opposition.[6] Ideally, under the act, inspectors would be freed of local political biases and thus able to offer objective assessments of the character of tavern keepers and their premises, and commissioners would act upon those reports and their own disinterested assessment of the needs of the district. Yet Jimuel Briggs's satirical inspector's report illustrated the concerns about how the Crooks Act could undercut grassroots Tory strength and boost Reform power by ensuring that most of the drinking places were run by loyal Grits or by Tories willing to keep their political proclivities in check. This in turn would weaken the ability of Conservative tavern keepers to sway votes in favour of Tories.[7] Indeed, reflecting on the early years of the Crooks Act, former journalist and eventual *Globe* editor Sir John Willison recalled that, under the act, liquor vendors had to mind their politics: "An adequate display of zeal for the Government was a fair guarantee of security when licenses were renewed. Inactivity was tolerated. Open rebellion was often punished."[8] Noel describes this as placing licensees in "a clientele relationship with the Liberal district bosses."[9]

Nevertheless, it would be a mistake to reduce the liquor system established by the Crooks Act and implemented over the next few decades to nothing more than a new opportunity for patronage. The numerous investigations of drinking practices across the province undertaken by Crooks's department indicate the Mowat government's interest in understanding and attempting to answer effectively the "liquor question." Their answer, the licensing system constructed by the Crooks Act, had to avoid compromising the government's relationship with a vocal cohort of electors, temperance advocates, or an important industry, the liquor trade. Indeed, whereas patronage was neither alien to the workings of the government nor entirely offensive in the way that the government operated, both Crooks and Mowat argued that the government would not seek to benefit politically from the appointments. Recall that Mowat had called the responsibility for liquor licensing "distasteful."[10] Moreover, although such an assurance might have been simple political posturing, commentators advised the government to tread softly in order for the system to be a success.[11] Besides, as Noel notes, there was an "ethical line" between corruption and patronage, "even if its precise location was unmarked and often hotly disputed."[12] Mowat biographer Margaret Evans argues that the premier had strict rules about using patronage in ways that did not damage the reputation of his party.[13] Using licensing simply as a patronage boondoggle would not reflect well on Mowat's government and contradict his claim to, and reputation for, managerial efficiency.[14] Nevertheless, patronage remained an important lubricant in the gears of the party machine. So, despite the claims of Mowat and Crooks that they were not aiming at building a new source of patronage, they could not escape the grasping of loyal party workers who believed that it was payback time; nor, it seems, did they try.

It is important, then, to examine the efforts to construct the licensing system as a process of expanding the rational apparatus of a growing state administration notwithstanding the patronage-driven politics of the time. A fundamental component of the liberal state is the implementation of an administrative system that can carry out the rationalizing operations of the government. Bruce Curtis contends that "liberal state formation is also a history of administration" and that this administration was necessary to fulfill the goals of the state.[15] The Crooks Act necessitated a complex network of disparate administrators – license commissioners and inspectors – whose loyalties were to the government but whose expertise was rooted in the license district. By considering the process of appointing these officers and implementing the legislation (especially selecting and rejecting licensees), and examining resistance to a law that had redirected systems of power from municipal governments to provincial patronage networks, we can see the challenges to building this liberal state apparatus. Establishing a functional regulatory bureaucracy required the Grits to negotiate a middle path between Wets and Drys, partisan loyalists and political enemies, and central and local power structures. From the initial correspondence between local party operatives, members of the legislature, and everyday residents, the complexities of establishing this system become clear. Then, after appointing its officers and establishing its processes, the License Branch spent several years comparing the effectiveness of the more centralized administration of the Crooks Act with the alternative way of addressing the liquor problem, local option, and finding the latter defective, to say the least.

***

When Benjamin Higgins was appointed as the license inspector for London, Ontario, in 1874, he was expected to clean up the city. The report of the provincial inspectors, submitted to the legislature in January that year, had presented a less than favourable assessment of London's licensed establishments. The existing inspector had not "succeeded in enforcing a proper respect for the requirements of the law," so the law was "inefficiently carried out." The city had thirty-eight shop licenses, many of them for businesses operating openly as barrooms "with all appliances or necessaries for selling by the glass ... in full view." One such shop was located within sixty-six feet of the inspector's own office.[16] By most accounts, Higgins had succeeded. Thus, when the Liquor License Act, 1876, came into force, Higgins applied to be appointed the city's inspector under the new provisions. He easily mustered supporting letters from influential people across the city with a variety of backgrounds. Although W.A. Gill, the issuer of licenses for the city whose job would end when the roles of inspector and issuer of licenses were combined, also sought the position, Higgins had a much stronger claim to the post.[17] The Board of Police Commissioners, to whom Higgins had reported, deemed him "the most suitable and efficient person to be ... continued and appointed" as inspector.[18] This endorsement was matched by that of temperate but uniformly supportive local clergy. W.R. Parker, the pastor of Dundas Street Methodist Church, testified to Higgins's "efficiency and fidelity... in the performance of his onerous duties."[19] John Gemley, minister of the local Anglican church, called him "in every sense a suitable person for this increasingly important office."[20] Gemley's boss, the bishop of Huron, concurred. Former mayor Benjamin Cronyn, who had appointed Higgins in 1874, explained his impact on the city's licensing situation:

> In the beginning of 1874 we reduced the licenses in the city from 149 to 110 which cut off at once 39 licenses. The commissioners had a most difficult and unpleasant duty to perform and we found it necessary to obtain the services of a reliable inspector. From a large number of applicants Mr. Benjamin Higgins the present inspector was chosen as a man of honesty and integrity and as one who would fearlessly perform his duties and it is freely admitted that the law was strictly and properly carried out during 1874 & 1875 ... [T]he leading temperance men and clergy men have frequently complimented myself and the other commissioners upon the satisfactory manner in which the law was enforced, the great evils which had existed in former years having been entirely removed principally by the manner in which the inspector performed his duties. At the end of last year there was not one unlicensed place selling within the city and I believe such is now the case.[21]

From these and other accounts, Higgins seemed to be a shoo-in.

Benjamin Higgins had one problem, and its name was Robert Henderson. Henderson had no experience as an inspector, but he had a crucial characteristic that Higgins, it seems, lacked: connections. Duncan Cameron Macdonald, London's mayor, wrote to T.B. Pardee, the commissioner of Crown lands, to inform him that Henderson "has the sympathy of the whole Reform party here," and "I really know of no one in London more deserving" of the position.[22] Note that Macdonald said that Henderson was "deserving" not "suited." A group of about twenty petitioners, including a physician and a Member of Parliament, also supported Henderson.[23] Moreover, London was traditionally and persistently a Conservative city, so placing a strong Grit supporter in this influential post could help the party's reputation there. So, when Henderson was selected to be the new inspector, it was with considerable political support despite Higgins's strong reputation and stellar record.

Henderson's appointment was not without controversy. T.C. Patteson, editor of the Toronto *Daily Mail*, railed against the appointment of "superannuated party hacks" to positions under the new law and pointed to the London case as a perfect example of how patronage corrupted the system.[24] Henderson, the editor reminded his readers, had been an Election Committee chairman who had admitted, in 1874, to committing bribery, among other illegal election activities. Found guilty, he had been "disqualified from holding office under the Dominion government."[25] The newspaper also erroneously stated that Henderson was the father of Arthur Sturgis Hardy, member for Brant, saying that this explained his appointment.[26] He was an insider, certainly, but patronage based upon party loyalty and deservedness, not nepotism, was the issue. Higgins might have taken cold comfort from the fact that his removal was nothing personal: the distribution of new offices under the Liquor License Act seems to have been, as opposition members had predicted, a patronage-driven feeding frenzy.

One reason that the Crooks Act did not depoliticize liquor licensing was due to the structure of the patronage system in Ontario. Local political associations had power, and the government would look to these associations for advice in finding the most suitable candidates for inspectors. In many ways, those local party officials could determine what "suitable" meant. Ottawa MLA D.J. O'Donoghue, in recommending John O'Reilly as that city's inspector, noted that, whereas there were several suitable candidates in nearby ridings, O'Reilly was his clear preference for Ottawa: "I would feel badly disappointed were he not to get the position ... as I feel that ought to be in my gift through the gov't of which you are a member."[27] For O'Donoghue, O'Reilly was suitable because he deserved a gift for his loyalty, so O'Reilly got the job. In Conservative Lanark County, E.J.J. Stevenson recommended Henry Stafford, whose family "have ever been true supporters of the present administration ... If office be the reward for political service rendered, for the former owing to the latter he has a just and positive claim."[28] Less verbose but equally effective, M. McMaster forwarded a letter of application from J. Maconchy to Crooks, scrawled on it a simple note that "he has all his life been a most influential supporter of the liberal party. His claims are very strong."[29] Another correspondent demanded that Maconchy's appointment "be carried out at once." And it was done.[30]

Yet O'Reilly's and Maconchy's successes were not experienced by all who offered partisan justifications for appointments. In a telegraph to Crooks, John Howell from Cobourg noted that in his seventy years he had always been a Reformer, "stumped county reform interests for 40 years[, and] never asked a favor from [the] government. [I] think I have ... a right [to] ask you [to] appoint [my] son Stanley [as] inspector [of] licenses."[31] Also promoting his son, Rev. C.V. Pettit in Carleton County noted that, since the local MLA was a Tory and had "no claims on you," Crooks should appoint Pettit's son. Pettit reinforced this assertion with the reminder that he had supported the Reform Party's appointment of a principal to the local normal school. "This ought to give me some claim on you. I will remember you for good if you will only give my son the office."[32] Lincoln MLA Sylvester Neelon justified his recommendation of A. Morse for inspector in consideration of "the length of time he has been in the reform Ranks which I think is about 45 years and always has taken an active part in elections."[33] Yet none of these partisan overtures was successful.

Indeed, partisan considerations and party loyalties were not the only factors in recommending inspectorships. Neelon, a Reformer, recognized that he should provide more than simple partisan loyalty, adding that Morse was "an honest man and fully competent and would discharge the duty ... with credit to the government."[34] Yet Neelon himself had been embroiled in election day shenanigans that involved liquor in taverns.[35] The idea of a competent inspector did underpin much of the contemplation of appointments, both partisan and those that seemed to be apolitical. Writing to Mowat as the Crooks Act was making its way through the legislature, the former warden of the Conservative-held riding of Carleton requested that "if any patronage is coming to these counties ... those friends who have been friends to us politically ... are not overlooked providing they have the necessary qualifications."[36] Recommending John Dawson ("a gentleman of sterling worth and integrity") to the inspectorship of North and West Middlesex, D. Eccles noted that Dawson was prominent within the local Reform association, "but I do not recommend him for that position ... I recommend [him] on account of being *sure* that he would discharge his duties faithfully and impartially without fear or favour."[37] Dawson was appointed a commissioner. In contrast, John Capron of Ingersoll was even better qualified but unsuccessful. A.H. Sorely told Crooks that Capron "was at one time a Hotel keeper and latterly has been a detective and is thoroughly capable of working up evidence in magistrates cases; is intelligent and trustworthy and has always been a thorough going reformer."[38] The ridings of Oxford South and Oxford North were highly politicized, being the ridings of Crooks and Mowat, respectively. Without more solid contacts, such qualifications do not appear to have been sufficient to get Capron the job.

Competence was a factor because an incompetent inspector might not effectively enforce the law, but also (and possibly more importantly), incompetence could bring disgrace on the party itself. The legislation's success was intertwined with the party's reputation. Probably unnecessarily, Simcoe County's Angus McKay explained this problem to Crooks:

> The government should be greatly interested in the successful carrying out of the law [because] if it proves a success it will [be] to the credit of the government as a whole and upon yourself in particular as the author of the bill, therefore the inspector should be a person who from principle is in favour of enforcement of the law and whose interest in and zeal for the government would be an incentive for him to do his duty.

Seeing himself as "interested in the success of this law and also in popularity of the government," McKay stated simply that "I should get it."[39] In a similar spirit, after the executive of the local Reform association of Kingston proposed two candidates for inspector, grocer William McCrae wrote to Crooks with advice "for the keeping of the reform party together." McCrae explained that one candidate, Samuel Shaw, already had benefited from considerable patronage, whereas the other, Thomas Connelly, the current inspector, "a decent man in every respect," had been the inspector prior to 1876 and was a "first class man fearless of any class or creed always found promptly at his post, and who has given general satisfaction to the citizens."[40] In this instance, too much patronage might have been a bad thing. Connelly did not suffer the same fate as Higgins of London and kept his job. P.C. McGregor, headmaster of a high school in Lanark County, an area that he described as having "fallen into the hands of the enemy & needs to be redeemed," was concerned about the rumoured nomination of Henry Stafford, whose "appointment I feel certain would be a very bad one and would create a great deal of dissatisfaction among the liberals of this county." McGregor insisted that "it is of the utmost importance that no appointment should be made that would alienate from the government any of its friends." Stafford was allegedly a liquor vendor who had been fined for illegal selling. Had he been fit for the position, McGregor argued, it would not be an issue, but "I, in common with most of the public, consider him very unfit."[41] McGregor's concerns were not heeded, possibly due to partisan and demographic rationales. As E.J.J. Stevenson confided to Crooks, Stafford was a dedicated Grit worker whose appointment would be supported by the local Catholics who were underrepresented in government appointments in that district.[42]

In many of these letters, recommendations channelled the values of the liberal state's need for rational actors to implement the authority of the government. Notwithstanding partisan expectations, many of the entreaties favoured political moderates best situated to support the government and navigate the rocky waters of municipal politics and power. This emphasis on moderation was not just about temperament or political views. It was essential when considering the substance legislated under Crooks's law. Few would argue that personal integrity, efficiency, and competence were not good qualities in an inspector, but less clear was the individual's relationship to liquor. Some argued that it was imperative that an inspector be a temperance adherent, or at least a sympathizer, whereas others were wary that overly zealous enforcement of the law could cause more problems than overly liberal liquor sales. Moreover, the inspector did not just inspect premises and recommend to the local Board of License Commissioners who would and would not receive licenses. The legislation assigned the inspector the additional task of undertaking investigations of illegality: accumulating evidence, launching convictions, and enforcing the law, often in lieu of a local police force. Commissioners, too, had to be men of strong convictions, and though they were not expected to prosecute cases, they needed to have a deep understanding of the dynamics of their communities and the stomach to make difficult decisions about individuals' livelihoods. So the ideal characteristics of inspectors and commissioners needed to suit the community contexts in which they were working, and each correspondent presented his or her own perspective on which personal qualities were paramount.

With their expansive organizational structure and experience in lobbying, along with extensive connections to the Reform Party, temperance forces defined an ideal inspector or commissioner as one who held abstemious principles. Before Crooks had even presented the revised legislation, the officers of the Durham County Lodge of the Good Templars wrote to remind him about "the *vital* necessity of appointing total abstinence men *only* as commissioners and inspectors." It was for "the cause of temperance and the welfare of the community" that the government should appoint "only tried and true total abstinence men with ability, honor, and judgement."[43] MLA Gideon Striker from Prince Edward County submitted a list of candidates that a convention of temperance people had drawn up for him before he even returned home after the license bill passed. All of the recommended individuals were "first class men and I could not have done better if I selected them."[44] The candidates for commissioners were all wealthy former farmers who "have sold out and are now living on their money" and, by implication, not corruptible. Since the Dunkin Act was to come into force in the Prince Edward County on 1 May, Striker might also have seen the value in a commission that held strong temperance principles. John Tierney from Carleton County presented his strong temperance views as a positive quality (along with a passing interest in payback). Noting that he had been defeated by the "whiskey influences" when he had run for the office of reeve, he argued that "there is a very strong feeling against me, particularly by the whiskey ring of this rideing [sic] for voting [sic] for [Liberal] John L. McDougall MP for South Renfrew as a benefit."[45] To Tierney, being a man of strong temperance convictions and a fervent enemy of liquor, not to mention a Liberal who had suffered for his allegiances, made him an ideal inspector, but these characteristics were not enough to get him the job.

Tierney's failed bid for an inspectorship might have been the result of his zeal in fighting that whiskey ring: numerous correspondents were less convinced that strong temperance values would make a good liquor license official. Indeed, overly zealous enforcement could be a dangerous thing. W.D. Lyon from Halton County wrote to Crooks in March 1876 to recant his recommendation of George Black as an inspector, saying that "there is a strong feeling against Black outside the temperance people, and his appointment might defeat the object of the new Bill."[46] Huron MLA Archibald Bishop considered temperance zeal when he recommended as commissioner Edward Cash over a man named Beattie: "It is thought by some Mr. Beattie would be too stiff, he being a very rigid temperance [man]. Mr. Cash being likewise a temperance man but more moderate and less prejudiced." Another correspondent concurred, suggesting that Beattie was "a rapid [sic] teetotaller and one of the most opinionative [sic] and impertinent men I know."[47] Isaac Aylesworth, secretary of a local temperance society, recommended a man named Lewis to be the inspector in Simcoe County, noting that he was a strong friend of temperance, although "he is no *fanatic* ... [H]e is a total abstainer ... who would as an officer be a credit to your government but no panderer to liquor sellers."[48] Pandering was not a good character trait, but being on good terms with the liquor sellers might have been. James Wiley from Lincoln County was a highly recommended candidate whom one correspondent described as a "grand worthy patriarch for the ... Sons of Temperance" and "favourably known to all proper hotel dealers and all proper liquor dealers as well as to the temperance men."[49] Wiley got the job.

Wiley's good relationship with individuals described as "proper" liquor dealers illustrates the broad grey area between fervent teetotalism and the spectre of an uncontrolled liquor system. In this grey area lay the moderates, those rational actors who would fulfill the aims of the state. Several correspondents to Crooks were convinced that people favourable to the liquor industry needed to be part of the new system. G.W. Monk endorsed William Corbett Jr., who had "kept a public house for several years" and was a respected member of the community.[50] Sorely's recommendation of former hotel keeper Capron has already been noted. James Brady, in Crooks's riding of Oxford South, offered to "rent or sell my hotel as I am anxious to go out of the business." He thought that he would be suited to the inspector position, and "if the salary would be worth anything I think I could carry out the law and would not compromise the government in this county."[51] Others in the community were not so convinced; James Moscow told Crooks that Brady would continue to own the hotel property and "continue to be with the liquor dealers," and W.S. King noted that Brady's "intimacy with almost every tavern keeper in the county would render it very difficult for [Brady] to perform his duties properly."[52] Such suspicion likely kept those with wet business interests from being liquor inspectors. None of these aspirants was successful.

Yet the Wets were not completely shut out of the system; indeed, Evans observes that Mowat was able to navigate the liquor question because he could balance the interests of the temperance movement with those of the liquor trade.[53] Certainly, comments by him (and Crooks) in the legislature noting that licensed victuallers were in favour of centralization of the licensing system indicated that the government was considering the views of others besides temperance advocates. So, although inspectors with roots in the tavern business might be unsavoury to the temperance community, a three-person Board of License Commissioners offered an opportunity to balance the various interests. To the chagrin of the Drys, some boards included commissioners known to be friendly with local liquor interests. For example, when the recommendations for commissioners made by Durham West MLA John McLeod met with "widespread dissatisfaction" in the riding, J.W. McLaughlin, president of the Darlington Reform Association, sent Crooks his organization's duly considered alternatives. He noted that, although Andrew McNaughton was "theoretically and practically in harmony with the liquor traffic," he should be allowed to remain as a commissioner to appease McLeod. The rest of the board, one of whom was a former municipal clerk "well versed in municipal law" and the third "a conservative but not a bigot," would provide a good balance.[54] All three recommendations were accepted.

As the Durham West case illustrates, the partisan nature of appointing inspectors could be balanced by the members of the three-person Board of License Commissioners. Just as the specific characteristics needed for an inspector were not defined in the legislation (it would have been unusual for legislation to be that specific), so too the ideal characteristics of the board members were yet to be defined. Each community had different characteristics that might need attention. For example, Ottawa MLA D.J. O'Donoghue explained that his recommendations had to be balanced based upon local demographics:

> In Ottawa the rights of *three* classes are tacitly recognized, namely *French Canadians, Protestants,* and *English speaking Roman Catholics.* The rights of all these are recognized in elections, *both parliamentary* and *municipal* and hence my recommendation of one from each element and I respectfully say that as the gentlemen [whom I have] named possess the full competence of the general public I expect and request that they be appointed commissioners for the city of Ottawa.[55]

O'Donoghue's recommendations appear to have been mostly heeded, though one correspondent advised Crooks that two of the three commissioners were Tories who "will do the reform party an immense damage if they are appointed and will not aid in the nice carrying out of the law."[56] In other communities, the board was seen as representing various geographic areas of the riding. When James Patton refused the position of commissioner for Simcoe, George Watson of Collingwood told Crooks that he should find a person living "in the centre of the division[, for] then the board could ... have an eye at all times on the whole west riding."[57] A similar concern about geographic balance was expressed in West Hastings, where a correspondent observed that none of the recommendations for commissioner lived in the town of Belleville and that "it would be better to have one" from there.[58] The interest in balance could take various forms, including political affiliation and temperament. William Hargraft, the Liberal member from Northumberland West, explained that "I have endeavoured to select gentlemen of standing in the community and at the same time who are not extreme in their views." He was conscious of the hazards of overly partisan decision making. "I have advised with my best supporters here, and in order to do away with the party feeling as much as possible I have recommended two Reformers and one conservative."[59] The need to avoid extreme views was important since the appearance of being fair could mute criticisms of overly partisan activities by the government.

Hargraft's explanation might also have been an attempt to mute simmering concerns about his own motivations and activities in making his appointments. Before the Liquor License Act passed third reading, but in the midst of the frenzy of applications for inspectorships, Cecil Mortimer wrote to S.C. Wood with a concern about one of the applicants. James Haig, he explained, was "not a British born subject." He was an American. Mortimer explained that he was writing "in justice to our government and town as well as to other applicants," but he was also concerned about the process of selection, stating cryptically that "improper financial and family influence is being brought to bear upon Mr. Hargraft to secure the appointment of the said Haig who is wholly unfit for the position."[60] Haig's pending appointment fired up the community. Several correspondents noted that Haig was a drunkard who "has the whisky compact in his favour"; others pointed out that he was married to the daughter of Peter McCallum, who financially supported Hargraft's political career and grain business.[61] John Hartman Clark summed up the situation clearly: Haig was not Canadian, had never taken "the oath of allegiance," and was "addicted to drinking intoxicating liquors to an alarming extent and has no influence, no stability, nor ability nor any other requirement for such an important position," and he was being recommended solely as a favour to the local MLA's patron. To appoint Haig, Clark explained, would be "a sad mistake for you, for Haig, for McCallum, and for the temperance cause besides being sure to defeat the grand object of your file."[62] To be sure, Hargraft might have had little enthusiasm for strict enforcement of the act in his riding. The year before the law passed, his daughter Ella married William George Gooderham, the eldest son of the influential milling, distilling, and shipping family.[63] Despite considerable opposition, Haig was appointed an inspector. Thus, although party loyalty, temperance sentiment, ethnic preference, and religious affiliation might all have come into play when individuals made recommendations for inspectors and commissioners, occasionally personal entanglements surpassed other considerations. In possibly an unrelated occurrence, Hargraft did not stand for re-election.

***

The appointment of inspectors and license commissioners to enforce the Liquor License Act was the first step in creating the new licensing system, and it was tricky enough; the next step was to determine who would receive the licenses. Under the population-based calculation in the Crooks Act, roughly one-third of all licenses were to be cancelled. Indeed, even before the law passed, residents across Ontario were paying close attention to how the act would change the province. For example, William Alger, justice of the peace for Northumberland, told Crooks that "the question of who will be [the] license inspector is the excitement of the hour."[64] Within about six weeks, the commissioners and inspectors determined who would and would not receive licenses under the new legislation. They reduced the number of tavern licenses by 33 percent from 1875 and the number of shop licenses by 37 percent.[65] As news circulated about which licensees were to retain the privilege of selling liquor and which would be denied, the Toronto *Daily Mail* printed a disgusted but vindicated editorial: "No reasonable mind could have doubted when the government changed the law that their great object was to make its operation subservient to their political ends."[66] Although some commissioners, editor Patteson conceded, "may have endeavoured to discharge their duty with fairness and apart from political bias or leaning ... the great majority of them have shown by their conduct that they were quite conscious of the nature of the duty they were appointed to discharge, and have discharged it to the entire satisfaction of their masters."[67] Their duty was to party, not to province. A few days later he railed against the fact that the new law, "so sweeping and harsh, and crude," could not be "carefully withheld from bigots, temperance and party, who sought for it as men look for a weapon of revenge."[68] In *Grip,* John Bengough represented such concerns in an evocative cartoon of Crooks ordering the beheading of Tory tavern keepers (Figure 3.1). Readers of the *Globe* were presented with a different perspective. A correspondent using the pseudonym "Temperance," who admitted to having been skeptical of the law initially, approved of the "very material reduction" made in the number of places licensed to sell liquor and argued that no respectable person saw a need to complain.[69] Editor George Brown, reading complaints in Conservative newspapers such as the *Daily Mail,* called it a "political outcry" rather than a public one and "upon the whole ... supremely foolish." The apparent culling of Conservative tavern keepers was an illusion, he noted, because of the disproportionate number of Conservatives involved in the liquor industry to begin with: "It does not then follow as a matter of course that when a conservative has lost his license, it has been because of his political leanings, as some would have us believe."[70] After the first year of operation of the Crooks Act, S.C. Wood, the provincial secretary whose office assumed the administration of the Liquor License Act from

Figure 3.1 "Off with his head! 'Richard III' as played by Mr. Crooks throughout the province" | *Grip*, 6 May 1876

Crooks, included in his report a table showing the party affiliations of applicants for licenses and how many were actually granted (see Table 3.1). It suggests that the retributive partisan cull of Conservative tavern licenses was illusory.

Table 3.1 Licenses granted and refused after passage of the Crooks Act

	Granted Reformers	Conservatives	Refused Reformers	Conservatives
Tavern licenses	852	2,017	316	758
Shop licenses	264	511	62	103
Wholesale licenses	30	90	2	8
Total licenses	1,146	2,618	380	869

Source: Ontario, Legislative Assembly, "License Report," *Sessional Papers of the Legislature of the Province of Ontario,* No. 42 (1877), 1–2.

Still, it was impossible to ignore the reported problems in the administration of the law. Again, and not surprisingly, the *Globe* suggested that all of this was understandable. Complaints about commissioners and inspectors being overly attentive to the demands of the temperance forces were indications that the system remained responsive to local conditions: "Where the temperance feeling has run very high the rule of conduct adopted has probably been more rigid than elsewhere. As the act left both to the municipalities and to the Commissioners a very wide discretion this was to be expected, and is quite in accordance with the intentions of the law."[71] Yet there would be mistakes as a result of the newness of the legislation and the problematic system that it sought to replace.

> The law as it now stands was being administered for the first time; the officials appointed to carry it out are new to their duties; and to make matters worse, the old system was so fraught with abuses that it was very difficult indeed to make people understand the new Act was to be something more than a dead-letter, and to be put in force without fear or favor for anybody.[72]

A stalwart Grit organ that opposed prohibition in favour of moderation, the *Globe* cautioned a temperate assessment of the outcomes of the Crooks Act.

Watching with amusement and disdain, prohibitionist John Bengough painted both sides as fools. In a scathing article entitled "Complaints of the Unlicensed," he saw the hypocrisy in the jeremiads.

> The Unlicensed Victuallers are complaining in all directions. There never was, apparently, so ill-treated a body ... They universally shout that to deprive a tavern-keeper of his license on moral grounds is rank tyranny;

but also let you know that it would have been all correct if it had happened to some other publican than themselves. In fact that would have been an improvement on the old law.[73]

In the same issue of *Grip* that included the cartoon of Crooks beheading a Conservative licensee, Bengough published a poem written from the perspective of a newly unlicensed Irish shopkeeper. It combined libertarian arguments against licensing that characterized the licensee as an innocent victim of the machinations of the state, rhetoric of liberalism that infused complaints about constraints imposed by the new licensing system, and attempts to corrupt the system by bribing influential individuals with booze:

Shure ivery man a right to life and liberty may claim
and to purshoo his happiness, if not to catch that same.
But here they've saized my manes of life, and liberty to sell
and Confishcated my purshoot of happiness as well.
...
Is not my vested intherests quite ruined and desthroyed?
My capital locked up, and all my property employed?
Decanthers – five, quite illigant – the one that's cracked made six,
Nineteen whole tumblers, and the pump that in the counther sticks.
...
And thin the drinks I did invist in influential min
To shpake for me whin it was time for licensing agin.
All them investments swallowed up complete, and no return.
St. Pathrick! But it makes my blood wid indignation burn.[74]

To Bengough, it was not about Reform versus Conservative, Catholic versus Protestant, British versus American, or any other handy binary; rather, it was about vested interests operating in a system that was far more corrupt than any mere adjustments to the licensing system could fix.

Evaluating the New System

Having cajoled its commissioners into service and hired the inspectors, the provincial secretary's License Branch attempted to construct a system that represented Oliver Mowat's goal of efficient management and to minimize the political damage that could come from the blatant partisanism that manifested itself in the selection process. This was important to Mowat, who thought that his reputation for honest government hung on his ability to ensure that patronage did not get in the way of efficient administration, notwithstanding his acuity in using patronage appointments to strengthen his party's power.[75] The combination of broad concerns about drunkenness and abuses of the licensing process, along with the political tension related to the new centralized licensing system, required the government to establish clear guidelines for the activities of the commissioners and especially the inspectors. These guidelines were set out in a series of letters sent in March and April 1876 to all newly appointed license officers. They described the process of assessing premises, developing recommendations, granting licenses, and documenting transactions. The government established a new bureaucratic system of accountability and oversight. Inspectors were to record all activities in ledgers provided by the provincial treasurer's office; commissioners were to sign off on all licenses granted, keep minutes of their meetings, and establish standards for enforcement of the regulations. Both inspectors and commissioners were also responsible for keeping an eye on local liquor businesses (in some communities, commissioners provided a secondary form of inspection and enforcement). Finally, inspectors were to gather evidence of establishments found to be in violation of the law and to initiate conviction proceedings. Then, at the beginning of 1877, the License Branch sent a circular to Boards of License Commissioners asking them to assess how well the new system was operating and to recommend changes to the law that would make the act more enforceable. The replies illustrate how cultures of drinking and local pressures challenged the new system and how officials, whether partisan appointees or otherwise, attempted to make it work.

Although the Crooks Act included some specific requirements for the enforcement of licensing in Ontario, such as the formula for a maximum number of licenses that could be granted in communities, many of its regulations were general, allowing for regional variations. The license commissioners established some of the basic regulations for their ridings, such as setting closing times (outside the statutory Saturday-night to Monday-morning closure of barrooms) and "other wholesome regulations for any locality in a License District."[76] Accordingly, in Lennox County, the commission set up "stringent regulations for the guidance of innkeepers." In South Simcoe, the board sent copies of the act to all licensed proprietors and "posted a large number of placards containing extracts from same, and a caution to the public respecting the license law."[77] Similarly, the Cornwall board drafted "a series of rules and regulations for observance by tavern keepers" and sent them to licensees with the intention "of preventing ... drunkenness, and ... securing orderly and well-kept houses."[78] Such initiatives met the intended goal of the Crooks Act, which allowed boards to respond to local situations.

This authority of each board of commissioners to set unique regulations in their license district was intended to respect the exigencies of local drinking cultures, economies, and demographics, underscoring the importance of local autonomy to the operation of the liberal state. Given how varied the attitudes toward drinking and temperance were across the province, such flexibility would allow better adherence to the new law. The commissioners in Elgin recognized that the lakeside town of Port Stanley, a popular summertime tourist destination, would need more licenses than the population-based maximum would permit because the town had such a large influx of excursionists in the summer.[79] They recommended that the government create a provision for summer hotels or an amortized payment system so "that a person applying for a license ... after say 3, or 6, or 8 months of the license year has expired ... should not be obliged to pay the whole year's duty." This sentiment was echoed by the commissioners in Welland, who had authority over the licensing in beach and cottage communities along the northeast shore of Lake Erie and of towns along the Niagara River.[80] The Crooks Act already granted an exclusive right for the town of Clifton (overlooking Niagara Falls) to have more hotels than the population-based formula would permit because of the number of tourists who visited the area each summer. Both Elgin's and Welland's commissioners saw that more flexibility in the law was required to meet local conditions, and accordingly an amendment to the law in 1877 included provisions for summer hotels, allowing a license to be granted for up to three months.

As the Port Stanley case suggests, the license commissioners were expected to make their best judgments on how stringent or forgiving they should be, a move necessitated by the lucrative nature of drink, the often large investments that proprietors had made in their premises, and the heavy reliance of many hotels on liquor revenues to keep them running. In Northumberland East, the commissioners decided "not to be too strict at first and to give parties who had been refused [a] license ... due notice, which was done." But after some time, the commissioners began to crack down on infractions.[81] Similarly, in York West, the commissioners decided "that no unfair advantage should be taken of those who were suddenly refused licenses," and they would delay enforcing the law, presumably so that the tavern keepers who had lost their licenses could get rid of their stocks and wrap up their businesses. The commissioners reported that, this consideration notwithstanding, when they began to enforce the law, they found that most unlicensed taverns continued to sell "with more or less secrecy."[82] Such stories, perhaps not surprisingly, were common in the reports of the commissioners. Indeed, subverting the system seemed to be generally accepted among the newly unlicensed tavern keepers – and for good reason. Until the passage of the Crooks Act, many tavern owners seem to have been able to violate regulations and get away with it. So, when license commissioners began to refuse licenses to a large number of drinking places, these newly unlicensed victuallers responded with a variety of strategies of resistance. Many of them simply kept selling liquor. In many parts of the province, the remoteness of the taverns and the recognizability of the inspector allowed unlicensed taverns to continue to sell liquor with few concerns. Popular tavern owners could rely on the complicity of their customers and at times other municipal officials to alert them when the inspector was in town. The commissioners in Huron West reported that "persons selling without a license … are scattered over the riding." Even when they were identified, it was difficult to obtain a conviction because "those who go there and drink will shield them in most instances by perjury. They soon know the Inspector; hence he loses his power to catch them." The commissioners also noted that, although licensed hoteliers complained about unlicensed hotel owners who continued to sell liquor, "they will give no assistance [in enforcing the law], and may go and drink in such places."[83]

This lack of assistance was not just hoteliers refusing to rat out their business competitors: in many municipalities, officials, including magistrates, simply would not enforce the legislation, or enforced it with reluctance. The commissioners from Elgin noted that "some magistrates have shown open hostility to the law, and have refused to convict on the plainest evidence." Some of these magistrates were known to have frequented unlicensed taverns, as the Elgin commissioners reported, and to have "bought intoxicating liquors, and drank them in unlicensed houses kept open in defiance of the law."[84] The Dundas commissioners reported that their inspector had difficulty "to get Justices to act; sometimes he has to travel 25 miles to get two justices to lay his complaint before."[85] Commissioners in Russell were likewise frustrated with the seemingly intentional slowness of a local judge named Ross, who, upon hearing an appeal of a conviction by a tavern keeper, "has not yet given his decision, which is causing a great deal of irritation and discontent among all classes for the tavern keepers are selling all the time without license." By the end of 1876, when they wrote their report to the License Branch, the appeal had been pending for about eight months.[86] In Ottawa, the inspector found that there was even a greater problem with magistrates not in favour of the Liquor License Act. The commissioners reported that some magistrates would throw out a case "with costs" and then refuse to admit that there "was reasonable and probable cause for preferring the charge." Apparently, without such a finding, the inspector was left to pay the costs of the abortive trial himself, "thereby deter[ring] him from prosecuting as vigorously as he otherwise would."[87]

The intransigence of some magistrates could also be found among other municipal authorities. No doubt some councils that had lost the power to appoint inspectors, and the political and sometimes financial benefits of such power, could be less than cooperative with the new Boards of License Commissioners. Commissioners from West Peterborough noted cryptically that "parties that should lend their assistance have not, but have taken the very opposite course; their influence seems to be with hotel-keepers."[88] Others were more precise in their concerns. The Elgin board noted that in communities where police officers were appointed by municipal councils rather than independent (or semi-independent) Boards of Police Commissioners, police officers might not enforce the license law with the requisite diligence. Citing their experience in the town of St. Thomas, where council appointed police officers, the Elgin commissioners noted that "it is useless to expect the officers to report breaches of the law and tavern regulations. Many of the councillors sympathise with illicit sales for the sake of ephemeral popularity, and assist to set the law at defiance, and threaten constables with dismissal if they dare to assist in carrying out the law."[89] The mayor of London had issued the order that the police force was to discontinue pursuing license law violations "on account of the force being so small as to require all their efforts to attend to patrol and other duties." Soon after, the police magistrate issued a contradictory order that the police should report all such offenders. The *Globe* noted drolly that "the chief of police has two orders on the subject."[90] In Toronto, where the municipal council was also generally hostile to the license act, the commissioners noted that problems with the law would continue "so long as the Police force have the instructions which now exist."[91]

Even where Boards of License Commissioners had the support of law enforcement agencies, the inspectors could face concerted and organized opposition from licensed and unlicensed tavern keepers. The Licensed Victuallers' Association of Ontario sought the legal opinion of John Hillyard

Cameron, noted lawyer and former Tory MP.[92] At a meeting of the Licensed Victuallers' Association a month after the Crooks Act came into force, Cameron asserted that the legislation was unconstitutional and that "every tavern-keeper who had the proper accommodation as required by the law of 1876 could not now be refused his license."[93] A few weeks later licensed and newly unlicensed victuallers met in Toronto to discuss whether or not to proceed with legal actions based upon Cameron's assessment. Unfortunately for them, Cameron had reconsidered his opinion and concluded that it would be unwise to challenge the law. The victuallers contemplated running a test case to see if they could get the law overturned but decided against it since the government could just change the law while their case was in the courts.[94] Instead of proceeding in the courts to challenge the law, the victuallers turned to exploiting a few key loopholes in the existing legislation. For example, a major problem with the new license act was the wording about an inspector's right to enter premises to investigate allegations of illegality. Section 56 of the license act of 1874 (which remained unchanged in 1876) allowed "any provincial officer, police officer, or constable ... at any time [to] enter into any tavern, inn, ale-house, beer-house, or other house ... wherein refreshments or liquors are sold, or reputed to be sold, whether under license or not," to inspect activities in the premises.[95] Attorneys for the victuallers convinced judges that "if the tavern keeper allows [officers] to enter inside of the front door, ... he can resist a further entrance."[96] Many commissioners commented on the problems of this section. The commissioners in Huron called the law "defective"; those in West Hastings called Section 56 "useless."[97]

This gap in the legislation was the first of two main problems that the inspectors faced when attempting to ferret out illegal selling. The second was the fact that unlicensed premises, by definition, were unlicensed. Although the Crooks Act mandated that inspectors should investigate liquor sales in both licensed and unlicensed premises, it seems that taverns without a license faced less scrutiny. Many hoteliers, denied a license, redefined their businesses to be "temperance hotels" and continued operations. In their now "dry" barrooms, they served "temperance drinks," but many commissioners learned that they were not as advertised.[98] In Wellington Centre, the commissioners reported that, although the act had generally had a positive effect, illegality continued in the form of temperance hotels, of which there were eleven in the riding,

> all of whom are suspected to be more or less engaged in selling contrary to law. They profess to keep temperance houses of entertainment, selling

whiskey under the name of ginger wine, and other mixed drinks containing a large portion of spirits. They also give false names to all such drinks believed to contain spirits, thereby rendering it extremely difficult in getting witnesses to prove in court what they really did drink.[99]

These hotels attempted various libatory subterfuges. In Dufferin, the unlicensed victuallers were known to "mix whiskey in soda-water ... [or sell] ginger ale with a 'stick' in the shape of whiskey."[100] In Halton, the commissioners believed that unlicensed victuallers were selling intoxicating liquors "secretly mixed in syrup."[101] The commissioners in Prince Edward County said that "liquors are being sold as mixed slops," suggesting a less than savoury mixture or dilution of spirits.[102] In Huron East, the most common way of subverting the law was to sell customers ginger beer, and then when they wanted "something strong," the proprietor would simply give, not sell, liquor, thereby avoiding charges of illegal selling.[103]

Temperance hotels were a significant challenge to the working of the law. Some municipalities licensed temperance hotels, thus making the proprietors beholden to municipal authorities and not provincial ones. This reproduced, of course, the sort of clientelism that the authors of the Crooks Act might have hoped to alleviate. In the city of London, temperance hotels required such a license, and the commissioners argued in their first reports to the provincial authorities that the law should be amended to forbid temperance licenses from being granted to hoteliers who had been denied liquor licenses.[104] Other Boards of License Commissioners recommended other approaches. The Dufferin commissioners argued that large purchases of liquor by owners of temperance hotels should be "*prima facie* evidence against them" and that all unlicensed hotels should take down their signs and dismantle their bars.[105] Several boards argued for some kind of inspection of temperance houses. Moreover, many temperance hotels, not bound by the closing hours of 7 p.m. on Saturday to 6 a.m. on Monday, began to fill that hospitality gap by acting as drinking places outside the times that licensed premises could sell liquor.[106] Thus, some commissioners argued that all hotel bars, wet or dry, should have to follow the same hours of operation.

These challenges, reported to the government at the beginning of 1877, did not stop the commissioners from giving generally positive assessments of the working of the Crooks Act. Most commissioners, replying to the second question of the circular ("what has been the effect of these provisions?"), noted that the law had improved the nature of tavern accommodation in their regions. In Durham East, the act's provisions resulted in "a decided improvement in the accommodation provided for the travelling public."[107] In Grey South, the result of the act was "to make the business of tavern-keeping a more respectable employment, by weeding out a great many of the way-side groggeries."[108] In North York, the act "raised the standard of the licensed taverns in the ridings. They are now cleaner, better kept, more orderly, and better provided with accommodation."[109] Even in Toronto, where there was considerable opposition from municipal officials, "the liquor traffic is generally being placed in the hands of the better class of men that engage in that business, and is being withdrawn from the low groggeries."[110] Such commentaries came from across the province, with few commissioners reporting that the law had resulted in no change. Although such reports might have been inspired by a need to protect the reputation of the government (even though not all commissioners were Grits, there was generally a government-positive bias in the boards), the consensus seems to have been a general improvement in accommodation across the province.

Although some commissioners agreed with those in Toronto that the result was to put the operation of taverns into the hands of "the better class of men," that change might have been the result not of weeding out "the low groggeries" but of making the license a more precious commodity. With the reduction of licenses across the province, hundreds of previously licensed taverns – "low groggeries" or otherwise – closed. Tavern owners either turned to illegal activities or, as the commissioners in Lanark South observed, gave "up the trade entirely, and in many instances have moved away."[111] In such a situation, the new licensing system, combined with the broad cull of taverns, might have encouraged those who managed to retain their licenses literally and figuratively to clean up their acts. Commissioners were aware of this effect of the law. Glengarry's board noted that "the fear that a license will be refused to any person who has been convicted of a breach of the law has undoubtedly acted as a wholesome restraint."[112] In North York, "shop and tavern keepers ... know that their business depends upon their good behaviour."[113] West Hastings tavern keepers "now desire to observe the law and regulations, knowing that, if they did not, they ran the risk of their license being refused another year." Consequently, "their houses are now kept more for the accommodation of travelers than for drinkers."[114]

The system created by the Crooks Act, then, can be considered to have been directly responsible for a change both in the material conditions of the licensed premises and in the attitudes of their owners. By significantly reducing the number of licenses and creating a licensing board and inspectorate less easily influenced by municipal authorities, the Crooks Act caused an immediate shift in the character of licensed premises, since "the low groggeries" tended to be those that closed, and a longer-term change in attitude among the tavern keepers who remained. This was a sort of internalizing of control in which the tavern keepers followed the rules for personal gain but knew that transgression was no longer a simple matter of just paying a fine and going back to business. With more taverns than licenses in an area, it could be more efficient for a board to grant a license to a properly constituted tavern that did not receive one the first time, although few commissioners reported that they refused to grant licenses to establishments that met the structural conditions and expectations of respectability set out, literally and by implication, in the Crooks Act.

***

In his report of January 1877, provincial secretary S.C. Wood, whose office took over the administration of the License Act from Crooks's office, presented an unsurprisingly positive assessment of the working of the new legislation. Wood argued that the Crooks Act was more efficient and effective in dealing with criminality related to liquor than the Dunkin Act. It was clearly a political assertion designed to favour a licensing system that encouraged moderation over local option that many saw as deeply flawed. First, the Crooks Act provided funds, through the license fees, that financed an enforcement mechanism. Second, the Dunkin Act seemed to be haphazardly enforced, whereas there was a certain "zeal" for enforcement of the Crooks Act. As many critics of the prohibitionists argued, the Drys pushed for local option but had little interest in helping to enforce it. "However powerful the public sentiment may have been in successfully carrying a by-law for establishing the Dunkin Act, ... this sentiment then ceases ... or becomes so diffused as not to sensibly ensure an equal amount of zeal in having the Prohibitory law enforced."[115] Wood based his assessment not simply on the reports from the commissioners across the province but also on an investigation undertaken by Henry Totten (who was becoming an essential member of the License Branch). Wood dispatched Totten to Prince Edward County to investigate how the Dunkin Act operated there, and his report underscored the illusory benefits of local option and the value of the revised licensing legislation.

Totten argued, bluntly, that the Dunkin Act had failed to prohibit the sale of liquor. He noted that, in most of the nearly 150 municipalities where the act was in operation, "with few exceptions it remained practically a dead letter." He then assessed the main weaknesses of that legislation. First, he said, in places where municipal councils were not supportive of the legislation, the Dunkin Act could not be enforced. In small towns, temperance supporters were well known to liquor sellers, so it was unlikely that illegal selling would have taken place within their sight. And, if so, it was not likely that they would have had the wherewithal to gather evidence for a prosecution. Moreover, Totten noted that temperance advocates, however zealously they pushed for a local option vote, often seemed to see a successful vote as the end of their work. "These temperance organizations exist for the sole purpose of securing the absolute prohibition of all traffic – wholesale and retail – in liquors. Their energies and means are almost exclusively devoted to this end, and they give very little assistance to, and in most places they ignore, the advantages in suppressing intemperance of the present Liquor License Law." Nevertheless, he noted that the Crooks Act required the Board of License Commissioners and the inspector to enforce the provisions of the Dunkin Act in the sections of a license district where local option was in effect.[116] So, despite potential inertia among temperance supporters, local option could still be enforced. Turning to the specific case of Prince Edward County, Totten provided damning evidence of the ineffectiveness of the Dunkin Act and in contrast the value of the Crooks Act. He dismissed the Dunkin Act in one sentence: "Every tavern in the town of Picton sells liquor at the bar openly." He found the same condition throughout the county: "In every tavern ... liquor may be freely obtained." Numerous residents told Totten that the Dunkin Act "did not advance the cause of temperance." Even some temperance supporters who had voted for the act "informed me that they did not think that it could be enforced." Digging deeper, he found that although the Dunkin Act had passed with a significant majority of votes, only 34 percent of potential voters had cast ballots. Many voters "were indifferent to the matter; ... if they wanted liquor they were well aware they could get it."[117] When Totten visited the Township of Lincoln in Lennox County, and Ernestown in Addington, he found comparable situations.[118]

Totten did not just offer a critique of the Dunkin Act but also illustrated how prohibition was impractical to the broader community. He noted that farmers did not support prohibition because when bringing their products to market, they needed taverns "where stables, sheds, and meals are furnished them at reasonable rates which the tavern-keeper could not afford were it not for the profit of the bar." He noted that even temperance people preferred staying at licensed taverns because "the accommodation is superior and the rates more reasonable."[119] The quality of accommodation could affect the broader community. In the town of Napanee, where the Dunkin Act was about to come into force, Totten found merchants concerned that "trade which now seeks Napanee as its centre, will be transferred to other places," notably Belleville and Kingston, neither of which was dry.[120] He concluded not only that the Dunkin Act was unworkable but also, more importantly, that it would "retard" the progress of temperance because the negative impacts were tangible and the positive impacts unrealized. His report was a reiteration of the importance of the Crooks Act to the orderly operation of the community. With license fees and fines providing revenue to fund enforcement, an inspectorate disconnected from local influence and incentivized to enforce the law, commissioners who had no financial interest in the operation of the licensing system or in the generation of revenues for the municipality, and licensed vendors who saw it to be in their best interests to see the law succeed, Totten concluded, the new system was far superior to the outdated pre-Confederation prohibition legislation. "One inspector, supported by the licensed dealers, can perform more efficient services than fifty inspectors under the Dunkin Act."[121] It was a vision of efficient governance in a liberal state, based upon reasonable regulation, citizen participation, and dedicated officials.

In 1880, the provincial secretary's office, now under Arthur S. Hardy, sent a letter to license inspectors throughout the province asking them to assess the impact, four years in, of the Crooks Act. The eight questions considered the state of the licensed premises, the character of the proprietors, the effect of the act on the drinking behaviour of the people, and public opinion about the value of the legislation, especially compared with the previous municipally managed system. With few exceptions, the responses were positive. Most licensed taverns that survived the cull were of higher quality than many before 1876. Proprietors were more consistently concerned about maintaining order and keeping their premises respectable. Drinking habits seemed to have shifted, with certain activities, such as drinking on Sundays and "treating" (buying rounds of drinks), diminishing or being eliminated altogether in many communities. Members of the public assured inspectors that the Crooks Act had instituted a system superior to that before 1876, a viewpoint held even by many who had originally been critical of the act. As the inspector for South Huron explained, people who had opposed the Crooks Act were telling him that "we cannot deny that taverns are quieter – less fighting about them, a great improvement over the former Acts."[122] The only people identified as continuing to be opposed to the law were vocal members of the Licensed Victuallers Association, some Tories whose opposition was aimed at the government and not the system (what one inspector called "political gealousy [sic]"),[123] and some municipal councils that wanted to restore the patronage system that they had lost. As the inspector for East Northumberland noted, "there are some aspirants for municipal honours who would like to have the patronage [of the tavern] to assist them at their elections."[124]

One area that several of the inspectors noted as needing additional attention, however, was the shop license. As the inspector for North Leeds and Grenville noted, since the law did not limit the number of shop licenses that could be granted in a municipality (leaving that decision to the municipal council), "a greater competition exists, and disposes the [shop] license holder to infringe the law." Moreover, he wrote, there remained an incentive for the municipal government to raise funds: "'Tis true the municipal council may limit the issue [of licenses,] but as they look upon this as a means of increasing their revenue, they never act upon it."[125] Another inspector noted that shopkeepers were more likely to continue to use the license as a means of attracting customers. In Kingston, the inspector argued that although shopkeepers "are certainly a very orderly and creditable class of citizens," they were still breaking the law.[126] The inspector in Toronto added that the unlicensed grocers were not happy with the fact that some grocers held licenses because "the large profits made from the liquor traffic by the licensed dealer gives him a sort of monopoly, and enables him to undersell his less favoured neighbours."[127] Most of the inspectors argued that it would be best to separate the sale of liquor from the sale of other commodities. As the Kingston inspector argued, doing so would allow the government to require liquor shops to close earlier on Saturdays, "thus preventing drunkenness on Saturday nights and Sundays."[128] Indeed, the inspector for South Huron noted that the town council of Seaforth required liquor to be separate from other commodities in the store; he called it "the greatest improvement in shops."[129]

The inspectors noted two main challenges that they had faced when instituting the new liquor regime. The first was the lingering effect of the overabundance of taverns that had flourished under the municipal licensing system. Several inspectors explained that it took a few years to weed out the problematic tavern keepers and other dealers; generally after the second year of operation of the Crooks Act, however, most illicit dealers who had been operating generally unimpeded had either been shut down by the law or left town. They might also have gone underground, for inspectors in some communities admitted that some illegal dealing remained, but it was confined to close friends and family members of illicit vendors, and it was nearly impossible to build sufficient evidence for a conviction. The inspector from East York noted that respectable members of the community kept away from such houses "as they consider it a disgrace to be brought up as witnesses against the offenders of the law."[130] Most inspectors agreed that illicit dealing – either licensed hotels selling liquor illegally or liquor sales in unlicensed hotels – was significantly lessened.

The second challenge was, ironically but not surprisingly, caused by the Dunkin Act. Numerous inspectors noted that rather than improving the liquor situation, local option caused far more illegality. The inspector for East York explained the challenges faced by Dunkin Act communities in his district:

> In the year 1878–9 we had the Dunkin Act in force, when illicit traffic in intoxicating liquors became general, the law itself giving general dissatisfaction, and was defeated by a large majority the same year. In the year 1879–80 about the same number of licenses were granted, but there was considerable trouble in putting a stop to the illicit traffic started under the Dunkin Act. During the present year things are getting into the old groove and the act is working more smoothly and the people seem better pleased with the present law after trying the Dunkin Act.[131]

The inspector in North Grey made a similar report, noting that "we lost so much ground during the time the Dunkin Act was in force, that we are only now regaining what we lost."[132] Addington's inspector explained that after the act was repealed, "it was found that many holders of licenses seemed not to realize that there was any law regulating their business. It was a hard year's work to bring to a moderate degree of order the unsettled state of the licensed liquor traffic."[133] The South Essex inspector noted caustically that "there are very few persons engaged in illicit traffic ... except in the municipalities ... in which the Temperance [Dunkin] Act of 1864 is in force."[134] South Grey's inspector characterized the latter months under the Dunkin Act as a time of "absolute free trade in liquor."[135] The conclusion of inspectors who had experienced the Dunkin Act was unanimous and coterminous with Totten's report of 1877: the Crooks Act was a far more reasonable and effective way of addressing illegality than local option. As the inspector for West Wellington explained, during Dunkin Act agitation those opposed to local option used the Crooks Act as "a text book ... shewing it to be such a perfect Act, if properly carried out, that no better Act was required."[136]

Positive assessments of the legislation were not without qualifications. The practices of treating and drinking at bars as well as drinking on the Sabbath could be affected by broader social trends. Several inspectors noted that recent economic downturns had affected drinking habits. The inspector for South Ontario attributed changes in drinking habits to the licensing regulations, public opinion, and "probably ... the hard times which have prevailed for the last few years."[137] The inspector for North Perth was less circumspect, saying that drinking had decreased steadily "during the hard times and scarcity of money but since the times have improved and money become more plentiful, within the last few months, evidently drinking seems to be increasing."[138] Some inspectors also pointed to a shift in the beverages that tavern patrons preferred. A few noted the increase in beer drinking, some referencing the popularity of lager beer, which supplanted the consumption of stronger spirits. The inspector for South Grey called this "a quiet revolution ... in the drinking habits of the people, [with] light wines and beer taking the place ... of stronger liquors."[139] The inspector for East Middlesex ventured the opinion that "since the introduction of lager beer, which is now fast becoming the principal drink (particularly during the summer season)[,] less drunkenness is noticeable."[140] Inspectors also noted an increase in the power of temperance ideals. In East Peterborough, the hard times were part of it, but the inspector also noted the impact of "temperance societies and moral suasion ... [that] have had the effect of keeping the young men from the tavern."[141] The inspector for East Durham concurred, noting that "the younger generation seem to take kindly to the temperance lodges, and to avoid at least any excesses."[142] East Huron's inspector demonstrated the power of economic scarcity in reducing drinking when he reported that tavern keepers had noted a decline in drinking, but "whether that is caused by the people becoming more temperate, or more unable to spend, is more than I can say."[143]

Although it is impossible to disentangle such economic, cultural, and social influences from the impacts of the licensing law itself, the broad conclusion was that the Crooks Act had altered the drinking landscape of the province, turning something that many saw as chaotic into a much better controlled liquor system. The reduction of licenses meant that tavern keepers were compelled to run more responsible businesses lest they lose their licenses to the many hotel keepers refused licenses in 1876. Increased fees and more attention by inspectors to the operation of the accommodation side of the tavern business made running them more costly, and many officials nodded approvingly that this resulted in a generally wealthier, and therefore presumed "better class," of tavern keeper. The improved drinking spaces appear to have resulted in a significant change in the behaviour of many thirsty Ontarians. The change was not entirely a result of the law since the depression and introduction of lighter drinks could have had effects, but the law did drive a change in the perception of drinking and the social and legal suitability of public drunkenness. The inspector for North York addressed this issue when he noted that "temperance organizations have doubtless done something towards educating public sentiment ..., but I am convinced that we are indebted to the present license law for a large part of the improvement."[144]

Yet the changes wrought by the Crooks Act, however positively viewed by the province's residents, did not solve the "liquor problem" in Ontario. Several key points of tension were growing and would manifest themselves over the next several decades. As the legal action contemplated by the licensed victuallers indicates, the law might have been passed, but it was not yet settled. Over at least the next decade, the authority over licensing the liquor trade would remain a point of jurisdictional tension between provincial and dominion governments. At a lower political level, but a level more culturally significant, prohibitionists who wanted more stringent restrictions were gaining social and political momentum. Notwithstanding Totten's assessment of the functioning of the Crooks Act versus the Dunkin Act in eastern Ontario, the push for local option did not diminish advocacy for provincial or dominion-wide prohibition. Prohibitionists continued to lobby both provincial and dominion governments to increase restrictions and point the country toward their dry utopia, one in which, freed from the predations of liquor, people could experience true liberty and personal economic growth. In response, members of the liquor industry and moderationists who saw prohibition as an improper and un-British imposition on the lives and liberties of citizens pushed against such efforts and articulated a vision of the state that remained based upon the principles of individual liberty, fairness, and protection of property rights. In these contrasting ideas of the role of the government in overseeing the liquor system in Ontario, the ideals of the liberal state would be assessed, confronted, and continually challenged.

4
Politics, Law, and the License Branch

Embedded in the Crooks Act was a revised relationship between the local community and the provincial government. The Boards of License Commissioners and the inspectors, appointed by the government but chosen to be responsive to their regional contexts, operated both as a buffer between the central administration and the people in their communities and as the government's representatives there. They were agents of the liberal state but members of their communities. Notwithstanding the roots of the selection process in patronage and clientelist precedents, the role of commissioners and inspectors was to apply the law effectively and rationally, responding to the many imputations and requests of community members, whose opinions on the liquor traffic had to be assessed and addressed within the confines of the law. This was a difficult task. When the Crooks Act was first passed, George Brown of the *Globe* described the ideal inspector as needing to be above reproach because he would be "assailed on all hands with temptation. Every kind of appeal – neighbourly, feelings, friendship, relationship, sheer importunity, political partisanship, and even gross bribery – will be resorted to in order to induce them to favour some at the expense of others and of the community."[1] Such fortitude was especially important for the appointees who claimed fealty to the party because the success of the system would strengthen the ability of the government to project provincial power into local communities. As both Bruce Curtis and Michèle Dagenais note, the administrations imposed on municipalities by the provincial governments reiterated and broadened the power of the state.[2] Since the Crooks Act was designed to remove power over liquor sales from a municipal council while respecting the uniqueness of the local context, it did not apply a unitary standard on liquor licensing in the province. It did apply, though, a more rational and ideally more objective system of licensing. Consequently, the bureaucracy that the Crooks Act created acted as a legally constituted and authoritative buffer between politicians seen to continue to operate in a clientelist manner and people who thought that their opinions should receive special consideration by their elected representatives. Examining the implementation of the Crooks Act reveals how the legislation in effect interrupted that relationship, further strengthening the imperative of the liberal state to manifest rational, reasonable, and consistent governance.

Excavating the early operation of the system that the Crooks Act created requires some sleuthing. The expansive License Branch generated reams of documentation, but much of it has been lost to the exigencies of storage limitations before laws required that such material be retained. Nevertheless, a few records permit a glimpse of the operation of the law. First, copies of a few records from the License Branch survive in the sessional papers of the province. When an MLA requested information about a situation related to licensing, the provincial secretary presented the records to the legislature, copies of which were filed as sessional papers. Second, some investigations undertaken by the License Branch were presented to the legislature and printed for public information. Third, some decisions of court cases that involved liquor licensing remain available through publications such as *Canada Law Review*. Finally, testimony to the dominion Royal Commission on the Liquor Traffic, which gathered evidence in Ontario between 1893 and 1894 (and which will be discussed in more detail in Chapter 9), provided many details of the operation of the Crooks Act, often in contrast to the prohibition implemented by local option. Although doubtless a drop in the bucket of decades of licensing records, these sources illustrate the challenges of administering the Crooks Act, the License Branch's attempts to balance local autonomy and centralized control, and the important role that the new legislation played in infusing the ideals of the liberal state in the lives of the people.

***

With the state's power radiating out to the community, and the understanding of the community mediated through the Boards of License Commissioners and the inspectors, the system's success hinged on the personnel chosen to do the job. Chapter 3 traced the process of selection and the attempts to find people who could represent the government's interests and simultaneously tread the middle path between Wets and Drys. They were not always partisan appointees, but partisanism, it seemed, had a functional value in the operation of the system. In the first year of the operation of the Crooks Act, the government led by Oliver Mowat included Conservatives on the Boards of License Commissioners.³ Yet a few years later, people were complaining that the boards were almost entirely dominated by Reformers. Mowat explained in the early 1890s that the attempted bipartisan system failed because many Conservatives on the boards tried to undermine the system to discredit the new licensing administration and make the Liberals look bad. Consequently, Mowat said, the government replaced the problematic commissioners with partisans who would ensure that the licensing system worked.⁴ Whether this explanation shows the complete picture is debatable. Sir John Willison contended that the entire liquor system created "an [a]rmy of officials in the service of the government [and] never was an army more faithful to the High Command."⁵ S.J.R. Noel holds the liquor licensing system up as an archetype of Mowat's blending of government bureaucracy and party machinery.⁶

Partisan or not, many hurdles remained in the efficient operation of the system, and inspectors and board members often clashed. In 1880, the commissioners in Lincoln submitted their resignations to Arthur Hardy, the provincial secretary, protesting "the inefficiency of the Inspector," Dilly Coleman, appointed the year before, and some of his activities, which they saw as undermining the board's work.⁷ The commissioners – John Orchard, James Morin, and James Henderson – explained that even six months after his appointment Coleman "took no pains to inform himself or make himself acquainted with the license Act." He seemed to be incapable of performing even the most basic aspects of his work:

> On one occasion he informed the board on his passing through the town of Thorold on Saturday or Sunday evening a large portion of the hotels had lights in their bar rooms and from all appearances were in full blast[;] when asked why he did not stop and attend to them [he] replied he did not want to bother with them.⁸

As a result of this negligence, Lincoln got a new inspector, and only Orchard resigned from the board.⁹

Some inspectors might have been incompetent, but many were overworked. In the autumn of 1882, the executive of the Lambton Prohibitory Association asked the local license commissioners to appoint a "sub inspector" for the West riding of Lambton. The commissioners thought that it was a good idea but suggested that the association send the request to the License Branch directly. The subsequent petition argued that "the enforcement of the liquor license law in the west riding of Lambton involves more work than one man can perform" and requested that David Deacon of Petrolia be appointed to undertake inspections in that town.[10] Petrolia was in the midst of a boom, having grown from 2,651 residents in 1871 to 3,465 in 1881, on its way to 4,357 in 1891, a far steeper rate of population increase than that of the entire province.[11] When two months later they asked why such a position had not been created, Hardy explained that "no sub inspector has heretofore been appointed in any license district." He noted that it might not be legal to appoint such an officer, and in any case it might not be economically possible. After all, if one community received a sub-inspector, then requests for others would follow, and soon there would need to be a sub-inspector "in nearly every town in the province in which an inspector does not reside."[12] At the same time, Henry Totten wrote to the inspector, R.C. Palmer, explaining that complaints had been received about poor enforcement of the law in Petrolia and told him to "see that the law is enforced in such a manner that the inhabitants shall have no grounds for complaint."[13] He recommended that, if necessary, Palmer should employ detectives.

Palmer replied the next day, explaining that he had done what he could to ensure that the law was enforced in Petrolia. It was challenging work because, as he explained, he had "found it difficult to reach such parties as violate the law during prohibited hours and such as keep shops and allow liquor to be consumed upon their premises." He assured Totten that the violations were not nearly as "flagrant a character" as suggested by the complaints sent to the License Branch. Nevertheless, his reply illustrates the difficulties that a single inspector faced when enforcing the law:

> Bar rooms are closed and kept closed in all directions which are exposed to public view and only opened at other points in the most cautious manner to [people whom] ... the proprietors think they can depend upon and further are so surrounded by other rooms and ways of ingress and egress that it is next to impossible for any suspected party to gain admission or detect what is going on sufficiently clear [sic] to make a case.

Moreover, even when he managed to identify places where liquor was being sold illegally, Palmer had trouble finding reliable witnesses to testify against the management of these taverns. People who patronized the illegal drinking places "usually make very bad witnesses and sometimes I have been made to feel quite foolish when one after another has been called and all declare they did not get any liquor ... [H]owever I am willing and anxious to do what I can."[14] Unable to secure effective evidence, Palmer agreed to Totten's recommendation that he employ detectives.

Dubious Detectives

The suggestion of using detectives offers a fascinating point of reflection on the limited apparatus of the state in reaching the less accessible parts of Ontario. Prior to 1910, there was no formal licensing system for detectives in Ontario, so anyone could call themselves a "detective" with few constraints upon their activities.[15] Detectives were controversial, and so employing them associated the nascent liquor administration with some of the most unsavoury characters in the province. For example, the "whiskey detectives" were individuals who, inspired by the provisions in liquor laws that gave half of the fine to the informant, made money by convincing sometimes well-meaning vendors to sell liquor illegally and then take them to court to earn the fine. By the 1880s, they were notorious for tripping up pharmacists or other shopkeepers into selling liquor illegally. In London in 1876, there was "great excitement ... concerning the operation of sneak whisky detectives who have been going about begging for small gifts of liquor to relieve sudden illness and then laying charges against their benefactors of giving liquor away in illegal quantities."[16] Barrie's Conservative *Northern Advance* called the employment of detectives "a course which no right thinking man approves of," likening their tactics to entrapment by the police.[17] The disfavour with which many people viewed whiskey detectives could rub off on license commissioners thought to have employed them. In the example from London, the *London Advertiser,* a Grit newspaper that supported temperance, attempted to cleanse the reputations of the recently appointed license commissioners when they were accused of hiring a former county constable, Charles Allen, to act as a whiskey detective. "To disprove this accusation, [Allen] has secured the written statement of two of the commissioners ... who testify that Allen has not been appointed 'whiskey detective' and that no information has been received from him."[18] Although the *Advertiser* opined that "this should settle the matter," a week later the proprietors of a store near the city's market, identified only as Bryce and Mills, said that Allen had come into the store complaining of "choleriaic diarrhea and begged that he might have a little brandy to allay the intense pain." When they provided the medicinal liquor, "sympathizing with him as we should with any one in a similar case," he went away and laid charges against the shop. They also argued that the letter from the license commissioners claiming that he was not working for them was falsified.[19] The whiskey detective was not someone with whom respectable individuals wanted to be associated. When the Ontario College of Pharmacy was thought to be employing a whiskey detective named John Mason to use similar tactics to encourage druggists to break the law by selling him medicine without a prescription, the college vehemently denied such an association.[20]

Nevertheless, detectives were soon found to be necessary for enforcement of the licensing law. Totten's letter to Palmer suggests a disinclination to employ such characters, a reluctance that likely went beyond the costs of such practices. At the Royal Commission on the Liquor Traffic, inspectors were frequently asked if they employed detectives, and most said yes. It was necessary, explained Toronto inspector Thomas Dexter, despite public disapproval. "People complain of our employing detectives; we cannot get on without them."[21] Dexter had been the inspector since the passage of the Crooks Act. He noted that in 1876, when seventy-four taverns and twenty-eight shops lost their licenses, "the great majority of the people whose licenses were taken away continued to sell, and we found it necessary that year to spend a good deal of money in detective service."[22] A police magistrate in Peterborough explained that the authorities needed to employ "unknown men" to secure evidence against illegal selling because the inspector, George Cochrane, lived outside the city, and everybody knew when he came into town to inspect the licensed premises.[23] Even in Hamilton, with two inspectors who lived there, the board still used detectives.[24] Despite their usefulness, they retained a bad reputation. In 1883, when A.G. Hodge of the Trades Benevolent Association spoke to a House of Commons committee, one of his complaints was the use of detectives to enforce the law. Doubtless many of his group's members had experienced their share of convictions through the work of detectives, and Hodge argued that police should be employed to detect illicit sales, "thus doing away with the irresponsible detectives who are now employed, many of whom are of the criminal class."[25]

Detectives were also useful given the many small and spread-out populations that made up many license inspectors' districts. In small towns, inspectors and police officers had the problem of being familiar to licensees in the community. Inspector George Cochrane, who lived nine miles outside Peterborough, told the Royal Commission that he was well aware how difficult it was to get around "without being seen. I have too big a body not to be seen, but I get around as quietly as I can."[26] In 1903, the License Branch received complaints about the ineffectiveness of Guelph inspector Walter Cowan. One correspondent suggested that Cowan's routines, intentionally or not, could alert licensees to an impending inspection: "When the inspector takes ten minutes to tie up his horse he naturally finds everything quiet and ship-shape in the hotel he has gone to inspect. When he makes his rounds at regular hours, and in a methodical manner, of course all concerned are ready to receive him."[27] County Crown attorney Francis Bell explained the dilemma:

> Of course the inspector has great difficulty in enforcing the law because he is well known, and without the assistance of people outside, both of the police and of the Inspector, it is utterly impossible to enforce such a law; because the police are well known, the Inspector is well known, and it is an extraordinary thing if he can catch them in the very act. He must depend upon the information that he receives from outside, and if people will not give that, then it is impossible to enforce the law.[28]

As Cowan explained, the "information ... from outside" could come from a variety of places. He could use detectives or simply use people hanging around the hotels who, "for the sake of a five dollar fee, would give information."[29]

However controversial, detectives became increasingly valuable to the functioning of the licensing law not despite their association with unsavoury activities but in fact because of it. Their work permitted the eyes of the state to penetrate the poorly lit parts of the community. When Conservative James Whitney became premier in 1905, promising to enforce strictly the licensing law, which he argued had been poorly run under the Liberals, he routinely sanctioned the use of detectives. One Conservative explained the difference between an inspector, a respectable government employee who had "never been in barrooms, [and] knew nothing of the seamy side of life," and a detective whose familiarity with such environments was essential to ferret out illegality: "It was very well to talk of appointing so-called respectable men to these positions, but such men could not be detectives."[30] For example, one report to the provincial inspector included a detailed account from a detective agency employed to investigate the Davey Hotel in Toronto. The detective, anonymized in the report as the "operative," detailed activities that he had observed and in which he had participated. These activities included drinking after hours, gambling with proprietors, and both observing extramarital coupling and possibly even being involved with prostitutes himself (the account is frustratingly unclear on this matter). A report of this nature would be valuable in prosecuting the hotel proprietor, but engagement in such activities continued to make the practice of hiring detectives akin to condoning rather than condemning immorality.[31] The detective's agility in negotiating spaces of disorder to inform a government interested in restoring order was a valuable, albeit problematic, enhancement to the operation of the liberal state.

Indeed, this intersection of individuals comfortable in legal grey areas with an apparatus intended to eliminate them illustrates a key tension in the operation of the licensing system created by the Crooks Act. The use of detectives created an uneasy relationship with the appropriate operation of the liberal state because, although detectives could provide insights into the shadows of life, they did so because they were more familiar with skirting the fringes of legality. The liberal state was strengthened by, indeed required, order created by the standardized application of a rational and comprehensible law. Numerous interactions between the license commissioners and the administrators and politicians overseeing the License Branch demonstrate how the ideal of objective enforcement, however illusory it might be, strengthened the operation of the licensing system across the province.

Some of this objective enforcement was in the way that the administration dealt with staffing. As already noted, there could be considerable tension between the work of inspectors and the way that commissioners sought to enforce the law. It could result in attempts at dismissal. Chapter 3 traced the various opinions of the suitability of a license inspector candidate based upon political affiliation or temperance sentiment; but what happened once an inspector was hired? How did opposition from the board manifest itself, and what could be done? The case of William Hogle of Lennox County provides a useful example of the complicated intersection of clientelism and administration, and the resolution illustrates how interest in fair and reasonable operation of the licensing law was an important aspect of its administration. Hogle was contentious from the start. He was a partisan appointment but described as someone who "would make a good man" for the job; local temperance advocates opposed his appointment because he was not zealous enough for their liking.[32] After his appointment, Hogle remained contentious, not for political reasons but because, according to some reports, he was not doing a good job. Since he did not live in Napanee, some thought that he could not concentrate on the parts of the district most in need of attention.³³ The following January two commissioners resigned, complaining to newly appointed Provincial Treasurer S.C. Wood not only that Hogle was a mediocre inspector but also that, since the Dunkin Act was coming into force in 1877, "with *him* as inspector the county Dunkin by-law ... will not be enforced ... as he is not capable of doing it."³⁴ The temperance forces suggested that both the board and the inspector needed to be entirely sympathetic to the prohibitionist goals of the Dunkin Act.³⁵

From a temperance viewpoint, all of this made sense, but from a bureaucratic standpoint it was anathema. It was a problem less with the inspector not doing his job than with the seemingly unfair exercise of power at the local level. Responding to these communications, Wood offered a muted and bureaucratic explanation of why he would not proceed as recommended.³⁶ First he noted that, apart from the issue of Hogle's residence, "no complaint was made against him ... of such a character as to justify his being superseded." In fact, when Hogle agreed to move to Napanee, "the government decided to retain him as inspector." Wood then turned to the broader principle of constructing an administration that strives to be objective. "I think you will agree with me," he explained to the commissioners, "that an official should not be dismissed unless for good and sufficient cause." No such cause had been provided in Hogle's case. Moreover, Wood argued for a degree of grace and opportunity for improvement. "An inspector may be somewhat lax in his duty, but upon complaint being made and he having knowledge of such complaint, may become vigilant and in several instances we have found such to be the case." He ended his letter with a none-too-subtle criticism of the zealous righteousness of temperance adherents who felt empowered to dictate policy through veiled threats:

> If it was now simply a question of choice, the resolutions passed at a public meeting of men interested and active in the temperance movement would have a very great influence in determining the decision of the government[;] in fact the decision of such a meeting would likely be [concurred] in, but it is not a matter of choice – it is one of dismissal; it is in effect [to] turn out an officer without a sufficient case having been made against him.³⁷

Wood's suggestion that Hogle might straighten up seemed to be prophetic. Between May 1876 and April 1877, he prosecuted nineteen cases and was successful in twelve, whereas between May 1877 and the end of the year he prosecuted twenty-eight cases with twenty-three successes.³⁸ Hogle remained an inspector for several years afterward.

The Hogle case illustrates a complication in the operation of the licensing system: the need for community members to support the licensing regime. Often license officers, especially inspectors, found little assistance from temperance adherents despite their often passionate criticism of the government and their active engagement when the time came to appoint officers. As noted above, the lack of community members willing to inform on hotels was a problem addressed by hiring detectives. At the Royal Commission on the Liquor Traffic, numerous inspectors and commissioners explained that they had almost no help from temperance adherents. In Hamilton, a former commissioner, John Murton, said that his board "received very little assistance from the temperance organizations" and that "nearly all the prosecutions failed which were undertaken on the evidence they were to produce."[39] Alexander Bartlett, Windsor's police commissioner, made a similar observation, explaining that "they do not assist us as much as we would like to have them."[40] Numerous temperance supporters at the Royal Commission were nonplussed when asked why they were not helping inspectors. As Woodstock Presbyterian minister William McKay explained, "I am not … duty bound to turn informer, or take a special part in enforcing this or any other law. We have paid officials to do that. I will do my duty as a citizen."[41] As discussed in subsequent chapters, this reluctance, if not outright hostility, among temperance advocates to assist inspectors in enforcing the liquor law was especially problematic under the Scott Act.

Temperance organizations such as the ad hoc Lennox group were not the only people to attempt to pressure the government to accede to local interests. Although the law gave to commissioners the authority to grant licenses using information gathered by inspectors, it did not stop people from attempting to circumvent the commissioners and use their influence, real or imagined, to get the politicians to grant them favours. In 1882, A.S. Conover, from the town of Bluevale, wrote to Provincial Secretary Arthur Hardy complaining that the commissioners for East Huron had refused to grant him a license when he moved from managing the Dominion Hotel to the Royal Hotel.[42] He complained that the manager of the Dominion Hotel had some influence on one of the commissioners and that this was simply a case "of spite and envy." Moreover, Conover explained, he had "my wife's mother, and a wife, and three children" to support. He asked Hardy to "use your influence and see me justice done." He added in a postscript, "I am your own party, a Grit."[43] Another community member, T. Farrow, wrote to Hardy to expand on Conover's situation, and the plot thickened. Apparently, the license that Conover requested was to be used by Mrs. Conover, who had the support of all the councillors in the Township of Turnberry "and all the leading men, nearly of the place."[44] This letter was accompanied by a petition explaining that two hotels were needed in Bluevale because it was on a busy road and had enough business to merit more than one hotel.[45]

In his reply to Conover, Hardy deployed the same administrative distancing that Wood had expressed in the Lennox case. He explained that it was not merely inappropriate for him to interfere; it was actually illegal: "The power to grant or withhold licenses is vested in the board of commissioners and the government are not authorized by law to override their discretion."[46] The board, however, substantially contradicted Conover's story, demonstrating to Hardy the importance of regional autonomy. The commissioners explained that Conover and his friends were misleading the License Branch. First, Conover no longer lived in Canada, "but [it] is reported and believed that he is running a saloon in Chicago." Second, they clarified that it was Mrs. Conover who was to be denied the license, not the hotel. The board did not see her as an appropriate licensee. Their assessment was based upon the "unchaste and immoral language she uses in the barroom [that] is very injurious and distasteful to society especially the youth of the locality in which she resides."[47] Hardy reminded his correspondents of the need both for fair application of the law and for the commissioners to operate with integrity, and nothing more was said.

Advocacy for or against a new hotel could be persistent to the point of dysfunction when community members refused to relent in their criticism of commissioners' actions and threats of political retaliation. This was especially the case with temperance supporters. In a case in Brantford, there was such repeated niggling that the respondents in the license commission became defensive and then defiant. In 1892, George Pike, the inspector for North Brant, wrote to the License Branch about a tricky case of electoral boundaries. When a section of the township was added to Brantford, its electors were no longer eligible to sign petitions against a new license in their neighbourhood. This denied them the provision in section 11(14) of the Crooks Act as amended in 1884 that denied a license if a majority of "persons duly qualified to vote as electors in the sub-division at an election ... petition against it."[48] Thus, when the board received an application for a new tavern license close to the boundary, the new Brantford residents had no legal recourse to oppose it.[49] Moreover, as the local inspector explained, until new electoral lists were drawn up, he would not be able to determine who was eligible to sign a petition and therefore could not assess whether the names on a petition were valid. Totten told the inspector that, until the electoral divisions were "rearranged by the municipal bylaw" the following April, there was little to be done. Only those electors remaining in that subdivision were eligible to petition under the parameters of the Crooks Act, and no provision existed for determining who had that right.

Waiting for the municipality to fix the lists was unacceptable to the residents of the new Brantford subdivision with the lofty name of Eagle Place. They were concerned about a local developer's plan for a tavern 200 yards from the boundary. After the board deemed their petition ineligible for consideration, J.E. Waterous wrote to Arthur Hardy, who by this time filled the influential position of commissioner of Crown lands and was MLA for nearby Brant North. Waterous noted that the hotel was "just on the dividing line between the City and the Township so that any Police protection we might have from the City would have no jurisdiction"; that the new tavern was opposite a school, "which, we think, is a very objectionable feature"; and that "on account of it being placed just outside the city limits it seems to us that it will be a harbor for all the sports and roughs of the city." Moreover, it was on a road that led to a nearby "Indian Reserve," and Waterous feared that "a drinking place in this locality would only be one where no doubt the Indians would largely congregate." He was not concerned about the welfare of the Indigenous people but saw the combination of "sports," "roughs," and "Indians" as a threat to neighbourhood peace.[50] Hardy repeated Totten's contention that there was nothing the License Branch could do: "The law vests the power of granting or withholding [a] license wholly in the Board of [C]ommissioners for North Brant."[51] Another resident, Joseph Hartley, wrote to Hardy claiming that it was the MLA's "duty as a prominent member of a government ... to oppose to the utmost of your ability the granting of such license." Hartley finished the letter with a threat: "If this crowning infamy is allowed to be perpetuated upon a long suffering and at present helpless community, the day will come ... when [people] not only in Eagle Place ... but in many a Christian home ... will show their disapprobation by marking their ballots in a way which will not be to your advantage."[52]

When responding to this correspondence, Hardy reiterated the importance of the rational administration of regulations and the primacy of law, although in the face of such criticism, he found it difficult to restrain himself. After explaining that "it would be an undue and improper exercise of authority on my part were I to intervene," and that in fact he would be "open to censure in the House" if he tried to influence matters, he assured Hartley that "the license commissioners for North Brant are men of intelligence, standing, moral character, and business capacity and I am strongly inclined to think that our good friends in Eagles Nest [sic] ... as in other parts of that riding can safely trust them to do ... what is just and right." Having presented the party line, Hardy then let his frustration show: "I am, you will pardon me therefore for saying, a little at a loss to know upon what ground it is assumed by your very friendly letter or by any of our friends in Eagle's nest [sic] that I should take the ground which you advise in the matter." After explaining that he was no more justified in attempting to influence commissioners than he would be in attempting to influence a judge, he concluded with an allusion to Hartley's attempt at partisan influence: "I write you thus fully as I know how warm and disinterested a friend you have been of myself and of the Mowat Government for so many years."[53] The subtext spoke volumes.

For Hardy and Totten, the law inoculated politicians from blame when decisions at the local level upset constituents, and the denouement of the story illustrates how administrative processes further served to distance politicians from blame. Three weeks after this exchange, T.H. Preston, editor of the *Brantford Expositor,* wrote to Totten clearly hoping to uncover administrative malfeasance. Preston asked whether Provincial Treasurer Richard Harcourt, whose office had taken over the License Branch in 1890, had been consulted about directions that Totten had sent to inspector Pike regarding Eagle Place. Totten's response was telling both in its use of administrative procedure to block the inquiry and protect Harcourt and in revealing the inner processes of the License Branch. Totten explained that "anyone at all familiar with this class of correspondence very well knows that the head of a department very rarely dictates or sees such letters before they are mailed." He assured Preston that on matters of policy or gravity, the "chief is consulted but the details are executed as a rule by the deputy." Totten noted that there was so much correspondence in the office that to consult the boss on every matter would grind the machine to a halt. In any case the letter between the office and Pike was privileged, but Totten assured Preston that the inspector had simply asked him for his opinion on the law. Finally, describing his substantial workload, Totten placed himself and the machinery of the bureaucracy between Preston and Harcourt:

> Several times daily I am called upon as the head of the branch to advise inspectors upon questions that have arisen or are likely to arise under the License Act. Cases occur in which it is impossible from the absence of any

ruling or decision of the courts to say what the law is. Directions of some kind must be given at once and the inspector is advised to do that which is for the time considered best under all the circumstances. To make public a letter of instructions or directions written in the usual official manner by an officer of a department to another official in the same department advising him how to proceed in a very difficult case and hold the head of the department responsible therefore at the same time questioning his legal ability does not seem to me to be very fair play at all.[54]

Totten then engaged in an extensive lecture on how the License Act worked, clarifying several minute points of procedure. This discussion of the secrecy of departmental correspondence might well have inspired the request for this file in the legislature, but there appears to have been no further action in regard to the controversy.

The Eagle Place case demonstrates the power of the bureaucracy emerging out of the Crooks Act as both administratively practical and politically expedient. As a key feature of the operation of the liberal state's power, the legally established administration served to separate the subjective demands of constituents and possibly the personal and partisan interests of politicians with a buffer based upon objective administration and legal requirements. Hardy referenced the legally imposed separation of authority to distance himself from attempts to influence commissioners. Totten embellished with the administrative procedures necessary in a system that was generating such extensive documentation. This, along with the rhetoric about the autonomy of the license boards and the integrity of their procedures, allowed the License Branch to stand between politicians and the operation of the law. By giving commissioners the power to grant or deny licenses, the legislation was an attempt to limit the potential for political influence, be it from the province or the municipality, to affect licensing decisions. Doubtless, license commissioners were open to local influence: the Lennox County case demonstrates how commissioners brought their own biases to the job and were affected by their own social and political networks. Yet the fact that commissioners, as unpaid appointees, were not beholden to any political masters for their jobs, and the fact that they did not need to look to the community for approval through elections, meant that there was a more independent body making decisions than had been the case before 1876. At least that was the theoretical construction of the political distancing of license operations.

This idealism does not mean, however, that commissioners were above temptation. For example, Dufferin County was rife with problems in the first iteration of its board. In November 1876, a group of locals describing themselves as "friends of the government" charged that the first year of the Crooks Act had been less than satisfactory. Two of the main concerns were that the board had not been firm enough and that hopes that the new act "if operated by conscientious and active men would arrest such glareing [sic] infractions of law and wipe out such dens of vice" had been unrealized. The correspondents noted that, although fewer licenses were being granted, "there are a large number selling without licenses and we shall not have any material change until it is understood the Board of Commissioners mean business."[55] When provincial inspector Richard Stedman investigated, he heard stories that "Dr. Corbal one of the commissioners and Mr. Dunbar the Inspector could be bought or turned for any small sum." Such rumours could be corrosive, and Stedman noted that "one can hear the name of Dr. Corbal connected with other things that are not very creditable to any gentleman."[56] Corbal's reputation, despite his professional status, was not a credit to a government commissioner. The next year the inspector and two of the three commissioners (including Corbal) were replaced.[57]

Even when their integrity was not being questioned by the License Branch or its officers, commissioners were not unimpeachable, and several found themselves in court as defendants as a result of licensing decisions that they had made. Early in 1889, William R. Pizer, a hotel keeper in the village of Essex Centre, submitted an application for a tavern license for his hotel.[58] The inspector reported that Pizer was a "fit and proper person to have a license," that his tavern had the proper accommodations, and that he was "known to ... be of good character and repute."[59] Yet, at the hearing for the application, the board received a petition from local ratepayers asking the commissioners not to issue any liquor licenses in the area. The commissioners concurred with that request, believing it to be conversant with the Crooks Act requirement that licenses be denied if electors opposed them by petition (the same section that the residents of Eagle Place were unable to use). In this case, it appeared to the board to be a clear case that a majority of electors did not want the license to be issued. Justices Falconbridge and Street came to a different decision. Looking at other parts of section 11 that set out more specific reasons for denying a license, they concluded that it was not enough for petitioners simply to say that they did not want a license granted in the area. They needed to give clear reasons for denying a specific license, justifying why either the premises or the applicant was objectionable. Both justices argued that such precision was necessary because section 11(14) gave electors a powerful veto. As Justice Street reasoned, "such a power ... should be exercised strictly in accordance with the statute."[60] The court found in favour of Pizer and concluded that he should be entitled to a liquor license.[61]

Many cases against commissioners involved perceived vested rights in relation to liquor licensing. The issue in *Pizer v. Fraser et al.* was the community's right to refuse any license in its area; this was also the case in Eagle's Place combined with the redrawn municipal boundary complicating the idea of vested rights to oppose local changes. In Blue Vale, the issue involved the suitability of the proprietor, the authority of the commission, and the ability of Conover and his friends to use their purported Grit bona fides to gain political favour. In 1890, the notion of entitlement and the authority of commissioners clashed yet again in Kent County, in southwestern Ontario, another case that ended up in court. In June 1889, James Leitch wrote to inspector Thomas Boon demanding "a certificate stating that I am entitled to [a] tavern license for ... Victoria House in the village of Highgate." His lawyer, N. Mills, referenced *Pizer* to argue that a general petition against a license in the area was not sufficient to block the application. The commissioners, he argued, had no valid reason to deny a license. Through his interpretation, "the applicant must have a license as provided by statute."[62]

It was a complicated situation, made more so by the timing of the repeal vote. Kent County had been under local option until a majority of over 1,500 voted to rescind the law on 4 April 1889.[63] The Crooks Act required that a meeting to consider license applications be held before 1 April each year, and all licensing decisions had to be made by that time. Not only had the local option vote happened after 1 April, but the results of that law were not official until the outcome of the vote was published in the *Canada Gazette,* a process commonly referred to as being "gazetted"; Kent County's Scott Act repeal was gazetted on 18 May.[64] There was no legal way to circumvent this timeline since, as Totten noted in a memo to the provincial secretary, "until it is gazetted no one could know when the Act would be repealed."[65] All licenses had to be issued by 1 May, but no valid meeting could be held before 18 May. In effect, legally, the Board of License Commissioners was unable to issue licenses until May of the following year. Nevertheless, Kent County's board began to consider applications in April, and continued deliberations into July, a process that involved increasingly intense lobbying and conflict. When community members petitioned the board not to grant any licenses in the area, the board considered the petition to be too general to be applicable. Consequently, when the commissioners issued licenses to Leitch and another tavern keeper, James Patterson, also of Highgate, a lawyer representing the petitioners applied to the courts for an injunction against the licenses. The case against Patterson was dismissed, and he was granted his license, but the Leitch case was more complicated. His property was adjacent to a school, and the petitioners had mentioned that they opposed one of the properties because it was close to a school, so according to the precedent established in *Pizer* the petition had credibility and was not dismissed.

The outcome was equally complicated but revealed a remarkable liberty that the law gave to license commissioners. Justice Robertson ruled against the petitioners, allowing Leitch's application to be considered by the board, but Robertson also questioned the procedures of the commissioners. He argued that the commissioners violated the Crooks Act by ignoring the various dates for considering license applications. Yet, in an extraordinary legal twist, he observed that the Crooks Act stated that "non-compliance [with such rules] ... shall not invalidate the action of the board ... [So] all the provisions which were thought necessary by the legislature to ensure the granting of licenses to respectable and worthy persons ... [might be] utterly ignored." In other words, the board could do what it wanted and not be held legally responsible. Unhappy with the decision that he was forced to make, Robertson refused to require the plaintiff to pay court costs, which was normal procedure (and a decision that concerned the License Branch because it now had to pay for the trial). The judge concluded with a pointed criticism of the license commissioners, saying that he was not satisfied that they had "faithfully discharged their duty as public servants ... [and that,] had the commissioners acted in terms of the statute, which gave their jurisdiction, no license would have been granted."[66] Totten called the judgment "unnecessarily severe," but the point was clear: the licensing system was designed to provide local boards with maximum leeway when administering the law in their districts, to a degree that boards seemed to be above the law that they were enforcing.[67]

The purpose of the Crooks Act was to establish a system that reduced the excesses of the liquor trade by implementing a centralized and ostensibly objective licensing administration across the province. By creating a system that was deeply partisan but sought to exemplify Mowat's self-declared preference for honesty and efficient management of the provincial government, the Crooks Act engaged that government more directly with the complications that liquor imposed on the liberal state.

The defence of local interests could be intense, and efforts to enforce the law and construct a system distanced from the exigencies of municipalities were repeatedly forced to engage in the minute details of municipal life. Notwithstanding the authority of the license commissioners to make decisions based upon their assessments of the local situations and the needs of the communities, bias, influence peddling, personality clashes, problems with partisan appointees, and sometimes intense political entreaties meant that liquor continued to be problematic. It would be easy to make a joke here about people being drunk on power, but it was not that simple. Rather, the personal stakes in and subjectivity of the liquor system, in which livelihoods hung in the balance and lives and lifestyles were threatened, could impair judgment and make the central administration reel with the toxic effects of such imputations, sometimes significant, sometimes petty, but always passionate. It is not surprising that governments, both at the provincial level and at the dominion level, found, in the last quarter of the century, that the complex and seemingly unsolvable liquor question caused headaches, giddiness, and a tendency to start fights.

Part 2
The Complications of Liquor in a Federal Liberal State

5
How Drinking Affects the Constitution, 1864–83

Liquor's political power was not simply a matter of municipal or provincial concern: it infiltrated all levels of government. When the speaker of Ontario's legislature ruled in 1873 that John Clarke's prohibition bill was outside the constitutional authority of the provincial government (i.e., ultra vires), the decision caused Dry legislators to halt their advocacy for provincial prohibition and push the dominion government for clarity on the issue. Liquor complicated the operation of the Canadian state, not only because of conflicting notions of how a liberal government should affect the lives of individuals, but also because of the way the Constitution apportioned authority to regulate the affairs of the people. Recall that the British North America Act imparted specific powers to dominion and provincial governments.[1] Section 91 outlined the powers of the federal government, including section 91(2), the power over "the regulation of trade and commerce." Section 92 listed the powers of provinces, including section 92(9) ("Shop, Saloon, Tavern, Auctioneer, and other Licences in order to the raising [sic] of a Revenue for Provincial, Local, or Municipal Purposes") and section 92(13) ("Property and Civil rights"). Anything not specifically listed in these sections, according to section 91(29), was within the dominion government's power. The distinctions were broad enough, and the liquor business was diverse enough, that dominion and provincial governments frequently clashed over which had responsibility for the liquor trade. Although section 92(9) seemed to be clear about licensing, even it was debatable since it described licensing only insofar as it could be used to raise revenue. Moreover, the preamble of section 91 assigned to the dominion government the responsibility to make laws for the "Peace, Order, and good Government" of the country, so licensing laws intended to impose order on a disorderly system could indeed be considered the responsibility of the dominion government.

You do not need to be a lawyer to see the complications in such overlapping jurisdictions, but even canny lawyers such as Oliver Mowat and John A. Macdonald could be engaged for decades in constitutional wrangling. The authority to legislate the business of liquor was a repeated source of legal debate, with several important cases making their way to the Judicial Committee of the Privy Council, the ultimate arbiter of constitutional issues even after the creation in 1875 of the Supreme Court of Canada. It might be just a coincidence that the first case heard by the Supreme Court involved provincial and dominion authority over brewers' licenses, but it is emblematic of the way that liquor would influence the interpretation of Sections 91 and 92 thereafter. Brewers in Ontario contended that they did not need to hold a license from the province to sell their beer because they already had to pay for dominion licenses to brew it, and the Supreme Court agreed with them.[2] This ruling, known as *Severn v. The Queen*, would resonate through discussions of licensing for the next few decades. The first half-century of the country's existence saw numerous constitutional challenges related to liquor, and although considerable clarity was created by successive judicial decisions up to the 1890s, such debates continue in the twenty-first century.

One of the most problematic overlaps in dominion and provincial powers lay in the operation of the Canada Temperance Act, 1864 (the Dunkin Act). This legislation had two main components. First, it gave municipalities the right to pass bylaws prohibiting the sale of liquor in small quantities in their jurisdictions. Second, it created a mechanism by which electors of the community could petition to have such a bylaw passed, along with the specific process to be followed when holding the vote. The act did not create total prohibition. It prohibited the sale of liquor for public consumption, for example, in a tavern, but it did not ban production. Brewers and distillers were still allowed to make and sell their wares in Dunkin Act communities, but they could do so only in large volumes. Distillers could sell in quantities of no less than five gallons at one time, and brewers could sell in no smaller volumes than one dozen bottles of three half-pints (thirty imperial ounces).[3] Similarly, retailers could sell alcoholic beverages at the same large volumes as long as the beverages were taken off premises.[4] The legislation included minimum and maximum penalties for violations, but it did not include the text of the prohibition bylaw to be passed in municipalities. The specific wording of the bylaw was up to individual councils.[5]

The Dunkin Act had several significant flaws. Although it included processes for prosecuting violators, it did not create a mechanism for enforcing the law on the ground. Its provisions simply compelled officers of the Department of Inland Revenue to cease issuing licenses for the sale of liquor where local option was in force. Numerous critics argued that unless prohibitionists were willing to take an active role in enforcing the Dunkin Act, they would continue to see it fail.[6] This was noted repeatedly even in newspapers sympathetic to the temperance cause. A correspondent from Alnwick in Northumberland County told the *Globe* in 1878 that the Dunkin Act was a failure in his community: "I have seen more people drunk here ... than I did before. The fact is we have a law but no one to look after it and see that it is carried out. What we want is a detective."[7] As Henry Totten noted in his report to the legislature after the first year that the Crooks Act was in place, whereas the Crooks Act license fees funded enforcement of the law, the Dunkin Act included no method to pay for enforcement; prosecution was simply an additional duty of the inland revenue collector or any private citizen who would collect part of any fine imposed.[8] Totten's characterization of the impoverished nature of Dunkin Act enforcement was not entirely accurate. The Crooks Act included a provision requiring municipalities in which the Dunkin Act was in operation to provide two-thirds of the costs of running the Boards of License Commissioners and the license inspectors who, presumably, would oversee Dunkin Act provisions (since Boards of License Commissioners operated throughout license districts, whereas the Dunkin Act could be in operation in townships or villages within those districts). However, the provincial secretary noted in his report to the legislature for 1879 that few municipalities actually paid this money. Of the thirteen counties that he noted in which the Dunkin Act had been in force, only three had paid the full contribution.[9] Rev. James Cameron argued that the problem with the Dunkin Act was its lack of enforcement mechanisms. Reminding his audience that the classic image of Justice was a blindfolded woman holding the scales in one hand and a sword in the other, Cameron noted that "in the Dunkin Act Justice has the scales all right, but it has no sword ... like many other good acts [it has] become a dead letter in the Statute book." The creation of the position of provincial license inspector, he told his audience, although not achieving prohibition, was "a step in the right direction."[10]

Cameron's muted support might have channelled that of temperance adherents who seemed to take a renewed interest in local option after the Crooks Act became law. Half a year after the Crooks Act came into force, *Globe* editor George Brown observed with approval that temperance advocates had begun agitating with some gusto for the Dunkin Act to be passed in their municipalities. He expressed some surprise, noting that the act "has, up to the present year, been, with a few spasmodic exceptions, left a dead letter."[11] Brown must have viewed this activity with some self-satisfaction, for the *Globe* had been reminding readers for years that there was already a prohibition act on the books and that temperance advocates needed to give it a good trial before they could claim credibly that the public was ready for prohibition. C. Blackett Robinson, editor of the *British American Presbyterian,* also observed with similar pleasure renewed interest in the Dunkin Act: "In a number of counties this by-law is now in force, because the people have been aroused to see the awful evils of drinking customs, and have been led in consequence to give their votes for shutting up all groggeries, and taverns, and saloon bars."[12]

It might not have been a coincidence that in Ontario the push for the Dunkin Act came on the heels of the passing of the Crooks Act. Temperance advocates might have believed that, as Cameron noted, the administration created by the Crooks Act would be able to enforce local option. Conversely, perhaps temperance advocates saw in the passing of the Crooks Act a victory for liquor interests since drinking places remained in operation. A third possible explanation for the increased energy in pushing for the Dunkin Act might be found in changes within the temperance movement itself. In 1875, various male-led temperance groups began to discuss combining their resources, a process that led to the creation in 1877 of the Dominion Alliance for the Total Suppression of the Liquor Traffic, modelled on the even more clumsily named United Kingdom Alliance for the Suppression of the Traffic in All Intoxicating Liquors. The Dominion Alliance had members from many temperance groups, including some notables from the Sons of Temperance and the Good Templars of Temperance.[13] Moreover, the Dominion Alliance formed only a few years after the founding of the first Canadian branches of the Woman's Christian Temperance Union (WCTU). The WCTU began in the United States in 1874, coming on the heels of and driven by the energy of the Women's Temperance Crusade in the US Midwest, which had captivated teetotallers in Canada.[14] Branches were formed in Owen Sound and Picton soon after the US organization was formed. The Canadian WCTU's torch was carried by Letitia Youmans, a resident of

Picton. The "temperance men," then, were joined by the vigorous energy of temperance women.[15]

Yet the rapid increase in agitation for the Dunkin Act was quickly followed by a rapid decline. Although thirteen counties passed Dunkin Act bylaws soon after the Crooks Act came into force, by the end of the decade it had been quashed by the courts in four and repealed in the rest.[16] Many commentators realized its weaknesses. Observing the push for the Dunkin Act in Toronto, Robinson of the *Presbyterian* listed several impediments to its passing there unrelated to the strong public opinion against local option. He noted that everything from the fact that electors had to express their opinions openly rather than using the recently introduced innovation of the secret ballot to the limited number of busy polling places could prevent Drys from heading to the polls. Robinson observed that although some might argue that the open declaration vote could have the same effect on the Wets, their interests were financial, and "the Anti Dunkinites, deeming the measure to be one that touched their pockets, were not deterred by the consideration of loss of time."[17] A year later the Committee on Temperance of the Hamilton and London Synod of the Presbyterian Church noted that the Dunkin Act was losing ground. The committee mentioned that this was not because of the lack of an "earnest desire in the public mind for legislation to curtail the traffic in strong drink" but because of "the manifest imperfections of the Act itself, and the want of efficient means for its enforcement." These rescissions did not mean, however, that soon there would be no dry areas left in the province. Under the Dunkin Act, when a county local option bylaw was rescinded, any municipal bylaw that had been in place prior to the county legislation would return to operation. Nevertheless, it was still a reduction of dry patches in a wet province.

The failures in Ontario illustrate the existence of strong wet sentiment, although it was less vocal, public, and organized than that of the temperance people. In several counties, agitation to repeal the legislation began almost immediately after successful votes in favour of local option. In others, local option lasted for less than a year because of legal appeals to have the results quashed, normally by showing that the voting procedures included in the Dunkin Act had not been followed properly. It was indeed a cumbersome process. The act required polls to be open for a certain number of days depending on the population of the area. For example, in Brant County, Wets charged that officials used incorrect voter rolls to calculate how many days the polls should stay open. Although they lost the ensuing court case, the trial delayed by three months the date on which the Dunkin Act came into effect: it should have been in operation in March 1877 but did not take effect until the end of June. So, when the act was repealed the following March, its proponents argued that it had not been given a chance.[18] In Frontenac County, the bylaw was held to be invalid because the court determined that in several townships notices had not been posted for long enough, and in others, "the postings had been irregular."[19] Similar cases were launched across the province, and many were successful.

A second way that opponents challenged the Dunkin Act in court was by exploiting discrepancies between the Crooks Act and the Dunkin Act. For example, some tavern keepers were convicted under the Crooks Act in jurisdictions in which the Dunkin Act was in force. In *Regina v. Prettie,* the defendant in a Dunkin Act municipality was charged with selling alcohol without a license, but "the conviction should have been under the Temperance Act of 1864 ... for keeping liquor at all"; the conviction of the lower court was quashed.[20] In other instances, licensees used similar conflicts to avoid prosecution. The Dunkin Act stipulated that its provisions were to take place on 1 March each year, whereas the Crooks Act operated from May to April. Thus, in several communities where the Dunkin Act came into force, licensees argued that they should be allowed to continue to sell alcohol until the end of April since this was the scope of their licenses. In one case, hotel keeper Joseph French was charged with selling liquor in a Dunkin Act district of Yorkville on 19 April 1878. He argued that, since he had a license under the Crooks Act that expired on 30 April, he was not in violation of the law. The magistrates could not agree on a verdict and dismissed the case.[21] The *Globe* noted that, in most Dunkin Act districts, proponents of the act simply turned a blind eye to the selling of alcohol, preferring to let licenses run out and allowing licensees to sell their stocks.[22] Other issues of incompatibility between the two laws included the different administrations to which they referred. Although according to section 129 of the BNA Act, legislation passed before 1 July 1867 continued to be in effect unless changed or repealed by the provinces, the Dunkin Act referred to different administrations.[23] For example, under the act, the collector of inland revenue had to be sent a copy of the bylaw, although after Confederation such financial arrangements were normally the purview of the provinces. Under the Crooks Act, license boards superseded collectors of inland revenue. In 1877, the Ontario legislature passed a significant amendment to the Crooks Act that addressed several cases of incompatibility in the legislation, including noting that, where the Dunkin Act was in force, selling liquor without a license remained a violation even though no license could be issued.[24]

A powerful case against the Dunkin Act was found in Prince Edward County, the home of Letitia Youmans. Although voted upon in 1875, the Dunkin Act came into effect in May 1876, soon after the Crooks Act became law.[25] As noted in Chapter 3, Henry Totten investigated local option in Prince Edward County and concluded that it was not working. Illegality remained rampant, and the inspector and commissioners could not keep it in check. This assessment was made only a few months after Youmans, president of the Picton WCTU, described in glowing terms to her like-minded sisters at the Women's International Temperance convention in Philadelphia in June 1876 the success in Prince Edward County: "With many prayers, tears and efforts, [the Dunkin Act] had been carried there, and ... now there were hopes, bright hopes, for its youthful sons."[26] Such hopefulness did not last. In 1880, the Dunkin Act was repealed, although not without considerable controversy.[27] By 1881, the government could claim that no license district in the province was entirely dry, reinforcing the opinion that a licensing law was better than total prohibition.

The legal problems with implementing the Dunkin Act drove temperance advocates to further action. In 1877, groups from across the province petitioned the dominion government to make changes to the act. Many were from areas such as Brantford, where legal challenges had hindered the operation of the legislation. Some requested that a vote by ballot replace the existing vote by verbal declaration.[28] Several temperance groups from outside Ontario and Quebec – notably Manitoba – petitioned to have the provisions of the Dunkin Act extended to their province.[29] The following year petitioning increased, with temperance groups requesting that the government further update its local option legislation. These efforts appeared to bear fruit when, in March 1878, Richard Scott, a Liberal senator from Prescott in eastern Ontario, secretary of state in Alexander Mackenzie's cabinet, and government leader in the Senate, introduced a bill to create the Canada Temperance Act (CTA). The CTA would expand the local option provisions of the Dunkin Act to the entire country and address many of the problematic provisions that had made the act ineffective in many jurisdictions. Once Scott's bill was presented in the Senate, petitioning ramped up, with dozens of petitions read in Parliament each day demanding that the legislation be passed.

Scott argued that his bill was intended to address both requests from residents outside the original Province of Canada who wanted it to apply to their provinces and significant problems in implementing the Dunkin Act itself. The 1864 act's plebiscite rules required polls to be open for one day for every 400 electors; thus, larger towns could have many days of polling. In Toronto, the Dunkin Act vote continued for nearly two weeks, "keeping the city in a state of ferment during all that period."[30] Scott also wanted to take the process of holding the vote out of municipal governments' hands because "the municipal machinery was the creature of the legislative bodies of the several provinces, and could at any time be changed." On top of the vote itself, the Scott Act would modify several of the restrictions in the Dunkin Act, mentioning specifically the provision that allowed wholesalers and distillers within a local option community to continue to sell their wares in large volumes. Under his proposed legislation, these businesses would be able to sell only in volumes of ten gallons or more and only to purchasers outside the local option community.[31]

The Scott Act faced several criticisms. Notwithstanding the extensive number of petitions received by Parliament, the fact that the government waited until just before it would have to call an election suggested to some, such as British Columbia Conservative Senator Clement Cornwall, that the bill was simply an electoral ploy. Cornwall did not support prohibition, seeing it as an imposition on individual rights. His fellow Conservative, Alexander Vidal, a prominent leader of the Dominion Alliance, defended the time that it took to put the act together but also was critical of it. To Vidal, the issue of constitutional jurisdiction remained unsettled. The Supreme Court had considered several cases related to liquor licensing and dominion/provincial jurisdictions over the past few years, and Vidal suggested that Scott, the secretary of state, should have been able to obtain an opinion on the constitutionality of the act from the Supreme Court or at least the minister of justice. Nova Scotia Conservative Senator Robert Dickey argued that the Scott Act would be dominion legislation repealing provincial licenses and that this was unconstitutional, arguing that if provincial governments "have power to grant licenses and the Dominion Government has power to take them away by this bill, it is a perfect mockery, and the conflict of jurisdiction is complete."[32] Dickey then concurred with Vidal: he, too, was not opposed to the legislation but wanted a straightforward legal opinion on the issue before proceeding.[33] Clearly, the strategy of the Conservative temperance faction was to paint the government as procedurally irresponsible, allowing the Tories to appear to support temperance and seem more able to pass legislation that would actually work.

One reason that this opposition had such power was that the Supreme Court itself had not been united in its decisions on jurisdiction cases with respect to intoxicating beverages. When pressed about the lack of clarity in Supreme Court decisions, Scott referred to *Severn v. The Queen*. He noted that the government had hoped that this case would clarify the issue in broad strokes but that the court had decided to deal only with the specifics of the case: "As those who have taken the trouble to read the dictum of the Judges know, they avoided all but the naked question. They have not given us very much light."[34] In his study of the Supreme Court, John Saywell argues that in its early cases its decisions were often specific, with justices refusing to rule on issues beyond the precise legal matter of the case.[35] Despite these concerns, and after some relatively minor changes to the bill, the Scott Act became law in May 1878. Immediately, temperance organizations across the country began working to have it implemented in their communities.

If the Scott Act had indeed been an attempt by Mackenzie's Liberals to shore up support from Dry electors in advance of the election, then it was a failure: Mackenzie lost the election, and it was up to Sir John A. Macdonald to deal with the Scott Act. The Conservatives faced a dilemma when it came to liquor. Macdonald himself had not supported the Scott Act, but the legislation was popular among influential temperance adherents such as Vidal. At the same time, Macdonald had close ties with liquor interests, including banker and brewer Eugene O'Keefe, who attempted to influence Macdonald through friendly but often impassioned letters about liquor laws. When the Scott Act was being debated in the House of Commons, for example, O'Keefe had sent a frustrated telegram to Macdonald asking him, "are the temperance people going to have everything their own way[;] will not Vidal and [Conservative ally James] Aikens ... make some concessions?"[36] They did not, and many considered the Scott Act to have been authored by the Dominion Alliance, to the frustration of the liquor industry.[37]

When he returned to power, then, Macdonald was faced with the challenge of dealing with an issue that divided both the country and his party. These divisions became so toxic that, apart from minor tweaks and fixes, numerous attempts to address the liquor issue failed for several years. In 1879, 1880, and 1881, bills were presented to amend the Scott Act, and in each session members introduced hostile amendments to the legislation that would fundamentally change it. For example, in 1879, during discussion of a relatively minor amendment that would fix some problems with the repeal of the Dunkin Act, Conservative Senator George Alexander proposed a change that would require those who petitioned for a Scott Act vote to pay the cost of the plebiscite if the majority of votes cast did not amount to a majority of electors in support.[38] This amendment would have addressed concerns expressed by members of the liquor industry that Drys had nothing to lose by repeated campaigns for Scott Act votes, whereas the liquor industry would be financially ruined. The amendment also would have addressed concerns that more than a simple majority of votes should be needed for such a change; a majority of all electors would be a more convincing representation of the will of the people. Alexander's amendment was defeated. In 1880, when the House of Commons was discussing a seemingly straightforward amendment proposed by Vidal that would have offered simple tweaks to the Scott Act, fellow Conservative Alfred Boultbee proposed yet another amendment to define a dry victory only when a majority of electors, rather than a majority of votes cast, supported local prohibition. This amendment passed in the House, but in the Senate it was pushed back until a date after the session was scheduled to end, a process known as "giving the bill the hoist."[39] In 1881, Boultbee proposed his own bill to require local option to be triggered only by a majority of electors. It also failed but not before one of Macdonald's temperance-supporting Tory correspondents warned the prime minister that if he supported the bill, temperance people would oppose him, and he would be "in real danger."[40]

This amendment was the least of the temperance advocates' worries in 1881. When Alexander Vidal again presented his bill, Nova Scotia Senator William Almon proposed an amendment to modify the Scott Act to permit the sale of beer, cider, and light wine. If this change went through, then the Scott Act would only prohibit the sale of spirits. It would be a major step backward for the temperance movement, although moderates, claiming the mantle of "true temperance," argued that it would encourage the consumption of lighter alcoholic beverages and reduce drunkenness. After the amended bill passed in the Senate, a deluge of letters poured onto Macdonald's desk. Wets wrote with support and praise; Drys wrote with opposition and threats. O'Keefe joined a hail of telegrams in March 1881 supporting the amendment as "the only sensible solution of [the] temperance question."[41] Toronto brewer Thomas Davies wrote that Almon's amendment was "just what is wanted by people generally [–] true Temperance at last."[42] Henry Cronmiller, a brewer from Port Colborne, expressed his concern about Scott Act agitation taking place in his Welland County neighbourhood. He asked Macdonald to back the amendment, "and by doing so you would much oblige a true supporter."[43]

Yet others warned that the party could lose votes. Hamilton iron foundry owner James Killey sent two letters in as many days asking Macdonald to "give the amendment the quietus." With an eye on the expected election of 1882, Killey argued that the temperance movement would pull any support that it had for the Conservatives and that "pettitions [sic] by the thousands will be sent in[, and] this will be made into political capital by the opposition as sure as you live." This was a staunch warning from a staunch supporter that "the temperance men are resolute and powerful."[44] George Jackson, a Conservative from Durham County, advised that the amendment would "emasculate" the Scott Act and that it would be less dangerous politically to repeal the act altogether. If the Almon amendment were successful, then "the result will ... confront us at the next general election with a well-organized temperance opposition."[45] These hazards were never risked, and the bill never reached a second reading in the House, thereby avoiding the perils of casting a vote in favour of or against it. O'Keefe wrote bitterly and with not a little venom that the "farce just ended will ... give intense satisfaction to your temperance friends, but not so to the general public, who regard it as a great act of weakness on your part."[46]

The intractable challenge of liquor regulation was presented by both sides as an immediate, practical problem as well as a philosophical one, indicating a core tension of the liberal state. Temperance advocates, drawing from decades of sensationalized literature illustrating the risks of falling from a precarious economic state into utter destitution, linked the liquor traffic to broader "evils" and perils to both the individual and the nation. The disorder found in the "low groggery" represented the rapacity of capitalism, the exploitation of the poor, and the danger of an unfettered traffic for the individual and the country. Moreover, the low groggery itself was the product of unenforced liquor laws and the political corruption that permitted such unsavoury places to proliferate. It was a threat to individual economic stability and to the strength of the nation. Beyond the economic problem was the ideological one: the liquor traffic enslaved the individual, and such enslavement was antithetical to a nation in which liberty was a fundamental value. Individual freedom and the role of the state in protecting the ability to enjoy life, liberty, and property were threatened by the traffic in alcohol.

Opponents of prohibition presented similar ideological dilemmas from a different perspective. Most did not advocate unfettered access to liquor, at least not those who presented themselves as respectable. Often they also claimed to be supporters of temperance, but their "true temperance" was based upon the notion that moderation was preferable to excess, and they opposed both excessive restriction and excessive indulgence. Typical of such arguments was the assertion by Boultbee that he was strongly in favour of temperance but not of the extreme approach of local option. Anti-prohibitionists' version of temperance advocated not only individual self-control but also a temperate government that did not go to the extremes of prohibition and constraints on individual liberty. Indeed, protecting liberty was a key issue in their rhetoric and even more salient because it linked the liberty of the individual to economic self-determination. In his angry letter to Macdonald after the 1881 amendment failed to reach second reading in the House, O'Keefe drew out the problem. He reminded Macdonald of "the amount of capital employed in our business – some fifteen millions of dollars" and contrasted this investment with the financial risks of temperance adherents, who had little to lose. Indeed, many of their speakers and organizers were "employed by the temperance fanatics at a fat salary." Success or failure did not have nearly the importance to these individuals as it did to the many respectable distillers, brewers, vintners, hoteliers, and wholesalers whose livelihoods were threatened. Win or lose, the temperance "agitators," as he often called them, would move on to the next battle.[47] However, if the Scott Act came into force, then respectable members of the liquor industry would suffer. As O'Keefe noted in 1880,

> the amount of money asked from us when we are called upon to contest the act is so large that we must absolutely give up business and lose our all whether the Act passes or not, inasmuch as we do not receive back any of the money we are obliged to expend in fighting against it, while on the other hand the petitioners lose nothing.[48]

Here liberalism – freedom of industry and individual self-determination – was threatened by the same kind of rapacious greed that "the temperance fanatics" saw in the liquor trade.

O'Keefe's use of the term "agitator" is significant. Along with the term "fanatic," it was a repeated trope in the rhetoric of the Wets and more than just a colourful way to characterize temperance supporters. Both terms were used to paint temperance as irrational and outside the social norm. For example, contemplating the passage of the Crooks Act in 1876, the Toronto *Leader* referred to temperance petitioners as "those afflicted with a mania."[49] Yet "agitator" had a more profoundly problematic connotation, especially in the land of "peace, order, and good government." In contrast to the disorder found in the low groggery, attributed to tavern owners or shopkeepers who sought profit at any cost, agitators profited by causing disruptions. O'Keefe contended that impassioned temperance speakers were "paid to keep the agitation up."[50] Similarly, Frank Smith, head of the Licensed Victuallers Association of Ontario, wrote in 1881 that the temperance campaigns were "a source of great annoyance to various municipalities and counties" and that it was "all caused by parties who make a living by agitation."[51]

O'Keefe, Smith, and their fellow Wets leaned heavily on another value of liberalism embedded in the ideal of equality: the principle of justice. If the temperance forces were to triumph, they argued, then the businesses closed and the lives shattered by prohibition would be a severe blow to the nation. Therefore, if prohibition did become the law of the land, then the government needed to be just in its implementation. Smith might have been deploying a *reductio ad absurdum* argument when he wrote to Minister of Finance S.L. Tilley in December 1881 contending that, if strict licensing could not work, then

> adopt another course – stop all manufacture and importing of strong liquor, after a certain date, then let the government take over all the property etc. used in the manufacturing get a valuation and sell it for other purposes. Let the country stand any difference in loss and have a uniform law. This could be tried for two years and everyone could then judge how it worked.[52]

True justice would be served only if those who lost in this prohibitionist push were properly compensated for their losses. Liberalism, in this way, would continue to protect property.

Just as Vidal and Dickey had predicted, the constitutionality of the Scott Act was quickly challenged in several distinct cases. The first was in New Brunswick after temperance advocates in Fredericton polled a nearly two-to-one victory in a Scott Act plebiscite in November 1878. Local option came into operation on 1 May 1879, and the following October Fredericton hotel keeper Thomas Barker was refused a liquor license. He took his case to the Supreme Court of New Brunswick, claiming that the Scott Act could not overrule a licensing law that was the purview of the provinces.[53] The court ruled in favour of Barker and forced the city to issue him a license. The city appealed the case to the Supreme Court of Canada, which heard it in February 1880 as *Fredericton v. The Queen*. Like many submissions to the Supreme Court, the arguments for the appellant (the city) and the respondent (the Crown) covered a broad range of legal issues. They included whether the dominion government's restriction of the trade in liquor was legal given that the BNA Act specifically gave the provinces the right to license taverns; whether it was within the dominion's power to delegate its authority to create laws for a portion of the population (in this case, electors of individual municipalities), in effect allowing a subset of voters to determine when an action is legal or criminal, the basis of local option; and whether the dominion government could create legislation that attempted to change individuals' behaviour in the guise of dealing with trade. This last point came from the preamble to the legislation, which stated that it was created because it was "very desirable to promote temperance."[54] Here the court did not avoid what Scott had called "all but the naked question" but zeroed in on the essential one: was "the Canada Temperance Act *ultra vires* the Parliament of Canada?" In a four-to-one decision, the justices ruled that the Scott Act was constitutional.[55]

The decision in *Fredericton* was soon tested in front of the Judicial Committee of the Privy Council. Since the initial appellant in *Fredericton*, Thomas Barker, died before the case could be taken to London, the liquor interests, as John Saywell words it, "seized the case of William Russell," who had also been convicted under the Scott Act, to test the authority of the federal legislation in contrast to provincial licensing laws. Thus, the principle on which the Supreme Court ruled in *Fredericton v. The Queen* was assessed by the Judicial Committee as *Russell v. The Queen*. Russell's case was supported by the liquor interests, and the temperance advocates pressed Macdonald to present a rousing defence of the Scott Act, claiming that the case was an affront to the sovereignty of the dominion government. Macdonald, never interested in robustly supporting the temperance cause, claimed there were no funds for such an appeal, and the Dominion Alliance ended up covering the costs.[56] This decision paid off and on 23 June 1882, the Lords upheld the Supreme Court's decision, confirming the right of the dominion government to create legislation to constrain trade in the name of "peace, order, and good government." In effect, this meant that the ability of a province to license taverns for the purpose of generating revenue could be constrained by the dominion government, so long as it was in the interest of peace, order, and good government.[57]

The decisions threatened to undermine the liquor licensing regime in Ontario (and those in all of the provinces) in practical and theoretical ways. These decisions – *Severn v. The Queen, Fredericton v. The Queen,* and *Russell v. The Queen* – seemed to confirm dominion authority over the liquor traffic and subordinate the provincial right of licensing to the dominion power over trade and commerce. It was a tricky distinction since, as several people noted during the hearings, in many ways trade and commerce could be seen to cover the powers of property and civil rights assigned to the provinces.[58] This was because an individual's ability to trade, or be involved in commerce, could affect his or her power over his or her property, and constraints on trade could be seen as constraints on an individual's rights.[59] This was more than just an academic distinction; it had a significant impact on legislation and the operation of the laws and reached to the heart of the liberal state. Does a system that prohibits the sale of liquor in a certain jurisdiction interfere unjustly with an individual's right to a livelihood? Conversely, does a licensing system that limits the number of places in which liquor can be sold be seen to interfere with commerce? The answer is a qualified "yes" in both instances, and the qualification was the subject of reams of arguments, counterarguments, and decisions at various judicial levels.

Since these court decisions seemed to place the responsibility for managing the liquor traffic in the hands of the dominion government, Macdonald seized the initiative. In the speech from the throne of 1883, the newly re-elected Conservative government argued that the outcome of *Russell v. The Queen* clearly demonstrated that the dominion had the legal right to impose a licensing regime on the entire country. It is not clear whether Macdonald wanted to legislate any further control over liquor, but he was decidedly against the strictness of the Scott Act. His disinterest in defending the act in London might suggest that he hoped that the act would be declared ultra vires, thereby allowing him to be rid of legislation that he never supported but that he knew would be politically dangerous to oppose openly. He was nevertheless aware of the dangers of thumbing his nose at temperance supporters. Something had to be done to deal with liquor consumption that would placate the temperance movement while not undermining – and politically alienating – the liquor industry. In any case, Macdonald was a shrewd political tactician, and he saw the outcome of *Russell v. The Queen* as an opportunity to deal a blow to political rivals. As Saywell argues, Macdonald used the *Russell* decision as an opportunity to stick it to Mowat, who had achieved several victories for provincial rights in various courts (although so far not with respect to liquor legislation). The Ontario premier's actions had been a constant thorn in the side of Macdonald, an avowed centralist. He made this motivation clear in a campaign speech in Yorkville in 1882 when he declared the Crooks Act "not worth the paper it was written on" and promised to pass a license law that would undermine the overly grasping patronage system of Mowat, "that little tyrant, who is trying to control public opinion in Ontario by getting hold of every little office from a bailiff ... to a tavern keeper."[60] Spitefulness aside, Macdonald's actions were pure political calculations. Mowat had become adept at using patronage of the provincial government to compete with the patronage provided by Macdonald's Tories. Until Mowat became premier, the dominion government had many more opportunities for patronage offices (e.g., postmasters and inland revenue collectors). As S.J.R. Noel demonstrates, Mowat built patronage networks at the provincial level that rivalled those that Macdonald had used to maintain his party's power at the national level.[61] The opportunity to assert dominion authority over the provinces – interrupting the patronage leverage of "that little tyrant" and strengthening support from the important cohort of tavern keepers, shop owners, and the liquor industry in general – was too tasty a dish for Macdonald to push away.

Mr. McCarthy's Act

In the wake of the *Russell* decision, few members on either side of the House of Commons seemed to dispute the constitutional responsibility of the dominion government to create licensing legislation. Indeed, Leader of the Opposition Edward Blake, former Ontario Reform leader and friend to Oliver Mowat, criticized John A. Macdonald not for the constitutionality of the decision but for foot-dragging on this important issue. Blake complained that, five weeks after the speech from the throne promised that a national license law would be a priority for the government, Macdonald had decided only then to establish a committee to explore what form such legislation would take. Given how important the law seemed to have been to the government, Blake asked, why did it need a commission? Clearly, he said, it had a capable cabinet including many brilliant legal minds who could draft a bill, and since Macdonald had made his promise to create a national liquor license system during the election campaign the previous June (prior, Blake reminded the House, to the *Russell* decision) there had been plenty of time to write a bill.[62] He framed his criticisms within a sense of urgency. Since the Privy Council's decision in *Russell* had suggested that it was not within the power of provinces to restrict the liquor trade, even though they had the power to license it, it was not inconceivable that people could open taverns contrary to provincial laws, arguing that legally provincial laws were ultra vires and that provincial licensing bodies were constitutionally required to grant them licenses. Nevertheless, a committee was struck to determine the best form that such a license should take. Chaired by Conservative heavyweight D'Alton McCarthy, the committee held few public consultations and appears to have done much of its work behind closed doors. It issued a report and a draft bill in May 1883.

McCarthy's committee seems to have been little more than symbolic consultation, with the predetermined outcome being a licensing law that looked remarkably similar to the Crooks Act. It was a clear case of policy being defined on a narrow field of conflict. The committee heard testimony from only three groups, two representing liquor interests and one representing temperance advocates, and most of the discussion included comparison with the Crooks Act. The first deputation represented the Ontario Trades Benevolent Association, a group claiming to include 2,500 "distillers, brewers, wholesale liquor merchants and hotel keepers." Their spokesman, A.G. Hodge, described this association as a group of respectable men who wanted to make sure that the trade remained in the hands of decent citizens who would follow the law as long as it was not too strict. He requested that the committee draft legislation that would reduce or eliminate the patronage system of the Ontario license law. His members wanted more openness in the work of license commissioners, arguing that many decisions were made in secret and that, when complaints were lodged with some boards, they acted like "a sort of Star Chamber and sitting with closed doors."[63] The term "star chamber" suggests a system that lacked transparency and in which the law was applied unequally.[64] Hodge also requested that the Saturday closing time be extended to nine o'clock. The current closing time, he said, was intended to keep recently paid workers from wasting their pay in bars, but he provided evidence that most workers were no longer being paid Saturday afternoons, so there was no need for bars to close so early. He also argued that the early Saturday closing time, along with the rule that prohibited bars from opening on Sunday, simply encouraged illegal drinking. Illegal taverns, Hodge explained, relied on the illicit Saturday-night and Sunday trade to remain in operation. If those laws were relaxed, then the respectable, legitimate trade would be able to drive away the law breakers.[65]

The second group to make a presentation to the committee was a deputation from the Dominion Alliance, led by Conservative Senator Alexander Vidal and New Brunswick Conservative MP George E. Foster. After mildly denigrating the members of Hodge's association, and noting how much bigger and more representative the Dominion Alliance was, Foster (also a member of the McCarthy committee) spoke to some of the points presented by the Wets' delegation. He agreed with the idea of removing partisanism from a Board of License Commissioners and argued that having the board select the inspector was more efficient than having the government appoint him. Whereas Hodge had argued that municipalities should have the right to apply to have an increased number of licenses in areas where there were seasonal increases in residents (e.g., summer holiday spots), Foster thought that this would just open the door to rampant abuse. He argued that shop sales of liquor had to be separated from sales of other products, something not specified in the Crooks Act. He advocated that the law should give more opportunities for residents either to block license applications or to approve them, suggesting that "a veto power be given to the people." Foster listed the various ways that this was applied across the country; for example, in both British Columbia and Nova Scotia, a license application needed to be accompanied by a petition signed by two-thirds of the adult residents (presumably male) in British Columbia and two-thirds of the ratepayers in Nova Scotia. Foster claimed that such systems "have worked well."[66] Finally, the Dominion Alliance deputation advocated significant penalties for breaking the law, noting that liquor sellers felt little more than inconvenience when they had to pay small fines: they just paid them and kept selling alcohol. "Liquor selling is such a profitable kind of business that there is no use passing any laws unless there are adequate penalties and a method of enforcement."[67]

Fully a month after these two groups spoke to the committee, a third deputation, representing the grocers of the Ontario Trades Benevolent Association, led by Joseph Kavanagh of Ottawa, and again including A.G. Hodge, made its case. This group was apparently motivated to action by rumours that the committee was going to recommend forbidding liquor sales in shops that sold other products and create a population-based cap on the number of shop liquor licenses that could be granted. Its members argued that most grocers could not survive without liquor sales, but neither could a shop survive on liquor sales alone. Rather than creating more temperance, such divisions would lead to more illegality. "It will do temperance a great deal more injury than good," they argued, because liquor stores that could not rely on some revenue from groceries would break the law to survive: "The great majority will become simply grog shops."[68] They supported their claims with a hastily assembled petition of ninety-six grocers from Toronto (saying that they did not have enough time to get petitions from elsewhere but that it would not be difficult for them to do so). In a series of interactions with a hostile George Foster, the grocers described how their low margins on grocery sales meant that liquor sales often made the difference between survival and business failure. When

McCarthy explained that the committee was trying to figure out how to reduce the temptation for shop owners to encourage drinking "as a means of inducing people to buy what they do not want" and to stop the "tippling and abuse in these corner groceries," Kavanagh said that "if the law is carried out, if the Inspector does his duty properly, there will be none of that."[69] It was not a satisfying answer for the committee. Kavanagh then explained to the committee how liquor was sold in shops. Most people preferred bringing their own containers to be filled from larger vessels because it was less expensive than buying sealed bottles. Whether this deputation's pleas were the reason that the McCarthy Act did not require the separation of liquor from other business is impossible to know. In any case, the grocers would not be entirely satisfied with the final law.

The bill drafted and presented by McCarthy's committee would create a uniform licensing system across the country. The preamble to the legislation indicates that its authors understood the tenuous constitutional status of such a licensing bill and the likelihood that it would end up in the courts. It specifically positioned the bill as relating to the dominion's constitutional responsibilities, stating that the bill was designed "to regulate the traffic in the sale of intoxicating liquors, ... for the better preservation of peace and order."[70] The provisions of the bill, presented as An Act Respecting the Sale of Intoxicating Liquors, and the Issue of Licenses Therefor [sic], copied many key elements of the Crooks Act. It created a three-person Board of License Commissioners in each license district (to be determined by the governor in council but expected to be cities, counties, or electoral districts). Premises were inspected by a license inspector, who recommended granting or cancelling licenses. The law set a population-based limit on the maximum number of licenses to be granted in each district. Most licensed places were to be hotels with accommodations for travellers, horses, and vehicles. A limited number of saloon licenses were available for places without lodgings. Licenses were granted annually. The decision on whether or not to grant a license included a subjective assessment of the "character" of potential licensees. The board had the power to establish further criteria for licensing in its district, and its operations were to be separate from those of the municipal government.

Beyond these similarities, the McCarthy Act represented a significant change from the licensing regime established by the Crooks Act; indeed, several of its provisions seemed to address directly complaints about Ontario's licensing law. The commissioners were not all appointed by the government: the chair was to be a judge, the second would be either the mayor of the town or the warden of the county, and the third was to be a government appointee who would hold the office only for one year. The inspector was appointed not by the government but by the board itself. All license fees would go to the municipality, although – likely in a nod to section 92(9) of the BNA Act – the provinces were allowed to levy a fee on top of the license fee for their own revenues. Any new license application had to be accompanied by a petition of at least one-quarter of the voters in the immediate vicinity of the premises. In a similar vein, the act made a license application invalid upon the receipt of a petition by two-thirds of the electors in the electoral subdivision.[71] The law also outlined in some detail how residents were to be informed of license applications, and it provided specific reasons for rejecting an application. Whereas the Crooks Act forbade any selling of liquor from Saturday night at 7 p.m. to Monday morning, the McCarthy Act permitted bona fide hotel guests to be served alcohol with their meals during specified mealtimes on Sundays; it also forbade selling liquor on other days from 11 p.m. each night to 6 a.m. the next morning, something the Crooks Act did not do.[72] Finally, and notably, the McCarthy Act included a proviso that permitted municipalities below the size of counties or cities to vote themselves dry, something that many believed was no longer possible under provincial law.[73]

The McCarthy Act was a direct response to the Crooks Act and flipped a triumphant middle finger at Mowat's patronage-based licensing system. This should not be surprising since Macdonald had promised to rid the province of the partisan licensing act introduced by "that little tyrant" Mowat. The details of the two acts are compared in Table 5.1.

Table 5.1 Crooks Act and McCarthy Act compared

	Crooks	McCarthy (as applied in Ontario)[a]
Number of licenses	1 per 250 up to 1,000 1 per 400 thereafter (5 for villages that were county towns)	1 per 250 up to 1,000 1 per 500 thereafter (5 for county towns regardless of size)
Makeup of commission	3 commissioners, appointed by the provincial government	1 county court judge 1 mayor of a town or warden of a county 1 government appointee
Appointment of inspectors	By the provincial government	By the commissioners
Authority to issue licenses	By the board, signed by the provincial treasurer or secretary	By the board, signed by the minister of inland revenue

	Crooks	McCarthy (as applied in Ontario)[a]
Board meetings open to the public?	No	Yes, specific method of giving public notice included in the law (s. 10(3))
Number of bedrooms in a licensed tavern	4	6
Number of stables for horses	6	6
Limits on shop licenses?	No, municipalities may pass bylaws	Yes, population-based 1 per 400 up to 1,200 1 per 1,000 thereafter
Resident input on licenses?	No	Yes, by petition to approve or reject licenses
Requirements for public approval?	No	License applicant to submit petition signed by one-third of the electors in the polling subdistrict in which the tavern operates
Municipal prohibition permitted?	No	Yes
Where does the money go?	Fees and fines go into a license fund. The license fund to pay the costs of administration. Residual amounts divided one-third to the provincial treasurer and two-thirds to the municipality in which the tavern operates	License fees go into a license fund. The license fund pays the costs of administration. Residual funds go to the treasury of the municipality[b]. Fines are divided between the license fund and the prosecutor

Sources: An Act to Amend the Law Respecting the Sale of Fermented or Spirituous Liquors [Crooks Act], *Statutes of Ontario* (1876) 39 Vic c 26; An Act Respecting the Sale of Intoxicating Liquors, and the Issue of Licenses Therefor [McCarthy Act]. *Statutes of Canada* (1883) 46Vic c 30.

Notes:
[a] Since the McCarthy Act was written to conform to different geographic and political divisions across the country, some elements of the law affected the provinces differently. The components listed here indicate how the law was to apply to Ontario.
[b] "Dominion License Act," *Globe* [Toronto], 5 June 1883, says that a license fund would never have a surplus to benefit the municipality.

The complaints that Ontario's Boards of License Commissioners and inspectors were all government appointees, with the potential for lucrative patronage, were assuaged with provisions making two of the three board members drawn from existing municipal officers, one of whom was a judge and considered by most in the House of Commons to be an ideal non-partisan participant. Having an inspector appointed by the board similarly undercut patronage. Concerns that taverns were being foisted on unwilling populations were addressed by the requirement that new applications for licenses be accompanied by petitions from one-third of the electors (increased from the proposed one-fourth). The petition affirming the demand for a license, along with the provision that half of the electors could quash an application (the proportion was amended in the House to two-thirds of the electors), paralleled practices in some of the provinces, such as Nova Scotia, Prince Edward Island, and New Brunswick, where – in the few areas not under the Scott Act by 1883 – more direct involvement by the residents had kept the number of licensed premises remarkably low. The formula used to determine how many licenses would be granted in a municipality was more restrictive than that of the Crooks Act. Although in both laws a community would receive one license per 250 people up to a population of 1,000, the Crooks Act assigned one license for every 400 after the first 1,000, and the McCarthy Act assigned one license for every 500 after the first 1,000 (see Table 5.1). The Crooks Act left it at that, whereas the McCarthy Act made further distinctions related to villages designated "county towns" (in which courts of the assizes were held). Both acts gave the town of Clifton near Niagara Falls an extra three licenses, and both acts created provisions for vacation towns to increase their number of licensed hotels in the summer.[74] In what must have been a shock to the grocers who had testified at the commission, McCarthy placed a population-based limit on shop licenses, one license per 400 up to 1,200 and one license per every 1,000 after that. The Crooks Act had placed no specific limit on the number of shop licenses permitted in a community, leaving that decision to the municipality.

Whereas these differences were mostly small variations of the Crooks Act, a few sections represented more considerable changes. Indeed, these changes were partly the result of attempts to represent varying approaches to liquor licenses across the country and partly the result of the authority of the dominion government to control or prohibit the liquor traffic. Section 46 of McCarthy's bill required that a board not grant licenses in a polling subdistrict if it received a petition against issuing new licenses signed by a majority of electors in that subdistrict. The board could grant licenses in that area only once another petition from a majority of the electors was received asking that licenses be granted there.[75] Since this provision allowed voters in an area to introduce prohibition through a petition, most MPs agreed that it was a poor way to gauge the opinion of a population, so an alternative was presented. Georges Auguste Gigault, the Conservative member for Rouville, Quebec, introduced an extensive amendment that created a mechanism for a local option vote in towns, incorporated villages, parishes, and townships, thereby restoring the type of municipal local option that had disappeared with the Scott Act.[76]

Gigault's amendment was discussed at length, first as a replacement for the mechanism allowing a majority petition to disallow all licenses, and in the end as an addition to the section, with the majority petition increasing to three-fifths of the ratepayers in that municipality. Much of the debate hinged on the propriety of reintroducing local option on such a small scale and on using plebiscites to institute prohibition. McCarthy admitted that he did not approve of the initial petition clause and preferred Gigault's amendment, which would require a proper vote. After Edward Blake opposed the amendment, embarking on an extensive discussion of the merits of temperance and the need to ensure that drunks had as little access to liquor as possible, McCarthy replied by reminding the House that Blake's concern was really that this bill was better than the one introduced by his friends in the Ontario legislature and that, "whatever view may be taken of this Bill, it is a great step in advance of anything adopted in that province."[77]

Considering the McCarthy Act from the perspective of partisan politics, it appears that McCarthy was right. The law was an attempt by Macdonald not to seize the patronage system that the Crooks Act had established to enrich Conservative political fortunes but to break Mowat's hold on patronage in the province. Although there was room for government appointments, the McCarthy Act returned some decision-making authority to municipalities but without tying the liquor license so closely to municipal politics that the corruption of the pre–Crooks Act system would return. Both in the composition of the board and in the numerous opportunities for electors to express their opinions on the propriety of a license, the McCarthy Act sought to restore the liquor licensing system to community members. So, although not directly partisan, the act was decidedly political. Macdonald had made taking control of liquor licensing an election promise, and many partisans encouraged him to undertake it with gusto. In January 1883, W.R. Davis of Mitchell, Ontario, had told Macdonald that such a move could favour the Conservatives in the province, set to face Mowat in an election that February: "Many will vote Conservative who never did before, if they are only assured that they will be safe in doing so."[78] Eugene O'Keefe underscored how important the issue was in Ontario since until then Conservative hotel keepers felt unable to speak their minds: "This commission of Mowat's is a terrible drawback, and presents the Hotel keepers not only there but throughout the country from working as they would wish for the Conservative cause."[79] A few days later he explained that dealing with the license issue would allow "many a poor fellow who has been literally ruined by the Mowat Gov't a chance to get even with him."[80] After the Conservatives failed to unseat Mowat, partisans were even more eager to see the license law return power to municipalities. As one correspondent from Brantford noted, this strategy "would aid the conservative party, as nearly all the cities and towns are conservative."[81]

***

The passage of the McCarthy Act was a political strategy to undermine provincial power, especially targeted at Mowat, and the outcome of ongoing legal debates about which level of government had authority over the everyday sale of liquor in the country. Various court challenges seemed to suggest that the "trade and commerce" and "peace, order, and good government" provisions of the British North America Act supported the dominion's efforts to regulate the trade across the country. Notwithstanding the different political systems created by the provinces, the Scott Act and the McCarthy Act created opportunities for the uniform regulation or prohibition of the liquor trade depending on the will of the people. Yet that is not to say that these legislative manoeuvres were non-partisan attempts to build a coherent legislative solution to the liquor problem. Both Macdonald and Mowat understood the importance of the liquor issue to many people, and both recognized how difficult it could be to manage sharply diverging interests between temperance and liquor interests. The McCarthy Act might have been a culmination of legal and social pressures to bring the liquor trade into some kind of reasonable and uniform shape, and framed as good government and fairness, but it was also a conscious power struggle between provincial and dominion governments. And it ushered in a new phase in the regulation of liquor, a phase in which the province, rather than the dominion, would ultimately prevail.

6

McCarthy and Crooks Enter a Tavern, 1883–85

The assertion that the Dominion of Canada had authority to enact a liquor license act for the entire country, repeated on both sides in Parliament, was on shakier legal ground than most commentators were willing to admit. Once the McCarthy Act became law, several correspondents to Sir John A. Macdonald, from both wet and dry sides of the liquor question, urged him to seek a legal test case to confirm whether the dominion in fact had the right to create a liquor licensing law. For example, Eugene O'Keefe complained to Macdonald that provincial license commissioners in Ontario were insisting that any hotelier who took out a license under the McCarthy Act "will be immediately proceeded against and put in gaol without the option of a fine."[1] It was not only the Wets who sought clarification. The Carswell branch of the Independent Order of Good Templars wrote to the prime minister to urge both the dominion and the provincial governments "to adopt such measures as will remove all doubts as to the legality of the liquor license to be issued for the year 1884." The branch demanded that the governments "submit with all possible dispatch ... the question of their respective rights to control and regulate the liquor traffic, to the courts in order that a final and binding decision ... may be obtained without further delay."[2]

The Good Templars' timing was impeccable, but their plea was unnecessary: the very next day the Judicial Committee of the Privy Council ruled that, in the words of some commentators, the McCarthy Act was "null and void."[3] The case in question, *Hodge v. The Queen*, began when Archibald Hodge, a tavern keeper in Yorkville, was fined on 7 May 1881 by the local (provincial) Board of License Commissioners for having a billiard table in his tavern. He appealed the conviction to the Court of Queen's Bench on the ground that the commissioners had no right to make such bylaws since the provincial government had no right to give a municipal body such powers. As the case wound its way through the courts, the divergent legal outcomes defined then redefined provincial jurisdiction over liquor licenses in general.[4] The Queen's Bench overturned the conviction, but Mowat took the case to the Court of Appeal, which overturned the Queen's Bench ruling. Hodge then appealed directly to the Judicial Committee, which issued its decision on 15 December 1883. The committee's ruling was characteristically brief. The lords recognized that although *Russell v. The Queen* (the case that had originated in Fredericton) had appeared to suggest that provincial governments had no authority to license the liquor traffic, that was not constitutionally sound. Whereas the judgment in *Russell* related to the authority of the dominion government to enact the Scott Act for the maintenance of the "peace, order, and good government" of the dominion, the BNA Act explicitly assigned the right to license taverns to the provinces. Moreover, the lords ruled that the Crooks Act conformed to provincial authority "to make regulations in the nature of police or municipal regulations of a merely local character for the good government of taverns &c. licensed for the sale of liquors by retail," thereby to preserve order, maintain public decency, and "repress drunkenness." All of these activities, the lords affirmed, were well within the scope of provincial responsibility.[5] So the license commissioners did indeed have the power to pass bylaws such as those under which Hodge had been fined. The Crooks Act was intra vires – within the power of – the provincial government.

Yet, as had been the case several times before, the decision in *Hodge v. The Queen* was far from definitive. A Judicial Committee ruling tended to be specific to the case at hand. The lords set precedents only for the precise issues dealt with in similar cases and rarely veered into clarifying broader areas of potential ambiguity in the law. Indeed, at times, they would clearly state that a decision was not to be construed as affecting broader aspects of the law or laws not being contested at that time. In cases in which barristers who argued in front of the lords attempted to speak beyond the scope of the case at hand, the lords might stop, ignore, or even upbraid them.[6] So the Constitution was being interpreted in specific cases and the decisions had a limited application. Thus, *Russell v. The Queen* upheld dominion power to pass laws for the "peace, order, and good government" of the country, which many argued was the purpose of liquor licensing, but *Hodge v. The Queen* upheld provincial rights not only to issue licenses but also to make laws constraining the issuing of those licenses, which appeared to be about peace and order but was framed as being about local issues of decency and order, which fell under the powers of the police. With a government in Ottawa dedicated to centralizing power, and one in Toronto actively seeking to decentralize it, these seemingly minor points of law related to jurisdiction became the beam-sized motes in the eyes of tavern keepers and liquor vendors as they attempted to negotiate overlapping and seemingly competing authorities.

The fact that this case originated in Yorkville was amusing irony for the supporters of Mowat's government. Recall that Macdonald was on the stump in Yorkville in June 1882 when he called Mowat "that little tyrant" and declared that the Crooks Act "was not worth the paper on which it was printed," paving the way toward the McCarthy Act. In typical campaign hyperbole, Macdonald asserted that the supposed invalidity of the Crooks Act meant that "any man in this city or in any other part of Ontario can open his saloon and sell liquors, and there is not a court in the world can prevent him [from] doing so."[7] The Hodge decision called into question this assertion, and, as numerous Grit papers gleefully proclaimed, it was the McCarthy Act that was not worth its paper, which John Bengough was only too happy to illustrate in *Grip* (Figure 6.1).

The *Hodge* decision did not mark the end of the jurisdictional dispute over liquor licensing. After all, as noted above, until the Judicial Committee ruled specifically on a law's validity, there were far too many ways to interpret the Constitution's assignation of provincial and dominion powers to be certain that a law would be clearly within constitutionally defined authority. Therefore, between the *Hodge* decision in late 1883 and the end of 1885 (when the Judicial Committee ruled the McCarthy Act ultra vires), Macdonald continued to insist that the dominion had the right to issue licenses because it had the authority to constrain trade. The province had the clear constitutional right to collect license fees, or duties (he used both words interchangeably), but could not restrict the number of taverns. That would be tantamount to restricting trade, a clear power of the dominion government. Macdonald explained this rationale to O'Keefe in 1883 as the McCarthy Act was being written: "Any man who pleases can open a tavern in Ontario except where prevented by the operation of the Scott Act (which as you know was passed by the Canadian Parliament). If however he does open a tavern he must pay the license fee as provided by the Act of the Ontario legislature."[8] In other words, Macdonald asserted hopefully, the province could not stop

Figure 6.1 "The smart boy takes a tumble" | *Grip*, 2 May 1885

someone from opening a tavern; the person merely had to pay the license fee to the province in order to open it. The same would apply to shops.

After the *Hodge* ruling, and having refused to rescind the McCarthy Act, Macdonald created an unusual situation for licensees in Ontario. Since the McCarthy Act's administrative structure of a three-person board, a paid inspector, and a population-based limit on licenses paralleled the licensing structure of the Crooks Act, the implementation of the Dominion Liquor License Act resulted in two boards existing in each license district. Moreover, the boundaries of the districts were not exactly the same (the McCarthy Act was administered in geographic counties and five cities, the Crooks Act in political ridings), the numbers of licenses were based upon different calculations, and the fees to be charged were different. The next two years resulted in considerable confusion, tension, and outright hostility in communities across the province as some tavern keepers anticipated the quantum dilemma of Schrödinger's cat, being simultaneously alive and dead, licensed and unlicensed, depending on who was observing them. Moreover, convinced that the provincial law was valid and that the dominion law would soon be overturned, Mowat proceeded to enact legislation intentionally hostile to the workings of the McCarthy Act. Further complicating the operation of the McCarthy Act in Ontario, an 1879 amendment to the province's Municipal Act included provisions that excluded municipal officials from the position of license officer, whereas the McCarthy Act required an elected official to serve as a license commissioner.[9] It did not help that Scott Act agitation was ramping up in counties across the province, that manufacturers and vendors were intensifying their lobbying for compensation given what some argued could be millions of dollars of lost productivity, and that Parliament continued to face a powerful push to allow beer and wine to be sold in Scott Act counties. Although in retrospect we know that Mowat was vindicated, between 1883 and 1885, this was not certain, and tavern keepers and the public faced a remarkably confusing situation. Our friend the Ontario drinker, nearly two decades after Confederation, might not have known if his tipple was even legal.

In Ontario, the *Hodge* decision provoked widespread speculation about what would happen next. Opinions on the meaning of the Privy Council ruling generally broke along party lines, with Grit papers saying that the ruling made the McCarthy Act null and void and Tory papers saying that the decision did not affect the general constitutionality of the law. The *Globe* wondered whether Macdonald would accept the decision of the Privy Council and repeal the McCarthy Act or "continue to harass the liquor trade and provoke legal controversy by putting his act into force."[10] The *Daily Mail,* in unsurprising contrast, countered the insistence of gleeful Grits that *Hodge* was a death sentence for the McCarthy Act, noting that all it did was reiterate what everyone already knew: the province had the authority to extend policing powers to municipalities and collect fees. The *Daily Mail* insisted that the *Hodge* decision "bears out fully and circumstantially the view we took" that "only the minor matter of police regulation was decided; the powers of the dominion parliament expressly stated to be supreme in regard to liquor treated as an article of trade and commerce, and the powers of the Local legislature expressly limited to matters of police regulation."[11] Over the next few weeks, the two newspapers, along with partisan periodicals across the province, continued to insist that *Hodge v. The Queen* was either fundamental or marginal in their attempts to clarify who had the main authority over liquor licensing.

The public debates between the papers were not the only forum for tense discussions on the meaning of *Hodge*. In his capacity as attorney general, Mowat wrote to the dominion government (via the lieutenant governor) insisting that Macdonald do the right thing and repeal the McCarthy Act "to prevent groundless doubts and useless litigation."[12] Apparently getting no response, Mowat wrote again (also through the lieutenant governor). He noted that, a month after his first message was sent, he still had heard nothing back from the government, but the newspaper reports made it clear that the dominion government "does not regard the decision to which I have referred as determining that the Province of Ontario has exclusive power to regulate the sale of liquors." Suggesting a compromise, Mowat had the lieutenant governor "respectfully" urge that the Crooks Act, "which is held to be valid and binding, be allowed to operate alone until the validity of the Dominion Statute is determined by the Privy Council and that your government be moved to suspend" the McCarthy Act.[13] In the House of Commons, Ontario Liberal MP Malcolm Cameron requested that all correspondence between the provinces and the dominion government related to the McCarthy Act be released, but Macdonald's government complied only after the session had finished.[14] This tardiness was likely to avoid what might have seemed to be damning correspondence; although the first two letters had already been released to the public by the provincial secretary of Ontario, the third was from Premier of Manitoba John Norquay, who was a Conservative in sentiment but ran a non-partisan administration.[15] He argued that the McCarthy Act was unworkable in his province.[16] Before the letters were released,

John Cameron, editor of the *Globe,* called the delay "characteristic trickery and cowardice" of the Tories.[17] After the letters were released, Cameron ambitiously took his characterization of the exchange further than only three letters might allow, describing them as evidence that all of the provinces rejected the legislation: "Thus Sir John Macdonald finds every province of the Dominion resisting his encroachments upon Provincial rights; but he still persists in his efforts to usurp the functions of the Local legislatures."[18]

Although Cameron might have seen the Manitoba letter as the final nail in the McCarthy Act's coffin, the legislation was not dead yet. During the 1884 session, Macdonald faced numerous calls to deal with the problems of the act, and he appears to have begun to question the confidence that he had expressed in Yorkville in 1882. In the middle of March, when Quebec Nationalist Conservative MP Frédéric Houde moved that the House repeal the McCarthy Act, Minister of Public Works Hector Langevin proposed an amendment that would moderate such an extreme reaction to *Hodge.*[19] Langevin's amendment recognized the legal uncertainty of the McCarthy Act and committed the government to submit it "with all convenient speed to the Supreme Court of Canada or the Judicial Committee of the Privy Council, or both."[20] The motion, the *Globe* was quick to remind readers, was essentially the same as the one made by Peel, Ontario, Liberal MP James Fleming when Parliament debated the McCarthy Act a year earlier. At that time, the government was confident that the legislation was legal and saw little need for the courts to affirm its authority over licensing matters. The debate sparked by Langevin's motion and its amendment stretched deep into the night, leading to a bleary-eyed suggestion by Conservative MP Joseph Ouimet that the McCarthy Act be modified to remove all components except for the sections regarding local prohibition and leaving the rest of the licensing elements to the provinces, in effect confirming provincial jurisdiction in the area of licensing. Ouimet's amendment failed, and Langevin's amendment passed, so the government was required to send the question to the higher courts for their assessments.[21] The fact that these motions and amendments were made by Quebec politicians should not be surprising: Quebec's legislature, politicians, and population, from all parts of the political spectrum, appear to have been overwhelmingly opposed to the McCarthy Act and repeatedly asserted provincial authority over licensing.[22] Until the test case was heard and all appeals were complete, tavern keepers and members of the liquor trade more broadly found themselves struggling to figure out how to act and who to believe.

The Tavern Keeper's Dilemma

By entrenching the governments of Ontario and Canada behind their license act barricades, the *Hodge* decision resulted in consternation and confusion for the liquor sellers of the province. Tavern keepers and shopkeepers faced the prospect of having to pay two license fees and to conform to two sets of requirements issued by two different boards. The problem was compounded by the facts that the license districts were not the same and that the two competing boards could impose regulations requiring different conditions for the establishments, such as the billiard bylaw that had caused Hodge so much bother and ultimate disappointment. Moreover, the Crooks Act required taverns to have four bedrooms for the use of customers, whereas the McCarthy Act set the number at six, immediately excluding numerous small taverns from acquiring the dominion license. On top of the legislative constraints, as O'Keefe's jeremiad to Macdonald had illustrated, the two boards and their two inspectors actively urged members of the liquor trade to follow their regulations alone. Finally, and to add another layer of baffling administrative complexity, the McCarthy Act required license applicants to submit their fees for *dominion* licenses to the *provincial* inspector, a clause that was necessary because provinces had the constitutional right to raise revenue through licenses but that still gave dominion authorities (commissioners and inspectors) the power to determine who would be licensed. It was a situation that likely drove many tavern keepers to drink, and fortunately neither law forbade them from keeping their own liquor for personal consumption.[23]

To be sure, Ontario was not the only province in which such dominion-provincial tension caused local consternation. The McCarthy Act and the *Hodge* decision spurred most provinces to reassert provincial rights and local autonomy for liquor licensing. We have already seen that the premier of Manitoba insisted that the McCarthy Act could not be operational in his province. In February 1884, the mayor of Saint John, New Brunswick, refused to sit on that city's dominion license board, claiming that the McCarthy Act contradicted the city's charter, which gave the mayor the right to issue licenses.[24] New Brunswick MPs and license officers also contacted Macdonald directly and explained how a lack of clarity in the McCarthy Act could throw the workings of the Scott Act in that province into disarray.[25] Similar messages detailed problems implementing the act in Nova Scotia.[26] In April, the government of that province announced that it would pass an act similar to the Crooks Act. Reporting on this development, the Kingston *Whig*, a Grit newspaper, noted that every province would "have the management of the liquor traffic ... before the close of the year."[27] In Quebec, even Tory newspapers argued that the dominion law was invalid. In February, the *Globe* noted that Montreal newspapers, including *Le Canadien,* a leading Tory organ, had asserted that the "only rational" course of action was for the province to follow the example of Ontario and assert its right to issue liquor licenses.[28] A month later, evidently with much satisfaction, the *Globe* reproduced an article from *Le Canadien* that criticized "the persistence of Sir John Macdonald in maintaining in force the Federal License Act – notwithstanding the incontestable right of the Provinces to legislate on the matter."[29] This reiterated an observation that the Toronto paper had made earlier that year about how Quebec was "jealous of any infringement on its rights" but that the Conservative MPs from Quebec had tried to help "Sir John to play his little game" by enacting various exemptions for that province.[30] Such exceptions were not enough. By this time, mayors of several Quebec communities also refused to sit on license boards.

Resistance was spreading across Ontario as well, and a central concern was the question of who could be a dominion license commissioner. Whereas the mayor of Saint John had the city charter to back his claim, in Ontario the issue was hindered by the legal restrictions placed on municipal officials. The Mowat government's 1879 changes to the Municipal Act prohibiting license commissioners and inspectors from being elected to municipal office caused confusion in the makeup of the McCarthy Act's Boards of License Commissioners.[31] The act required either a city mayor or a county warden to be an ex officio member of the licensing committee, thus creating, if you pardon the anachronism, a legal Catch-22. As the *Whig* explained it, when Kingston's mayor refused to sit on the city's board, "his being mayor or warden is the qualification for his office of License Commissioner, by the Dominion Act, and as this qualification disappears as soon as he accepts the latter office, he ceases at once to be in either office, and is out of both in the cold, on the now-you-see it and now-you-don't principle."[32] The *Whig* wondered whether the boards were even legally constituted if they lacked a mayor or county warden.[33] On top of that, the paper questioned what an appointment to a dominion Board of License Commissioners would mean for judges, suggesting that accepting the jurisdiction of the dominion legislation would render questionable any of a judge's previous decisions on the Crooks Act: "To accept membership commits him to the provisions of the new Act and thereby stultifies him, from the fact that he has, by his past actions in connection with the Crooks Act, acknowledged its constitutionality ... [If he accepts the board position, then he] condemns all judgements given by him under the Ontario law."[34] Mayors and wardens across the province acted similarly. Grit newspapers reminded readers that, lest Conservatives complain that this was another Grit plot to mess with the dominion act, William Meredith, leader of the provincial Conservatives, had been adamant about excluding license commissioners and inspectors from serving on municipal councils before the changes to the Municipal Act were made in 1879.[35]

Although some municipal officials who were Grits might be expected to have engaged in acts of civil disobedience through legal obedience, licensed victuallers had the further challenge of a paralyzing paradox of their own. Not being lawyers, and having little insight into the seemingly capricious decision making of the Privy Council, proprietors of licensed taverns, saloons, and shops could find little definitive advice from the entrenched partisan opinions around them.[36] Tory newspapers, which generally sided with the liquor trade, argued that the *Hodge* decision did not negate the authority of the McCarthy Act, whereas Grit newspapers argued that *Hodge* rendered the McCarthy Act not worth the paper on which it was written. To make matters worse, licensed victuallers, many of whom were Conservatives, were also nursing the injury that they felt when the McCarthy Act became law. Unlike the Crooks Act, which had heavy partisan leaning, the McCarthy Act was to be operated mostly by people who already held some municipal office. Many of them were Grits, and an increasing number seemed to be teetotallers. So, despite arguments by the government that the licensing was being undertaken in a politically non-partisan way, the political leanings of two of the three commissioners were not in control of the Tories in Ottawa. Robert Henry of Brantford wrote to Macdonald describing the problems that he faced under the legislation. The local warden had refused to act as a commissioner, and Henry explained that "he is a papist Grit and doubtless has been advised by [Provincial Secretary Arthur] Hardy ... to take the course he has taken." But removing this unseemly character from the board would not help Tories in the area since the now two-man board was divided between a Tory loyalist, W. Palmer, and "Judge Jones," "a narrow minded bigot in the temperance question and ... a thorough grit" who was the statutory chair of the board.[37] Moreover, a Grit-leaning board would tend to hire a Grit-leaning inspector. So the hoped-for relief in the Conservative McCarthy Act was evasive.

The licensees' plight was made especially difficult because a proper answer could not be obtained from the authorities who should have had one: the license commissions themselves. Charged with collecting fees and enforcing the law, the dominion and provincial inspectors engaged in disinformation campaigns against each other. O'Keefe told Macdonald that hotel keepers and other members of the liquor traffic "are showing evident signs of dissatisfaction" because the government had not yet, at the end of January 1884, appointed commissioners: "Not one in twenty believe that they will ever be appointed."[38] Patrick Kelly, a hotel keeper in Renfrew, wrote to Macdonald in mid-February asking if it was necessary for a hotel keeper to take out a dominion license, a pressing question because "we have got notice over a month ago to file application by the first of April with local [provincial] government."[39] When Kelly received no reply from the prime minister, he wrote to the provincial minister of public works, who "immediately replyed [sic] instructing Kelley [sic] to take out a Provincial license and that he would protect him." This information came to Macdonald from John Harvey in nearby Arnprior, who explained that Kelly "feels sore" and that "we cannot afford to lose any of our former friends if it can be avoided." Harvey added that the hotel keepers were being told by the provincial inspector and license commissioners "not to heed the federal act but stick to them and they will protect them."[40] Another correspondent informed Macdonald that a circular had been sent to tavern keepers in his district explaining that hotel keepers who applied for the dominion license were permitted to do so but had to submit all of their money in cash to the local inspector. The inspector's note reiterated (accurately) that "this is the law," but the inspector took it further when he said that if licensees sent their fees to the dominion inspector, then the provincial inspector would "arrest him [the dominion inspector] for obtaining money on false pretenses and summon you before the police magistrate for a violation of the license act."[41] Dominion inspectors were also known to undertake what appeared to some to be less than forthright tactics to convince hotel keepers to take out dominion licenses. The Kingston *Whig* reported that "the new license Inspector for the County of Frontenac appointed ... by the unorganized Dominion License Board ... has notified the present holders of licenses under the Ontario government not to apply to the latter for their license ... but to himself. In doing this the officer exceeds his duty. He has no right to do anything of the kind."[42]

Given the conflicting and contradictory information, members of the liquor trade faced three options: take out a dominion license, take out a provincial license, or take out both. It was clear to most observers that relying solely on a dominion license would not be a safe bet (although it did not stop one correspondent from telling Macdonald that he refused to take out an Ontario license, even after being rejected by the dominion board, because he was "too good a conservative to take anything from the Grit party"[43]). Most licensees already had administrative relationships with their provincial license officers, so renewal of the provincial license was generally painless, except in areas where the number of provincial licenses was reduced either by decisions of commissioners or by municipal bylaws. In these cases, reportedly, some former licensees, having been denied a provincial license, turned to the dominion boards. In Toronto and London, there were suggestions that the dominion boards would issue licenses in areas where, it seems, there was a common understanding that licenses should not be issued. For example, the provincial Board of License Commissioners in Toronto had decided not to license any establishment on Toronto Island, a place of mixed recreational and residential use. In April 1884, the dominion board decided that it would issue licenses on the island "after the question had been thoroughly discussed last year that the Ontario License Commissioners, in deference to overwhelming public sentiment, decided not to issue licenses there."[44] Condemnation was swift and broadened the discussion. One correspondent to the *Globe* noted that the decision was but one of a number of licensing rulings resulting from "thoughtlessness, or it may be indifference." The correspondent reasoned that a board chaired by a judge should realize that certain taverns in mainly Italian neighbourhoods should not be granted licenses given "our late experience with the Italian temperament when under the influence of liquor."[45] In September, the dominion board elicited more protest when it contemplated moving the license granted to a Mrs. Meade on the island to the exhibition fairgrounds, a move supported by the exhibition association itself. The mayor, who did take his seat on the dominion board, supported the move as long as only beer and light wine were sold. A few days later the directors of the Western Fair in London, Ontario, perhaps anticipating the issue coming up in that city, voted to prohibit liquor sales on its fairgrounds.

The third option, to take out both licenses, was made even more viable when it was recommended to licensees across the province by the central committee of the Ontario Trades Benevolent Association.[46] When the Kingston branch of the association met on 1 March 1884 to consider the proposal, its members recognized that it was a logical and simple way to protect their businesses and allowed them to hedge their bets. They reasoned that it cost only fifteen dollars more to take out a dominion license; moreover, if the dominion law were found to be unconstitutional, then the fees, collected by the provincial authority anyway, would be refunded to them. As one tavern keeper explained to the reporter from the Kingston *Whig*, "the fee ... is not large, and we pay it, under protest of course, rather than be placed in a position both embarrassing and annoying."[47] Moreover, dominion inspectors had suggested that there was no guarantee that those licensed only under the provincial act would receive a dominion license should the Crooks Act be declared ultra vires. Despite this resolution, when the boards tallied up their license applications, the *Whig* announced, far more applications had been made for provincial licenses than for dominion ones.

The results in Kingston were symptomatic of the fact that by the middle of March 1884, the licensing issues were even more complex than they had seemed at the beginning of the year. At the end of February, the Mowat government had introduced legislation that placed significant additional fees on any tavern that applied for a dominion license. Provincial Secretary Arthur Hardy told the legislature that the top-up fees were based upon calculations of the expected loss of revenues from the McCarthy Act (should it be found to be constitutional). Since the McCarthy Act's population-based license limits were different from those of the Crooks Act, the result would be fewer tavern licenses in each community. The requirement for more bedrooms would further reduce the number of taverns in the province. Thus, even if the per-license revenue for the province were the same as with the Crooks Act, the McCarthy Act would reduce license-based income by 20 percent. Finally, if the two acts were to continue to operate concurrently, then they would increase the costs of inspection and enforcement.[48] In the legislature, the reaction of the opposition was predictably against expanding fees, although the *Globe* was pleased to see opposition leader Meredith contradicting Macdonald and defending provincial rights.[49] Instead of merely condemning the legislation, Meredith proposed an amendment that accepted provincial jurisdiction in licensing issues and rejected the increased fees because they were unnecessary since the dominion law would soon be rendered invalid:

> Inasmuch as this house is of [the] opinion that the right to regulate the liquor traffic by license laws belongs under the British North America Act exclusively to the Legislature of the Provinces, it is not expedient to settle a scale of duties under the Dominion License Act which this House believes to be beyond the jurisdiction of the Dominion Parliament.[50]

Grit newspapers were surprised by this apparent weakening of Tory unity. For example, the Barrie *Examiner* called Meredith's admission of provincial authority "slapping Sir John Macdonald's face with a vengeance" and, like other newspapers, congratulated the leader of the opposition "on having at last shown he has a backbone."[51] His amendment did not pass, though; when the fees bill became law, a dominion license increased from $15 to $315.[52]

The increase in fees was not the final complication faced by members of the liquor trade, who had to navigate the licensing labyrinth and the accompanying bullheadedness. In Ottawa on 10 April 1884, a little more than a week before the end of the session, the government introduced a bill to amend the McCarthy Act. Along with enshrining in legislation the resolution to submit a question of constitutionality to the Privy Council, the bill, as is often the case the year after a major law comes into force, addressed aspects of the legislation that had been found to be unworkable and about which Macdonald had received letters from across the country.[53] He was not in the House during the discussion on 15 April, so D'Alton McCarthy responded to questions. Initially, the government had intended to advise the governor general to "remit" any fines that might be incurred upon prosecution. Yet, in discussion in the House, several members noted that this was a problem. First, a portion of the fine was to go to the person who prosecuted the case, and that person could not well be asked to give the money back.[54] Second, they noted that McCarthy had promised to suspend prosecutions pending a decision by the higher courts. He refused to honour this promise. Two days later, when the bill came to third reading, a series of amendments was proposed that sent the House back into committee to discuss the law further. Macdonald was back in the House and addressed the issue of remission of fines versus suspension of prosecutions. He explained that it was not realistic to suspend prosecutions because if a prosecution was suspended, then it would not be possible to take a case forward to higher courts.[55] Moving a case into higher courts was deemed essential by this time by all of the members who weighed in on the matter. In the end, the legislation suspended prosecution of specific clauses in the McCarthy Act that had made selling without a dominion license subject to prosecution.[56]

The Grit press took this in with some amusement. The *Globe* called the bill to suspend the penal clauses an emasculation of the McCarthy Act, arguing that it was "so far as the holders of Provincial licenses are concerned ... practically repealed ... [B]eyond question it is now a dead letter."[57] The Kingston *Whig* quoted Conservative Alphonse Desjardins explaining that, having been promised that there would be no penalties under the McCarthy Act, many people simply ignored the dominion law and applied for provincial licenses.[58] The *Whig* quoted McCarthy himself attempting to explain the necessity of the suspension of prosecutions and remission of fines. McCarthy said that the original law "was intended that those who had taken out Provincial licenses should not be prosecuted, but if a person took out a Dominion license he must comply with the Dominion law." The *Whig* crowed that the government had realized that "there was no concurrent jurisdiction and that if the Federal Government had power to deal with the matter the Local governments had not that power and vice versa."[59] It was a far cry from Macdonald's claim in 1882 that the Crooks Act was not worth the paper on which it was printed and signalled a painfully slow death for the legislation. The Barrie *Examiner* gleefully reminded readers of that speech, observing that "Sir John must have had many a bad quarter of an hour, and all because of the foolish boast he made in Toronto that he would take the control of the liquor traffic out of the hands of 'that little tyrant,' Mowat."[60] The McCarthy Act was deemed ultra vires first by the Supreme Court in December 1884 and then a year later by the Judicial Committee. By that time, the act had been a so-called dead letter for two years. Apart from occasional gasps of life, such as in September 1884 when the dominion boards issued liquor licenses to the exhibition in Toronto, the activities of the various Boards of License Commissioners seemed to have become inconsequential.

The weakening of the McCarthy Act did not signal a complete retreat of the Dominion government's interest in licensing. Macdonald especially remained committed to protecting the legislation against the predations of Mowat, specifically against the provincial legislation that tacked high fees onto dominion licenses. At the end of April 1884, Macdonald recommended to Minister of Justice Sir Alexander Campbell that Ontario's fees legislation be "disallowed." Disallowance was a legal priority for the dominion government, empowering it, through the governor general, to declare a provincial law invalid. Macdonald based his argument upon the fact that Mowat's law seemed to be more than just a means of ensuring a consistent revenue stream:

> It is clear ... that this differential duty is imposed or enforced not for revenue purposes but as a penalty on any person who dare[s] to take out a Dominion license ... Now the idea that any subject is to be punished in a heavy fine for obeying the Law of the land ... cannot be put up with ... [T]he federal government is imperatively called upon to protect the legislation of the Federal parliament and to disallow this act.[61]

Disallowance was gazetted on 30 April 1884.[62] Tory newspapers such as the Toronto *Daily Mail* cheered the decision, noting, probably accurately, that Mowat's legislation "was inspired by the very worst spirit of partisanship" and that "it was a menace to all business men holding licenses under the McCarthy Act."[63] The Reform papers, of course, were outraged. The *Globe* called it a "despotic disallowance" by an "autocratic" prime minister and "another invasion of Provincial rights."[64] The Kingston *Whig* was less histrionic, arguing yet again that the McCarthy Act would be found to be ultra vires the dominion but informing readers that, apparently upon the news of this disallowance, the dominion license inspector began warning licensed victuallers once more that if the McCarthy Act were to be upheld, then those who held only a provincial license had no guarantee that they would receive a federal one from the dominion board.[65]

***

The jurisdictional conflict in early 1884 between the dominion and the province, far from being a mere constitutional blip, contributed to the shape of Ontario's licensing regime for years to come. The legal wrangling led to precedents that shifted the power over liquor sale and consumption into the hands of the provinces. The several decisions in favour of the dominion government began to be less significant as the provinces, often led by Oliver Mowat, continued to chip away at constitutional authorities previously assumed to belong to the federal government. Moreover, the McCarthy Act had a material impact on the Crooks Act. After the events of 1884, the Mowat government introduced several amendments that increased the involvement of the community in both opposing and proposing license applications. Some of the changes were direct quotations of passages in the McCarthy Act. Many of the changes, especially those that gave the community more say in whether a license would be granted, were supported by the temperance movement. Nevertheless, adding new elements of direct democracy had its own challenges, as license commissioners, inspectors, and central administrators would soon learn. The temperance community was becoming stronger, and their ability to influence the government was becoming more refined. In Ontario , the temperance movement was gaining momentum, as illustrated most powerfully in the prohibitionists' efforts to see the Scott Act passed across the province, efforts that ran parallel to Macdonald's attempts to weaken local option even after defending a law that had in effect strengthened it.

If it is remembered at all, the McCarthy Act is often little more than a footnote in Canadian history, yet it was an important moment of constitutional conflict and had a serious impact on the members of the liquor trade. The confusion created by the overlap between dominion and provincial jurisdictions illustrates a complicating feature of liquor in the Canadian liberal state. The relationship between different levels of government, established by the Constitution, but defined through legislation and legal decisions, combined with the competition between the provincial and dominion leaders, served to undermine the pillars of liberty, property, and equality. The struggle for control of the laws overseeing the liquor trade led to a situation that, although in retrospect might be simply amusing and odd, caused tremendous problems for residents who happened to earn their livelihood from liquor. In the liberal state, equality is often equated with justice, the concept of equal treatment under the law. Yet the intense partisan machinations revealed by the overlapping jurisdictions of the boards of license commissioners, the conflicting messages from inspectors, and the actions of provincial and dominion governments to use licensing to screw with each other created an intense sense of injustice among many licensees. Their property and livelihoods were threatened, and their freedom to act was constrained by often subjective and contradictory legal systems. Members of the liquor trade were pawns in a much larger political game, and one that was playing out under the guise of imposing more order on the liquor business. Indeed, the manoeuverings around the McCarthy Act shows how liquor in the liberal state can result in a decidedly damaging *dis*order.

7
Attempting to Water Down the Scott Act, 1884–92

The slow death of the McCarthy Act did not remove the liquor issue from the dominion government's attention. The growing success of Scott Act campaigns worried the liquor industry and its allies in government, especially the prime minister himself. John A. Macdonald supported, however surreptitiously, attempts to amend the Scott Act that would limit the destruction that local option could wreak on the liquor industry. Modifying the Scott Act in favour of the liquor industry was politically important since the liquor licensing system created by the McCarthy Act had not been popular among, or beneficial to, liquor vendors, let alone brewers, distillers, and the few vintners of the nation's nascent wine industry. Many Tory tavern keepers were dissatisfied with the McCarthy Act since, even when it was in full operation, it did not reproduce the sort of partisan favouritism that they saw in operation under the Crooks Act.[1] Indeed, under the McCarthy Act they could feel worse off than before. John Seaton, a hotel keeper in Strathroy, Ontario, told Macdonald in March 1885 that among the numerous grievances that the liquor industry had against the government's management of the drink issue, hotel keepers were angry that "agents of the Dominion license commissioners came around and took $15.00 ... for nothing."[2] When Macdonald moved to suspend the operation of the McCarthy Act pending the Privy Council decision, Kingston resident A. MacCormack suggested that it would be better to let the McCarthy Act remain active since licensees who had held a dominion license in the past year would be unlikely to obtain a license from the provincial government.[3] Yet hotel keepers elsewhere would have told them to count their blessings because at least they were not living in Scott Act communities.

Although several counties in the Atlantic provinces were quick to adopt the dominion local option legislation, it was not until the middle of the 1880s that enthusiasm for the Scott Act intensified in Ontario.[4] On 19 April 1881, the electors of Halton County voted in favour of the Scott Act, earning Halton the nickname of "Banner County" among Ontario's prohibitionists since it "carried the banner" of local option. Local prohibition came into effect there on 1 May 1882. The confusion of *Russell v. The Queen* might have put a damper on temperance organizations in other counties that campaigned for the Scott Act; however, once the Privy Council upheld the authority of the dominion to implement such legislation, jurisdictions in Ontario quickly followed Banner County's lead. From 1884 to 1885, an additional twenty-four counties in Ontario passed the Scott Act (see Figure 7.1). By 1886, a large swath of the province operated under local option. These victories did not parallel the successes garnered by temperance forces in the Maritime provinces which, by the middle of the decade, were almost completely dry, but it was nevertheless a significant achievement.

Still, the Scott Act quickly came to be seen as flawed legislation that caused a variety of problems across the country. For example, it was to be operated at the county level, but British Columbia did not have counties as political districts. The act also stated that, once voters passed it into law, it would come into effect when liquor licenses in their jurisdiction expired. This became a problem in the Maritimes, where, with numerous counties already under some form of local option, there were no licenses to expire, and thus the timing of the implementation of the Scott Act could become a focus of debate. Much more contentious and politically tricky for Macdonald was the impact of the Scott Act on the liquor industry. Letters and reports to the prime minister suggested that local option would be destructive to the country, paralleling prohibitionists' claims about the destruction caused by the liquor industry. Many correspondents told Macdonald that the rapid increase of Scott Act counties meant a consequent contraction of the economy, rippling outward from liquor production to associated industries. Ontario Conservative MP and physician George Orton saw a dire outcome of the Scott Act, which would destroy erstwhile respectable businesses both directly and indirectly related to the production of alcoholic beverages. Brewers, maltsters, distillers, farmers, tavern keepers, and liquor dealers, as several correspondents noted, would be "ruined and turned virtually into the

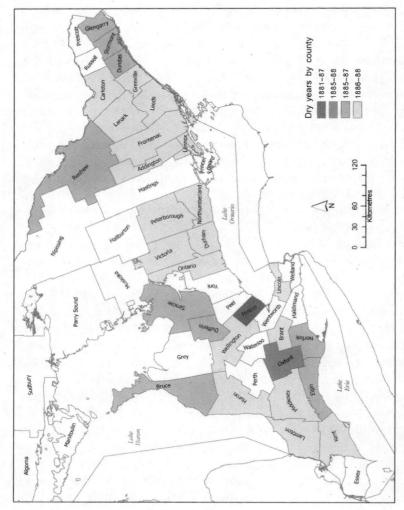

Figure 7.1 The Scott Act in Ontario | Brock University map library, used with permission. Map modified to fit county boundaries in the 1880s.

streets with no other means of livelihood."[5] Thomas Davies of Davies Brewing and Malting in Toronto, where the Scott Act never came into effect, informed Macdonald in early 1884 that the Canada Temperance Act exacerbated the business situation of brewers and maltsters already facing high tariffs from the United States and negative effects of Macdonald's National Policy: "Borrowed capital and [a] high rate of interest payable make the condition of most of the Brewers anything but satisfactory and if any relief is to be given us we want it now."[6] As the Scott Act campaigns ramped up, so did the panic among the liquor industry. In March 1885, Eugene O'Keefe illustrated the impact of the Scott Act with a story about a cooper delivering barrels to O'Keefe's Toronto brewery. The cooper stated that "the 100 (or more) casks I ordered are the only ones he has made for a brewer this year and has not one order on his books. In ordinary times this man ... could scarcely handle the orders." Moreover, equipment that the cooper had ordered to improve his efficiency was now "lying in his shop wasting."[7] In May, O'Keefe wrote that "should the abominable measure be operated much longer universal disaster ... will be the inevitable result" for brewers. "Our trade at the present time is in a most precarious position and it will be but a very short time until matters will assume alarming proportions."[8] In March 1886, Thomas Macdonald of Belleville noted that most of the farmers were "against the Scott Act for they know it will hurt their barley trade and their taxes will be higher if this Scott Act passes it will be the ruination of Canada."[9] Belleville, located in Hastings County, was not dry, but counties on either side of it saw the Scott Act implemented in 1886.

Along with the troubling economic toll was the associated personal impact of the drying up of counties. Macdonald received some heart-wrenching stories, such as the one told by Elizabeth Temple, a widow whose husband had left her with a tavern property to support her and her daughter, "who will never be able to help herself." She explained that if the Scott Act came into force in Grey County, where she lived, it would destroy her only source of income. "I can't call it a law that would take [a] woman's thirty years hard work and destroy it ... I am an aged woman and that place was my only support."[10] Fortunately for Temple, Grey County did not pass the act. She was not alone. J. Calcutt of Port Hope explained that "to be deprived of all is a terrible prospect to those amongst us that have families dependant [sic] upon our exertions, and who are too old or too infirm to begin the world again with nothing!"[11] They were powerful narratives, although it is difficult to determine if they were genuine.

In many letters, the impact of the Scott Act on the economy of the nation and the personal lives of its citizens was joined to a philosophical perspective that invoked liberal ideas of the negative impacts that immoderate measures such as prohibition would have on the country. Essentially, people argued that because the Scott Act was too extreme in its prohibitions, illegality would increase. Alex Turner of Hamilton called the act "a most iniquitous measure ... having a very immoral tendency as leading to False swearing [in court], smuggling, and illicit distillation without any benefits to the district where the act is in force as any one with an honest desire to beget actual facts can ascertain ... the only difference being the drinking is done on the sly in place of openly."[12] Professed teetotaller Thomas Conant from Oshawa said that he was not in favour of prohibition since, in his experience, under local option even "the decent hotels were brought down to low illicit groggeries."[13] Many argued to Macdonald that the Scott Act did not support "true temperance," the moderation of liquor consumption rather than absolute prohibition. Indeed, many saw beer, cider, and light wine as not antithetical to the ideal of temperance.

Solutions to these problems generally followed four threads. First (and ideally for many Wets), repeal the Scott Act and enforce a consistent system of licensing. Perhaps that was Macdonald's intention with the McCarthy Act, but repealing the Scott Act might have damaged his support from Dry conservatives. Second, revisit the failed amendments of the first part of the 1880s to allow beer, cider, and light wine to be sold in Scott Act communities. Since most of the businesses affected by local option were brewers, maltsters, hop farmers, and tavern keepers, this would mitigate most of the problems. Moreover, spirits were more powerful and thus more portable, and they were often the choice tipple in Scott Act communities. Thus, allowing people to continue to drink "light" alcoholic beverages would reduce the need for surreptitious liquor consumption and thereby encourage moderation. Third, be prepared to pay for prohibition. The liquor industry demanded that compensation be offered to those businesses whose value was destroyed by the Scott Act. For the most part, this argument would allow the original Scott Act to continue but modify it to require compensation for lost business or for equipment rendered useless as a result of the Scott Act. A final suggestion, often pressed by moderates, was to modify the Scott Act to ensure that it was supported by a larger proportion of the electorate than a simple majority of votes cast. This was seen as a way of minimizing the impact on the liquor industry since it would mean that fewer, if any, counties would pass the legislation, and those that did probably would not have had a large customer base for the liquor trade anyway.

These suggestions underlay the dominion government's attempts to address concerns about the Scott Act beginning in the session of 1885; over the next few years, a number of bills to amend various aspects of the act were presented in both the House of Commons and the Senate. The process was complicated, and for several years it resulted in few changes to the legislation. This lack of progress was the result of three main factors. First, Macdonald himself did not support the Scott Act and had repeatedly spoken and voted against it when he was in opposition. Nevertheless, he understood that killing legislation that had the support of the temperance movement, a good number of whose members had voted for his party, could be politically problematic. As a result, he let Conservative MPs vote as they wanted. As he explained to J.R. Dundas, who implored the prime minister to support the temperance views of dry Tories,

> the Scott Act itself has never been and is not now a party question. There are Conservatives as well as Grits [who are] noted Scott Act men, and people must be allowed to vote according to their own opinions without any dictation on the part of the government ... [A]s you know the government has never been a unit as to tem[perance] legislation[;] each member of the government and each member of the Conservative Party in the House of Commons vote as they please.[14]

Second, as Macdonald intimated to Dundas, these bills were usually private members' bills rather than "government" legislation, so there was no effort to whip the vote in one or the other direction because a defeated vote would not affect the government. Some thought this approach problematic, and in 1886 Senator Billa Flint from Belleville suggested that Macdonald make prohibition a government bill in order to undermine the Grits' electoral platform.[15] Third, as illustrated in Chapter 5, the approach to ameliorating the legislation to support the liquor trade, at least in the first few years, involved hijacking bills dealing with seemingly minor functional changes to the legislation and adding amendments that would alter the essential character of the Scott Act. That way, if Drys wanted to pass changes to make the act more easily enforceable, they would have to support amendments that minimized its impact on the liquor trade.

In 1885, Parliament experienced a flurry of activity related to the liquor question. Nearly every day, the House and the Senate received petitions from temperance groups, most of them from Ontario, demanding that

Parliament not change the Scott Act and pass broader prohibitory legislation (most petitions made both requests). A smaller number of petitions asked the government to loosen Scott Act provisions.[16] This intense petitioning was matched in the House by a series of bills addressing various aspects of the Scott Act. In February, D'Alton McCarthy presented a bill to allow brewers, distillers, and wholesalers operating in Scott Act counties be allowed to manufacture and sell their products locally. He argued that it was only fair since the law allowed people to buy liquor in Scott Act counties as long as they took it out of the counties, and people living in Scott Act counties could buy liquor outside their counties and take it home. "It appears to me that this is a manifest absurdity, and I propose to permit those who have a right under the act to sell ... to do so to those who reside in the county."[17] Later that day Waterloo North MP Hugo Kranz moved that the House agree that, should it pass national prohibitory legislation, brewers, distillers, and maltsters be compensated financially.[18] After extensive discussion, the motion was amended to affirm that the issue be discussed if and when such prohibition was contemplated. The wishes of the temperance movement were embodied in a much more complex amendment bill drafted by the Dominion Alliance and presented in early March by Lanark North (Ontario) Conservative MP Joseph Jamieson. He explained that the bill was designed to strengthen the provisions of the Scott Act, which he called "necessary to the effective working" of the law.[19] Two weeks later fellow Conservative Georges Auguste Gigault presented a bill decidedly at odds with the spirit of his party colleague. His bill would allow electors to vote for "partial prohibition," meaning that cider, beer, and wine would still be permitted.[20] Other bills to amend the Scott Act included one by Quebec Conservative Désiré Bourbeau that would allow ministers and priests to issue certificates for medical alcohol in Scott Act communities and one by Nova Scotia Conservative Charles Townshend that dealt with the process of petitioning for a referendum.[21]

Temperance supporters might have been heartened to learn that the only bill that made it into second reading was Jamieson's, but over the next few months they would learn how much trouble could be wrought by a master of the parliamentary process. While contemplating second reading, the House rejected an amendment presented by Quebec Conservative William Bullock Ives that would have modified the Scott Act to make it operative only upon agreement by a majority of electors. After a fraught process of moving the bill through second reading, it was modified in committee and contemplated anew in third reading. Here, parliamentary process allowed numerous attempts to change and augment the Scott Act.[22] To see more clearly how this process unfolded, consider the following exchange dealing with whether or not new measures affecting prosecutions should be applied retroactively:

> Mr. Jamieson moved, seconded by Mr. Fisher, ... that the bill be now read the third time.
> Mr. Weldon moved in amendment, seconded by Mr. Mills[,]
> That all the words after "now," to the end of the Question be left out and the words "recommitted to a committee of the whole House, in order to add the following proviso at the end of the 6th section: 'provided this Act shall not apply to any prosecutions or proceedings heretofore commenced and now pending, and notwithstanding the repeal of the said Section, the provisions of "The Canada Temperance Act of 1878," relating to offences, penalties and punishments, and the procedure relating thereto, shall, as to prosecutions and proceedings commenced after the passing of this Act, *be in full force*.'"[23]

Parliamentary process required that the House debate this motion and decide by vote whether it was proper to consider the proposal in committee. If the members agreed, then the speaker would leave the chair, the House would go into a "Committee of the Whole" with a different chair, and this committee would debate the amendment. When this process was completed, the speaker would return to the chair, and the chair of the Committee of the Whole would report any change to the bill. If the bill had been changed, then the House had a new motion to accept a third reading of the altered bill; if it had not been changed, then the House considered yet again a third reading of the unaltered bill. At this point, someone could again propose a motion to go into committee and make further changes. Any such motion proposed and seconded was then debated and voted on, and depending on the result, another Committee of the Whole was struck; if the vote was negative, then the initial question was considered again. At this time, a member could also move to delay the reading for three or six months, giving the bill "the three- [or six-] month hoist," which effectively would kill the legislation. It could be painful, onerous, and frustrating, but it was parliamentary democracy at its most meticulous; it also suggests why the speaker refused to close the bar in the parliamentary restaurant.

During the third reading of Jamieson's bill, eight motions were made to recommit and consider changes to it. Some of the proposals were relatively benign, whereas others, such as McCarthy and Cameron's motion to include beer, cider, and wine, were decidedly unfriendly to the original bill. Bourbeau presented his amendment to allow ministers to issue medical certificates for alcohol, which, though not necessarily hostile, required extensive debate, with most Drys arguing that experience had already shown that overly permissive dispensing of medical liquor would undermine the spirit of the Scott Act. Despite such parliamentary shenanigans, Jamieson's legislation finally did pass third reading after a raucous debate that began in the afternoon and finished after midnight on 14 April 1885.

Members of the Dominion Alliance who might have celebrated this late-night third reading would have been getting ahead of themselves, for the legislation still had to face the Senate. Unlike members of the House of Commons, senators were not concerned about being re-elected, and as Macdonald informed J.R. Dundas, anyone who thought "that the Senate is under my control and at my beck to command" would be mistaken. Although most senators were Conservatives, "they would resent any attempt at dictation from me."[24] Such protestations were not likely to have satisfied disgruntled Drys, such as a correspondent to the *Globe* calling himself "Spectator" who argued that "Sir John has only to hold up his finger and the Conservative Senators go in the way he points."[25] Nevertheless, it is clear that in the Senate, even more than in the House, liquor-related legislation resulted in members from different parties aligning along dry and wet lines. Liberal Richard Scott, for example, usually allied with fellow Dry Conservative Alexander Vidal. Indeed, contrary to Spectator's assertions, there was more cohesion among Liberal senators than among Conservatives on the liquor issue, but Quebec Liberals often voted for less restrictive liquor policies.

Whether or not they were receptive to Macdonald's entreaties, most senators were willing to modify the legislation in a way that made it unpalatable to the Dominion Alliance members who had drafted it. It took four days of debate before the Senate even allowed the bill to be read a second time, during which time many senators waxed eloquent on ideas of liberty, morality, and the future of the nation. After the Senate voted for a second reading, it took another two weeks before the bill moved into committee, where several amendments rejected by the House reappeared. Nova Scotia Liberal Senator Lawrence Power moved that any vote in favour of the Scott Act pass only when three-fifths of the votes cast supported it; his motion was ruled out of order. Ontario Conservative Senator Donald McMillan added a clause that made the Scott Act not apply to physicians or pharmacists; the clause was hotly debated but remained in the amended bill. Most problematic for the Dominion Alliance, Senator William Almon, drawing from his greatest hits playbook of earlier in the decade, moved "that the dealing in ales, porter, lager-beer, cider and light wines containing not more than twelve per cent of alcohol, be exempt from the operation of the Canada Temperance Act of 1878."[26] This amendment was supported in the Senate by forty-two votes in favour and twenty against.

The inclusion of Almon's amendment caused rapid defensive action by the Drys. The next day Vidal moved that the third reading be pushed back, likely to allow more consultation and to give opponents more time to voice their displeasure through letters, telegrams, and petitions sent to legislators. The Senate received fourteen petitions after Almon's amendment was approved, "praying that no alteration be made in the Canada Temperance Act, 1878, lessening its prohibitory character or making it more difficult of adoption or enforcement."[27] Yet it was not only the Drys who were mobilized. Likely having had prior notice that the motion would be made, the Wets jumped into action. Over eighty petitions received by the Senate voiced their support for the beer and cider amendment. On 26 May, for example, petitions with over 36,640 signatures supporting Almon's amendment were received by the Senate; three days later another 3,340 signatures joined that number.[28] Despite several efforts by Vidal and Scott first to have the clause removed and then to give the entire bill the six-month hoist, the clause remained in the bill and became a key factor in the now fundamentally changed amendment. It passed third reading in the Senate on 27 May 1885 with a vote of thirty-three for and nineteen against and did not split along party lines.[29] It was sent back to the House, where amendments added in the Senate needed to be debated and approved or rejected.

Not surprisingly, the success of Almon's amendment created an uproar and drew criticism of the Senate and concern about the fate of Macdonald's party. Opponents of the now "mutilated" bill criticized both the Senate and Macdonald for what seemed to be nefarious tactics. Liberal Senator Billa Flint (who had opposed the Almon amendment) warned Macdonald that it "has brought the Senate into disrepute." He predicted that the value and necessity of the upper chamber would be increasingly questioned unless "the majority retrace their steps and allow that amendment to drop ... [T]he Senate will now have few friends left except the Liquor dealers and those who imbibe to [sic] freely."[30] Indeed, these sentiments were echoed in the *Globe,* which asked, "[W]hat is the Senate for?"

It proceeded to criticize comments made by Senator Almon that it was not the job of senators "to do what the people think best; we are here to do what we think best ourselves," a decidedly undemocratic utterance.[31] At a mass meeting in Brantford a few days later, former Waterloo South Liberal MP James Young described the Senate as "a dull, dead, dark lagoon that never stirs unless Sir John Macdonald steps into it."[32] Victoria South (Ontario) Conservative J.R. Dundas sent Macdonald a letter from "our best friends in Victoria" expressing "the sentiments of the temperance people, who form no inconsiderable portion of the conservative party ... I submit earnestly Sir John this matter, for it is very important."[33] Thomas Dight, a miller in Lucan, Ontario, wrote, "I am very much afraid that the Senate amendment to the Scott Act will injure our party at the next election unless very carefully handled."[34] William Campbell, president of a Conservative association in Goderich, Ontario, predicted that if the bill in its revised state "should be carried by the House ... there would be a large defection from the Conservative ranks at the next election."[35] Several MPs wrote to urge Macdonald to delay a vote because of impending by-elections in their communities, the results of which could be affected by the final decision on the bill.

Wets issued similar warnings. Throughout the session, members of the liquor trade wrote to remind Macdonald that failure to satisfy the liquor interests would result in a weakening of his party's prospects. Strathroy's John Seaton advised Macdonald to "take notice that nine tenths of the License [sic] victuallers are conservatives and strong supporters of your government and they are greatly dissatisfied."[36] An anonymous correspondent calling himself "Rate Payer" warned Macdonald that "the Brewers and liquor [dealers] and also the hotel men of Ontario are about to have a meeting to vote for reform candidates ... for there is no reason why they should voate [sic] conservative."[37] An anonymous letter from Toronto predicted that "the conservative government will be left in the shade if the Scott Act is not stoped [sic] either by making it not law or by passing license for wine & beer."[38] As the amended bill returned to the House for final approval, O'Keefe advised Macdonald to ensure that the beer and cider amendment "not be killed when it reaches the Commons" and contradicted party stalwarts who predicted a mass exodus of dry Tories from their ranks: "Those who have voted on a straight party ticket up to the present will not change to please the temperance party ... [W]e have a striking illustration of this fact in the late election in Northumberland where the Temperance party ignored their cold water principles and ranged themselves on their respective sides." Echoing Wets who had been warning Macdonald against upsetting the trade, O'Keefe reminded him of the power of liquor interests in local politics, noting that the amendment "would give universal satisfaction and secure to the Conservative party the honest support of the Hotel Keepers and the other branches of the business throughout the Dominion. With these ... the present gov[ernmen]t can hold power as long as they please."[39] A few weeks later an anxious O'Keefe wrote as the bill was scheduled to be deliberated again in the House: "The brewers have acted as you advise to rouse the country on this question, we have done our best and feel satisfied that the country is with us on the exemption clause."[40] Macdonald was not so optimistic: "I shall be very glad indeed to see the Senate amendment to the Scott Act carried in so far as it relates to beer and light wines. I have however no great hope of its success in the commons." He noted that a significant portion of the house is "fully under the control of the Alliance."[41] The prime minister was correct. In mid-June, the House removed the beer clause as well as a few other disagreeable amendments added by the Senate. In July, the Senate rejected those changes. Without concurrence, the bill died.

The next five years saw similar glacial progress in changes to dominion liquor legislation. Macdonald's continual backroom arrangements to scupper the Scott Act, along with partisan loyalties sometimes dividing Drys, meant that in both 1886 and 1887, although numerous bills to amend the Scott Act were proposed, and several received vigorous debate, none passed into law. It was not until 1888 that things began to change, when a modified version of Jamieson's bill and McCarthy's bill to clarify the process of repealing the Scott Act both received royal assent. After these amendments passed, the temperance-oriented members of Parliament shifted tactics to seek movement toward national prohibition, with Wets, and even those who believed in moderation rather than prohibition, continuing to push back. By this time, the Scott Act was in significant decline in Ontario, and all Scott Act communities were either rescinding the law or becoming involved in intense campaigns to do so. The act would be rejected in all Ontario counties by 1889. That year Jamieson presented a motion urging the House to support prohibition. Of course, it resulted in more attempted amendments. One changed the wording so that the House agreed that prohibition would be advisable "when the public sentiment of the country is ripe." That amendment passed. Failed amendments included one that would have instituted prohibition only after a clear majority of qualified electors voted for it and another that sought yet again to amend the Scott Act to allow beer and cider sales. The latter motion was ruled out of order. In the end, the House agreed to the motion that, "in the opinion of this House, it is expedient to prohibit the manufacture, importation and sale of intoxicating liquors ... when the public sentiment of the country is ripe for ... such a measure of prohibition."[42] Such motions had no legal force, and over the next few years Jamieson sought a stronger measure. In 1891, he moved that "the time has arrived when it's expedient to prohibit the manufacture, importation and sale of intoxicating liquors for beverage purposes." Amendments to this motion were different from those in the past. One member moved to strike a select committee to investigate the economic impact of any prohibitory bill, but that amendment failed. Then, in a move that would affect the direction of debates on the liquor traffic for the next few years at least, Conservative temperance stalwart George Foster suggested the creation of a royal commission with the mandate to investigate the following:

1. The effects of the Liquor traffic upon all interests affected by it in Canada
2. The measures which have been adopted in this and other countries with a view to lessen, regulate, or prohibit the traffic
3. The results of these measures in each case
4. The effect that the enactment of a Prohibitory Liquor Law in Canada would have in respect of social conditions, agricultural business, industrial and commercial interests, of the revenue requirements of Municipalities, Provinces, and the Dominion, and also as to its capacity of efficient enforcement
5. All other information bearing on the question of Prohibition.[43]

The motion was accepted by the House with a vote of 107–88 at 1:40 in the morning of 25 June 1891.[44] On 23 March 1892, the government struck the Royal Commission on the Liquor Traffic. Further combative motions in Parliament, to weaken, strengthen, or undermine the Scott Act, and dealing with the liquor traffic in general, appear to have been suspended while the commission undertook what ended up being a three-year endeavour.

***

The attempts to amend the Scott Act demonstrate how intractable an issue the liquor question had become by the last part of the nineteenth century. Opponents and supporters of prohibition drew from core values of the liberal state to press their arguments. The appeal to the rights to property and freedom to trade and have a livelihood, the need to liberate the excessive drinker from the bondage of alcohol, and even the principle of equal treatment under the law were fundamental to the ideas about local option. Yet the central governing body of the nation was unable to move in any direction that strengthened or weakened constraints on the liquor trade. Again, the machinations of partisan politics undermined the apparent reasoned operation of the liberal state, and the complications presented by Drys and Wets within their parties led to legislative gridlock. Temperance supporters on both sides of Parliament pushed for changes that would make local option more powerful, whereas opponents – also in both parties – sought to undermine such efforts. But legislative problems were not the only challenge that the Scott Act created. In Ontario, the surge of support for the act, followed by a rapid decline in support, indicated the difficulty in crafting a functional law that implemented the prohibitionist dream, even at a local level. It seemed to be clear that local option caused problems worse than those that it was designed to solve. Apart from a few relatively minor amendments, the Scott Act remained essentially unchanged from its original form in 1878 and thus difficult to enforce. Partisan self-preservation, tensions between Wets and Drys, and skepticism among many moderates meant that the intractable challenge presented by liquor in the liberal state persisted well into the last decade of the century.

8
Plebiscites as Tools for Change? 1883–94

The conflict between the governments of Oliver Mowat and John A. Macdonald over the fate of the McCarthy Act was one of several issues that shaped the direction of liquor licensing in Ontario at the beginning of the 1880s. At the municipal level, the difficulty in enforcing the Crooks Act and the activism of the temperance movement drove demands to introduce more stringent restrictions on liquor while giving communities a more direct role in determining whether and where licenses would be granted. There was also the persistent argument that the best solution to all of this would be total prohibition. Those who opposed prohibition, both representatives of the liquor industry and moderates who saw it as an extreme, unenforceable, and counterproductive act of government overreach, did not remain silent. To a government that saw total prohibition as both impractical and outside its constitutional purview, appeals to moderation were attractive; they also fit within a liberal view of limited state involvement in the lives of individuals. Nevertheless, some issues the provincial government found it increasingly difficult to ignore. First, agitation to remove liquor sales from grocery stores, which Drys had argued were loci of surreptitious drinking, gained significant success in the middle of the century. Second, prohibitionists urged Mowat to challenge the assumption that province-wide prohibition was ultra vires the provincial government, resulting in a move to address this lingering area of constitutional uncertainty. The implementation of these changes involved a persistent and often contradictory discussion of the place of the liberal state in the lives of individuals, drinkers or otherwise.

Although the Mowat government passed several amendments to the Crooks Act in the years after it became law, major changes did not appear until the early part of the 1880s. Most early amendments dealt with technicalities of enforcement and conviction rather than components of the law that affected the availability of liquor, such as reducing the number of licenses, increasing license fees, limiting the types of businesses where Ontarians could buy liquor, or giving the public input on the process of granting licenses. One notable change to the Crooks Act in the early 1880s involved the role of community members in the application process, permitting local electors to express their willingness to allow new license applications to stand. This change was likely inspired by similar provisions in the McCarthy Act. Along with drawing license commissioners from local officials rather than making them all political appointees, the McCarthy Act required more transparency and public input in licensing decisions. It was a response to criticisms of the secrecy of the operations of local Boards of License Commissioners. Recall that, when speaking to the McCarthy Committee in 1883, A.G. Hodge of the Licensed Victuallers Association had complained that the Ontario commissioners sat "like a star chamber behind closed doors," and this lack of openness added to the impression that decisions were biased and unfair.[1] The secrecy itself was cherished by some license commissioners. In 1880, when Lincoln County commissioners John Orchard, James Morin, and James Henderson tendered their resignations to the provincial secretary, they explained that the inspector had disclosed, among other things, "the conversations of the board meetings, which above all things should be secret."[2] The original Crooks Act had made no provisions for licensing boards to consult with the community, presuming that the commissioners were capable of making decisions that suited the community's needs. In contrast, the McCarthy Act required inspectors and commissioners to publicize notices of applications and dates of board meetings and included provisions requiring commissioners to deny licenses if enough electors petitioned against them. In 1884, the Mowat government proposed legislation that inserted similar forms of administrative transparency into the operation of the Crooks Act. Had they still been commissioners, Orchard, Morin, and Henderson would have been incensed because the amendment required inspectors to post notices about impending licensing board meetings and gave electors in any polling subdivision the right to petition against applications. The new clauses provided specific reasons that a license could be contested, reproducing verbatim the similar passage from the McCarthy Act. Indeed, the Toronto *Daily Mail* complained that the amendment was "a transcript of the McCarthy Act of 1883."[3] The amendment would also phase out shop licenses for grocery stores by forbidding new licenses to be issued to stores that sold liquor along with anything other than "mineral and aerated waters (not containing spirits), ginger ale, liquor cases, bottles, or liquor baskets, or packages, taps or faucets." If the proprietor of a liquor shop decided to sell other products after receiving his license, then the license would be invalid.[4]

The decision to separate liquor sales from general goods was the result of agitation against "grocers' licenses" that had been simmering in several Ontario communities for some time. With the number of licensed taverns severely cut in the province, the temperance movement had begun targeting grocers' licenses as a cause of problematic drinking. Temperance petitioners urged councils in municipalities – including Toronto, London, Barrie, Bowmanville, and Orangeville – to pass bylaws eliminating grocers' licenses.[5] Temperance speakers took issue with how the licensing law created a situation in which grocers had to sell liquor in order to survive. They argued that liquor-selling grocers had an unfair advantage over their unlicensed competitors, so the unlicensed felt compelled to sell liquor illegally to remain competitive. This tendency to break the law cast aspersions on these otherwise upstanding shopkeepers, and it bled into other aspects of their businesses. After all, licensed or not, grocery stores in which liquor could be purchased were frequented by women and children, thus placing a dangerous temptation, so the argument ran, in front of those who were most in need of protection from the predations of King Alcohol.

The situation in Toronto, the centre of much temperance and liquor industry activity, was especially volatile. In 1883, temperance supporters sent a resolution to Toronto City Council arguing "that the sale of liquor in stores where other commodities are sold is attended with serious evils, resulting in intemperance in the homes of the people, and greatly aggravating the social disorders arising from drinking habits." They reminded the councillors that the Crooks Act gave municipal councils the right to impose restrictions on what liquor dealers could sell in their shops.[6] Debate in the council then included concerns about the impacts that such a law would have on grocers, their rights to relatively unfettered commerce, and jurisdictional confusion about how far a municipality could go. In response to a bylaw to eliminate grocers' licenses, proposed by Alderman Peter Ryan, the council received a petition from eighty-three grocers who argued that they were respectable members of the community, contributed tax revenues to city coffers, and could not survive without continuing to sell liquor. When proposing a motion to delay a decision until the bylaw could be scrutinized by the city solicitor to ensure that it did not violate the Crooks Act, two aldermen called the law imposing such restrictions on respectable merchants a "manifest injustice." This appeal to property rights and justice resonated with the council. Alderman H.E. Clarke, although claiming to be a "professed temperance man," supported the motion to delay the bylaw, explaining that he opposed "any legislation which would take away any rights enjoyed by any number of men in the city."[7] The council gave Ryan until 26 February to present a legal opinion on the issue, but he missed that crucial deadline because of illness. Since the Crooks Act required municipalities to pass bylaws by 1 March, to be implemented on 1 May, the issue was dropped.

The following year, however, things had changed to strengthen the temperance position. The *Hodge* decision of December 1883 confirmed the right of the province to download certain responsibilities to the municipalities, including allowing them to pass bylaws limiting the sale of liquor in shops. Moreover, the temperance forces were able to draw from evidence from the temperance movement in the United Kingdom, which was agitating for an end to grocers' licenses there. The UK Alliance's campaign against grocers' licenses was extensive. It published tracts such as *A Cloud of Witnesses against Grocers' Licenses: The Fruitful Source of Female Intemperance* (1883), connecting grocers' licenses to an increase in female drunkenness, a major concern for evangelical temperance forces.[8] In late 1883, the Church of England Temperance Society had introduced a bill "for the abolition of grocers' licenses" to Parliament in London.[9] In January 1884, the *Canada Citizen and Temperance Record* (edited by Dominion Alliance Secretary Frank Spence) published two short articles on grocery store liquor sales using data from the United Kingdom; this material set the basis for much of the agitation about shop licenses in 1884.

The anti–grocery store sales agitation focused on two favourite themes of the temperance movement: the role of drink in degrading women and the connection between drink and crime. The *Canada Citizen and Temperance Record* prefaced its articles with an editorial claiming that "the facts and arguments in regard to [grocery store licenses] have been fully and frequently laid before our readers," so "it is not needful for us to discuss further the question." Somewhat redundantly, it then proceeded to do just that, claiming that "female intemperance – the result of the grocers' license system – is assuming alarming proportions and calls for immediate and decisive action."[10] The first article, entitled "Intemperance among Women," used police reports from Manchester that linked the increase in female committals for drunkenness to the granting of liquor licenses to grocers and shopkeepers in 1861. "The most piteous result of the Act was the marvelous increase of female intemperance that followed its introduction." The grocers' license undermined the otherwise upstanding women of all classes: "Wives of respectable mechanics, domestic servants, and even those of a high class … somehow or other learned to drink, and then went to the public house, and subsequently helped to swell the terrible array of convictions for drunkenness." The article concludes with a cry for action in Canada: "A million times better than such degradation come upon us would it be that the license of every grocer, confectioner, restaurateur and saloon be repealed throughout the broad Dominion of Canada."[11] The second article, from the UK *Temperance Record,* was less histrionic, providing a range of data on the increase in offences, prostitution, drunkenness, and associated vices, with only a brief mention of the increase in drunkenness among women. As well as illustrating support from the centre of British democracy, this material provided data to support the arguments of Canadian temperance advocates.[12]

To temperance forces, the grocers' license presented a clear threat to the viability of a liberal state, especially because of how it corrupted women. Soon after the articles mentioned above went to print, the *Globe* published another extract from the UK *Temperance Record* arguing that "secret drinking is far worse than drinking openly." The subsequent explanation made a none-too-subtle gendered slip indicating the severity of the problem: "When a man or woman drinks in the presence of others, there is always some little restrictive influence till the drink gets the upper hand, and the poor victim then disregards the opinions of others, and even her own convictions, to quench the consuming fire which rages within her."[13] The use of the gendered pronoun clearly acknowledged that, although either men or women might drink openly, secret drinking appeared to be a female pastime or at least problematic only when women did it. When a delegation of temperance luminaries brought its petition to Toronto City Council in early February 1884, it explained the problem in similar terms. The bishop of Toronto noted that "the effects of the practice [of secret drinking] were most apparent among women." One delegate, Mr. Hoyle, referred to the UK example. As a result of William Gladstone's Licensing Act, he explained, women "were compelled to go to the grocery stores where liquor was kept in stock. It was a great temptation to them. From some merchants liquor was obtained, delivered secretly, and charged as tea and sugar. The results which accrued from this practice were terrible, and not unfrequently the husband was drawn into the vortex of intemperance by these means."[14] Hoyle's image of a naive wife who also functioned as a temptress for the unwitting husband had deeply rooted misogynistic scriptural origins and carried considerable weight. Honouring and protecting the home were fundamental to the cult of true womanhood and pervasive in the temperance movement.[15] As Rev. G.M. Mulligan noted, "some people argued that if the sale of liquor in grocery stores were abolished men would not be able to drink at home, they would be compelled to go to the taverns. That was right. If they wanted liquor let them go to the taverns and keep the home pure."[16] Another speaker of the delegation reiterated the point that the unbalanced nature of liquor licensing meant that some vendors had an advantage over others. This perspective, drawing from the liberal value of fairness in trade, however, was secondary to the protection of the home in this delegation's arguments.

Facing pressures from both sides, the council resorted to the type of decision that would become typical of governments that dealt with the liquor question: it decided to hold a plebiscite. The *Globe* thought that this was a cowardly dereliction of duty, putting the decision onto the shoulders of ratepayers and subjecting the city to added expense.[17] It was also concerned because the liquor industry was strong in Toronto, as demonstrated by the failed attempts to achieve local option there. In a subsequent editorial, the *Globe* reminded readers that the liquor industry would do everything that it could, legal and illegal, to try to defeat the measure. Nevertheless, it did note that there was some hope since the issue of grocery store licenses did not cleanly follow the dry/wet cleavage:

> Many who are abstainers neither in theory nor [in] practice are strongly in favour of the measure in question, they believe that the present arrangement is ... injurious to customers, especially to women and children; the fruitful parent of tippling on the sly; and the means of actually cheating the regular tavern-keeper by such places being turned, as they too often are, into regular drinking saloons.[18]

Protecting the home and the honest merchant were key arguments in the temperance campaign, although the emphasis would soon shift.

During the plebiscite campaign, the theme of women drinking secretly was initially the strong rallying cry of the "no license" forces. At a mass meeting, several speakers noted the deeply troubling rise in drinking among women in the United Kingdom. Rev. R. Wallace explained that the law in England had led to the situation in which women would "carry [liquor] home and drink who would be ashamed to walk up to a bar and take their drink there." Rev. F. Sweeney noted that, "as bad as this was, it was not so dark a picture as that of the young girls who are being led into drinking habits. The number of young girls under 17 ... committed in one day to Westminster House of Correction for drunkenness was 14, and the number was increasing." Drawing direct links between what had been observed in the United Kingdom and what was going on in Toronto, and possibly appealing to English Canadian prejudice about the immorality and drunken tendencies of French Canadians, Sweeney observed that "drunkenness in Montreal was not half so barefaced as here."[19]

The problem, of course, was not just women drinking but also their secrecy. John Cameron, editor of the *Globe*, claimed that he did not wish to focus only on women drinking; rather, "we are quite sure that for one woman thereby led astray there are ten men." He proceeded to indict the character of grocers across the province, who all seemed to be culpable in the spread of surreptitious drinking:

> We doubt if there is one licensed grocery in the Province which does not keep a free bottle for its customers, from which they may take an occasional "toothful" when so "dispo[s]ed" with the understanding that the grocer *recoup* himself by more respectable entries in the family pass book ... It is also a matter of notoriety, especially in country towns, that there are certain passwords which drouthy souls and accommodating sellers have agreed upon to keep everything serene. "There's a parcel for you down in the cellar." "Would you like to see our stock?" "Have a cigar?" "Would you speak a minute?" etc. There is not a town or city in Ontario where this sort of work is not going on, and where men in scores and hundreds are not being prepared slowly and surely to "graduate" in due time in the taverns and the gutter. All this is beyond reasonable question. Nobody who knows anything of the real facts of the case would even think of denying it except with a wink.

Cameron concluded by reminding readers, many no doubt already true believers, that it would be a hard fight, the liquor interests were notorious for vote tampering and other nefarious election shenanigans, and thus temperance supporters needed to do more than speak or cheer at rallies: "Work – hard, earnest, and united – is much more important, and will be found much more effective."[20]

Such imputations of the grocer's character were not ignored by the liquor interests, and their counterattack was swift, pointed, and based upon ideas of justice that seemed to have eluded the temperance advocates. There were many examples of this appeal to justice, or fairness, the most vivid of which took place during a mass temperance meeting on 12 February 1884. As the chair was beginning to wrap up the meeting, a group of Wets from the back of the room began to chant, "Fahey! Fahey! Fahey!" The chair, somewhat reluctantly, allowed Toronto *Daily Mail* journalist and notorious anti-temperance campaigner James Fahey to take the stage.[21] His arrival was met with "a torrent of hisses and applause," and a reporter attending the meeting said that it would be difficult to know which predominated. Fahey did not have an easy time speaking to the loud and hostile crowd of temperance supporters. At one point, "hisses," which the chair had a difficult time controlling, "interrupted the speaker for several minutes." When some semblance of order had returned, Fahey made a "well merited rebuke": "He said he had always understood that temperance men were supposed to be temperate in language as well as in eating and drinking, and the temperate manner in which his [wet] friends had listened to the gentlemen who preceded him should meet with a similar acknowledgement from the opposite side."[22] In other words, we respectfully listened to you; why can't you do the same for us?

Fahey's reproach typified the way in which Wets approached the criticisms of Drys in this and other debates, characterizing them as irrational zealots without a sense of the practicalities of commerce or governance. The day after the *Globe* published its editorial about the secret bottle held by every grocer in Ontario, two grocers named Jaffray and Ryan sent a brief letter taking umbrage at the accusations "that drinking is general in grocers' cellars, that liquor is frequently bought and charged as groceries, as a blind, and that 'nips' of whiskey brandy etc. are frequently given to customers with all the other charges of that kind." Repeating the argument of respectable merchants, they insisted "that it is not true as respects the great bulk of the respectable grocers of Toronto."[23] The next day the *Daily Mail* published a letter from W.J. McCormick, president of the Licensed Grocers' Association, defending the city's grocers. He argued that the charge that grocers kept a private bottle for customers – "whether male or female" – was patently untrue and that this was an ongoing slander against the men and women of the community.[24]

Supporters of grocers' licenses further argued that temperance claims about the women lured into drinking in grocery stores insulted the respectable women of the city. Another correspondent to the *Daily Mail*, T.H. George, decried "these cowardly libellers of our wives, sisters, and daughters [who] have not had the manliness to apologize for the outrage.

If such creatures are temperance men, I am proud to say I am not one of them."[25] William Kyle, a Toronto merchant, voiced similar offence, suggesting that the temperance forces had gone off the rails:

> They are not attacking intemperance, the evils of which are too notorious to be insisted upon; they are not even attacking those drunkards who are the terrible examples of one form of vice; their abuse is directly levelled at the women of our city, the wives of our workingmen. If a stranger were to read a report of some of the speeches of some of the advocates of liquor stores, for that is really what they are, he would imagine that the majority of our women are given over to drunkenness and debauchery, and that no man can trust his wife or daughter to go to a licensed grocery lest she become intoxicated. This is outrageous slander against which the manhood of Toronto should rise up in indignant protest. There are bad men and women of every class, but they will not be made good by shifting the sale of liquors from one building to another.[26]

In this letter, Kyle, a frequent correspondent with Sir John A. Macdonald and a passionate Tory, saw the insults to working-class men and women uttered by middle-class, mostly Reform-voting, temperance supporters as indicative of the overly zealous, even radical, prejudice that many Wets found troubling in temperance rhetoric.

The criticism of the "slander" of women of the city was part of a multi-pronged attack that, as James Fahey's statement illustrated, charged temperance advocates with uttering rhetoric that itself was hardly temperate. The counterargument was that a moderate approach, based upon the values of fairness and justice rather than hyperbole and histrionics, was a more appropriate way to deal with the purported excesses of drinking. At a mass meeting the same day that Jaffray and Ryan's letter appeared in the *Globe,* a number of opponents of the bylaw claimed a right to speak, arguing that since it was a meeting of all citizens to discuss the bylaw, it was only fair that both sides should be heard. When inviting Fahey to the platform, the chair, Rev. Dr. Castle, said that if Fahey "could show him that the sale of liquor was good for the mothers and sons of the city, he would shake hands with him." Fahey was nonplussed by the taunt and countered the stereotype that liquor dealers were not interested in temperance by saying that "it would take an abler man than anyone present to prove that temperance was not better than intemperance." He then challenged the speakers to provide evidence that removing liquor from grocery stores would stop the sale of surreptitious liquor:

> Is it possible ... to aid the cause of temperance by transferring the sale of liquor from one corner to another? It is a notorious fact that many grocers who have no licenses have customers who require liquors sent home with their groceries. Of course they do not keep the liquors themselves, but they know where to get them, and the order is filled. You say that by depriving those people of licenses you are going to do justice to those who have not been so successful. But will it be justice?[27]

Another speaker, a Mr. Griffiths, added that the argument that it was unjust that some grocers were able to sell liquor and others were not had little to do with fairness and everything to do with the judgment of license commissioners, appointees of a government that also supported temperance. The persistent theme of the Wets was that respectable liquor dealers, far from wanting to corrupt and undermine the morals of the citizens of the city, were interested in temperance but not in illiberal restrictions.[28]

The debates in the letters to the editor of the Toronto *Daily Mail* were especially heated and illustrative of the complicated wrestling with liberal values manifested on each side. Although it was a Tory newspaper that supported the Wets, the *Daily Mail* tended to publish more letters than the *Globe* representing all sides of the argument (although doubtless there was some editorial preference for opinions against temperance). A correspondent calling himself "A YMCA Secretary" illustrated the problem with grocery stores' selling of alcohol by telling of a time when he himself witnessed corrupt practices. He was speaking to a young man at a grocery store and claimed that in a span of forty-five minutes,

> fifteen persons came in to obtain whiskey in quantities ranging from five up to twenty cents' worth. Eleven of these customers were children, certainly under fifteen years of age, and several of them so young they could scarcely reach the counter to place the jug or bottle upon it; some even had not to ask for what they needed, as it was distinctly understood when they laid the money down.[29]

The next day, George S. Michie, one of the most vocal licensed grocers in the city, criticized YMCA Secretary for his inactivity in the face of blatant disregard for the law. "The man who will stand by and see whiskey sold to children as he says he did, without informing the proper authorities, is a poor apology for a temperance man, a bad citizen, and a worse Christian."[30] Michie argued that it was likely a false characterization of the events at the grocery and challenged YMCA Secretary to provide proof.

This wet counterattack appears to have moderated the rhetoric of the temperance forces. In the same issue in which it printed Jaffray and Ryan's letter, the *Globe* offered a half-hearted backpedal, explaining that "we have no wish to do the slightest injustice to anyone, and are only too glad to be assured that some, at any rate, of the licensed grocers do not keep a free bottle. But as to such a state of things being exceedingly common there seems to be a considerable accumulation of evidence."[31] Others also attempted to give some evidentiary support while dialing down the histrionics. James Knowles wrote in the *Daily Mail* that the separation of liquor from groceries deserved a fair trial since licensed groceries had a worse reputation than saloons: "It was only the other day that a lady informed me that she was ashamed to enter a licensed grocers, and facts prove that many of these stores are little better than taverns. For my own part, I would just as soon enter a saloon as a licensed grocery store."[32] J. McLean Ballard suggested that Wets had misunderstood the issue:

> What I have heard said is this, that carefully-prepared statistics in England have shown an increase, since the issuing of grocers' licenses there, of convictions for drunkenness among women in something like the ratio of thirteen to one. And to save the women of Toronto from a temptation which has been thus disastrous in its effects elsewhere ... is one of the reasons now urged for the abolition of grocers' licenses. Who then, I would ask, is the true friend of the wives and daughters of Toronto, those who would remove temptation out of their way or those who would leave them in it, when they know what have been the appalling results in England?[33]

To Ballard, the insult to the women of Toronto was not as important an issue as the entreaty to the men of the city to defend those women from temptation.

Nevertheless, despite such attempts to contextualize the issue of women drinking as a matter of supporting them rather than attacking them, the prohibitionists shifted their rhetoric back to the classic liberal values of justice, liberty, property rights, and fair trade. Consequently, when the campaigners in favour of the bylaw issued a circular a few days before the vote, women were not mentioned at all, and the issue of justice returned to the forefront. They based their arguments on five key points:

1. It is wrong in principle to allow a business that requires a license to be carried on in the same premises with a business that requires no license.
2. The licenses of 100 of the 500 groceries in the city are a grievous injustice to the 400 that cannot be licensed.
3. The cover of the grocery business prevents the license inspector and the police from discovering illicit selling.
4. The selling of groceries and liquor in the same premises places a strong temptation in the way of those who are victims of intemperance.
5. We have the strongest official testimony that the passing of this bylaw will greatly assist in the prevention of intemperance that all good citizens equally deplore.[34]

Whether the issue that appealed to voters was women drinking, fairness to unlicensed grocers, or concern that the licensed grocery was a place of secret drinking and corruption across classes and genders, in the end the supporters of the bylaw prevailed. In a vote that reportedly had a greater turnout than any other plebiscite to date in Toronto, a majority of 362 voted to separate sales of liquor from sales of groceries.[35] Even though the votes by ward had been evenly divided – five wards voting against the bylaw, five in favour of it – the issue seemed to be settled. Toronto City Council sensed the danger in countering what many saw as a clear majority opinion. After some last-ditch attempts by grocers yet again to delay the bylaw vote past the 1 March 1884 deadline, council passed the bylaw and advised license commissioners that thereafter grocers would not be licensed to sell liquor. In a display of reconciliation, temperance supporters agreed to an extended timeline before the law would come into effect, allowing grocers to sell off their stock. In April, the implementation of the bylaw was pushed back until 1 May 1885.

The agitation against grocers' licenses saw a gradualist response from the provincial government. In 1884, it amended the Crooks Act to deny shop licenses to new applicants if the shops sold goods not related to alcoholic beverages and associated activities.[36] Two years later, the Mowat government strengthened the separation between the sale of liquor and the sale of other goods by prohibiting internal communication between liquor and non-liquor departments of any licensed shop and establishing a fine of between twenty and fifty dollars for every day that "such communication remains open." Not paying the fine would result in imprisonment for at least a month.[37]

Revisiting Provincial Prohibition

Changes to the Crooks Act affected the operation of licensed places in wet counties, but they did little to deal with the ongoing challenges in Scott Act communities and the legacies of the McCarthy Act. As more counties passed the Scott Act in the middle of the decade, the Mowat government tried to address problems created by restrictions caused by the implementation of the law. A main issue was the uneven enforcement mechanism of the dominion legislation. The Scott Act required dominion collectors of inland revenue in Scott Act districts to enforce the law. However, many of those officers, Conservative appointees, appeared to be reluctant to act against illegal selling, and doubtless their political masters placed little pressure on them to do otherwise. At the same time, when an Ontario county passed the Scott Act, the provincial government disbanded the Board of License Commissioners and dismissed the inspector. In many communities, the variation in provisions between the McCarthy Act and the Crooks Act led to further problems with administering the licensing laws. This process was in contrast to that under the Dunkin Act because that law applied to smaller units within a license district, so the commissioners and inspectors remained in place. Even when the law was being enforced, courts were finding it difficult to secure a conviction when a violator was apprehended (e.g., by temperance groups who organized to enforce the law in lieu of, or in combination with, government officials). As a correspondent from the Bruce County Scott Act Association complained to the *Globe* in early 1886, "the changes from Crooks Act to McCarthy Act, thence back again, ... together with the fact that we cannot get a Police Magistrate, makes [sic] it impossible to enforce the Act."[38] Recognizing the different legal systems across the country, the Scott Act included provisions for prosecuting offences in each province, and in Ontario it was especially confusing. In places without a police magistrate, someone who hoped to make a conviction could go to a mayor, justice of the peace, or stipendiary magistrate. Under the current regulations, a police magistrate could be appointed only upon the request of a county council. Yet many members of a council were afraid to make such an appointment, reportedly fearing retribution from liquor interests.[39]

Many of these concerns were expressed in February 1886 when a deputation from the Dominion Alliance met with Oliver Mowat and Arthur Hardy, the irascible provincial secretary. The deputation was pleased to learn that Mowat had decided to reappoint license commissioners and inspectors in Scott Act counties. Hardy cautioned the temperance supporters against thinking that this would solve the problem of enforcement. He reminded the deputation that it was incumbent on supporters of the Scott Act to "supplement the work of the inspectors and commissioners." He recognized that an inspector's ability to enforce the law often hinged on geography and topography, which increased the onus on temperance people to support the officials:

> One inspector, in a district say thirty miles by twenty miles, or even half that size, cannot properly cover the ground. I receive letters now and then saying that an inspector is worthless, that liquor is being freely sold in a certain place. Well, the inspector probably lives in some other part of the county and he cannot be in two places at the same time ... Unless you aid him perhaps get the County Councils interested in supplementing his efforts, he won't be able to discharge his duties as you and I would like him to do.[40]

Hardy was repeating a concern expressed by numerous observers that it was irresponsible for temperance people to petition for prohibition but not work to support its enforcement. It was a lesson that they found difficult to follow.

Such challenges in the enforcement of the Scott Act led to its rapid decline in Ontario. By the end of the decade, all counties in the province had rescinded the act, even the Banner County of Halton, which had been under local option since 1881. Although prohibitionists also lobbied the dominion government to fix the Scott Act, the persistent challenges, amendments, and inaction discussed in Chapter 7 provided little reason for optimism compared to Mowat's promises to fix the enforcement issue. Indeed, even though temperance advocates continued to be frustrated with his limited support for outright prohibition, they did find him a sympathetic leader who offered encouragement to the temperance cause. Mowat was also motivated by political threats from the breakaway farmers' party, the Patrons of Industry, which was siphoning off support for the Liberals and advocating a number of policies that directly threatened Mowat, such as a repudiation of patronage.[41] The other motivation, of course, came from the growing power of the temperance movement itself. Thus, by the middle of the decade, Mowat had returned to an unresolved but early discarded issue in the constitutional division of powers: the right of the provinces to institute prohibition.

This renewed drive toward prohibition began in 1890. Immediately before the legislature was prorogued and an election called, Hamilton MLA and Provincial Secretary John M. Gibson presented a bill to amend the Crooks Act that introduced a few important changes to the liquor trade in the province. The amendment continued the trend initiated in 1884 of adding components from the McCarthy Act to the Ontario legislation, although whether these amendments were consciously or unconsciously reflections of that federal legislation is difficult to say. The legislation raised the minimum drinking age from sixteen to eighteen but also allowed parents or guardians of someone up to the age of twenty-one to request that an individual be refused the sale of liquor. The *Globe* noted approvingly that the change would make it "increasingly difficult for young men to contract habits of intemperance."[42] The bill also required a new license application to be accompanied by a petition from local residents approving of the application (rather than changes in the early 1880s allowing residents to petition against the application). Increasing restrictions on access to liquor, the law also prohibited liquor sales on ships travelling on rivers or the Great Lakes. Finally, and not insignificantly, the bill inserted into the license law provisions permitting councils of "every township, city, town, and incorporated village" to pass prohibitory bylaws.[43] These changes were driven by the Dominion Alliance, members of which had advocated raising the drinking age, removing liquor from inland waterways, and allowing local option in smaller geographic divisions than counties and cities. The failure of the Scott Act in Ontario might have suggested that county- or city-wide prohibition was not viable, but the persistence of the Dunkin Act in municipalities across the province gave some confidence that achieving local option at the town, village, or township level might be a way of slowly spreading the prohibitory drought across the province.

This expansion of local option began a legal chain reaction that ended in expanded rights for the province in the area of prohibition. The preamble to section 18 of the bill justified the change because of the fact that similar provisions had been part of the Municipal Act at the time of Confederation and were included in the Tavern and Shop License Act of 1869 but removed "in subsequent consolidations of the Municipal Act and the Liquor License Act."[44] This preamble was important for the constitutional battle that the Mowat government anticipated. In deciding jurisdictional issues, both the Supreme Court and the Judicial Committee of the Privy Council often took into consideration pre-Confederation jurisdictional rights and authorities.[45] Since the British North America Act did not specifically describe the powers of municipalities – leaving it to the provinces to assign powers as they saw fit – the preamble argued for the authority of the province to give these powers back to municipalities because of pre-Confederation precedents.

The bill was also intended to shore up support for the Liberal government in advance of an election to be held the next year. The advocates of the New Party, a small breakaway temperance-oriented provincial party, goaded Mowat's Grits for not being sufficiently supportive of the temperance cause. Up to this point, many temperance supporters had seen the Liberals as the only one of the two major parties amenable to strong temperance measures, notwithstanding the numerous temperance advocates who were avowed Tories.[46] In the face of New Party criticisms that Mowat was too friendly with liquor interests, the *Globe* repeated the assurances of *The Good Templar* that the Mowat government had been able to place the liquor traffic under tight control, a point that "should never be forgotten by enemies of the saloon."[47] Yet still it wondered why some temperance men continued to campaign for the Tories. When Conservative leader William Meredith repeated the claim that Mowat's liquor laws put the government further into the pockets of the liquor traffic, the *Globe* editorialized about the various "concessions to the liquor traffic" that the government had just made. It concluded, facetiously, that "the public will be surprised to learn that The Good Templar and The Citizen are organs of the liquor traffic" since the amendments "have been praised by The Good Templar, The Canada Citizen and other Temperance journals."[48] The local option clauses were bold attempts to give back to the municipalities the power to determine whether liquor would be sold within their borders, and numerous municipalities passed such legislation within a few months of the enactment of the provincial bill.

According to Mowat's biographer, Margaret Evans, the 1891 election was the first in which the liquor question was a major issue, and Mowat's victory came with increased pressure from prohibitionists to make their dream his reality.[49] Initially, Mowat balked, reasserting his claim that the province's authority to enact such legislation remained uncertain. This uncertainty was reiterated in April 1891 when Chief Justice Thomas Galt quashed several municipal local option bylaws passed under the authority of the 1890 amendment.[50] Almost immediately after this judgment, on 28 April, the government introduced a bill to clarify some of the problematic sections of the 1890 legislation, including section 18, the municipal local option measure. Clearly referring to Galt's decision, the bill recognized that "doubts have arisen as to the power of this legislature to enact the provisions of the said section 18," and the government would submit a question about its constitutionality to the Court of Appeal.[51] That court heard the case on 28 May and rendered its decision in September. The court determined that it was within the authority of the province to empower municipalities to pass prohibitory bylaws. The main limit that it placed on local option was that municipalities could not decide on their own what volume of liquor could be prohibited. That had to remain the authority of the province.[52] The *Globe* celebrated that Mowat was "once more sustained in the courts."[53]

Although a victory for temperance, the expansion of local option was of limited value to prohibitionists who were building alliances across the country and saw the liquor problem as a national, indeed a global, scourge. They continued to dial up the pressure on the provincial and dominion governments. Near the beginning of the 1893 session and after dozens of petitions from temperance organizations across the province were presented to the legislature, Toronto North Conservative MLA George F. Marter introduced a private member's bill to extend local option provisions to the entire province, in effect creating province-wide prohibition.[54] The bill led to extended discussion among prohibitionists about how best to proceed and revealed significant cracks, mostly along party lines, in an organization that labelled itself an "alliance." It also suggested to critics a certain duplicity in the activities of the ruling party, which claimed to hold temperance sentiments but did not support a Tory temperance measure. Although Marter's bill had broad support from the temperance movement, some argued that prohibition on only the sale of liquor would undermine the push for prohibition of its manufacture and importation; many prohibitionists saw "total suppression" of the traffic as their ultimate goal. On 10 April 1893, at a meeting with members of the legislature, these divergent opinions on strategies, normally discussed behind closed doors, became public. The disagreements among prohibitionists, aired in front of the press, created what the *Daily Mail* labelled in a cheeky understatement "a warm gathering." It in fact became quite heated.[55]

The meeting had been called by the Dominion Alliance ostensibly to discuss the idea of urging a prohibition plebiscite in Ontario. The main defender of a plebiscite was Frank Spence, the secretary of the alliance and a powerful voice in national temperance debates. Spence was also a known supporter of the Mowat government. He noted that Macdonald's decision to strike the Royal Commission on the Liquor Traffic was an example of how demands for prohibition at the federal level were repeatedly "sidetracked by motions of various kinds" and that the commission was simply an "evasion" by the federal Conservatives. Spence criticized those who supported a measure for provincial prohibition, such as the bill proposed by Marter, arguing that it was not total prohibition since it applied only to retail sales (constitutionally appropriate for a provincial law). He insisted that a strong showing in a prohibition plebiscite could be leveraged to convince the dominion government that prohibition of the manufacture and importation of liquor was widely supported.[56] Finally, Spence appealed upon a strategic basis, noting that the riding-by-riding results of a prohibition plebiscite would "also enable them to see just where the liquor traffic was firmly rooted, and where to go in and work."[57]

Spence's speech resulted in a flurry of responses. Those who supported Marter's bill argued that since a prohibition on retail sales was constitutionally the most that a provincial government could achieve, it was time to get it done. They also noted that a plebiscite would delay productive measures to curtail the traffic. Many also chafed against Spence's claim to speak for all prohibitionists. As W.W. Buchanan from Hamilton, a well-respected Grit, member of the Royal Templars, and editor of *The Templar*, explained, "it was not to be understood that the sentiment of the temperance societies of the province was in favour of taking a plebiscite."[58] He also pointed out that, at a meeting of the Dominion Alliance, Spence had called a motion for a plebiscite "stupid," although Spence repudiated this claim.[59] Supporters of the plebiscite were no more diplomatic than Buchanan. As the Conservative Toronto *Empire* characterized it, Spence had set the stage for contentious assertions by "referring somewhat contemptuously to a motion adopted by the grand council of the Good Templars asking for the Local Government ... to grant prohibition."[60] Malcolm Gibbs, a man claiming to represent the WCTU, challenged the utility of a provincial law that prohibited only the retail sale of liquor and argued that "a plebiscite would demonstrate to the weak-kneed and faint-hearted the strength of the cause" and show the government that the province was ready.[61] At the same time, the disagreements, although heated, were not evidence of a complete schism within the movement. Many speakers supported both Marter's bill and the idea of a plebiscite. Noting that he favoured "any measure which looked for the restriction of the liquor traffic," John McKendry of Picton argued that his support for Marter's bill "did not prevent him [from] favouring the taking of a plebiscite afterwards," an assertion that received a hearty "hear hear."[62] While the meeting debated a motion proposed by Rev. J.W. Bell of Hamilton to "heartily endorse" Marter's bill, Spence moved that the group appoint a member from each side of the legislature to press for a plebiscite, recommending Marter for the Tories and E.J. Davis for the Liberals. Marter was reluctant, but he said that if his bill were to pass, he would be happy to support a plebiscite.[63] The committee passed both motions and left the partisan press to debate how much support each measure had received.[64]

By supporting both strategies, the temperance leaders appeared to be divided and confused about the best way forward. Reports of the meeting of 10 April 1893 did not help matters, and – when a notice appeared in the papers announcing a meeting at Toronto's Richmond Hall to support Marter's bill and urge the premier to allow it to pass – Dominion Alliance leaders quickly clarified that they had not called this meeting.[65] The meeting was the initiative of the Royal Templars of Temperance. Although the circular announcing it claimed the support of the Good Templars, Spence (a member of that organization) denied this connection.[66] Two days later J.B. Brooks, a leader of the Sons of Temperance, added to the evidence of dissention in the ranks by contesting publicly that his organization also had not called for such a meeting.[67] Although key leaders of the temperance movement thus distanced themselves from the meeting, Spence and alliance president Dr. J.J. Maclaren participated in the Richmond Hall gathering, facing derision from a hostile crowd that supported Marter's bill and was unreceptive to any discussion of a plebiscite. Rev. William Kettlewell kicked off the meeting by impugning the motives of the Dominion Alliance, suggesting that its strategy was a partisan attempt to dismiss Marter in favour of a plebiscite that would buy time for the Grits. Likely knowing that he faced a tough crowd, Spence reined in his derision of Marter's bill but presented an argument that partial prohibition could damage both the province and the cause. He explained that if the bill passed, then the licensing law would be repealed; however, if Marter's bill was then struck down by the courts, then there would be no effective check whatsoever on liquor. Spence reminded the crowd that something similar had happened in Prince Edward Island, where "the Scott Act was carried ... and the Local Legislature repealed the license law. When the Scott Act was repealed in that province, there was no local law to take its place, and liquor was sold everywhere."[68] The same, he warned, could happen in Ontario.

After considerable discussion, the meeting was suspended to allow a deputation to meet with the premier. Mowat was diplomatic but blunt, explaining that he would not support Marter's bill because

> it would be worse than useless to pass a law that could not be enforced. He referred to the passing of the Scott Act in Woodstock [in his own riding], and said that after it was passed there was no denying the fact that the temperance cause was worse off than ever. (Cries of "No, no"). [Mowat said:] That is my deliberate opinion, arrived at by a consideration of all the facts that came before me. If there is any doubt about the validity of any law it is hopeless to try to enforce it ... Everyone would like to see Mr. Marter's bill pass if they were sure of its validity.

Mowat finished his address by opening a small window of hope to the dedicated prohibitionists: "If we have the power to pass a prohibition law I am prepared to support it. I have not spoken things you would like to hear, but I have spoken the truth."[69] Back at Richmond Hall, the assembled prohibitionists were generally unswayed by the premier's promises. Spence asked for a resolution that was supportive of the premier and encouraged the Drys to elect dedicated prohibitionists to the legislature. Rev. W.J. McKay of Woodstock proposed a motion to support Marter's bill. McKay's motion passed; Spence's motion did not.[70] It appeared, from the results of this meeting at least, that the temperance forces were becoming weary of Mowat's vague promises and defence of what seemed to be an increasingly unpopular status quo on the liquor question.

The agitation around Marter's prohibition bill exposed Mowat to persistent criticism about his claims of support for temperance. Although the premier, now twenty years into his mandate and himself a non-drinker, professed temperance sentiment, many commentators observed that his words needed to be supported by his actions. Compared with his vehement defence of provincial rights in areas such as boundary disputes, insurance regulations, and liquor licensing, his reluctance to move forward on prohibition seemed to be out of character. At the 10 April meeting, Rev. Kettlewell had suggested that all that was needed to get a clear expression of the will of the people was "a convention of temperance societies ... held in Toronto during the sitting of the Legislature."[71]

At the Richmond Hall meeting, J.C. Miller announced that "he was a reformer ... but that if Sir Oliver Mowat would not support the Marter bill he would change his politics."[72] At a meeting two days later, when Toronto Liberal MLA Joseph Tait reiterated the concern that there was no point in passing a prohibition law if it was not enforceable, someone in the crowd shouted, "[W]hat are the legislators for if they cannot make laws and enforce them?" That question received a hearty "hear hear."[73]

The opposition newspapers picked up on and embellished this sentiment. Not surprisingly, the accounts of these meetings were significantly different in the various papers, with the *Empire* and the *Daily Mail* seemingly more interested in giving fuller accounts of how the temperance movement (and its support for Mowat) seemed to be falling apart and the *Globe* reporting more selectively, presenting the disagreement more as a collegial debate than a death knell for temperance or the Mowat government. Calling the premier's temperance sentiment into question, the *Daily Mail* reminded its readers that the premier "is a great constitutional authority ... who in the past has claimed for the province all possible rights which are pleasant to exercise." In a searing understatement, it labelled "rather unfortunate" Mowat's "doubts on the prohibition question" and his unwillingness to "seize upon the power to prohibit in the interest of local [provincial] autonomy not less than public morality."[74] When the bill faced second reading, the *Empire* noted that the temperance mantle with which the premier had wrapped himself was illusory: "For twenty years Sir Oliver has fooled the temperance sentiment of this province, [and] now he has deserted it while still claiming to be its friend." It reminded readers that the Liberals had never really supported prohibition and that earlier proposals had seen a response that was almost the same: a plea that the constitutional authority was uncertain and a promise to test it through a case in the courts. "Sixteen long years have elapsed ... and Sir Oliver once more scrambles behind this flimsy pretext. Have the temperance people of the province had enough of this? Nay have the honest men of the province had sufficient of this quibbling, this double dealing, this hypocritical shuffling?"[75]

True to his word, Mowat ensured that the prohibition bill did not pass and offered a plebiscite instead. During second reading of Marter's bill, Mowat's minister of education and prominent Dry George Ross proposed an amendment to give the bill the six-month hoist. His amendment contended that it would be premature to introduce prohibitory legislation before knowing for certain whether it was intra vires the legislature, but at the same time it bound the government to pursue prohibition if the courts determined that it was within the provincial government's purview.[76] Most notably, the amendment asserted that in the meantime the government would hold a plebiscite on the question of prohibition.[77] The day after his amendment passed, Ross introduced An Act to Enable the Electors of the Province to Pronounce upon the Desirability of Prohibiting the Importation, Manufacture, and Sale as a Beverage of Intoxicating Liquors. The *Empire* contended that such a complicated bill, already printed for distribution, could not possibly have been drafted in the twenty-four hours after Ross's amendment killed Marter's bill. It sneered at the attempt to suggest "the spontaneity of the government's amendments to the prohibition bill, and conversion in favor of a plebiscite," since "it took two weeks at least to draw up that bill," which was ten pages long. It also argued that the language of the plebiscite was a further indication of duplicity. The question on which electors would vote was "are you in favor of the immediate prohibition by law of the manufacture, importation, and sale of intoxicating liquors for beverage purposes?" Noting that importation and manufacture were not within the ambit of the provincial government, the *Empire* concluded that the wording was intended "to shift responsibility from the shoulders of Messrs Mowat and Ross to those of the authorities at Ottawa."[78] The *Daily Mail* was similarly dismissive, noting that Ross's measure made meaningless promises and equating it with the motion passed in Parliament that committed it to legislate prohibition "when the country is ripe for it."[79]

Despite the divisions among the temperance forces on the best way to move forward, when the plebiscite was held, they united in their support. To do otherwise would have been a disaster for the cause since a poor showing at this plebiscite would have suggested that temperance sentiment was not as robust as supposed. There were several factors in the temperance movement's favour. First, the plebiscite was held on 1 January 1894, coinciding with municipal elections, so there would be a good showing at the polls. Second, the same voters in municipal elections were to be enfranchised for the plebiscite, and consequently women who held property were able to vote. In a move that might be seen as mitigating the effect of the women's vote, the province colour-coded the ballots based upon the sex of the elector. Also, the question was non-binding, so some argued that people could vote according to conscience without being worried that doing so would have immediate effects. The *Ottawa Journal*, which generally did not support prohibition, made this argument, noting that the plebiscite had "no legal effect ... [and was] simply an expression of opinion" and suggesting that when it came time to contemplate actual prohibition legislation, issues such as compensation of the liquor industry for lost revenue would need to be discussed, and the real impacts of prohibition would need to be understood.[80]

Debates about the plebiscite continued to engage in the often-contradictory nature of the liberal state with respect to liquor. What was the role of the government in constraining an industry that might negatively affect individuals? Which was worse: risking damage to individuals (and some argued the strength of the nation) by permitting the liquor industry to proliferate or risking damage to the economy and the livelihoods of thousands of people by prohibiting liquor entirely? Both ideals were supported and challenged. At the same time, the very nature of the type of liberal government that operated in Canada was debated since a plebiscite seemed to many to be contrary to the representative democracy of the British parliamentary system. Plebiscites were more appropriate to the republican liberalism of the United States. Under the British system, many argued, legislators are elected to do what is best for the people, so how could such a system exist when the government shirked its duty and put important decisions onto the shoulders of the people themselves? Some also noted that a Royal Commission was under way and would offer a much broader understanding of the effects of liquor production and consumption on the country, and the evidence would lead to a clearer legislative direction than a popular plebiscite. In contrast to a republican plebiscite, a parliamentary commission was decidedly part of the representative "modern" liberalism upon which Canada was supposedly founded.

Nevertheless, prohibitionists were elated at the outcome of the vote. Across the province, including in many cities, electors expressed a clear preference for prohibition. The *Globe*'s editorial on 2 January 1894 noted that what prohibitionists would find especially satisfying was that "the sentiment is so general, and that no considerable part of the Province gives a hostile majority."[81] The final majority in favour of prohibition was 81,769, with majorities polled in thirty-five of thirty-eight counties, all six northern districts, five of seven "separated towns," and eleven of the twelve cities (only Windsor voted against prohibition). It seemed to be a clear indication that Ontario was a prohibitionist province and that, were the will of the people to be followed, it would soon be a dry one.

There remained, however, that sticky question of constitutional jurisdiction. The amendment that killed Marter's bill also required the province to seek clarity on its authority to implement prohibition, so Mowat headed back to court. Instead of trying a test case in a lower court, he opted to submit the question directly to the Supreme Court, a process that required the support of the dominion government. Prime Minister Sir John Thompson agreed to the plan in October 1893. The case was heard in May 1894, and the decision was rendered in 1895. The justices ruled that province-wide prohibition was ultra vires the provincial government because, as the speaker of the legislature of Ontario had ruled two decades earlier, prohibition was a matter of trade and commerce, a dominion responsibility. Mowat appealed this decision to the Judicial Committee of the Privy Council. In a complicated ruling that upended much thinking on the constitutional divisions to that point, the Privy Council disagreed with the Supreme Court. It ruled that it was within the power of the provincial government to prohibit the retail sale of liquor but not its manufacture or importation. It considered retail sale to be an extension of licensing provisions and therefore rightly a matter that the province could delegate to municipalities. Importation and manufacture, however, were dominion responsibilities, and the provinces could not tamper with those activities.[82] As John Saywell argues, the decision written by Lord William Watson "reconstructed sections 91 and 92 of the constitution ... strayed far from precedent and ignored previous judicial comment ... With something less than the precision of a scholar, Watson had written the text for symmetrical federalism." Saywell contends that this decision achieved what Mowat had been trying to do in various constitutional challenges since early in his tenure as premier: assert a more federalist interpretation on the Constitution that had been written by devoted centralists. This ruling gave provinces far more power than previous decisions had allowed and indeed went beyond what the original authors of the Constitution likely intended.[83]

***

By the middle of the 1890s, the liquor question had become a major irritant to both dominion and provincial governments. Tweaks to the Crooks Act, including a major concession to prohibitionists to restrict liquor sales in shops, did little to mollify an increasingly vocal minority, the temperance movement. The prohibition plebiscite of 1894 further spurred prohibitionists' agitation, allowing them to argue that the time was indeed ripe for the government to do something more significant to chase King Alcohol from the land. The Judicial Committee decision to uphold the provincial right to institute province-wide prohibition further amplified arguments to dry up the province. Yet, despite these changes, the liquor industry remained powerful and continued its lobbying efforts. It contradicted arguments that the liquor traffic threatened the liberty of the people and the integrity of the nation with assertions that unnecessary overreach by any government, regardless of its constitutional right to do so, would undermine the values upon which both the province and the nation had been founded. Freedom of self-determination, property rights, and equal treatment under the law meant, for them, that any attempt to kill the liquor industry would counteract these ideals, not to mention undermine the economy. Moreover, neither the provincial government nor the dominion government really had much appetite to put a stake into the heart of the saloon and saw the idea of prohibition as both economically and socially untenable. The conflict within the temperance camp, the slow changes and unclear promises, and especially the tendency to evade the issue through plebiscite meant that, by the middle of the 1890s, even though some Drys might have been optimistic that significant changes were afoot, those feet continued to drag.

9
Talking and Blocking National Prohibition, 1891–99

By the 1890s, many discussions about answers to the "liquor question" had become discussions about prohibition and how such an extreme measure of restriction might weaken the pillars on which rested, sometimes precariously, the liberal state. Two major events at the dominion level in that decade illustrate well the breadth and complexity of the relationship between the restriction of trade and the vision of a free nation. First, the extensive evidence gathered by the Royal Commission on the Liquor Traffic revealed how citizens from a range of backgrounds framed the issue of liquor – its regulation, sale, consumption, and possible restriction. Second, the campaign and results of the dominion prohibition plebiscite, held in September 1898, involved extensive discussion about the viability of prohibition and the nature of Canadian parliamentary government in handling such a complex issue. From debates about the very wording of the plebiscite question to the philosophical ponderings on the viability of prohibition itself, people presented varying, and often contradictory, notions of whether it is possible to restrict trade and limit individual freedoms to achieve some greater form of liberty while not undermining the principles of equality and justice. These debates, which raged in newspapers across Ontario, illustrate how liquor affected, for some people fundamentally, the integrity of the liberal state. Moreover, they show how the management of the liquor traffic often defied partisan allegiances and, conversely, how partisanism could weaken government efforts to address the problems that many perceived in the persistence of the liquor traffic.

The Royal Commission on the Liquor Traffic

Even though Prime Minister John A. Macdonald struck the commission as a way of deferring persistent calls for action on prohibition, and although he selected the commissioners to skew the results against prohibition, the commission engaged in an extensive examination of the liquor question across the country. Chaired by railway executive and Conservative supporter Sir Joseph Hickson, the commission included Ontario Judge Herbert S McDonald, Ontario MLA Edward F Clarke, former Conservative MP Georges Auguste Gigault, and Rev. Joseph McLeod of Fredericton, NB. Although guided by five main principles (see the end of Chapter 7), the commissioners were free to ask any question that they found germane to the topic. They did not follow a script; they wrote the play as they went along, integrating information that they gathered in one community into questions that they would ask in another. For example, when the commissioners learned that distillers in Brockville had seen their revenues increase while the Scott Act had been in effect in many communities in Ontario, subsequent hearings in other communities in the province usually included questions about whether local distillers or brewers had seen similar revenue increases. Normally, the answer affirmed that the Scott Act did not diminish revenues, which led to questions about how sales could continue in a dry community. When witnesses suggested that some town councils used the fines under the Scott Act as an ersatz licensing system, fining vendors until the fines roughly equalled the cost of a license and then leaving them alone, the commissioners thereafter asked questions in most communities about such questionable practices. (Most respondents said that this did not happen.) As a result, the Royal Commission followed several major lines of inquiry, each commissioner having his own area of interest. The proceedings interrogated in detail the rule of law and the role of lawmakers in the liberal state.

Since the commission was dedicated to investigating the potential prohibition of liquor, in Ontario the commissioners focused many of their efforts on examining whether the Crooks Act was more effective than prohibition in reducing the problems associated with drink. The Scott Act had been in place and rescinded in many of the communities that the commission visited, and the commissioners sought to understand its effects and why it failed. In Woodstock, for example, they asked James Hay, the town's mayor and a furniture manufacturer, about his experience with the Scott Act. Hay argued that it had been repealed because of "its unsatisfactory working, and the very poor results, from a temperance standpoint, that the law produced."[1] When asked how he compared the Scott Act with the Crooks Act, he said that, "without any question, I think the license law is much the better."[2] George Roach, the former mayor of Hamilton and a director of a bank, said that the license law was "the best system we can have."[3] George Inglis, the clerk of the county court in Owen Sound, testified that "a good license law properly enforced is far better than any prohibitory law that could be passed."[4] Toronto brewer William J. Thomas concurred, arguing that the license system raised the quality of all drinking establishments, noting that

> the License commissioners seem to be raising the character of the individual who holds the license; and where a man is liable to let his place run down, either by having excessive drinkers there or by keeping what they do not consider is a first-class house, they put him out and put in a man that is a fit and proper person to run it.[5]

Robert Reid, a customs officer in London, said that "the present license law has been a wonderfully beneficial thing for this town, and I am perfectly satisfied that every step made in connection with it has been a step in advance for both the moral and [the] intellectual welfare of the people, particularly the young men."[6] For these and other witnesses, prohibition was a much less satisfying measure than a licensing law, properly managed.

Other witnesses were not so supportive of licensing. In London, Reid's testimony was contrasted with the evidence of D.H. Williams, a former license inspector for East Middlesex and an avowed prohibitionist. Williams argued from his involvement with both the Scott Act and the Crooks Act that local option was easier to enforce "after we once got them broke down to it." He explained that in his experience, first as a commercial traveller and later as a license inspector, restricting liquor sales to a certain place at a certain time was ultimately more problematic than outright prohibition.[7] "Any man who has been a commercial traveller for five years on the road from here to Quebec ... knows that there are mighty few hotels that keep the Sunday law" prohibiting liquor sales.[8] Similarly, William Bowman, a London manufacturer, argued that with the licensing law, "matters could not be made worse, and I think prohibition is the coming law for our land and all civilized society."[9] Joseph Jamieson, a county judge in Guelph and a former Conservative MP who had persistently pushed Parliament to support prohibition, not surprisingly noted that "the beer traffic is creative of crime." He took issue with the general assumption that the failure of the Scott Act could be considered an example of the effectiveness of prohibition: "I do not think the Scott Act was even a fair test. Very few people favoured the Scott Act except as a partial measure ... I think the effect of a general law would be much more beneficial."[10]

Despite such cautions, most witnesses who had experienced licensing and local option tended to find the latter too deeply flawed, and the former a better system, at least partly because licensing was not such a harsh interference with individual liberties. In Brockville, former MLA and county clerk William Richardson argued that the Scott Act would have failed even if it had been better enforced because people who "otherwise were considered good citizens" simply continued to violate the law.[11] The lone temperance advocate on the commission, Rev. Joseph McLeod, asked Richardson if this was the result of what he interpreted to be a very illiberal characteristic of the license law, "which so controlled them that they must gratify the habits by violating the law." McLeod was implying that the license system encouraged drinking, building those habits that needed gratifying. Richardson did not see it that way, suggesting that "there were many men who felt that it [the Scott Act] was a little infringement upon their personal liberty, their personal rights." Rather than the license system creating a habit for drink, it may have created an understanding that access to liquor was a right: "Those things that they considered their rights may have been the outgrowth of the license system."[12] In Windsor, the commissioners asked Crown prosecutor Eudo Saunders, who had also served as police magistrate in Grenville County during the Scott Act, why erstwhile honest people were found to be unreliable in Scott Act cases. Saunders opined that people did not believe that they were under the same obligation to tell the truth because "they think prohibition an interference with their liberty, and they take greater latitude. They say we are prying into what they eat and drink, and that it should not be done, and in that way they excuse their conscience."[13] Mayor of London Emmanuel Essery concurred, noting that people tended to complain that the Scott Act was "interfering with personal liberty and not ... a proper law."[14] In Owen Sound, which had been under the Dunkin Act but not the Scott Act, Archdeacon Arthur Mulholland observed that the drunkenness during local option seemed to be of an unusual character. He claimed that he had never seen much drunkenness until the Dunkin Act was in place, noted that the drunks whom he saw under local option had been otherwise temperate men, and surmised that "there seemed to be a determination to show that they would not allow their liberty to be taken away by an Act of Parliament."[15] Such was the fundamental dilemma of a liberal state: the properly constituted government, elected by a majority vote, seemed to be empowered to constrain the liberties of its citizens. McLeod criticized Richardson for his concern about personal liberty, asking where the liberties of the individual ended and the rights of society began. When Richardson said that he favoured prohibition of liquor sales on Sundays, McLeod asked whether this was not also an interference with personal liberty. "If an interference with personal liberty is permissible in the public interest on one day, why not on other days, if it is in the public interest?"[16] (Richardson refused to engage in a philosophical debate, replying simply that he was just giving his own views.) McLeod was similarly critical of Archdale Wilson, a druggist in Hamilton who advocated higher license fees (called "high license") instead of prohibition. McLeod asked Wilson whether this did not simply make it difficult for poor men to get a drink, thereby "interfer[ing] with their rights to get it conveniently and cheaply." Wilson did not see any hypocrisy; he replied that he was in fact advocating precisely that, because he did not see whiskey as a necessity. He did not, however, favour laws that would increase the prices of beer and light wine.[17]

The issue of treating, which observers from dry and wet perspectives had identified as a major challenge in reducing drunkenness, also appeared in the Royal Commission testimony. Here the idea of the freedom to treat (in other words, the freedom to spend one's money as one wanted) was scrutinized as another freedom that legitimately could be constrained. McLeod used the example of treating to underscore the flimsiness of arguments that personal liberty should not be limited by prohibition, since practices acceptable to moderates could also be framed as limiting freedom. When Wilson, the Hamilton druggist who supported high license, noted that he advocated the abolition of treating, McLeod attempted to paint him as a hypocrite by suggesting that this was a further interference in personal liberty. Wilson agreed with McLeod's assessment but clarified that "inasmuch as that liberty is, to my mind, a very dangerous one, I would deprive the country of it."[18] Although he did not mention J.S. Mill, Wilson was alluding to the liberal philosopher's "harm principle," seeing treating as a form of liberty that by implication could cause harm to others. Judge McDonald posed a similar question to Rev. J.C. Farthing of Woodstock, an avowed total abstainer, who thought that treating customs were dangerous. Farthing, a minister of the Church of England, which tended to eschew organized prohibitionism, noted that the combination of temperance education and the reduction of licenses meant that "the social drinking customs of private houses have wonderfully improved." In keeping with his church's perspective, he maintained that this approach, rather than prohibition, was much more effective. Prohibition, he argued, "is taking away the Christian liberty of a man."[19] When McLeod attempted to link the duty of a Christian to follow the law, to the need for laws to restrict an individual's liberty for his or her own good, Farthing refused to be swayed:

[FARTHING] I do not see that it gives you any degree of liberty in the matter, because you take away from them their liberty at once. You make the use of liberty a one sided thing.

[MCLEOD] But they are unwilling to exercise their Christian liberty – if you like to talk of Christian liberty – in the interest of their weaker brethren. Would it be well in that case to have a law to force them to do it?

[FARTHING] I do not think so. I have not so read the Scriptures, if you put it on Scriptural ground.

[MCLEOD] The question I asked was whether laws against acknowledged evils have any effect in creating and strengthening public opinion against those evils?

[FARTHING] They no doubt have, if they are founded on a sound moral basis; but to found a law on the assumption that it is a sin for a man to drink a glass of wine, would be, to my mind, of very doubtful wisdom of the question of prohibition.[20]

The complexity of the idea of freedom was repeatedly discussed, with the limit to freedom, the role of the government in restricting freedom, and the justice of prohibition limiting such freedoms reappearing in various aspects of the liquor issue.

The commission engaged in an extensive examination of how prohibition was incongruous with the ideal of the liberal state when it examined Victoria College Professor Goldwyn Smith. Oxford educated and an internationally respected liberal philosopher, Smith presented a sophisticated approach to the moderationist views of many anti-prohibitionists.[21] In his testimony, we can see many of the key contrasts between the operation of the state and the value of individual liberty. He had been the president of the Liberal Temperance Union (LTU), an organization formed in response to the Scott Act to offer a moderationist alternative to prohibition. The LTU preferred "a good license system, and a discrimination in favour of the lighter drinks against ardent spirits, which appeared to be the main source of the evil."[22] Smith was guarded in his testimony, refusing to enter into discussions in which he thought that he had little expertise, such as the effect of alcohol on the body, but he was willing to discuss in some detail the effect of immoderate laws on the body politic. Most notably, he was concerned about the impact of the law on the reasonable function of the legal system. Smith explained that his opposition to the Scott Act was "on the ground that it has a tyrannical provision in the arbitrary power which it gives over property, liberty, and reputation, to magistrates of an inferior order, thus warranting conviction on hearsay evidence." Moreover, the law could be "injurious to marital peace" because it "gave power to use husband and wife as witnesses against each other." But the main reason was simply that it contradicted key liberal values in that it "broke through the principles of justice and liberty, which are as stable as temperance itself."[23]

Smith had expressed his reservations about prohibition in a letter to the *Globe* (reprinted in a number of other newspapers), to which the commissioners referred and which Smith agreed to have appended to the commission's published evidence. In his letter, he argued that a prohibition law was both impractical and unenforceable because "you cannot make people believe that drinking or selling a glass of wine or beer is a crime." Moreover, without public concurrence, the law would be ineffectual. He referred to examples in several American states where the law did little to eliminate the types of crime associated with liquor. He concluded that a prohibition law was simply unnecessary in Canada, a point that he repeated to the commission: "If Canada were sinking into an abyss of drunkenness, as some temperance orators would lead us to believe, [the] resort to extreme measures might be necessary and right. Canada ... on the contrary is temperate, and has been growing more so for many years past."[24] He attributed this temperance to the positive work of churches, schools, voluntary associations, and medicine. To Smith, moral suasion and nurturing a sense of individual responsibility were the best ways to encourage the temperate use of liquor. This perspective was a key element of the liberal order, encouraging the state to remain distant from the affairs of the individual citizen.[25] Nevertheless, there was a limit to the individual rights of citizens. When Rev. McLeod asked Smith if the prohibition of ardent spirits would be "an interference with personal rights," Smith hedged his statement behind his deferral to medical science: "If medical science pronounces that the use of ardent spirits is really noxious, ... then I do not think that personal liberty would be interfered with by prohibiting it." Liberty was a matter of degrees, and protecting physical health seemed to trump the freedom to poison oneself.[26]

This perspective on the role of the state was taken up when discussing the responsibility of a government to protect the property rights of individuals, most notably in the issue of compensation. Judge McDonald asked Smith about whether he thought that, were prohibition to be enacted, businesses should be compensated for losses. Smith said that of course they should "because these men have entered this trade under the State's sanction and authority, they have been encouraged to invest their money in this plant, and I do not see how you can escape the necessity of remunerating or indemnifying them."[27] When McLeod asked Smith whether he thought that such remuneration meant that individuals had "vested rights in the saloon," Smith reiterated the value of justice and fairness with respect to the degree of criminality in the sale of liquor: "I think when you abolish a man's trade and turn him out without the means of a livelihood you must deal fairly and justly with him." Referring to the rhetoric of some temperance people who vilified saloon keepers "as if they were criminals and murderers," Smith called foul: "It seems to me that a man who has been licensed to ply his trade by the State is not a criminal or a murderer."[28] The state's responsibility to respectable, legal trades was decidedly different from its responsibility to capital criminals.

Smith's philosophical liberalism that placed property along with liberty and equality as central to the liberal state's mission could be challenged by stories of the criminality and even violence that numerous witnesses described taking place under prohibition. When discussing the operation of the Scott Act during its popularity in the middle of the 1880s, numerous witnesses to the commission outlined how manufacturers sought either to manipulate the law or to circumvent it completely in order to get their products to market. Since the commission had been struck to determine the potential effectiveness of prohibition, the commissioners actively questioned witnesses about how the Scott Act worked and why it seemed to lose favour. One factor that did reflect poorly upon the liquor system in general came in evidence about how brewers and distillers sought to get their products into dry communities.

Many witnesses to the Royal Commission argued that the Scott Act did not work simply because people still wanted to drink. They testified that the act seemed to change the culture of drinking in newly dry communities. Stinson Bradley, the police chief in Milton, argued that respectable (i.e., wealthier) people would either get their liquor "in a dive" or buy it wholesale and take it home.[29] Other people began carrying flasks. The police chief in Woodstock also observed that the act "revived the custom of carrying flasks." Others noted that the law shifted the location of liquor consumption. According to William Grey, justice of the peace for Woodstock, "when people came into town, instead of going to a hotel and getting a glass of beer, they would get a bottle of whisky and drink that, which would cause a great deal more intoxication than there was before."[30] Berlin Mayor Henry G. Lackner described how he travelled to Woodstock to do his own investigation of the workings of the Scott Act. He and some colleagues entered O'Neill House "and were asked if we would like to see how the Scott Act worked ... [W]e were asked to step through a sort of sub-way ... [T]here was a dance going on in the Town Hall, and I was amused to see them drinking in lager beer glasses."[31] Robert Philips, the license inspector for Brockville, called the Scott Act "an evil in some cases," explaining that "young boys imagined it was very cunning to get hold of a bottle of whisky, and we found it scattered about in places where we do not find it now, and we found men drinking whom we do not find drinking now."[32] Journalist John Motz explained that in Simcoe County under the Scott Act, "you could get liquor in any place." At a dinner that he attended, "they had something they called Scott Act punch, with the pudding. That pudding contained a great percentage of liquor of some kind, but they all partook of it, and in our company were six temperance men, prohibitionists, ... and the temperance men relished it just as well as the rest of us moderate drinkers."[33] In Owen Sound, where the Dunkin Act had been in force for several years, the president of the Board of Trade, James McLaughlin, noted that during local option, "every person seemed to take delight in using ardent spirits; they avoided drinking the lighter drinks. They seemed to take perfect delight in violating the law. Men who at other times would be ashamed to be seen the worse of liquor rather gloried, at that time, in being seen the worse of liquor."[34] Such a cultural shift seemed to be evidence to these witnesses that the Scott Act was having the opposite effect. Many argued that licensing was a far better way to deal with the liquor traffic.

Stories of increased drinking were not simply matters of opinion and perception; manufacturers had statistics to show that during the Scott Act period their sales had increased. People "who were determined to buy it" apparently bought more alcohol than before. The contention of Essex County distiller Franklin H. Walker that he had filled large orders for whiskey in Woodstock during the Scott Act period were not accompanied by evidence, but others were.[35] G.T. Labatt, a brewer in Prescott, saw an increase between 1886 and 1887 of 25,400 gallons; in 1888, production increased by 19,425 gallons; in 1889, it increased by 22,075 gallons. In 1890, it decreased for the first time, by 7,700 gallons, the first full year

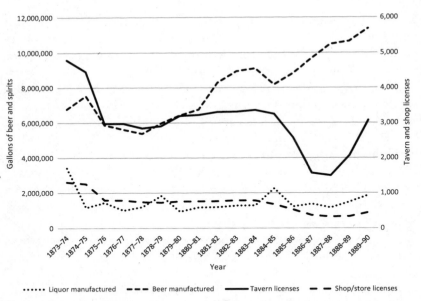

Figure 9.1 Licenses issued and liquor consumed throughout the Scott Act period

Sources: License numbers from Ontario, Legislative Assembly, "Report of the Provincial Treasurer on the Working of the Tavern and Shop Licenses Act," *Sessional Papers*, No. 14 (1891), 19; alcohol consumption numbers from Trade and Navigation Tables, in *Sessional Papers of the Parliament of Canada* (1867–1901).

Note: The data provided by the License Branch merged the number of regular tavern licenses with the far less numerous "beer and wine" licenses, and that combination is retained here. For this figure, I combined domestic manufacture with imports and subtracted exports.

during which the Scott Act was fully repealed throughout the province, and it decreased further by 41,250 gallons in 1891.[36] Toronto brewer Lawrence Cosgrave provided similar numbers, showing an annual increase in production after the low of 1886, to a high of 454,000 gallons in 1889, before dropping to 363,000 gallons.[37] W.L. Cummer showed a comparable increase, although not as steep, in the production of Hamilton's Grant-Lottridge Brewing Company.[38] George Sleeman provided output numbers to show that his production was flat for 1884 and 1885 but then began to increase steadily. In his history of Labatt's, Matthew Bellamy has described the challenges the Scott Act presented to manufacturers, and the strategies they adopted to ensure that their products could reach Scott Act counties. His account confirms what the brewers' data indicates, but what they may have been reluctant to admit to the commissioners: the

Scott Act caused a change in distribution tactics, not necessarily a decline in sales.[39] Distiller George Gooderham contended that the Scott Act "did not affect the business of Gooderham & Worts ... As much liquor as ever was being consumed, and one way or the other it was finding its way into the Scott Act counties."[40] He did not clarify whether his company had any role "one way or the other" getting liquor into dry counties. Figure 9.1 supports these assertions, illustrating that beer production increased throughout the Scott Act period and that spirits distillation seemed to be generally unaffected.

Infiltrating dry counties might have been simply the cost of doing business, and generally without significant legal ramifications, but the high stakes of the liquor business in an environment in which some people actively worked to shut it down could have more dire implications. The commissioners learned of several episodes of violence related to the enforcement of various liquor laws, and those stories confirmed suspicions that, rather than creating a more orderly and respectable outcome, prohibition could introduce even worse problems than liquor licensing. Numerous witnesses to the Royal Commission alluded to the dangers confronting inspectors, magistrates, and zealous temperance informers from vigilant enforcement of the laws, whether during local option under the Dunkin or Scott Act, in the course of campaigns to pass these laws, or even in the case of licensing under the Crooks Act. Peterborough physician Joseph Fife told the commissioners that members of the "Scott Act party" had their houses set on fire and red pepper thrown in their faces.[41] Fife claimed that a fire started in his own house was an attack by the liquor interests, although he admitted that he had no evidence.[42] Woodstock Mayor James Hay said that temperance people who were known to have informed on illegal liquor selling were attacked. He explained it as an understandable though inexcusable reaction: "Those people who were losing their property and who were compelled to make their living in an underhand way ... felt very bitter against the people who were trying to destroy their business of selling liquor."[43] Crown attorney Francis Ball mentioned "two or three serious riots" that occurred in Woodstock during the Scott Act period. He explained that the riots were reactions to "fellows coming in from a distance, going around and professing to get liquor at almost every tavern in town, and then laying information ... [I]t was a very serious unpleasantness."[44] He elaborated:

> There was a gang of fellows, I think, that came down from London on the first occasion, and they laid information and swore to the facts before

the Police Magistrate. They were driven up to the office of the lawyer who was acting for the temperance association at the time, and privately kept there. I went down in the afternoon and there was a crowd of two or three hundred people gathered along the street here. I observed the two tavern keepers who were complained of, and upon my remonstrating with them, I think they went up and insisted that the crowd should disperse, and they dispersed, and the thing ended in five minutes.[45]

When pressed to explain why this happened, Ball, like Hay, argued that it was entirely understandable: "The mass of the people of this town were very much opposed to the law from beginning to end, and there had been more or less of that going on, respectable people who had shop licenses and tavern licenses being fined on the evidence of these informers, evidence that, I confess myself, I would not believe."[46] The experience of these informers, whether they were actual detectives or just hired outsiders, demonstrated the challenges of building a case against violations of the law and the extremes to which both temperance supporters and opponents would go to push their agendas.

It was rare that violence could reach the level of being life threatening, with attempts to beat or intimidate witnesses being the key strategy, but the Royal Commission also heard shocking stories of violence in Ontario. In Owen Sound, for example, inspector Charles Pearce told of a riot in the community when it had been under the Dunkin Act in 1877. He explained that during the magistrate court sessions in which several liquor cases were being tried with evidence gathered by several detectives, "the liquor men hired a crew of Yankee sailors belonging to a schooner or barge that was lying in the bay to go to Chatsworth to mob the detectives who were attending court, and we afterwards made application to the proper authorities and had a company of militia called out and sent to Chatsworth for our protection." When asked if he had prosecuted the rioters, Pearce said that he had not been able to get evidence but elaborated that "I shot one of them." Pearce, who had been the license inspector in the community since 1876, took one detective back to his house, escorted by a hastily deputized militia. Pearce guarded the detective in his house for the next six weeks, explaining that the detective was valuable to the prosecution since he "got evidence in sixty cases."[47] It is uncertain whether Goldwyn Smith, who argued that legally licensed liquor interests were not criminals and murderers, would have been given pause by some of these stories or pointed to them as further examples of the corruption that prohibition could cause in the liberal state. Regardless, the final report of the commission included discussions of the preferability of a well-operated licensing system and the unsuitability of a prohibitory regime, which could provoke violence and illegality.

The commission's final report was a light read of 1,200 pages, providing a comprehensive digest of the information that the commissioners had gathered over three years. Perhaps fittingly, there were actually two reports: a majority view penned by Sir Joseph Hickson and signed by four of the five commissioners arguing against prohibition and a minority report written by Joseph McLeod arguing for its necessity. Both drew from ideas of a properly constituted liberal state to justify their perspectives. Hickson's report provided masses of data on the value of the liquor trade to the country's economy, the apparent ineffectiveness of prohibitory measures elsewhere, and the converse effect of increases in problematic drinking and law breaking under prohibition. McLeod's report was shorter and zeroed in on the problems caused by liquor as reiterated in the evidence presented to the commission. His conclusion was that, notwithstanding any initial negative economic impact, prohibition would elevate the country. The commission had been formed to gather evidence on five points, and its divergent conclusions on the final two – to explore "the effect" that prohibition would have on the country and "any other information" – illustrate clearly the contrasting perceptions of the liquor traffic and how increasingly irreconcilable solutions to the "liquor question" had become.

Hickson's report admitted the stark differences between how Wets and Drys viewed the potential impacts of prohibition on the country. Drys, he noted, saw "material benefits ... [T]he customs of the people have improved, the condition of the community [has] been greatly advanced, the moral tone raised and marked social advancement made." Wets, in contrast, saw prohibition as leading to "the development of other evils" mostly because the liquor traffic was not suppressed but simply driven into "corners, back alleys, and other hiding places." The opponents of prohibition noted further problems in the state apparatus in that prohibition "produces perjury and hypocricy [sic] amongst the people, corruption among officials, [and] tends to increase drunkenness in homes and the sale of adulterated and poisonous liquor."[48] Moreover, Hickson contradicted the argument that prohibition had a positive educational effect on people even when it did not work to suppress liquor sales. His evidence suggested that the inverse was more accurate: in places where there was higher education and "accompanying improved civilization," there was less drinking and drunkenness. Furthermore, he criticized prohibitionists who could give no evidence of any place where total prohibition had seemed to work.[49] Hickson concluded that "progress towards the suppression of intemperance, the curtailment of offences against the laws, and the suppression of vice generally ... has been greater and more solidly satisfactory in Canada than it has been in any of the neighbouring states." He quoted Goldwyn Smith's condemnation of coercive temperance, noting that "temperance implies self-restraint and self-restraint ends where coercion begins," and Professor W. Clarke of Trinity College, who said that prohibition was "quite inconsistent with the divine government of the world ... God does not make us good and strong by locking up all the cupboards ... which may contain anything hurtful." Both of these assertions alluded to the need for a free individual to make choices without constraint in order to strengthen her or his character.[50] Prohibition would not allow that growth.

Hickson anticipated and, in many ways, undermined the assertions that McLeod made in his minority report. McLeod argued that prohibition would be educational, but education would not be effective without bringing the law "into harmony with right principles." The law had to parallel the moral good.[51] He argued that it was impossible to conclude anything other than that "the effect of prohibition on the social condition of the people would be good" as long as it was well enforced and that the evidence heard by the commission "unmistakeably demonstrates that the liquor traffic is invariably productive of terrible evils."[52] In providing "all other information" on prohibition, McLeod stated that there was no question that "the liquor traffic is a public enemy" and should compel a government to act against it. A government dedicated to "the peace, safety and prosperity of the people" must be bound to "the protection of the possessions, rights, industries and virtue of the people from the lawless and mischievous."[53] He concluded by restating the common temperance argument based upon his reading of the evidence: "The effect of the liquor traffic has been ... seriously detrimental to all the moral, social and material interests of the nation," and the potential loss of revenue should not justify the "continuance of an admitted evil."[54] For McLeod, to protect the people and guarantee true liberty, the state needed to free itself from liquor.

The National Plebiscite

Sir John A. Macdonald did not live to see the outcome of his commission, passing away in June 1891 soon after winning a strong, though reduced, majority. He likely would have been satisfied with the commission's results, a firm and evidence-drenched repudiation of the idea of prohibition. Although it is problematic to engage in metahistorical supposition, we can imagine that – had Macdonald lived long enough to read the reports – he would have scoffed at McLeod's obviousness and obliviousness and nodded at the arguments that prohibition would be economically disastrous and not solve the problems that many argued were caused by the liquor traffic. Indeed, he might have even grunted his agreement with the notion that prohibition caused more problems than liquor did. Still, the commission, its two reports, and five volumes of evidence seemed ultimately meaningless. Its majority report did not give a final word on prohibition; it hardly dulled the increasingly loud roar of the Drys.

The general ineffectiveness of the commission might be explained partly by the rising popularity of the dominion Liberal Party, traditionally more receptive to temperance. After Macdonald's death, the Conservative government was led by a series of short-term prime ministers. The party was so conservative that it elected two more Sir Johns to lead it – Sir John Abbott and Sir John Thompson – before choosing someone else, although still of Scots descent, Mackenzie Bowell. Yet the Conservatives could not hold back the tide of support for the Liberals under Wilfrid Laurier, whose party made a pathway to prohibition part of its national platform.[55] During the election campaign of 1896, Laurier promised that a Liberal government "would take the opportunity of ascertaining by means of a plebiscite what are the views and wishes of the Canadian people in regard to that question."[56] When the Liberals came to power, they had to reckon with that promise. Yet, as Sir John Willison observed, leaders often used plebiscites to delay or avoid making a decision on prohibition. "Plebiscites or referendums," he wrote, "were refuges for Governments rather than concessions to prohibitionists."[57] In the implementation and outcome of dominion prohibition, we see the difficulty that the Liberals, purporting to hold progressive ideals but wedded to the ideas of the liberal state, had with the strengthening ability of prohibitionists to rally their supporters.

Soon after taking office, Laurier admitted that he would not be able to enact plebiscite legislation in the first session, pushing back the expected plebiscite to 1897. That year, however, he also delayed it. The bill that would enact plebiscite legislation left the decision of the date to the governor in council, allowing Laurier to choose a date that was most politically ideal. By the time the plebiscite was held, on 29 September 1898, Laurier had been in power for two years, during which time, in anticipation of the plebiscite, discussions about the place of liquor in the liberal state intensified. Commentators on both sides of the issue spilled considerable ink debating the merits of a plebiscite, the necessity and implications of prohibition, and whether there were alternatives to this seemingly drastic measure. In these discussions appeared a range of ideas on what the modern state should look like, how it should operate, and how citizens and governments should manage their affairs.

The simple promise of a plebiscite opened a range of complexities, especially related to the precise wording of the question on which electors would vote, what a vote in favour of prohibition would mean, and what type of majority would trigger national prohibition. At a meeting with the new prime minister in September 1896, a delegation of leading prohibitionists asked for a clear "yes" or "no" question and a commitment from Laurier that a vote in favour of prohibition would lead to a bill on it. The prime minister was reluctant to make such a promise. He noted that prohibition was a complicated issue, that "temperance" meant different things to different people, and that in some jurisdictions, notably in Quebec, the idea of a nationally imposed prohibition regime was anathema. That was to say not that Quebec was full of drunkards but rather that many municipalities in Quebec preferred the autonomy of enacting local option, and many had done precisely that.[58] Nevertheless, Drys were prepared to campaign, as they had at the provincial level, to convince their fellow citizens that total suppression of the liquor traffic was the best hope for the future of the country. The liquor interests also made clear statements about how they expected a plebiscite to be run. Meeting with Laurier in May 1897, a delegation representing both manufacturers and licensed victuallers demanded that support for prohibition be based upon a clear majority of electors (not just upon a majority of votes cast). Drawing upon the calculation in the Royal Commission report estimating the economic cost prohibition would have on the country, the liquor men argued that voters should be made aware that prohibition came with a significant price tag. Many estimated lost revenue to the country at about $8 million per year. They suggested that the prohibition plebiscite include a question asking voters if they were prepared to supplement the loss in revenue through direct taxation. The Wets also contended that those whose livelihoods would be severely affected by prohibition should be fairly compensated. Laurier, again offering platitudes and few concrete promises, seemed to be amenable to adding a question about making up lost revenue but was not ready to make any promise either on direct compensation or on the proper proportion of votes that would lead to prohibition.[59]

Debates about the nature of the plebiscite question itself drew from extensive discussions about how fair the vote would be. Since Laurier had explained that the plebiscite would provide a fair assessment of the will of the electorate, commentators from both wet and dry camps insisted on different notions of such fairness. For the Drys, their insistence on a simple "yes" or "no" vote was paired with apprehension about the politics behind Laurier's plebiscite promise. The reservations of Drys about the value of a plebiscite was understandable: Oliver Mowat's plebiscite earlier in the decade had shown strong support for prohibition but resulted in nothing but more broken promises. W.A. Mackay might have been thinking about that plebiscite when he argued in a letter to the *Globe* that "the country expects the Liberal government without any dilly-dallying ... to take a plebiscite on prohibition, and then in good faith to go forward and carry out the will of the people."[60]

Yet gauging the will of the people was more complicated than many prohibitionists were willing to admit. Laurier himself noted in his response to the liquor delegation of May 1897 that he was unsure whether a simple majority of votes cast would be enough to convince him that the country was ready for prohibition. As the Winnipeg magazine *The Commercial* observed when reflecting on his meeting with the Drys, "it would be [a] great mistake to try to enforce such a measure, unless it can be shown that public opinion is overwhelmingly in favor of prohibition."[61] But what would "overwhelmingly" mean? Walter Street, an anti-prohibitionist from Montreal, insisted to Laurier that prohibition could be determined only on a two-thirds majority "of actual voters" rather than a majority of votes.[62] Street's assertion was in keeping with debates on other prohibitionist measures, including the one held in Ontario earlier in the decade, as well as attempts to impose a higher percentage of the vote triggering local option under the Scott Act. But expecting two-thirds of all electors to support prohibition, as some had noted during Ontario's discussions on local option, was tantamount to killing prohibition since it was unlikely to have that many people support it. Still, even prohibitionists were not always convinced that a simple majority of votes cast would be sufficient support to trigger prohibition. In a meeting that the Dominion Alliance held with prohibitionist MPs in March 1897, its president, Dr. J.J. Maclaren, proclaimed that "prohibition cannot be enacted in Canada on even a large majority of votes cast in the plebiscite unless that majority embraces more than half of the electorate of Canada."[63] Not surprisingly, many of his prohibitionist colleagues disagreed with him outside the House, believing that a simple majority of votes cast was a sufficient indication of the will of the people. As a letter from the Uxbridge District of the Methodist Church explained to Laurier in March 1898, the decision to enact prohibition "should be estimated by a majority of those voting[;] if not the Government will I fear be blamed for shirking and taking this means of avoiding the logical result of a majority vote."[64] As we will see, the results of the plebiscite put even that simple equation into question.

Beyond the issue of what constituted an "overwhelming" majority was the issue of whose majority it would be. Several commentators were concerned that the vote could be skewed by people who supported one side or the other but otherwise were unfamiliar with or ignorant of the issues. For this reason, J.C. O'Neil insisted in the *Globe* that there was no reason that "any person but a property-owner should be entitled to vote." Prohibition, he asserted, "should not be decided by irresponsible voters." Although blatantly elitist, O'Neil's reasoning was about the problem of enforcing prohibition. Property owners would have more at stake, he reasoned, and thus would be more inclined to enforce the law: "If only property-owners are entitled to vote, and a good-sized majority are in favour of prohibition, then the Government know they have the right people at their back if they pass a prohibitory law."[65] William Houston of Toronto explained to Laurier that he was continuing to assess the opinions of constituents in that city. He explained that some people had favoured allowing women to vote on the plebiscite, but "most are willing to leave it to the ordinary parliamentary voters, as they must decide in the matter of revenue."[66] W.E. Norton, a Baptist minister who called himself "just as ardent a temperance man as a Liberal," saw the matter as one not only of property holding but also, more crucially, as one of ignorant versus enlightened voters:

> There is a wide difference between the *sentiment* that will prompt thousands of men to vote "yea" on a simple yea or nay plebiscite, and the conviction necessary to cause the same men to support their vote with their money and their action and energetic efforts to see the law enforced ... [T]he vast number of the people who have no conception of the magnitude of the position will vote "yes" and consider that they have thereby discharged their whole duty.[67]

If prohibition were to become law through the votes of ill-informed, unpropertied voters unaware of the implications of the law, both Norton and Houston feared, then the results would be catastrophic for the Liberal

Party. Neither seemed to be aware that during the Royal Commission it was the middle-class temperance adherents who were often blamed for not enforcing local option rather than the ignorant, unpropertied masses.

Fears that a result favouring prohibition could be politically disastrous for the Liberals if it were not followed by effective enforcement were not without some basis. The party's decision in 1893 to add a prohibition referendum to its platform might have seemed to be a strategically sound way of gaining votes, but it also created a politically tricky situation. Before he became prime minister, Laurier had explained the plebiscite pledge as an attempt to remove a vote on prohibition from other political activities. The Ontario plebiscite, for example, had been held in conjunction with the municipal elections of 1894, and several commentators had noted that this might have skewed the results. "We deem it wiser," Laurier asserted, "to separate it from all other considerations and test public feeling on the matter." He also vowed to honour the results of the plebiscite, noting that "I am by nature a democrat ... [T]he people must govern and ... their command must be obeyed."[68] In the months after taking office, he learned that such a noble sentiment could lead to complications. It was not that Laurier was naive but that the liquor question was so intractable that it could be used by each side in an attempt to bolster its political support. So his assertion that he wanted to remove the issue of prohibition from other political considerations, whether or not it was a genuine sentiment, soon became a victim of intense turn-of-the-century politics. It did not help that his government had a credibility problem since, although it held the majority of seats in the House, it had not received the majority of votes cast.[69] To some, his government was already illegitimate and undemocratic.

Consequently, many commentators, professing their devotion to the Liberal Party, cautioned Laurier against putting too much stake in the plebiscite's outcome. A correspondent to the Toronto *Globe*, using the pseudonym Presbyter, argued that "Mr. Laurier should know that the conservative 'temperance' agitators regard the plebiscite as a powerful instrument, which, in the absence of others, may be used to harass and if possible overthrow his government."[70] Edward Williams, identifying himself as a "Loco Engineer," told the prime minister that he was skeptical that the plebiscite could give a clear idea of the will of the people because Conservatives were planning to vote in favour of prohibition simply to "endanger the permanency of the present government." The solution proposed by Williams was to take the plebiscite by an open vote, making every elector declare his preference for or against prohibition.

"Their failure to go on record might cause the whole question to be removed from practical politics until public opinion was more matured on the question."[71] In August 1898, two months before the plebiscite was to be taken, Charles McLelland of East Huron made a dire prediction. He warned Laurier that people "say the [Manitoba] school bill defeated Sir Chas Tupper and Prohibition will defeat you."[72] The suspicion was that Tories would vote for prohibition and then force Laurier to renege on his promise to institute it. A few days before the plebiscite, the editor of the Conservative *London Free Press* urged readers not to make such a strategic vote. He explained that whereas Conservatives might see such a vote as a way to "embarrass" the Liberals, it would also allow the Liberals to present a prohibition bill but delay passing it until the next election. Laurier could thereby retain the support of the Drys without having to enact prohibition.[73] Again, the observations of Sir John Willison, by then editor of the *Globe*, were cogent expressions of twenty-twenty hindsight: "There was a desperate apprehension that under evasive plebiscites the popular majority for prohibition would be decisive enough to require actual legislation."[74] These concerns of the Liberals illustrated that sentiment.

Yet the Tories were not alone in plotting such political duplicity. The *Ottawa Journal*, independent in politics but anti-prohibition in sentiment, suggested that Liberals might be similarly strategic in their votes. Repeating a story from the *Hamilton Herald* in which a group of Tories out drinking were overheard planning to vote yes to the plebiscite for partisan reasons, the *Journal* suggested that "there is no doubt that thousands of Tory votes will be cast for prohibition" but also that "it is not less doubtful that thousands of Liberal votes, influenced by party considerations, will be cast against prohibition." Liberals knew that "a large majority for prohibition will place the government in a position from which it cannot retreat or advance without a great loss."[75] In December 1897, before the plebiscite bill had passed, the Toronto *Evening News* called foul when the *Globe*, a Liberal newspaper with skeptical views on prohibition, published a series of letters by Principal George Grant of Queen's College in Kingston. Grant was staunchly against prohibition, a view that placed him at odds with the Presbyterian Church, of which he was a lauded member. The *Evening News* characterized the *Globe*'s publication of Grant's repudiation of many of the key arguments of prohibitionists, not as an attempt to generate informed debate or sell more papers but as a way of turning Liberal readers against prohibition. "As another session approaches The Globe begin[s] a second effort to defeat the ends of the prohibitionists by publishing articles from the pen of Rev. Principal

Grant ..., in which this eminent Presbyterian politician renders valiant service to the Laurier government and against the prohibition cause."[76] Either the Conservative, anti-prohibitionist *London Free Press* did not catch the strategy, or it did not care. Two weeks before the plebiscite vote, it published all four of Grant's letters in one issue.[77] Never one to miss a business opportunity, brewer Eugene O'Keefe wrote to Wilfrid Laurier with concern about how Conservatives were encouraging him to vote in favour of prohibition "in order to defeat your government." Apparently concerned about such "wire pulling," O'Keefe explained that he wrote "with a view to upsetting the calculations of unscrupulous politicians ... [T]he only way I can see at present of accomplishing this end is to get your friends to vote the measure down."[78] Whether O'Keefe, generally a Conservative in politics, expected Laurier to believe that his goal was entirely for the benefit of the country, or whether he thought that he was offering Laurier a way out of a political bind, is difficult to say, but he did have much to lose if prohibition passed. Such machinations, steeped in strategic thinking about how best to undermine the reputation of the other side, were offset at times with some substantial considerations of what prohibition and indeed the plebiscite itself meant to the nature of the country.

Such concerns about the future of the party made pragmatic issues such as how to deal with the impact of prohibition on the revenue of the country much more significant. The matter of direct taxation was indeed potent. Following up on a meeting with the prime minister, J.H. Carson of the Dominion Alliance repudiated Laurier's suggestion that it would be prudent to include a question about direct taxation on the referendum, explaining that "the introduction of any method of taxation was entirely foreign to the question at issue in the plebiscite." He offered an alternative question – "are you prepared to meet any increased taxation that the enactment of a prohibitory law might involve" – that he called "the least objectionable form" of a revenue question, although he also admitted that he preferred no revenue question at all.[79] When they met with Laurier and Minister of Trade and Commerce Sir Richard Cartwright a week later, the liquor men had insisted that a question of direct taxation was fair to voters since they needed to know to what they were agreeing.[80] Laurier seemed amenable to the suggestion, leading to a brief flurry of reaction against the idea of a revenue question. Frank Spence roundly condemned the idea of any such question. In an extended letter to the *Globe,* he noted that the liquor traffic was already a tax collector of sorts but that the money spent by drinkers went nowhere. Offering baffling mathematics, he argued that "the people pay forty million dollars for which they receive seven million dollars' worth of services. The loss involved in the transaction is about thirty-three million dollars, for which the Government has no value, for which the tax payer has no value." Not willing to recognize that the businesses to which drinkers gave their money were legitimate tax- and license-paying enterprises, Spence used his new economic math to argue that the $7–$8 million lost under prohibition would be more than made up through other forms of commerce, a position that had been dismissed by the Royal Commission.[81] Privately, however, he confided to Laurier that should a revenue question be included, it should offer the choice of having "the lost revenue made up by customs duties or by direct revenue."[82]

Other Drys were also unwilling to compromise, at least publicly. P.L. Richardson, a secretary of the Montreal District of the Methodist Church, sent Laurier a resolution of his organization that called the question of direct taxation "a direct subversion of the distinct pledge given by the political party now in power," that pledge being to seek input on prohibition separate from all other considerations.[83] William Kettlewell, a past grand councillor of the Royal Templars of Temperance, explained to Laurier that such a question was simply unnecessary: "A readjustment of financial methods is involved in the main question of prohibition – an affirmative vote necessarily carries with it consent to share the burden or readjusting taxation." He added, nevertheless, that "methods of taxation are divisive issues" and that "it will be a great disappointment to the temperance men in the ranks of the Reform Party if the government handicaps the main issue by introducing the question of direct taxation."[84] When the Hamilton *Templar* complained about the direct taxation question, the *Ottawa Journal,* politically independent but lukewarm on prohibition, rushed to Laurier's defence:

> The violent tone of the Templar ... give[s] one the impression that the Templar is bound to have prohibition by hook or by crook, by fair means or foul – ready, if necessary, to swindle unthinking temperance people into it under the idea that they won't have to risk any consequences. Better to face the issue manfully ... That would sound much honester [sic] than howling intemperately at the premier because he has suggested that the people should face the issue squarely.[85]

Underlying many of the arguments about the issue of taxation lay a question about fairness, a manifestation of the liberal principle of equality and its associated concept of justice. The *Ottawa Journal*'s criticism of the *Templar* was based upon the assertion that voters should be provided with all of the information necessary to make an informed decision. Others concurred. Rev. J.S. Ross of Brantford argued from the principle of fairness when he insisted that the revenue question should not be included in the plebiscite. Prohibitionists, he explained, might simply refuse to take part in the plebiscite "on the ground that the Government placed such a handicap on prohibition as to ensure its defeat in any case. From a thousand and one pulpits and platforms such unfairness would be denounced, and if there is anything the average Britisher likes and demands it is 'fair play.'"[86] Ross argued that there were better ways to raise revenue that did not interfere so directly with individual lives, such as increasing duties on items such as sugar, tea, and coffee. A correspondent under the pseudonym Excise pointed out that Ross's suggestion was anything but fair. Increased duties would force grocers

> to explain why they had advanced their teas 13 cents to 15 cents per pound, and give 4 or 5 pounds less sugar for the dollar. They would maintain that it was an increased duty put on by the Government, but in no way to associate it with "prohibition" ... Does Mr. Ross esteem it as "fair play" to create conditions ... and leave others to assume the responsibility for them?

Excise saw things differently: "It appears to [this] writer that 'fair play' demand[s] that the public shall not vote ignorantly or at blind dictation, but that they shall know just what is involved in this question."[87]

Others took the matter of fairness further, suggesting that, whereas the liquor industry would be destroyed by prohibition and that associated businesses would be seriously crippled, perhaps it was fair that only those who voted in favour of prohibition should pay for its costs. Cymric, a pseudonymous correspondent from St. Catharines, suggested that,

> should this revolutionary measure obtain, it follows as a matter of justice, that its opponents whose privileges would be thus curtailed, should be exempt from any form of taxation to cover the reduction in revenue resulting from this policy, and that the deficiency should be provided for by a direct tax upon that portion of the electorate voting for the measure.

Indeed, Cymric suggested, such a provision would be a good test of the resolve of prohibitionists.[88] The *Ottawa Citizen*, a Tory newspaper clearly opposed to prohibition, agreed. When the issue came up in January 1898, it noted that "a man who votes for prohibition and at the same time declares by his cross [on the ballot] that he agrees to pay his share of the cost will respect a prohibitory law and will do what lies in his power to make others respect it." Nevertheless, the *Citizen* argued, "a single vote on Prohibition is the 'fairest' because it is what the government promised."[89] Sydney Fisher, the minister of agriculture and a temperance supporter, agreed, telling Laurier that it would be "a very serious blunder if we do not put the plain question in the Plebiscite bill." He reasoned that putting any additional question about revenue would not gain the party support from the liquor interests, nor would it likely affect the outcome of the plebiscite vote, but it would "be held up as a violation of our pledge to the temperance people."[90] From both sides, fairness, clarity, and an informed electorate were debatable points in the two years leading up to the plebiscite.

When the plebiscite bill finally appeared in April 1898, Laurier conceded that the question simply would be "are you in favour of the passage of an act prohibiting the importation, manufacture or sale of spirits, wine, ale, beer, cider, and all other alcoholic liquors for use as a beverage?" There would be no supplementary question about revenue. Even this wording faced criticism from temperance advocates. Spence told Laurier that he would prefer a question that did not mention specific types of alcoholic beverages.[91] W.E. Saunders, a pharmacist from London, Ontario, and a prominent temperance reformer in that city, explained to Laurier why people in his community were concerned about the mention of cider: "It has been freely stated to me here that the word 'cider' was added ... with the direct object of rendering the bill unpopular among the farmers; that this is so, I am inclined to doubt, but the effect stated we all anticipate."[92] For their part, the Sons of Temperance of New Brunswick lauded the inclusion of a straight yes-or-no question but were concerned about the layout of the ballot, fearing that it would cause confusion.[93] By this time, Laurier probably needed a drink.

Debates raged for the next few months. People repeated many arguments about the importance of prohibition to the economy and morality of the country, the value of a plebiscite as a tool in a British democracy, the validity of the actual question, and the need to compensate affected businesses should prohibition become law. Early in August 1898, Laurier announced that the plebiscite would be held on 29 September, suitably removed from any by-election or other contest that could pair it with partisan political activities. That deadline focused both sides, and meetings, letters, articles, pamphlets, and other forms of argument circulated through the end of the summer. The prohibitionists seemed to be highly motivated and active, many pouring themselves into the work, opening offices, holding meetings, printing pamphlets, and writing long and detailed letters in the popular press.

Yet, despite this activity, as the date loomed, several commentators suggested that there was not as much interest in the topic as Wets and Drys might have expected. The Toronto *Evening News* predicted that fewer votes would be cast than in the previous provincial plebiscite, reporting the "lukewarmness of erstwhile friends of the cause."[94] The newspaper suggested that this was because of Liberals' fears that a positive result in the plebiscite could endanger their party's government. Other observers did not see politics, just lack of interest. The *Toronto Star* columnist The Casual Observer suggested that the campaign was nearly invisible: "I would say that outside the circles of persons who live by the liquor business on the one hand, and of persons who are conscientiously devoted to the cause of prohibition on the other, there are few people who know just what the plebiscite is, or just what is the question which is to be put to them."[95] The weekly magazine *The Monetary Times, Trade Review and Insurance Chronicle* reported mixed emotions: "On the side of prohibition is enthusiasm; on the other side there is some zeal, much resentment on the part of really temperate people at the prospect of being deprived of malt liquor or wine, but a great deal of indifference." As the plebiscite neared, *The Monetary Times* expanded its analysis of why people did not seem to care: "Intemperance is no longer the devouring monster it once was ... Those who desire strong drink believe that under prohibition they would have no insuperable difficulty in obtaining it ... There is no party spirit in the contest to give it zest and energy." This apathy was of concern to the editor because "all who abstain from voting run the risk of investing a minority with the rights and powers of a majority. It is a majority of the electors who vote, not a majority of the whole electorate, who decide."[96] Regardless of the reason, on the day of polling, the *Toronto Star* reported its dismay at "a depressing lack of excitement."[97] The majority, however small, would rule.

Such predictions appear to have been justified: when the votes had been counted, fewer than half of the electorate had cast a ballot. Whereas the general election of 1896 had seen 835,600 votes cast, only 543,058 voters had shown up for the plebiscite.[98] The result was a slim majority in favour of prohibition, but that majority varied across the country (see Table 9.1). Quebec polled overwhelmingly against prohibition. In Ontario, no city favoured prohibition, a result in contrast to the surprising support for it registered in Ontario cities in 1894. The fact that all other provinces

Table 9.1 Results of the dominion prohibition plebiscite, 1898

Province	In favour	%	Opposed	%
British Columbia	5,731	55	4,756	45
Manitoba	12,419	81	2,978	19
Nova Scotia	34,646	87	5,402	13
New Brunswick	26,911	74	9,576	26
Ontario	154,499	57	115,275	43
Prince Edward Island	9,461	89	1,146	11
Quebec	28,582	19	122,614	81
District of Alberta	1,706	56	1,331	44
District of Assiniboia	3,919	77	1,166	23
District of Saskatchewan	611	65	327	35
Totals	**278,485**	**51**	**264,571**	**49**

Source: Canada, Parliament, "Report on the Prohibition Plebiscite Held on the 29th Day of September 1898 in the Dominion of Canada by Samuel E. St. O. Chapleau, Clerk of the Crown in Chancery for Canada," *Sessional Papers*, no. 20 (1899), 312.

had voted in favour of prohibition was also a surprise to many since few expected voters in British Columbia to support the measure.

The initial response from the temperance leadership was measured but generally not positive. An article entitled "Cannot Ask Prohibition" in the *Toronto Star* a day after the vote included interviews with several notable prohibitionists, many of whom agreed that the majority was "too small to justify a law." This perspective converged with Laurier's statement that only an overwhelming display of support for prohibition would convince the government to introduce prohibitory legislation, as well as with experience from the past few decades of local option that a significant majority of the population was necessary before prohibition could work.[99] The *Star* was a Liberal newspaper, but it seemed to be equivocal on prohibition, so the title of the article was belied by the interviews that it reproduced. Numerous prohibitionists refused to comment on the results, whereas others thought that a majority, even a mere 51 percent, was a satisfying expression of the will of the people. Rev. W.J. Barkwell suggested that the small majority did not represent the actual large majority that existed across the country, and Dr. J.J. Maclaren observed that the majority was larger than the one that had elected Laurier to power (which might have been a joke since his Liberals did not receive a majority of the votes cast in 1896). Still, other prohibitionist leaders were not convinced. Rev. William Patterson noted that the majority vote in Quebec and in cities would make prohibition, if it were enacted, difficult to enforce, and J.S. Robertson, the secretary of the Canadian Temperance League, did not think that prohibition would be justifiable with such a thin majority and a small turnout.[100]

Nevertheless, prohibitionists soon united behind the argument that a simple majority should carry the day. Those who had refused to comment to the *Star*'s reporter on 30 September had been waiting not for the results of the vote but for the Dominion Alliance to craft its response. This emerged five days after the results were announced at a hastily organized meeting of alliance leaders. They resolved "that one isolated province should not be allowed to control the destinies of six others and of four Territories [and that] we feel fully warranted ... in urging upon the Dominion Parliament the duty of enacting a measure entirely abolishing in The Dominion of Canada the manufacture, importation or sale of intoxicating liquors as a beverage."[101] A month later a large delegation of prohibitionists met with Laurier and several members of his cabinet to present their case. Laurier agreed to consider their arguments but also commented on some delegates' views that Quebec's overwhelming vote against prohibition should be dismissed. He argued that his home province was a temperate province and that roughly two-thirds of the municipalities there were already under local option. He also chided the delegates about their dismissal of Quebec. Laurier observed that, whereas the temperance forces had put a lot of effort into prohibition education and campaigns in English Canada, "I am not aware that there has been any general agitation in Quebec for prohibition; I am not aware that there has been a meeting held outside of Montreal or St Hyacinthe, nor am I aware that there has been a newspaper outside of Montreal advocating the cause."[102] If Quebec was not ready for prohibition, he argued, then at least in part it was because the prohibitionists had neglected it.

Laurier promised to give the Dominion Alliance a speedy decision, but nothing was forthcoming for another five months. The delay might have been caused partly by the political calculation to hold off any decision that could influence upcoming by-elections. James McMullen from Mount Forest advised Laurier that if the prime minister decided against prohibition, then temperance people "will go into those constituencies and defeat us if possible."[103] At the same time, Laurier received numerous letters from supporters making their cases for or against prohibition. Many of them insisted that if the government were to pass prohibition, it would be playing into the Tory plan to embarrass it.[104] Others offered alternative approaches, permitting Quebec to retain its licensing system but freeing up the other provinces to pass prohibition if they wished to do so, suggestions that seemed to require little more than an expansion of the Scott Act to permit provinces to enact local option.[105] Many other correspondents wrote in with accounts of their own experiences of the terrible effects of drunkenness, urging Laurier to pass prohibition and save the country from the ravages of liquor.[106]

On 9 March 1899, Laurier sent his response to the Dominion Alliance; it was not what the Drys wanted. Outlining his concerns about the low number of votes cast in favour of prohibition, he confirmed that he could not justify introducing such a measure at that time. He emphasized that only 23 percent of electors had voted for prohibition and that he could not rationalize the imposition of such a law on the other 77 percent. It was not a question of whether a majority of votes should decide the issue; rather, "in our judgment the expression of public opinion recorded at the polls in favour of prohibition did not represent such a proportion of the electorate as would justify ... a prohibitory measure."[107] The Drys were disappointed, to say the least, and in letters to the editor, editorials, and letters to the prime minister, they voiced their dismay. Yet, despite all of the rhetoric, campaigning, and passionate arguments that prohibition was the only way forward for the young country, the relatively low proportion of votes in favour of total suppression of the liquor traffic – as the *Evening News, Monetary Times,* and others had observed – was indeed too small to justify such a significant change. Although it is tempting to interpret Laurier's rejection of the plebiscite results as a base political calculation by a government that saw much of its support resting in Quebec, this perspective would overlook decades of discussion about how prohibition could be implemented and what degree of support would be required for it to be effective. In many of these discussions, the practical considerations of implementation ran alongside nuanced and passionate arguments about what a prohibition amendment would mean to the country and how it would affect the future. The next section reviews the rhetoric during and after the plebiscite to illustrate how the type of nation envisioned was decidedly a British state formed and informed by enlightened, educated, and appropriately modern citizens.

Prohibition, Plebiscites, and Prejudice

The future of the country, after all, was what was at stake, and, along with presenting ideas about the impacts of liquor production and consumption on the nation, debates during the plebiscite campaign reflected on what the whole affair meant to the country. Numerous discussions in the popular press referred to the nascent identity of the nation. Here we see the intermingling of sometimes contradictory ideas of the liberal state: progressive and traditional, free and fair, and a moral leader. Temperance advocates saw prohibition as a way of defining Canada among Western countries. Mrs. M.A. Colby from Winnipeg wrote to Laurier after reading his speech endorsing "Lady Aberdeen's memorial of the Queen's Jubilee." Colby had "a flash," she said, and thought "what a grand memorial for Canada to give us Prohibition. Nothing grander has ever gone before[, and] it would be worthy of the noble good Queen." Prohibition, she said, would "let Canada take the lead in the march of the world's progress in these last years of the century."[108] William Frissell of Toronto wrote to the *Globe* in response to Principal Grant's letters on prohibition, noting that it would be essential to the progress of the nation. Grant had said that prohibition would remove temptation and thus that it would be no gauge of morality because a moral person can resist temptation. Frissell turned this argument around, saying that if it were true that prohibition would remove temptation, "for the sake of the young men and women of Canada ... and for humanity's sake, let us have prohibition!"[109] As the date of the plebiscite approached, the *Globe* congratulated Canadians, noting that "it must be gratifying to all patriotic Canadians to see in the discussion ... no sign of party spirit ... but rather a desire to raise the question above the level of partisanship and deal with it solely from the standpoint of good citizenship."[110]

Yet such high-minded ideals were set against considerable invective characterizing all who opposed prohibition as somehow morally bankrupt. In a circular published in the *Toronto Star,* the Dominion Alliance argued that prohibition was fundamental to "the moral welfare of this young and promising country," for prohibition would fight "against the forces of avarice and appetite [that] ... are content to have us continue to suffer the sin and woe of intemperance, that not only bears heavily upon us to-day but mortgages the future of the young and innocent."[111] The Montreal weekly magazine the *Northern Messenger,* in urging readers to vote in favour of prohibition, lamented that the argument that the liquor traffic provided important revenue to the country remained a prominent defence of the Wets: "Canada is not so financially straitened that she must mortgage childhood, character and home for rum revenue. Nothing that pauperizes the home and dethrones the character can ever be of benefit."[112] On the evening of the plebiscite, Frank Spence (who well might have penned the Dominion Alliance circular) characterized the issue as having two sides: "the side that is seeking to uphold and strengthen the liquor traffic and the side that is seeking to uphold and strengthen the church, the law, the school, the home, and all that helps to make men nobler." The liquor traffic, he reminded readers, "is an evil," and no argument about how prohibition undermined individual liberty could contradict its evil influence.[113]

Spence's concern about liberty was a challenge to the often-used argument that prohibition interfered with personal liberty and that, in a British country, freedom and liberty were paramount. In response to the speech from the throne of 1897, in which Laurier's government promised to present a plebiscite bill for the first time, Hamilton Liberal MP Thomas Macpherson noted that the plebiscite was un-British because it was "a direct interference with the liberty of the subject."[114] C.E. Toye drew from the words of John Stuart Mill, noting that "any properly controlled Government cannot enact a law that interferes with the personal liberty of the citizen. Government must be kept at a minimum of power. Freedom must be the rule."[115] Walter Street of Montreal informed Laurier simply that the plebiscite was "an insult to ask us to vote on the matter affecting our freedom of person."[116] At the top of a list of ten reasons to vote against the plebiscite, the *London Free Press* noted that "it is an infringement on British Liberty."[117] In an editorial expanding on this argument, the *Free Press* noted that prohibition would fail because of that appeal to liberty: "The attempt to make everybody virtuous in the temperance sense by act of parliament, and severe restrictive laws, will fail as fail it should. The spirit of personal independence and freedom which is shared by Canadians in common with the British race generally will forbid the effective working of a prohibitory law if carried."[118]

Supporters of prohibition viewed liberty as equally important to their struggle and argued that the liquor traffic interfered with an individual's ability to experience true liberty. A correspondent to the *London Free Press* challenged writers whose opposition to prohibition was based upon an appeal to liberty by asking what kind of liberty they wanted: "Liberty to drink whiskey. This they claim is their right, only they are to do it in moderation." For this writer, that was the problem, since "prohibitionists ... know very well, as all sensible people do, that if moderate drinking cease[s], drunkenness will cease."[119] Spence challenged a simplistic notion of what liberty meant by suggesting that in a civilized country personal liberty was constrained by the rights of others:

> Under civilization liberty means freedom to do right. Freedom to do wrong must interfere with the rights of others and therefore destroy their

liberty ... If the liquor traffic is good it is an interference with legitimate liberty to suppress it. If the traffic is bad then true liberty demands its prohibition. Liberty for men to injure others is a condition that pertains to barbarism and savagery.[120]

Spence, it seems, had also studied his Mill, since Mill also placed the limit of an individual's freedom at the point where it results in injury to others.[121] Nevertheless, Mill saw some nuance between wide open sales and complete prohibition, which the prohibitionists refused to include in their form of liberalism.

Such binary arguments were fundamental to the temperance worldview. The opposite of liberty was slavery, and enslavement to liquor was a common trope in temperance rhetoric. In an editorial responding to Principal Grant's first letter, the *Globe* contradicted his assertion that prohibition was contrary to personal liberty, because "it is fair to point out the enormous gain in real liberty that would be effected by emancipation from a terrible form of slavery."[122] This was a similar position taken by Rev. Dr. D. McTavish at a meeting in Toronto a week before the plebiscite vote. Whenever he was asked to provide a scriptural basis for prohibition, he replied that, "as far as he could remember, Biblical teachings did not prohibit slavery, but in all enlightened Christian lands slavery was abolished. Who would say strong drink was not the most acute form of slavery?"[123] One person's liberty had to be constrained in order that it did not enslave others, as the *Northern Messenger* reminded readers:

> The foes of liberty are those who for greed or lust or ambition would enslave or oppress their fellow men. Heartless avarice, chafing under the restraints that true Liberty imposes upon it, often prates of "Liberty" as if the sacred word meant the unbridled tyranny of reckless selfishness ... [L]iberty of the citizen, of conscience, of religion, always and forever; but no liberty to do wrong, to make slaves, no liberty to poison liberty – no liberty for the liquor traffic![124]

The desire to ensure that all could experience this form of true liberty was thus at the heart of temperance arguments supporting a liberal state's restriction of the basest of individual liberties.

Yet this was a specific form of liberty, British liberty. It was liberty defended by the British Empire, which represented the type of civilization to which many commentators alluded, aspired, or hoped to defend. On both sides of the debate, an abstract form of "Britishness" was manifested as a core trope. The *Northern Messenger*'s article on liberty referred to it as being heroically defended: "To gain, retain, and enhance it, countless battles have been fought, blood has been poured out like water, lives have been freely given. The world's noblest and bravest and best have been its most ardent champions." It would not be lost on readers that those heroes were British or at least defenders of a British way of life. Yet this appeal to Britishness also worked against prohibition. Wakefield Hardgrave, the lawyer for the Licensed Victuallers Association in Toronto, wrote to defend Principal Grant's letters against a flurry of what he characterized as unconscionable attacks: "It is quite evident that the British spirit of fair play does not count for much with the advocates of prohibition, and so clerics and laymen and even women who join in the fray with particular unction, incontinently fly at one man – and he an old man, at that!"[125] James Haverson, a solicitor for members of the liquor industry, responded to critics of Grant, who had compared sobriety to freedom, by reminding them of the famous words of Britain's bishop of Peterborough. During the prohibition debates in Britain, the bishop had said that "it would be better that England should be free than that England should be compulsorily sober ... because with freedom we might in the end attain sobriety, but in the other alternative we should eventually lose both freedom and sobriety."[126] Even apart from the question of the value of prohibition, an appeal to Britishness resulted in a challenge to the very notion of a plebiscite. The *Toronto Star* columnist The Casual Observer noted that some would call the plebiscite "entirely foreign to the British scheme of government" since it was a foreign type of direct democracy rather than the (clearly) preferable form of British parliamentary democracy.[127]

This appeal to Britishness, as noble as it seemed to its Anglo-Canadian correspondents, was used against their French Canadian compatriots, whose ideas about prohibition were thought to be less advanced. When the plebiscite results began to be posted, and it became clear that only Quebec rejected prohibition, temperance advocates characterized French Canadians as less developed, indeed less British, than people in the rest of the country. Whereas nationalist Quebeckers might not blink at being considered less British than Anglo-Canadians, the critics equated Britishness with a higher form of civilization, so this was an interpretation of Quebeckers as less evolved members of the nation. The *Ottawa Journal* said that the plebiscite was "emasculated by but a single province," suggesting that somehow Quebeckers had diminished the manliness of the prohibition thrust. Gendered language was eclipsed by racialized notions of Quebeckers as backward, often using patronizing language to explain the dilemma of Quebec's perspective. May Thornley, the president of the Ontario WCTU, suggested that many residents of Quebec, being illiterate, were tricked into voting against prohibition. Generally, according to Thornley, ignorant Quebeckers were ripe for exploitation, exacerbated by their national character: "Adding this lack of intelligence to the mercurial disposition of the people, you have just the soil in which the demagogues and political trickster would flourish."[128] In other words, Quebec voters were not acting as free informed citizens because their low levels of education made them less capable of independent thought, and their "mercurial" character meant that they could be easily manipulated. Others were less prejudiced but just as concerned about the negative effects of Quebeckers' different natures on the fate of the country. Frank Spence lamented the loss using language that, although couched in patronizing sympathy, similarly characterized Quebec as less advanced:

> The progressive spirit and high moral aims of the Anglo-Saxon race are in advance of those of our fellow-citizens of continental origin. We must live side by side in unity, sustaining and aiding each other, sacrificing personal prejudices to amity and the broad, high patriotism that sinks individual preferences for the common good. There cannot, however, be any sacrifice of principle. No progressive Canadian community must be subjected to peril of property or character or life, because a minority lags behind in the march of progress.[129]

To Spence, Quebec's rejection of prohibition should not stop the rest of the country from adopting it. Such perspectives meant that Quebec could be a persistent hindrance to the ongoing "march" of prohibition. Rev. Dr. A. Carman explained in the *Globe* that if liquor interests "succeed in holding their heads above water, it is only as they are steadied on one arm by the mediaevalism and backward-bracing power of Quebec and by the whisky wards of rum-drenched cities on the other." Carman was more equivocal about Quebec's chances to improve itself. Despite the "mediaevalism" and "backward-bracing" tendency, "Quebec ... is not inaccessible to the approaches of freedom, nor forever doomed to moral and political immobility or retrogression." He recommended more education in Quebec to ensure that support for prohibition increased.[130]

The characterization of Quebec as backward played on both sides of the debate. When Laurier decided that the results of the vote did not justify prohibition, the staunchly Tory Toronto *Evening News* used the Quebec vote to criticize him as weak and corrupt. Although in the rest of Canada a majority of 107,000 had supported prohibition, "the Premier shelters himself behind the tremendous vote against prohibition that was cast in his own province by his own followers." The *Evening News,* suddenly a passionate prohibitionist, saw this as worse than just racial nationalism – it was an example of ruling based upon the weakest part of the country and therefore inherently undemocratic:

> Sir Wilfrid Laurier, in refusing the request of the prohibitionists, is not only arraying himself on the side of the minority, but is assuming that it is all right for the entire dominion to be governed by the most backward province in the dominion. It is only one more instance proving that the dominion of Canada is ruled by the descendants of the conquered Frenchmen who were unwisely conceded lingual and religious privileges at the time of the conquest that should never have been granted.[131]

Clearly adopting the strategy against which many concerned Liberals had warned Laurier, that Tories would use the prohibition result to "embarrass" the prime minister, the *Evening Star* employed Anglo-Saxon ethnic nationalism to question the prime minister's ability to govern the entire country.

In his response to such criticisms, and to the characterization of Quebec as a lesser partner in Confederation, Laurier countered with a clear statement of how he viewed his role as prime minister. When prohibitionists wrote to complain to him directly, he responded to most of them with an assertion that such was the nature of democracy. He told Rev. C.R. Morrow from Alma, Ontario, that

> in a free country we must be prepared to [accept] such difference of opinion. It would be vain to hope that in all questions, men will see their duty in the same light; but it is not vain to hope, I am sure, that in all such differences of opinion, there is on all sides, the same honesty of purpose and intention.[132]

Laurier reiterated this sense of the role of freedom in governing his decision in a response to the editor of the *Christian Guardian,* A.C. Courtice. Whereas Courtice opposed the decision, Laurier insisted that they were not so far apart since they shared core values: "We agree upon those broad principles, which construe what we understand by Liberalism, freedom of conscience, freedom of speech, to talk of nothing else."[133] Regarding criticisms that he was considering the opinions of French Canadians more than those of English Canadians, Laurier told J.R. Dougall, the editor of the Montreal *Witness,* the founder of the *Northern Advance,* and a devoted Dry, that the same kind of tyranny would result if he forced prohibition on Quebeckers:

> The object which I have had in view in my political career ... has been to unite the different elements of our population. That object you have yourself most ably and constantly seconded. Is it not to be feared that ... if a prohibitory measure were forced upon the French population before any attempts have been made to persuade them, before the ordinary means whereby public opinion is swayed, have been resorted to, is it not to be feared that such a course would be resented as dictatorial and likely to produce estrangement instead of union?[134]

As Laurier had explained to the Dominion Alliance soon after the vote, education should come before legislative change.

Contemplating the Future of Liquor

For the time, prohibition might have been thwarted, but even many of those who had opposed elimination of the traffic in liquor understood that an unfettered trade could cause problems. Many people offered alternatives to the absolute measure of prohibition, suggestions and observations that would be contemplated in more depth over the next decade. Some Ontario prohibitionists suggested that they needed a local option that applied to the province. Others were concerned that, just as during the Scott Act legal liquor from wet counties was brought into dry counties, keeping Quebec wet while other provinces were dry could create the same problem on a national level. One suggestion to deal with this was to institute state-run distribution (or even manufacture) of liquor, which would ensure that it was sent only where it was legal.[135] Others, during and after the plebiscite campaign, suggested a form of liquor distribution based upon the Gothenburg model, adapted as a dispensary system in South Carolina. Under the Gothenburg system, the state gave monopolies for liquor sales within specific jurisdictions to individual companies. These companies were expected to sell liquor based upon principles of sobriety and moderation rather than profit and drunkenness. Under South Carolina's dispensary system, the state managed the sale of liquor through regional stores to which a central dispensary would ship products. A correspondent to the *Globe* signing her name A Mother argued that such a system should expand well beyond liquor: "The government should have the control, with salaried men, who can have no selfish aim in selling for medicinal, mechanical, or sacramental uses, or for use in the arts. Also to sell opium, chloral and morphine. Coffee houses should take the place of the saloon."[136] In an article weirdly predictive of the situation that most provinces faced in the 1920s, the *Northwest Review,* a Catholic journal, also supported a Gothenburg-style system but argued that prohibition needed to come into place first: "We do not think it will prevail for very long, but it will sweep away the present system, and make it possible to introduce afterwards something after the manner of the Gothenburg system."[137] James Douglas from Dobbinton, Ontario, suggested to Laurier that, given how treacherous the political landscape had become with the thin majority in favour of prohibition, he might consider "a state dispensary system (in force in Sweden, South Carolina and some other places) coupled with a local option law."[138] Interest was growing in these alternatives, which would face more scrutiny in the new century.

Looking away from the broader regulatory system, others considered the practice of drinking itself, identifying the most troublesome aspects of drinking culture. James Spencer of Toronto suggested to Laurier that a better approach than prohibition would be to "make it a criminal offence for one person to purchase (to treat as it is termed) strong drink for another ... Put a stop to the treating system so common throughout our country. Then should a man be so unfortunate as to overestimate his capacity too frequently, have him placed under a physician. Instead of a jailor."[139] The *Globe* opined that a further step would be useful: "In the matter of treating, therefore, which is the commonest road to intoxication among those who are not habitual drunkards, half the battle is won by the removal of the saloon."[140] The *Evening Star* agreed; in an editorial a week before the plebiscite, it contended that eliminating "dives" would go a long way toward dealing with problematic drinking: "Let us have the open bar suppressed, and let us deal as we can by wise legislation and judicious law-enforcement."[141] John A. Cooper, editor of the *Canadian Magazine,* thought that prohibition would go too far and agreed that it was better to deal with the problems within the drinking spaces: "If [prohibitionists] would ask for the closing of saloons and barrooms they might succeed; and most of the evils of which they complain would be eradicated. It is the treating system which ruins the young man, and the weak adult. Do away with treating and these will be saved from temptation."[142] Eliminating treating and the proliferation of problematic drinking spaces, in the eyes of many observers, seemed to be a more reasonable approach than the complete eradication of the liquor traffic. This had been the plea for decades, and some noted that the system created under the auspices of Sir Oliver Mowat had done "much for true temperance in this great Province of Ontario."[143]

***

In the evidence and reports of the Royal Commission on the Liquor Traffic, and the extensive discussions on the dominion prohibition plebiscite, the role of the state in managing the affairs of the citizens and the viability of an extreme measure such as prohibition were given extensive airings. The fact that both the commission report and the plebiscite did not result in the restrictions that prohibitionists had wanted does not diminish their importance in the national and provincial discussions about liquor. Excessive interference in the liberty of the individual remained problematic, although the impact of the liquor industry on individual freedom was also an important consideration. Through both episodes of extensive national consultation, the balance between the role of the state in the life of the individual and the responsibility of the individual to the future of the state was thoroughly explored. Many considered a system of licensing to be both a reasonable constraint on the liberty of individuals and a valuable progressive measure to protect the freeborn individual from the predations of what seemed to many to be an unscrupulous industry. The types of liberalism manifest here were diverging, with the prohibitionist view being clearly collectivist in nature: the liberty of the individual had to be subsumed under the interests of the whole society. As Stuart Hall notes, this type of liberalism encouraged "much greater state intervention especially in the fields of welfare and redistributive justice."[144] In contrast, the Wets continued to articulate the classic liberal values of individual liberty and protection of property rights. Nevertheless, the result of the plebiscite, yet again showing a significant majority in favour of prohibition, provided further ammunition to Ontario's Drys and an ongoing dilemma for a government playing both sides of the court. As the century came to a close, the provincial government continued to wrestle with how to placate the seemingly implacable prohibitionists but not so constrain the liquor trade that it would lead to the sort of lawlessness that many had ascribed to the Scott Act. Ideas about innovations in liquor distribution joined the persistent political inertia of provincial policy makers.

10
Dodging Decisions at the End of the Liberals' Era, 1894–1905

By the end of the nineteenth century, prohibitionists were putting increased pressure on Ontario's government to legislate an end to the liquor traffic despite, or possibly because of, various governments' repeated rejection of the idea that a complete ban on liquor was a reasonable solution to the liquor question. The negative majority report from a Royal Commission created by a prime minister who was hardly a teetotaller might have been expected, but it was the rejection of prohibition by Liberal leaders (Mowat and Laurier) who had positioned themselves as friends of temperance that was a more profound disappointment. Still, the 1890s provided Drys reasons for optimism as the courts confirmed the authority of the province to institute some form of prohibition. When in 1894 Premier Oliver Mowat agreed to take Marter's prohibition bill to the Privy Council, he promised that, depending on the outcome of the case, he would give prohibitionists the most restrictive law that was constitutionally possible. The Privy Council decided in 1896 that a province could prohibit the sale but not the manufacture of liquor, as long as it did not interfere with trade beyond the province.[1] Yet, despite this ruling, Mowat did not follow through. He resigned in 1896 upon being appointed to the Senate by Prime Minister Wilfrid Laurier, serving briefly as Laurier's minister of justice before his selection as the lieutenant governor of Ontario in 1897. His departure left his promise about prohibition hanging over his administration. Through the 1890s, and well into the new century, both of Mowat's successors as Liberal premiers, Arthur Hardy and George Ross, continued his pattern of promising prohibition while strengthening the licensing system and increasing restrictions on liquor in the province, tactics that did little to satisfy the prohibitionists.

These political machinations took place despite the growing volume of the temperance voices. Membership in the temperance movement was broadening, with the political activities of the Dominion Alliance at all levels of government increasingly augmented by the expansive organization of members of the Woman's Christian Temperance Union. The WCTU's work harnessed the experience of women as mothers and caregivers in the home to enable them to take on a variety of educational, social, and political roles. Although the WCTU was often marginalized on the platforms of temperance meetings, its influence on younger generations might have been significant. Indeed, even outside the formal, evangelically led temperance movement, there seemed to be a general acceptance of the principles of temperance, if not outright prohibition and abstinence, in respectable society.[2] Faced with persistent pressure from prohibitionists on one side and from those who continued to maintain that prohibition was governmental overreach and unworkable on the other, Mowat's successors continued to negotiate an increasingly narrow middle path.

If prohibitionists were encouraged by Arthur Hardy's ascension to the premiership, they would soon be dismayed. Hardy's familiarity with the liquor issue was deep. He had been the provincial secretary in the early years of the Crooks Act, charged with administering the licensing legislation and overseeing the intensification of licensing restrictions before moving on to the post of commissioner of Crown lands in 1889. As the member for Brant South, Hardy represented a strongly prohibitionist riding. When he became the provincial secretary, Brant County was under the Dunkin Act, and Hardy used his position to send in detectives to enforce the law (in 1898, Brantford polled strong support for prohibition in the dominion plebiscite).[3] When Hardy took over as premier in July 1896, he insisted that his government would honour Mowat's prohibition promise.[4] Yet Hardy was not Mowat either in political savvy or in temperament. He had been notorious as an aggressive defender of the party, apparently referred to as "the party virago" by the *Daily Mail*, but he was also highly adept at manipulating the license act for partisan gains.[5] At the same time, some of the vigour with which he had pursued his early activities as provincial secretary had waned. Stricken with diabetes, Hardy recognized that his physical condition left him vulnerable, and reportedly he accepted the premiership with some hesitation. He consequently relied heavily on the support and assistance of George

Ross, the long-time minister of education and temperance stalwart. Thus, despite familiarity with the issue, experience mollifying prohibitionist sentiments, and reassuring Drys that he would keep Sir Oliver's promise, Hardy appears to have had little energy for or interest in pressing forward with provincial prohibition, which soon became clear to the Drys.

In 1897, Treasurer Richard Harcourt introduced a License Amendment Act, and the temperance leadership voiced surprise and frustration that it fell far short of Mowat's prohibition promise. Nevertheless, the bill had several key components that would appeal to the opponents of the traffic. By increasing the population-to-license ratio, it further reduced the number of licensed hotels in the province. The bill gave local ratepayers the right to petition against the renewal of a license in their electoral subdistrict, an extension of the power in the law of 1884 that allowed them to petition against new licenses. It established hours of operation for barrooms; whereas previously the legislation required them to be closed only between Saturday night and Monday morning (although municipalities could pass bylaws restricting hours further), under this amendment liquor could not be sold between 10 p.m. in rural areas or 11 p.m. in cities and towns and 6 a.m. every day except on weekends. The bill also increased the legal drinking age to twenty-one by making it an offence to sell liquor to anyone younger than that. It denied pharmacists the right to sell liquor without a physician's prescription.[6] Finally, and for some at long last, the bill included a provision that would eliminate the stand-alone saloon. In this final provision, the Liberals focused on one issue in drinking culture that continued to be seen as the centre of social disorder: the saloon. By the 1890s, the saloon, a tavern that did not require hotel accommodation, was a feature only of the larger cities, but it remained the focus of much temperance opprobrium. So, in the minds of many Drys, the clause to end the saloon license was long overdue. The initial bill would eliminate saloon licenses in phases, halving the number that would be issued in 1898 and eliminating them entirely in 1899 except for "eating houses at railway stations now under license."[7]

These temperance-friendly elements notwithstanding, the Drys were incensed by the legislation for two major reasons. First, they claimed that Hardy's government had reneged on the premier's assurances that he would honour Mowat's promise and pass legislation that "would go forward as far and as rapidly as public sentiment would warrant, and the jurisdiction of the Province would allow."[8] The Drys saw the provisions of Richard Harcourt's amendment, despite the elimination of saloons, as meagre half-measures rather than the vigorous pursuit of prohibition that Mowat had promised. Second, the Drys thought that their input was being ignored. In November 1896, after a meeting with the newly appointed premier, the Dominion Alliance had presented a list of twenty-three changes to the licensing law that they thought were both reasonable in their demands and essential to address the persistent problems that they saw with the liquor trade. They identified five fundamental changes: devising a more stringent population-based limit on licenses; setting earlier closing hours (7 p.m. during weekdays and 4 p.m. on Saturdays); allowing a petition by a simple majority of electors in a voting subdivision to prevent the issuance of new licenses; reducing the rampant problem of liquor being sold in private clubs (outside the scope of the licensing law); and fixing problems with the local option provisions. Yet none of these five most important "modest" recommendations was included in Harcourt's bill, and only two of the original twenty-three changes (increasing the minimum drinking age and abolishing saloons) found their way into the proposed legislation.[9]

The ire of prohibitionists was further drawn at a meeting with the premier on 11 March 1897. Whereas Mowat normally would have been conciliatory, or at least offered platitudes, Hardy appeared to be combative. He argued that the license amendment did not violate Mowat's promise because the former premier had been talking about prohibition, the issue in the case decided by the Privy Council, not about licensing. He then proceeded to outline some of the intricacies of parliamentary government, noting that his government should not be censured for taking into consideration the broader public sentiment, that the opposition was hostile to prohibition, and that, if he were to present a prohibition bill with the thin majority of "eight or nine at most," his government would fall.[10] The *Ottawa Journal* called Hardy's retort, at which the crowd literally hissed, "a cold douse for temperance people."[11] The *London Free Press* noted that Hardy lacked the finesse of Mowat: "He could not keep his temper before the temperance delegates ... but tried to browbeat and contradict their speakers." A Tory newspaper far from friendly to prohibitionist sentiments, the *Free Press* used the chance to advocate for change in government, noting that "all parties are weary of the trickery and trimming on this and other public questions. The time has come for a change of rulers in Ontario."[12]

It might have been an even colder douse for the temperance people when they learned that Hardy was less combative with a deputation of 200–300 representatives of the liquor industry who met with him a week later. This group, consisting of manufacturers and vendors, couched its arguments in the issues of economic fairness and numerical disjunction. It noted that the amendment would result in the cancellation of 153 licenses and that those licensees would receive no compensation for the loss of business. Moreover, the group explained that given how the law calculated limits to licenses, some smaller towns would actually be eligible for more licensed hotels than larger ones, a situation that they saw as unfair. Yet again drawing provisions from the long-dead McCarthy Act, the law allowed "county towns," in which county courts of assizes were held, more hotel licenses than other towns with similar populations, presumably because more lodgings would be needed when courts were in session. Consequently, county towns with small populations might have up to five licensed hotels, whereas equally sized towns not so designated might be permitted only two or three. The liquor men were also concerned about inequities in closing times. The provision that hotels in cities and towns could close at 11 p.m. but those in rural areas had to close at 10 p.m., and that municipal councils could set earlier closing hours, created another unfair situation. The Wets used the example of the area around London: within a radius of twenty-five miles, there were three different closing times, thus disadvantaging those places that had to close earlier. Finally, the group argued that the temperance people had a distorted understanding of what went on in saloons. It contrasted the temperance view of saloons as dens of iniquity and immorality with the contention that these establishments provided inexpensive meals to workers and were easier to regulate because, not being hotels, they were closed on Sundays and thus less likely to be sites of illegal selling. Hardy's reply to this delegation was brief (the *Ottawa Journal* called Hardy "very guarded"): he assured the members that their perspective would be considered while neither arguing points of detail nor really expressing any interest in the issue.[13] Telling, however, was that, as one newspaper reported, nearly the entire cabinet attended the meeting (as opposed to only a few at the temperance delegation a week earlier), and the leaders of the delegation introduced all of the ministers by name, ending with Treasurer Harcourt, who laughed "with evident enjoyment" at a joke made at his expense by one liquor representative.[14] A few days later, when brewers and maltsters met with the premier to argue that they would lose money if so many licenses were cancelled, because many hoteliers were in debt to brewers, the irascible premier seemed to be nearly as dismissive as with the temperance folks. Hardy responded that he had already heard from temperance and liquor delegations, and as the *London Free Press* paraphrased, "he did not know that he could say anything further than promise that their statement ... should be considered."[15]

Despite Hardy's hostility to the temperance forces and general ennui when it came to the issue at hand, when the bill was presented for second reading, Treasurer Harcourt announced notable changes, many of which appeared to cater to the wishes of the Drys. Hardy prefaced the announced changes with an extended discussion about the validity of licensing and how the Liberals' increasingly stringent liquor licensing system had resulted in a significant decline in crime and drunkenness. He also addressed again the charge that his government had contradicted Mowat's pledge. Hardy explained that the pledge had been about instituting prohibition and that this amendment applied to the licensing law. He implied that prohibition was not off the table, but in the meantime issues with licensing needed to be addressed. Hardy presented to the legislature a letter by Sir Oliver himself, who supported his interpretation. His reluctance to address prohibition likely stemmed from the upcoming prohibition plebiscite, which would have made any policy decision on that matter seem to be premature.

In the legislature, the law faced a thorough working-over, and in many proposed amendments temperance perspectives prevailed. The right to set closing hours was returned to municipal governments; private clubs whose charters did not specifically include the right to sell liquor were thereafter required to apply for and receive a license; a petition to have a license denied now needed signatures from only 50 percent of electors in a subdistrict, down from the original three-fifths; no new licenses were to be granted within 300 yards of churches or schools; the minimum legal age to buy alcohol remained set at twenty-one; and the regulations were made more stringent by eliminating an exemption for people under twenty-one staying at hotels. The contentious clause that would require any cap on the number of new licenses to remain in place for three years was also removed, so municipal councils could change annually the maximum number of licenses in their communities. In a nod to the wishes of the liquor men, liquor dealers or tavern keepers were now allowed to sell a maximum amount of cigars or loose tobacco along with liquor and to sell liquor in containers as small as one half-pint (as opposed to three half-pints in earlier legislation). In what might have been an orchestrated political set-piece, on the same day that the second reading was held, a group of Methodist ministers, who were visiting Queen's Park ostensibly to meet with the premier about the legislation, voiced their unabashed support for the changes.[16] It was, as the Toronto *Daily News* observed, "a temperance victory."[17] The amendment that restored the right of municipalities to set closing hours was lost during debate in the Committee of the Whole, an outcome that prompted opposition leader James Whitney to demand that Hardy resign (while earning the premier unusual accolades from the *Evening News* for not bowing to pressure from the liquor interests). Otherwise, the bill passed without further changes on 10 April 1897.

In the tension between prohibitionists and Hardy's government, the Tories found an opportunity for political gain. Conservative newspapers, generally opposed to prohibition, suddenly showed sympathy for prohibitionists and made much of what many saw as Hardy's decision to break Mowat's promise to enact as strict a prohibition law as possible. The papers presented this as an undemocratic tendency of a tired government. With the Liberals vulnerable because of their thin majority, several major Conservative dailies reminded readers that the Liberal Party was no friend of prohibitionists; indeed, they suggested that the Liberals were playing the prohibitionists for fools. Reporting on the initial bill, the Toronto *Evening News* argued that "it is … difficult to imagine how any sincere believer in prohibition can be hoodwinked into the acceptance of such a measure." It chided prohibitionists for being chumps in their support for the Grits: "The Mowat Government has jollied the temperance people along for the past ten years with little dabs of restriction and the alluring promise of ultimate prohibition. If the Hardy-Ross combination can hold their support after the present exhibit of infinitesimal temperance sentiment in the cabinet, the only conclusion will be that there is no sincerity whatever in the movement."[18] The *Ottawa Citizen* published an editorial from the *Canadian Presbyterian* that characterized the bill as a "secession from the solemn pledges of the government" and "a thwarting of the popular will." It speculated that whether or not the bill would succeed depended on "the promptitude with which the temperance people realize that they are betrayed to the Licensed Victuallers."[19]

This approach – criticizing the temperance movement for supporting the Liberals – indicated a persistent challenge in Ontario politics: despite many threats, individual temperance advocates generally tended to vote for their preferred party notwithstanding its actions on the liquor issue. As Eugene O'Keefe's reassuring letters to Sir John A. Macdonald had indicated, people tended to continue to vote along party lines even when a party, or more importantly its leader, was not considered a friend of temperance. This remained relatively consistent throughout the period under consideration. After a particularly raucous series of speeches at a major prohibitionist rally, where, according to the *Globe*'s report, the participants navigated poorly the rocky terrain of partisan affiliation, a correspondent to the *Globe* calling himself Eye Witness called out prohibitionists for not breaking ranks at election time. He reminded readers that after the majority voted for prohibition in the 1894 plebiscite and Mowat promised to pass as strict a prohibitory law as constitutionally possible, he still nearly lost the next election: "Where was the 82,000 majority vote for prohibition? Did they march to the ballot-box in a solid body in each constituency and vote for Mowat? Not a bit of it. Would they do it to-morrow for the Hardy cabinet if they gave temperance men all they asked? Not likely."[20] This was the crux of the political dilemma, presented during the license amendment agitation in 1897 and again during the dominion plebiscite the following year. Promises about prohibition, made or broken, often were not enough to convince people to vote for the other party. When Hardy explained to prohibitionists that if he tried to pass a prohibitory law his government would be thrown out, he was wildly hissed at and decried. Clearly, he understood the strength of the party loyalties of prohibitionists better than they cared to admit. His frank assessment of political reality contradicted the idealistic musings of virulent temperance advocates.

Yet again the leaders of the temperance movement demonstrated a degree of inflexibility when faced with the tricky policy construction required of balanced governance, and this bloody-mindedness spurred considerable criticism from the opposition press. Although arguments about the value of prohibition could be built on logic and rhetoric, the language that some temperance speakers used was increasingly *intemperate* to some. The *London Free Press,* a Tory newspaper in a city with a strong temperance movement (it was the home of Ontario WCTU president May Thornley), challenged the language of temperance speakers as far exceeding the limits of genteel discourse.[21] The editorial argued that "all sober-minded citizens must regret the intemperate language that is used in some of the city pulpits." It lamented that

> one minister gravely assures our law-abiding people that nearly all of them are on the broad road to hell ... [A]nother goes so far in his denunciation of the drinking customs of many of the people as to express the hope that the property of several of the largest ratepayers might be burned to the ground ... [W]ith minds undisciplined and imaginations heated by intemperate bigotry, which is worse than wine, they talk in a way that only offends and seldom convinces or persuades.

It noted that expressing the hope that businesses would be burned down was in point of fact incitement to crime and thus illegal.[22] The Toronto *Evening News* was similarly critical though less detailed when it reflected on the poor manners of members of the temperance delegation that waited on Hardy: "Some of the hot headed members ... so far forgot themselves as to hiss the Premier's utterances ... The cause of temperance reform cannot be advanced by ebullitions of this character."[23] Reporting on the same meeting, the *Ottawa Journal* referred to the "nasty things [that] were said" about Hardy by "Mrs. Rowley" of London (probably Thornley).[24] In an evening meeting, Thornley had stated that Hardy apparently would not "keep any promise that might endanger his political life," a comment that, however honest, was so politically immoderate to Grit prohibitionists that they jumped in to correct her.[25] (The Tory *London Free Press* called the utterance by a hometown notable "far and away the best speech" in the batch.[26]) In contrast, when representatives of the liquor industry met with Hardy, the *Globe* described the meeting as "a counter to the prohibition demonstration ... [I]n point of numbers, its representative character and the ability with which the arguments were adduced, it was certainly impressive ... [T]he best of order prevailed throughout the hearing, there being no interruptions or objectionable demonstrations and no intemperate language."[27] And nobody hissed.

Such allusions to the intemperate comportment of the temperance advocates, balanced against the apparent respectability of the liquor industry, suggest yet again one of the key issues in the debates about liquor: the importance of order and the fundamental idea of establishing or maintaining an orderly society. From even before Confederation, agitation against saloons was driven by concerns about the drunkenness and debauchery loosed upon the streets of the province. Temperance advocates clamoured about the dangers of the tavern, the immoderation represented by the drinking place, and the incitement to consume excessive amounts of liquor manifested in the practice of treating. In contrast, the liquor industry referred to the economic dangers of legislation that would take away a person's livelihood without any recompense, the immoderate language of the temperance orators, and the incitement to violence and uncitizen-like behaviour of the passionate prohibitionists. Politicians, finding themselves in the maelstrom where the warm and cold fronts of the liquor problem collided, were thrown in every direction.

The Ironic Waning of Prohibitionism under George Ross

The complicated partisan politics of prohibition became more complex under the leadership of George William Ross, who replaced Arthur Hardy as premier in 1899. Ross's ascension to the premier's office must have encouraged prohibitionists that, finally, they would see real change and actual prohibition rather than the gradual tightening of controls over liquor and empty promises. Ross was a vice-president of the Dominion Alliance and had always been seen as a voice of prohibitionists in the legislature. Moreover, like Hardy, Ross confirmed that he would adhere to Mowat's promise to bring in prohibition to the extent that the Constitution permitted. The decision of the Judicial Committee that the province could prohibit the sale, just not the manufacture and importation of liquor, which many called "partial prohibition," was the new goal of prohibitionists since they knew that it was the best that they could expect from a provincial government.

Yet partial prohibition could have problems of its own. Many commentators pointed to experiences with prohibition in US states, notably in Maine, as a caution that partial prohibition would simply result in the problems of the Scott Act writ large. Both Drys and Wets held up Maine as a study in the best and worst case of legislated prohibition in operation. The "Maine experiment" began in 1851 when Neil Dow, president of the Maine Temperance Union, became mayor of Portland and successfully lobbied the state legislature to ban both the production and the sale of alcohol.[28] The "Maine Law" was contentious both inside and outside that state. At the Royal Commission hearings and again during the dominion plebiscite campaign, prohibitionists contended that Maine had seen a dramatic reduction in problems associated with the liquor trade, including insanity, drunkenness, crime, and destitution. Such contentions were often combined with personal testimonies of visits to Maine by the speakers or their acquaintances and stories of Dow's state as a radiant dry city on a hill. Many Wets contradicted the utopian dream with their own evidence – partly testimonial, partly based upon data – that the positive impact of the Maine Law was an illusion.[29] Moreover, Treasurer Richard Harcourt in the Hardy government had argued during debates about the amendment of 1897 that Ontario's licensing system had seen far better outcomes along the lines of social order and a decrease in drunkenness and crime than had Maine's prohibition.[30] Prohibitionists knew that, like it or not, since the Constitution restricted a province from interfering with the manufacture of and trade in liquor, a prohibitory regime akin to the contested Maine law was the best that Ontario Drys could hope for.

Ross took his time responding to the demands of prohibitionists and found little support within the party for a push toward prohibition. In his memoirs, he explains that he was aware that prohibitionists expected great things from him but that, since prohibition had not been a plank in the Liberal Party's platform, he needed the support of his party members in the legislature to implement the measure. He was unable to achieve such concurrence: "Out of the fifty-two members present [in the caucus meeting] only fourteen had any confidence that they would be supported by their constituencies if prohibition were made a political issue."[31] Action, when it came, was prompted by events outside the province. In July 1900, the government of Manitoba passed an Act for the Suppression of the Liquor Traffic, which would have banned completely the sale of liquor in the province outside liquor for "the arts, medicine, and sacraments," sales of which would be the purview of druggists.[32] The legislation passed under the leadership of Conservative Premier Hugh John Macdonald, but when he resigned to run for Parliament, his successor, Rodmond Roblin, was less than enthusiastic about proceeding with the law.[33] The constitutionality of the legislation was immediately challenged by the Manitoba License Holders Association, whose contention that the law was ultra vires the provincial government was upheld by the Court of King's Bench of Manitoba on 23 February 1901. The government appealed this decision to the Judicial Committee of the Privy Council. Likely to Roblin's chagrin, the lords ruled that the law was within the jurisdiction of the provincial government because of clauses ensuring that commerce between businesses in the province and those elsewhere in Canada would not be affected by the ban on liquor sales.[34] To delay, Roblin turned to that old standby strategy: he held a referendum to gauge whether electors in Manitoba were amenable to the act even though two previous referendums had supported provincial prohibition.[35] The lords' decision in the Manitoba case encouraged Ontario Drys to seek yet again a prohibitory law for their province even though they were already bolstered by the Judicial Committee's decision in 1896, which had confirmed that partial prohibition was intra vires the province.

Ross concurred but with a major caveat: the prohibition bill he presented in February 1902 included the proviso that prohibition would have to be approved by yet another popular vote: this time a referendum (which was considered a binding expression of popular opinion), not just a plebiscite. His explanation was straightforward. Although it was true that in two previous plebiscites Ontario had voted in favour of prohibition, Ross argued that the type of prohibition supported in those cases was *total* prohibition, including banning the manufacture of alcohol. The electors of the province, he claimed, had never weighed in on the issue of partial prohibition. Moreover, he explained to a delegation of frustrated prohibitionists as the bill wound its way through the legislature, given that the experiments with partial prohibition of the Scott Act in the 1880s had been overwhelming failures, it was reasonable that the people should be asked to judge whether such an act, covering the entire province, was really what they wanted.[36] He further contended that ensuring the people supported such a law was essential since previous experiences with local option had demonstrated that without a significant majority in favour of the measure, it would fail: "It would be the maddest move ... to abandon the license system for a law which would have to be repealed, if they were to judge from every instance in which prohibition had been carried on a bare majority."[37] Such arguments did little to placate perturbed prohibitionists.

To complicate an already problematic situation, Ross introduced clever calculations to determine the type of outcome that would lead to prohibition. As experience with local option had demonstrated, if a simple majority of votes cast could carry the day, then it was feasible that relatively few electors could force prohibition on the whole province. By 1902, even highly placed prohibitionist leaders argued that a substantial majority favouring prohibition was necessary for such legislation to have a hope of being effective. In early 1902, the Presbyterian newspaper *Westminster* asked notable Protestant leaders what percentage would be needed. Most gave proportions such as 60 percent (three-fifths of the votes) or even 75 percent to carry prohibition.[38] Probably knowing that asking for anything more than a majority would create an uproar from prohibitionists, Ross decided that a simple majority would carry the day but only if that majority was at least as large as half of the votes cast in the most recent provincial election. Appealing to the principle of democratic governance, he reasoned that it would be appropriate for the same number of votes that put a party in power to put prohibition in place. In other words, if 500,000 people had voted in the election, then 250,000 had to support prohibition in the referendum, even if 500,000 people did not vote in it. Originally, he proposed that this majority would be based upon the number of votes in the 1898 provincial election, but in a stunning move of political manipulation Ross decided to call an election before holding the referendum and to use the turnout in that election to determine the required size of the referendum's majority.³⁹ It was clear to most observers that he was hitching his reputation as a prohibitionist to his party's prospects: if the Liberals lost the election, then there was no reason for the Tories to honour the promise to hold a referendum. In an attempt to put a positive spin on his political strategy, Ross explained to angry prohibitionists that, given the usual low numbers of votes cast at many elections, it was possible that "three out of every eight voters on the list" would be enough to make prohibition the law: "Now I want you to think that over; three men who go out and vote for prohibition can force it on the other five."⁴⁰

Not surprisingly, such reasoning did little to satisfy the Drys. Many argued that a vote held outside the regular election cycle likely would not register enough votes to carry the law. Calling an emergency convention in response to this plan, the Dominion Alliance executive argued that "prohibitionists will be handicapped so as to make their success almost impossible. The vote of a liquor favoring minority will prevail unless the prohibition majority is of great and unusual magnitude."⁴¹ At a meeting a few days later, the executive strategized about how to deal with the bill. Rev. Dr. A.C. Courtice claimed that Ross had violated promises made to him in two separate letters. As a result, he argued, "the time had come for the Alliance to send a deputation to see where [Conservative leader] Mr. Whitney ... stood." He then called for all Dominion Alliance members to "concentrate their energies upon the government which had betrayed them."⁴² Frank Spence, Liberal stalwart and secretary of the alliance, protested that any decision of this nature should wait until after the upcoming alliance convention. Courtice agreed but still intended to take some colleagues to speak to the opposition leader.⁴³ At the end of this meeting, the executive passed three motions, one of which was "that it will be the duty of prohibitionists in the coming campaign to oppose any member of the legislature who supports the unfair conditions of the proposed referendum."⁴⁴ In a similar vein, the Grand Council of the Royal Templars of Temperance announced that it could not consider "the bill now before the legislature as a fulfilment of the government's pledges inasmuch as responsibility is evaded by the proposed referendum ... [and made] its emphatic protest against such an evasion of responsibility."⁴⁵ A multi-denominational committee of the Toronto General Ministerial Association also protested the referendum's conditions, couching its concern in the recognition that there was "a crisis in the temperance situation in Ontario."⁴⁶ At the Dominion Alliance convention, partisan tempers flared, with numerous delegates wanting to read amendments and resolutions amid loud protests, while alliance president Rev. Dr. W.A. McKay attempted to maintain order. Some members spoke passionately in favour of the referendum, whereas others criticized the conditions that it would impose. Some questioned the government's intentions, with one member arguing that there was a conspiracy "on the part of the Liberal press to defeat prohibition." In the end, the members agreed to the resolutions to demand that the government remove the most egregious aspects of the referendum rather than repudiate a referendum altogether.[47]

The anger of the temperance people was exploited yet again by the Conservative press, which used it to characterize Ross as duplicitous at the least. The *Ottawa Citizen* trumpeted on its front page the referendum decision as "subterfuge."[48] Reporting somewhat gleefully on the Dominion Alliance executive meeting, the *Citizen* entitled its article "Ross Not Honorable," ostensibly because the alliance motion had referred to the proposed legislation as "not ... an honorable carrying out of the government's pledges."[49] Some surmised that the temperance people could give the prohibition referendum a better chance of success simply by failing to vote in the provincial election so that the majority would be lower and that the winning conditions for the referendum would be within reach. As several commentators argued, if 100,000 temperance voters stayed home, and only 300,000 votes were cast, then the magic referendum number would be 150,000, which seemed to be more attainable. The *Hamilton Spectator* noted that prohibitionists were in an impossible situation since the choice was either to vote at the general election and increase the size of the majority that they would need to poll in the referendum or to "refrain from voting in the general election" and reduce the required majority but risk Ross losing the election and Whitney not calling a referendum at all. "And there," the *Spectator* explained, "is where Mr. Ross has the advantage of his honest prohibition brethren."[50] The *Globe* argued that such political calculations were foolish since Whitney was unlikely to hold a referendum were he to win. Indeed, Ross unwittingly admitted his political calculation when defending his legislation to the Dominion Alliance: "I simply propose to ask for an expression of opinion of the whole community, and to see that the law is enforced if I am in power."[51] The implication was clear, that his defeat at the polls would cause more damage to prohibitionists than the referendum's majority conditions.

Many Drys knew that if they hoped to see prohibition become the law of the land, they had little alternative but to support the Liberals in the election. Conservative leader Whitney minced no words in his opposition to prohibition. As he stood in the legislature to oppose the referendum during debates on the 1902 Liquor Act, he reminded listeners that his policy was to strengthen the licensing laws, and that prohibition would not work, so there was no point in continuing to push for such a measure: "We cannot have prohibition in the Province; therefore it is idle to discuss that question. I believe the remedy is rather in using the powers that we possess, namely, wholesome restriction, decreasing the number of licenses, removing those charged with the administration of the law from political influence, and honestly enforcing the law."[52] Conservatives saw their chance, after three decades of Liberal rule, to take power. The *Ottawa Citizen* applauded Whitney's performance as "able and statesman-like." Noting that Whitney made no qualms about his opposition to prohibition, the editor averred that his "decided and manly attitude on the question will commend itself to the people and contrasts favorably with the insincerity and absence of good faith which has characterized Premier Ross's course, his record of unfulfilled promises and trifling with the temperance vote."[53]

If Ross had intended to use the promise of a referendum to bolster the Liberal Party's performance at the polls, the results of the election in May 1902 suggested that either he was not successful or the Liberal Party was more unpopular than ever. The prohibitionists, tired of Liberal double-speak, and fired up by Rev. S.D. Chown, organized a Union Prohibition Committee to run candidates to oppose the Liberals. Although six independent prohibition candidates ran, none won.[54] Still, it had a notable effect on Ross's party. The Liberals retained a bare majority of only one seat. In many ways, this victory was hollow: in power for over three decades, the party of Oliver Mowat was reduced to a precarious majority with limited party discipline. The prohibition referendum was held on 5 December. Unsurprisingly, and predicted by the two previous plebiscites, a significant majority supported the legislation. However, the votes in favour of prohibition were fewer than the number required to put the law into force. Whereas in 1898 the Drys, after initially conceding defeat, began to press Laurier to enact prohibition, in 1902 the clear victory conditions of the referendum law meant that few attempted to push Ross in a similar direction; it was clear that the measure had failed. The outcome of the prohibition referendum of 1902 was yet another blow to the temperance cause.

Interest in Disinterested Management

In the debates on the 1902 referendum, two issues continued to reappear: first, the validity of a referendum in a British democracy; second, the option for a potential third way between prohibition and private liquor sales: disinterested management. Both issues scrutinized the role of government in the liberal state, and both had detractors and supporters. As had also happened during the 1898 plebiscite, many argued that a referendum was a foreign innovation, with numerous commentators saying that it was something undertaken by the Swiss but that there was little place for such direct democracy in the British parliamentary system. During the Dominion Alliance meeting of 25 February 1902, one speaker likened a referendum to "placing a Swiss patch upon a British garment."[55] When introducing the Liquor Act in the legislature, Ross addressed the worries that many had voiced about the validity of a referendum as a process of governance, noting that "they were being charged with merely shirking the question, and that the method was un-British and unconstitutional." He assured members of the legislature that he had consulted Sir John Bourniot, considered "the greatest constitutional authority in the dominion," who concurred that "the referendum was not inconsistent with sound constitutional British procedure."[56] Yet the idea of a referendum was never so contentious as the conditions for victory that the premier had established.

Ironically, another innovation from outside the British Empire had gained considerable attention among those concerned with moderationist approaches to the liquor problem. Notwithstanding the challenge to the legislative mechanisms, by the turn of the century the idea of disinterested management, normally through some kind of government control of the liquor system, was gaining some powerful followers. Most prominent was the Gothenburg system, which had two distinct forms. The city of Gothenburg, Sweden, had decided in the 1870s to give the license to sell spirits to one trust company (a *bolag*). The company's shareholders would receive a maximum of 5 percent return on their investments, and any further profits would be used by the municipal government to improve public facilities such as roads and libraries, which in turn could result in the lowering of taxes for ratepayers. In contrast, under disinterested management in Norway, the company, the *samlag*, directed profits into projects outside the control of the municipality, thereby not reducing taxes. Supporters of the *bolag* system argued that by reducing municipal taxes, the Gothenburg system created an incentive to increase sales of liquor: higher liquor sales meant lower taxes.[57] Other forms of disinterested management involved direct government management of liquor distribution. In South Carolina in the 1890s, Governor Benjamin Tillman had introduced a "dispensary system" that closed all taverns and put the sale of liquor in the hands of government agencies.[58] It was a highly contentious move and ultimately declared to be unconstitutional, but that modification of the Gothenburg system had made it a viable option for people who continued to be concerned about the ongoing problem of uncontrolled liquor consumption.[59]

Although the South Carolina Dispensary languished under what many considered to be remarkable corruption, government control of the entire liquor trade was repeatedly cited during the referendum debates in 1902 as a potential method of dealing with the worst excesses in Ontario's liquor system. Contemplating the prohibition bill, the Presbyterian journal *Westminster* argued that government control was a far superior option than outright prohibition. The *Globe* provided a positive view of that journal's perspective:

> Government control of the entire liquor business ... would utterly abolish the saloon, the bar, and the treating system, give absolute prohibition wherever it could be made reasonably effective, reduce the number of selling agencies to a minimum, take away the commercial interest on the part of the man who sold and the incitements to drink from the man who bought, make adulteration and illicit selling impossible and so prepare the way for such further legislation as the evolution of circumstances might make necessary.[60]

The *Globe* editorial noted that such an option seemed to be the best choice.

Certainly, the notion of government involvement in the liquor trade, however it might contradict laissez-faire ideals, was becoming mainstream. In early February 1902, before the Liquor Act was presented to the legislature, a group of prohibitionists met with the government to ask that, if prohibition were to pass, the government would establish stores from which liquor would be dispensed for "mechanical, scientific or sacramental" purposes; pharmacists would retain the sale of medicinal liquor, but they would need to obtain supplies from government stores.[61] That such government control had ceased to be such a contentious topic was made clear by the *Toronto Star*, which, in reporting on the meeting, noted that people originally had thought that prohibitionists would be asking for government control of liquor instead of prohibition, a request that would have been much more significant and newsworthy.[62] The blasé tone of the reporter indicated that government management of the sale of permitted forms of liquor was much less of an imposition on liberalism than it once might have been. Indeed, government monopolies on certain industries had become more acceptable at the end of the century.[63] Numerous correspondents to the newspaper reiterated the potential for government control, although the number of supportive letters might have been skewed by editorial selection bias. Charles Richardson of Morpeth, noting that the partisan nature of the liquor question remained a barrier to finding an answer to it and that the liquor interests insisted that their business amounted to "seventy-odd millions of vested rights," argued that the government should take the business over entirely:

> It follows ... that the state is empowered to make fair compensation, take over the business for better, for worse, and dispense wine, beer, and other spirituous liquors for the benefit of the commonwealth. This plan is perfectly feasible and, moreover, takes all the details of the drink habit out of the realm of politics, and the profits revert to the public exchequer, and the State is held directly responsible for the consequences.[64]

A correspondent named Medicus went further, detailing the type of people who should be empowered to manage such an operation:

> Let men of the very highest character be placed in charge of these agencies ... [W]ith the sale of this dangerous commodity in the hands of such men, Toronto could breathe more freely ... [F]athers and mothers of this good city could go to their rest and sleep soundly, for they would not have the haunting dread that their sons were being corrupted in the saloons and barrooms of the city.[65]

Another correspondent, M. Rainey, noted that some kind of government control could eliminate the worst features of the saloon:

> Under these laws the barroom is abolished, and with it the treating habit is scotched. Liquor stores are established, where liquor may be purchased in stated quantities, but not to be consumed on the premises. These stores are kept open during limited hours and are free from any temptation to conviviality or "loafing" ... [T]his system largely accomplishes the great end of removing temptation from the young.[66]

The interest in the Gothenburg system was bolstered when Albert Henry George Grey, the fourth Earl of Grey, visited Ontario in the midst of the referendum campaign. Grey was president of the People's Refreshment House Association, a British trust association organized to create a network of pubs operated under the principle of disinterested management. It differed from the Gothenburg system in that these pubs did not have a monopoly in the community but competed with other pubs. Ideally, public houses operated by these schemes offered food and beverage services, sold alcohol but did not push those beverages over other refreshments, and hired staff whose job was to ensure that no overconsumption took place. As historian Maggie Brady explains, "if the manager thought a drinker had had enough, they pre-empted harm by putting their finger up as a warning sign that they would refuse further service."[67] Earl Grey visited Toronto in March 1902 and spoke on the public house trust system at the invitation of Toronto's Anglican Synod, which had its own Gothenburg Committee. Premier Ross briefly attended the event but "slipped away before discussion began."[68] The *Toronto Star* reported that some audience members liked the idea, but others were more interested in a more complete Gothenburg system in which all taverns would be run under disinterested management. Speaking at the meeting, Liberal Mayor of Toronto Thomas Urquhart gave his general support for the trust system but noted that critics had pointed out that "in seeking to make drinking unattractive, it might end by driving away business."[69] Nevertheless, Earl Grey's visit, and the interest that it demonstrated in some form of disinterested management to deal with some of the worst aspects of the existing liquor system, suggested an alternative to prohibition that might be more palatable to the overall population.

The Gothenburg system received additional support from Principal George Grant. During the referendum campaign, Grant wrote another series of letters to the *Globe* expressing yet again his reservations about prohibition. These letters were more specific and constructive than those that he had written during the dominion plebiscite campaign, which had been more philosophical. Grant evaluated the different forms of management of liquor in an attempt to advocate for both the rejection of prohibition and the acceptance of what he called "a more excellent way."[70] In one letter, he reviewed positively the Gothenburg system and several variations, noting that in both Britain and the United States, similar schemes were under way.[71] In a subsequent letter, published after tantalizing delays and numerous critical letters in response to his criticisms of prohibition, Grant endorsed "the Company system," which combined the trust system that Lord Grey was promoting with some type of government initiative. His idea was closer to the one established in Gothenberg than many of the innovations that he had discussed in his earlier letter:

> To establish a Scandinavian system all that is needed in addition to the present local option law ... is that power should be conferred on the authorities of towns and cities to hand over the licenses, allowed in each case, to a company consisting of persons who would undertake the business, not for the sake of profit, but for the public good.

The system took innovations from capitalism and funnelled any benefits to the community: "Shareholders should not derive profit beyond the ordinary rate of interest on the capital invested; and ... profits should be devoted ... to the municipality, or to the promotion of temperance, and the establishment of reading rooms, coffee-houses, and other philanthropic objects." Grant assured readers that such a system was never abandoned in communities in which it had been adopted and, moreover, that he was prepared to "invest liberally" in such a company.[72] Rather than strict government control, his system would create a low-profit joint stock company. Responses were pointed, with correspondents likely already familiar with the system and pointing out some of its potential problems. G.G. Huxtable was surprised that Grant would endorse such a scheme while "the town council of Gothenburg, alarmed at the frightful increase of drunkenness in that city, are appointing a commission to investigate the causes of that increase."[73] W.C. Good of Guelph saw merit in the system, "provided [that] there were some guarantee as to the good character ... of those in the 'company' ... [C]ompanies and corporations are proverbially soulless, and consequently there is some risk of having the same present condition of affairs continue under a new name." Without such guarantees, Good concluded, "public ownership is by all odds to be preferred."[74]

Many temperance advocates, well aware of disinterested management systems, were skeptical of their promised benefits. Reporting on the Dominion Alliance meeting of 25 February, the *Ottawa Citizen* noted that alliance President McKay had said of the system "that the liquor men were behind it and that the ears of the ass were to be seen under the lion's skin."[75] This statement was not mentioned in other reports of the meeting, but there was similar skepticism of the Gothenburg system among prohibitionists. The *Camp Fire*, a monthly temperance magazine edited by Frank Spence, scrutinized both forms of disinterested management, the joint stock company system and government ownership. In May 1900, the journal reported some dire statistics from the company system in Sweden and Norway: "Since the establishment of the companies, the number of paupers per 1,000 of the population has increased fifty per cent. The number of convictions for drunkenness has nearly doubled, the cases of delirium tremens have more than trebled."[76] A month later the *Camp Fire* published an article on the Gothenburg system that seemed to contradict these assertions. Contending that it was difficult to assess the effects of the company system in Sweden and Norway, it chose instead to compare arrests for drunkenness in Gothenburg to those in Toronto. Illustrating the familiar error of mistaking arrest statistics as indicative of drinking rates rather than simply representing policing activity, the author observed that "it is instructive ... to note that the number of arrests per thousand of the population has been diminishing in Toronto and increasing in Gothenburg."[77] One article in July 1901 speculated that a government monopoly would not be free of the evil of patronage, and that there might be some attempt to reduce the price of liquor, "followed by results that every good citizen would shrink from inviting."[78] In contrast, a story in the *Methodist Magazine and Review* of December 1902, the same month as the referendum, cautioned readers that the Gothenburg system "does not ... prevent or abolish the [liquor traffic] evil, but it is nevertheless a wholesome check upon intemperance."[79]

Thus, although not considered ideal, disinterested management generated discussion among prohibitionists as a better approach than the current privatized and "interested" system, but certainly they were a far cry from complete prohibition. At a meeting held by the Deer Park WCTU, Liberal stalwart and former candidate for federal office Newton Rowell pointed to the Gothenburg system and government control to characterize Tory leader James Whitney as no friend of temperance. Observing that prohibitionists frustrated with Ross's referendum had considered seeing whether Whitney was more open to their pleas, Rowell reminded his audience that Whitney stood by the existing licensing system and had "inferentially opposed government control and company ownership, and he and his followers, with two or three notable exceptions, voted against all of the amendments ... desired by the prohibitionists." Whitney would not, Rowell argued, be amenable to any system that might reduce the worst problems of the existing regime that permitted liquor to be sold by private individuals focused on profit. An individual who would not even consider a measure such as the trust system or government control, Rowell implied, was no friend of temperance.[80] Whitney, it seemed, was too much of an advocate of the form of liberalism that emphasized laissez-faire economics and limited government involvement in trade to suit prohibitionists.

The End of Liberal Party Rule in Ontario and the Turn of the Prohibitionist Tide

George Ross's weakened government and the failure of prohibitionists to meet the rather lofty conditions for victory in the referendum meant that prohibitionists' prospects for Ontario diminished even further in the next few years. The government floundered, wracked by several scandals that threw the integrity of the Liberal Party into question. Ross called an election in late 1904, possibly viewing the success of the Liberal Party in the federal election in November that year (in which it increased its majority) as an encouraging sign of his party's prospects. If this had been his hope, then it was dashed and in spectacular fashion. The campaign immediately became a contest between corruption and integrity, with Conservatives arguing that the various scandals that had manifested themselves under Ross's leadership demonstrated that the Liberal Party was spent. A clear illustration of the weakness of the Liberals and the allure of James Whitney's claims on integrity and "clean government" might have been seen in Ottawa, where J.P. Ross, editor of the independent *Ottawa Journal*, agreed to run as a Conservative, with the caveat that Whitney should let him vote independently were the Tories to form the government. The *Journal* spent much of the campaign defending its erstwhile independent editor's decision by repeating that the Liberals were no longer a party with integrity and that Whitney was a better choice for all independent-minded electors; it implored Liberals who read the paper to vote for the Conservatives, for the sake of the province and in the name of clean government. Whitney won by a landslide.[81]

Whether the end of the Liberal regime in Ontario had anything to do with Drys' frustration with Liberal intransigence on the issue of prohibition is difficult to say. Certainly, numerous prohibitionists wrote that the Liberals were no longer a political horse worth backing. At the same time, supporting Whitney must have been difficult for many prohibitionists. He had clearly stated his opposition to their cause, arguing that it was better to have a strong, well-enforced licensing system that worked than to have prohibition that did not. Moreover, during the election campaign of 1905, Whitney was accused of violating the liquor laws in a minor scandal in a hotel in Napanee. He allegedly ordered whiskey to his room after the legal hours of sale, and a number of his friends continued to drink in the beverage room late into the night.[82] The story was problematic enough that Whitney repeatedly defended his actions during the campaign. Such tales might have concerned temperance advocates, but whether they caused them to recoil from voting for the Conservatives was not seen in the election results. Whitney's Conservatives crushed Ross's Liberals, winning sixty-nine seats to the Liberals' twenty-nine. Given Whitney's lack of interest in prohibition, it was with some irony, then, that Drys would see their dream come to fruition under a Conservative government. But prohibition would take another decade, further investigation of new ways to manage liquor in the province, a different premier, and the national emergency of the Great War. In the meantime, a generation of Liberal rule was over, and it was the Conservatives' turn to be caught up in the complications of liquor.

11
Drinking in Whitney's Conservative Liberal State, 1905–07

The Conservative victory in 1905 saw not merely a change in the party in power but also a change in the approach to governing. James Pliny Whitney, by many estimates, was a different type of politician from those to whom a generation of Ontarians had become accustomed. As Jeffrey Simpson states, "the rather dour new premier always found distasteful electoral chicanery and the partisan clamour for appointments."[1] Whitney might have been dour, but another interpretation is that he was pragmatic, systematic, and intolerant of the subjectivity of personal politics. Indeed, as historian Charles W. Humphries notes in his biography of Whitney, from assembling his cabinet, through filling the many government positions across the province, to implementing his active agenda in the 1906 session, the new premier sought balance in his approach to governance.[2] He hoped to create, as much as possible in the highly patronage-laden bureaucracy that Mowat's Liberals had exploited for decades, a system shorn of the most corrosive elements of patronage. Whitney's style was captured during the election campaign in 1902 when he called himself and his party "bold enough to be honest ... [and] honest enough to be bold," a phrase that, Humphries notes, "stuck to him like glue for the balance of his career."[3] That honesty was indeed bold, at times to the point of bluntly stated disregard for those who opposed him or threatened to withhold their support if he did not implement policies that they wanted. Whitney's steadfast pursuit of a singular vision was based upon an understanding that, as premier, his job was to make good on the policies that he had promised to the electorate rather than be an inconsistent respondent to the whims of various interest groups. His vision of the liberal state was based upon British traditions, the rule of law, and the fair implementation of regulations, all of which were especially important when dealing with the divisive liquor question.

Well in advance of ascending to the premiership, Whitney had made clear his position on the liquor traffic. As noted in the previous chapter, during debates on the 1902 Liquor Act and in the subsequent election campaign, he presented four key principles with which he would approach the liquor question. He rejected prohibition as unworkable, supported the strict enforcement of the licensing laws, believed that high license fees would eliminate the worst abuses of the local liquor trade, and insisted that politics be removed as much as possible from the licensing system. These promises were more difficult to keep than he might have expected. Just as the License Branch had learned in 1876, the license inspector gig was a plum patronage position. It was relatively well paid; it did not require one to move far from home to make a comfortable living as would positions, for example, in the rapidly expanding mining, forestry, and railway sectors in northwestern Ontario; and it did not require heavy physical exertion.[4] It was thus suitable for people of many ages and backgrounds. Given how lucrative the liquor business was, the inspector appeared to have considerable social power in the community, although how much power an individual inspector had was debatable since he had to report to the Board of License Commissioners. Nevertheless, in the first month of his premiership, Whitney received scores of requests from loyal Conservatives to be appointed license inspectors and a flood of recommendations from influential Tories for those who would be most deserving of the position.

Public discussions from all political sides supported Whitney's goal of removing partisan considerations from the licensing system. Numerous commentators saw as a key to this promise the elimination of the "spoils system" from the appointment process. The Toronto *Telegram*, a Tory newspaper with independent leanings, paid careful attention to the expectations of Conservative workers of their newly elected members of the legislature. In February 1905, the paper printed a series of comics that lampooned the scramble for patronage, with one showing the "Unemployed Grafters Association" in a parade led by prominent Tory "wire puller" Dr. Beattie Nesbitt declaring that "we've got a pull all right" (Figure 11.1).[5] Another comic showed people, including members of the "Grafters Club" and the "United Order of Office Hunters," picketing the home of Commissioner (later Minister) of Public Works Dr. J.O. Reaume and clamouring for "any jobs that are going" and "them jobs we're lookin' for" (Figure 11.2).[6] The *Telegram*'s editorial commentary argued that, for

Figure 11.1 "Welcome to Whitney" | *Telegram* [Toronto], 8 February 1905

Figure 11.2 "There's no place like home" | *Telegram* [Toronto], 16 February 1905

the sake of the party's future chances, partisanism be subdued. In the *Telegram*'s estimation, the Tories won the election because many erstwhile Liberals voted Conservative. When Whitney confirmed that he was not going to remove all Liberal office holders from their posts, the *Telegram* was relieved, for "a party that requited the independence of thousands of Liberal voters by conducting the official slaughter of thousands of Liberal office holders would suffer for its bigotry at the polls." The newspaper noted that when the federal Liberals gained power in 1896, there was no such "official slaughter" of Tory postmasters and customs officers, so it would be best that the provincial government followed suit.[7] The Liberal *Windsor Record* argued that a wholesale dismissal of inspectors would "demoralize our civil service."[8] Some looked to the British Civil Service reforms that had been in place since the 1870s, which sought to establish a politically neutral cohort of bureaucrats whose appointments were based upon merit and not connections.[9] The Conservative *Toronto World* argued that it was time to implement a similar system in Ontario.[10]

When responding to many of the correspondents clamouring for the spoils of power, Whitney expressed similar views, arguing that he had to proceed in an honest and non-partisan manner. Within the first few months of his tenure, he had developed a standard response to partisan complaints: he was upholding the British system of government, in contrast to what he referred to as "the American system which has, however, been partially abandoned by them." He insisted that "the British system must govern, no matter what our opponents have done."[11] This was not just lip service: as Humphries notes, Whitney went so far as to insist that about 30 percent of the magistrates appointed across the province be Grits.[12] Such an even-handed approach to appointments was not roundly applauded, as Bernard McAllister made clear in an angry response to being added to a list of justices of the peace that included "some of the worst heelers in the grit party." Instead of being honoured by the appointment, McAllister considered it "an insult to have my name on the list with these [names]" and demanded that Whitney "take my name off and make room for another Grit heeler."[13]

Indeed, Whitney was not afraid to criticize those who thought that they deserved special treatment and who threatened to work against the Conservatives if they did not receive what they believed to be their due. To James York of Brampton, who penned at least five letters to the new premier making the case that he deserved some patronage appointment, Whitney observed, pointedly, that "it is astonishing the number of bright, intelligent men who seem to think that because they have done good

Party work or work for some one man that therefore there is a good paying Government position for them all ready to be handed out." Referring to the allusions that Whitney owed York for all the work that he claimed to have done for the Conservatives, Whitney facetiously apologized: "I am very sorry indeed that you supported me at a great loss to yourself ... and I am still sorrier to notice your suggestion that your actions in the future will be determined by what I do in this matter." Having been beaten down by such persistence among many loyal Conservatives now joining the parade of spoilsmen, Whitney concluded with the assurance that "I shall be very glad indeed if anything turns up that will be of use to you because I do not care to be in anybody's debt, especially when that person takes care to remind me from time to time of what I owe him."[14] He expressed similar frustrations over the next few months as the demands for offices far outstripped the available positions. In a letter to H.H. Ross of Iroquois, in Whitney's home riding, the premier commented that he had not much time to enjoy his new position since

> I have had about one and [a] half hour each day in which to do necessary work. The remainder of my time has been taken up with interviews and in reading and answering correspondence on the great overwhelming question of patronage. It has been wonderful to observe the unanimity with which hundreds of our friends have desired to get some position, something that will bring say about $100 per month.[15]

To Whitney, the meagre spoils of power did not merit the corruption of the system against which Tories had argued for decades. As Humphries explains, Whitney rejected such entreaties because "he was not in power 'to follow in [Liberals'] footsteps.'"[16] Nevertheless, requests and outright demands for some kind of reward continued. By June, Whitney told one such correspondent that there were "upwards of 1000 good men – good friends of the Government looking for public positions." Moreover, they were not just "hangers on ... [but also] good, intelligent deserving men like yourself." He explained that, if he and other MLAs had to find positions for all of them, they would never get any other work done.[17]

Requests for spoils included not only positions for Tory stalwarts but also retribution for Grit office holders who had demonstrated especially problematic partisanship when engaging in their duties. Whitney was more sympathetic to such overtures but even then insisted that a process of gathering evidence and making a case needed to be followed before considering outright dismissal. Conservative A.E. Donovan, who had lost the election in Brockville, wrote to Whitney with a hit list, recommending a purge of many of the officials in his town. Three-quarters of the government officers in Brockville, he argued, "are the most enthusiastic, fighting kind of partisans, and in our last election they were out upon the streets buying votes openly and driving at race neck speed to get voters to the polling booths to vote against me." In his view, his defeat was attributable to the fact that "from the highest to the lowest officials they are a well equipped, well organized band of political experts, and have for many elections past assisted in robbing the Conservatives of this Riding of their just rights."[18] Whitney supported Donovan's contentions, although he suggested that there needed to be some due process: "They must be dealt with ... [based] upon facts which will justify there [sic] being dealt with."[19] In this contention, Whitney drew from the Garrow Resolution, a precedent set in the legislature in 1897. In March that year, Liberal MLA James T. Garrow moved that government employees "who solely or for the most part obtain their livelihood in the Public Service ... should not actively participate in Provincial or Dominion Election Campaigns" or become candidates for municipal office.[20] It was a clear concurrence on the principle of the equitable application of the law, one that placed the apparatus of the government above partisan interests. Although members of the legislature agreed to the resolution, it did not have the force of law, and as the Liberals admitted at the time, it would be up to the government of the day to enforce it.[21] Whitney explained the notion of due process to W. Gibbons of the Cornwall *Standard* in July 1905: once somebody "formulates a charge [about a government official's partisan activities] ... we will do the rest, but we must in the meantime assume, as a government, that there is no charge against any of these gentlemen."[22] His liberal state included a clear interest in justice: due process and legislated precedent.

Whitney was not alone in his understanding of the toxic effect that unfettered partisan patronage could have on the province. Some Conservatives recognized that a wholesale elimination of all Grit office holders and their replacement by Tories would reflect badly on Whitney and his party. After all, he had presented himself as someone who would bring professionalism to the operation of the government and asserted that this professionalism should transcend party lines. Soon after the election, W.D. Hogg from Ottawa offered advice to the new premier on how to approach the spoilsmen:

> There is here, as no doubt in many other places, a great deal of talk as to clearing out officials and appointing new men. As President of the

conservative association here and having some regard to the decencies of life, and the best interests of our party, I feel that a reasonable discretion will have to be exercised and that the extreme demands of some of our friends will require to be set aside as they would, if followed out, do more harm than good."[23]

Whitney agreed and often noted that the staffing of government offices should follow principles of British fair play and the spirit of the Garrow Resolution. In a letter to Joseph Goodwin of Palmerston, who was lobbying for a position, Whitney saw this as a matter of integrity to electors: "The people who spoke on the 25th of January will expect honest and straightforward action."[24]

Nevertheless, soon after the Tories came to power, Whitney's promise to end the partisan nature of the licensing system was tested. Tories who thought that they had been wronged by overly zealous Liberal license commissioners sought redress by appealing to the premier's sense of fair play and partisan loyalty. Tavern keeper R. Lawrence of Toronto claimed that he had lost his license because he was a vocal Tory: "If I had supported and subscribed to the Reform Fund, as I was advised to do by my reform friends – and as most of the hotel men did – I would have owned the Black Bull Hotel to-day."[25] Similarly, Mrs. J.H. McKnight of Brouseville asked Whitney to help her sister-in-law, who had owned a hotel "far superior to other Houses that have been granted licenses" but lost her license "on account of our politics."[26] Whitney was sympathetic but repeated the well-honed mantra, also deployed by Liberals for decades, that the license commissioners had control over the issuance of licenses and that she needed to take her case to them.[27]

If Tory hotel keepers were lucky, then the license officials would be more sympathetic than Whitney, because most Liberal-appointed inspectors were quickly replaced by partisan supporters. It seemed to break Whitney's promise to remove partisanism from the liquor system but was rationalized with the argument that, unlike many other government offices, these positions were renewed annually. Since the appointments of license commissioners and inspectors were reviewed each spring in time for the 1 May license deadline, a few weeks after Whitney took power, all of the license appointments were open for consideration. By March, reports emerged of Conservatives being appointed as commissioners and inspectors. As local Conservative committees began the task of selecting staff for various government appointments, both Liberal and Conservative newspapers began to express their concerns. Two days after arguing that the government should avoid an "official slaughter" of positions, the *Telegram* criticized the decision to appoint a Conservative license commissioner in Toronto, noting that the city "will not regard such an appointment as a satisfactory first payment upon Mr. Whitney's promises of reform in the administration of the license law."[28] Conservative "patronage committees" were tasked with the job of filling both the unpaid commissioner positions and the paid inspector positions, as Liberal committees had been for the past three decades. As more reports of partisan appointments emerged, the *Toronto Star* argued that the system of having local Conservative committees recommend license personnel would not lead to the ideal non-partisan licensing system that the premier claimed to prefer: "How does Mr. Whitney propose to 'remove' these men from the influence of the Conservative member or the defeated candidate, who, along with his most intimate advisers, selected them for appointment?"[29] When the Conservative *Hamilton Spectator* argued that critics needed to wait until Whitney had a chance to pass a law removing partisanship from the system, the *Toronto Star* balked: "How does he propose later on to extract the saturation of partisanship which is now one of the chief merits entitling them to appointment? ... Has Mr. Whitney got the secret for causing leopards to change their spots?"[30] Such vitriol was aimed at the staffing changes in the public positions of license inspectors; there was little turnover in the administrative staff in the head office of the License Branch, and the highly influential post of chief officer remained held by someone appointed by the Liberals.[31]

The arguments against partisan appointments were not just about holding the premier to his election promise: critics also argued that appointments made by Conservative Party members would ensure that inspectors (paid employees) remained both beholden to the government and supportive of its continuation during an election. The *Toronto Star* argued that being appointed by the party meant that

> the license inspector will have as much at stake in an election as the candidate of the riding ... The new inspector ... will expect to hold office as long as his party is in power, no matter how loosely he does his work; and he will expect to lose office when his party loses power, no matter how well he does his work. The laws may be well enforced under these conditions but if so it will be in spite of the conditions.[32]

It was a concern not only of temperance-oriented and Liberal newspapers such as the *Toronto Star* but also of Tory editors worried about the effects of partisan appointments in the liquor system. Reflecting on decades of Liberal patronage, the *Toronto World* and *Toronto Telegram* urged Whitney to implement a system of liquor administration that emphasized the record of the inspector instead of his party affiliation. The *World*, more supportive in general of Whitney than the *Telegram*, still argued that it was a mistake to remove good inspectors merely for the sake of partisan rewards: "Those inspectors who have honestly discharged their duty and held aloof from active politics cannot be dismissed without loss of prestige in the Ontario government. It does not matter whether their sympathies are with the government of the day or against it provided they are kept within proper control. What Ontario wants is honest and capable inspectors."[33] The *Telegram* compared the temptation to acquiesce to the spoilsmen with the spurious reputation of the previous government and urged Whitney to remain above the fray: "The Ross Government became weak and contemptible by surrendering to every 'patronage committee' that could take it by the throat." This failure of Ross's government notwithstanding the patronage system that it had harnessed, the *Telegram* argued, suggested that Whitney would do well to resist the temptations of patronage, because the public was tired of the corrupting patronage network: "The Whitney Government need not hesitate to offend every 'patronage committee' in the province in order to keep faith with the public sentiment that put the Conservatives in power."[34] Seeing himself as having been elected to clean out government corruption, Whitney expressed similar sentiments often in his public and private communications.

Anticipating the criticism that a Board of License Commissioners dominated by Tories would support Tory licensees, Whitney and Provincial Secretary William Hanna insisted that their loyal followers make recommendations to the licensing system that would put effective administration above partisanship. In a circular to local Conservative committees, Hanna requested "that the persons recommended [for commissioners] should, as far as possible, be men the very mention of whose names in your community would carry with it the assurance that the Act will be strictly enforced."[35] Ironically, this would mean Tory commissioners to fulfill Tory promises to remove party politics from local licensing; it was not impossible but certainly smelled weird. The *Toronto Star* suggested that this was evidence that the "spoils system" was functioning in the licensing department.[36] Possibly to address that funky odour, the day after releasing the circular, Hanna announced in the legislature that he was drafting an additional circular to all newly appointed license commissioners insisting that "no man should be granted or refused a license on account of his politics."[37] The letter, released a few days later, emphasized several key considerations that license commissioners needed to keep in mind when assessing hotels. First, politics should not be a determinant in granting licenses. Second, Hanna decried the process by which, in some communities, patronage committees were "assuming to direct the boards as to what licenses shall be issued and to whom." He reiterated that the government "is sincerely anxious that the license laws shall be strictly administered, and on a non-partisan basis." Moreover, all inspectors were expected to make "a fair and impartial report" of every hotel premises. Finally, and most notably to many observers, Hanna insisted that too many drinking places were hotels in name only, and that had to end. "Make the licensees of such places live up to the requirements," he said, "or refuse their licenses," emphasizing, with capital letters, what would soon function as a kind of mantra for liquor license reform: "MAKE THEM KEEP HOTEL!"[38]

Whitney repeated this interest in non-partisan administration and the interest in respectable commissioners when soliciting potential appointees for his riding. Offering the position to Charles Patton of Dundas, Whitney explained that every license commissioner

> should look upon it as his duty to have the law enforced not in any hesitating or uncertain manner, nor on the other hand in a way which might be termed persecution. No license should be granted and no license should be refused for political reasons. No matter what a commissioner's individual opinion may be of the License Law he should endeavour faithfully to carry out the law as it is upon the statute book. Once the commissioners take office they are practically supreme and cannot be interfered with, either by the government or by any other influence. This is why I am particular in stating to each gentleman who is being appointed the course of action which the Government thinks he ought to pursue.[39]

Such qualifications made the task difficult. Whitney informed T.S. Edwards from Dundas that he had already approached four men from the county and that all had declined the offer. He was becoming desperate, noting that "I am very anxious indeed that good men will accept these positions as a matter of duty, although as far as our county is concerned it seems doubtful whether we will do so."[40] The reasons for this difficulty are uncertain, although the lack of remuneration and the general understanding of how time consuming the duties of commissioners could be might have repelled some of those "good men."

Appointing new commissioners was not nearly as contentious as appointing new inspectors. Since a liquor inspector was a paid and highly visible government official, many sought the position. Conservative patronage committees saw the position as a reward for worthy party workers. Immediately after Hanna released his letter emphasizing the non-partisan nature of the licensing system, Methodist social reformer S.D. Chown wrote to the *Globe* that the pledge of making non-partisan appointments was already a failure: "Utterly regardless of the pledges of the Government, and of the interests of society, in quite a number of instances these men, sometimes backed by the Conservative Patronage committee of the riding, have pressed or are pressing for the appointment of men entirely unsuited, and in some cases positively antagonistic to the duties that would devolve upon them."[41] A few days later the *Globe* noted, possibly with the pun intended, that "license inspectors are being liberally removed" and suggested that this was unfair and possibly contrary to accepted employment practice.[42] The *Toronto Star* editorialized that the "spoils system" remained intact when it reported that Hanna "informed the caucus in so many words that all the inspectors would be removed and new ones appointed." This meant that "men, all over Ontario, are being asked to resign, no reason being given," even though they "are not supposed to be dismissed without cause," a further reference to the Garrow Resolution.[43]

Such criticisms also reached Whitney from party loyalists concerned that, by completely replacing the inspectorate, he would be seen as trading good men for bad. Since the work of inspectors included both evaluating the suitability of a license applicant and prosecuting transgressions, the ability to prosecute cases successfully was a good indication of an inspector's success. Soon after the government led by Whitney took over, he asked the MLAs and the defeated Tory candidates (in the few places where Conservatives had not been elected) to recommend local people to fill positions, including those of license commissioner and license inspector. Although few argued to retain the commissioners who had been appointed by the Liberals, several commented that Grit inspectors in their areas were doing good jobs. James Leitch, Whitney's friend from Cornwall, suggested that the local license inspector, Thomas McNaughton, should be retained: "I need not tell you that Mr. McNaughton is a liberal but I can tell you that he has never been an offensive partisan and that so far as the administration of his office is concerned there has never been any complaints."[44] Similarly, A. Johnston from Clinton advised Whitney that the people there would "have less trouble" if they retained the local inspector. He "is certainly a good one[;] he has collected near[ly] $700 on fines last year[;] he and the chairman of commissioners have been in about 18 years well liked by both parties as men who fearlessly do right as far as we know."[45] Despite such recommendations, Whitney and Hanna undertook a nearly wholesale replacement of the inspectorate, explaining that they needed inspectors who could work well with the new commissioners. Such arguments were contradicted by several bitter former inspectors who noted that they had been able to work perfectly well with their new boards.[46]

The limited number of patronage positions and the lucrative nature of the inspector's job led to some tension within Conservative circles. Stories of Conservatives fighting over the spoils of office began to put the lie to any assurance that politics would be removed from the system, at least from the appointment process. When members of Kingston's Conservative executive learned that the town's former mayor had been appointed liquor inspector without their consultation, they balked, and the previous inspector was reappointed. In St. Catharines, an alderman known to have been an advocate for licensed victuallers scored the position of inspector; local Tories were divided over his appointment, temperance folks were united in their displeasure, but he kept the gig.[47] Similarly, when the defeated Conservative candidate in South Essex recommended James A. Smyth, the principal of a public school, as the inspector, some local Conservatives were unhappy. The *Globe* reported that the appointment "is likely to cause trouble," and soon, according to the *Windsor Record*, the area was embroiled in "seething political turmoil" over the appointment.[48] As with the case in Lennox, the appointment stood.[49]

These rough starts aside, when the license boards began their work, many seemed to take seriously the directions to be non-partisan and rigorous. The emphasis on the need to "MAKE THEM KEEP HOTEL!" seemed to capture the attention, and in most cases the admiration, of the press. In both Hamilton and Toronto, the license commissioners undertook a systematic, first-hand examination of hotels. The *Ottawa Citizen* called the Hamilton board's process "business like" and resulting in "something of a revelation as to the manner in which many licensed places under the old regime qualified as 'hotels.'"[50] In West York, the new chair of the Board of License Commissioners issued a circular explaining its expectations of hotel keepers: "Improvements in sanitary conditions and general conveniences of hotels will be strongly insisted on," sales to minors or after hours on Saturday night would not be tolerated, nor would "interference by brewers who own or control hotels."[51] A month later a meeting of a local Young People's Christian Union passed a resolution "expressing confidence in the West York license commissioners."[52] In Peel County, the commissioners similarly announced that "every man who has a license must keep a hotel." Consequently, over half of the existing licenses were eliminated, dropping the number of licensed hotels from thirty-five with one licensed shop to sixteen hotels and no licensed shop.[53] The Toronto *Telegram* explained this change as a direct result of Whitney's expectation that commissioners would be men who commanded respect and that the commissioners and inspector were not "temperance cranks." All four "of course" were Tories. The *Telegram* also observed that the cuts affected "Grit and Tory alike," noting that in Brampton, "at least two out of three licenses cut off were held by Conservatives." In echoes of 1876, when there had been more Tory hotels closed because there had been more Tory hotel keepers, the *Telegram* observed that across the province more Liberal hotels had been closed simply because more hotel keepers had been Liberals, "either from conviction or [from] expediency."[54] Similar stories were reported across the province.[55] Unfortunately, Whitney did not follow Mowat's example in 1876 of reporting on the politics of hoteliers who had their licenses renewed or cancelled, so we have only observational evidence of some attempt at balanced administration.

Despite much cynicism about assurances that the licensing law would be applied in an even-handed way, many observers, including temperance-minded ones, admitted that the licensing situation had improved under Whitney's watch. The *Toronto World* reported that Toronto's Municipal Reform Association "warmly commended" the city's license board, noting that "the board had begun its official career in a manner worthy of the highest praise."[56] Two weeks later the *World* opined that, since the new board had taken over, "a drunken man is a rare sight on the streets on Saturday evenings and Sundays."[57] Even the temperance-supporting and Liberal *Toronto Star* was cautiously optimistic, as far as its partisan eyes could see. In an editorial a few weeks after the license board began operations, it described the commissioners as "representative men who will be most anxious to do their duty by the public ... [T]hey will want the law enforced, and will seek to make themselves morally useful to the community." Nevertheless, it gave its strongest endorsement to the fact that the license inspectors from the old regime had been retained, and contrasted the upstanding members of the board and the inspectorate with what it saw to be the situation elsewhere, where "commissioners of another stamp have been appointed, the old inspectors have been dismissed peremptorily," and new inspectors had been appointed "who are in no fear of dismissal unless they offend the local party organization that selected them for office."[58]

Nevertheless, Liberal and temperance-sympathizing newspapers remained prepared to provide examples of appointments that contradicted Whitney's promise of a non-partisan licensing system. The *Globe* noted that the mayor of Port Hope said that "the liquor license act was being laughed at" and asked his council to hire a deputy inspector to pick up the slack left by the "partisan appointment of a non-resident inspector."[59] When the *Windsor Record* reported that the license commissioners had increased the number of licenses in the town of Tecumseh, it concluded by observing that whether or not more licenses would be issued "depends upon the political pull the applicants have."[60] In a story tellingly entitled "New Government's Methods," the *Toronto Star* reported that "the best hotel" in the town of Wahnapitae, north of Sudbury, had been denied a license in favour of a smaller building with fewer rooms and substandard amenities located "in a perfect boghole."[61] Such accounts are difficult to corroborate, however, and should be balanced against the many reports of a much improved system.

Whitney received many observations about the reformed licensing system, running the gamut from concerned to elated. In early 1906, M. Bailey, the chief license commissioner in Whitney's home riding, reported, perhaps with not a little self-satisfaction, the "wonderful change [that] has been made in the hotel business in our county ... [T]he law is respected and kept and it is a common thing to hear people remark on the difference in improvement under your government." He advised Whitney to point to his county as an example of the success of his changes.[62] A much less biased assessment came from Rev. S.D. Chown. Although commending Whitney for shutting down a notorious pool hall in Toronto Junction, he advised him that "such energetic administration will commend itself and secure the good-will, not only of so-called moral reformers, but of all right thinking people in the community."[63] Nevertheless, Whitney also heard complaints about unfair partisan actions taken against liberal-leaning hoteliers. Jennie Brander informed him that in Wallaceburg, "we see no improvement as yet rather the reverse," reporting "many men foolishly drunk on the streets."[64] When Thomas Flynn's hotel was cut off, also in Dundas County, O.D. Casselman, who had rejected an invitation to become a license commissioner, complained that "supporters of both political parties" thought that Flynn was being treated unfairly.[65] Whitney replied that he would not intervene despite repeated entreaties to do so.[66]

The Liquor License Amendment Act of 1906

Although Whitney's promise of strict, non-partisan enforcement of the licensing law had a rocky reception because of the long tradition of partisanism and clientelism in Ontario, his longer-term effect on the liquor system in the province came through legislative change. Whitney repeatedly argued that he had no allegiance to either the temperance people or the liquor trade and thus could carve a middle path that would be the best outcome for the people of the province as a whole. Here his attempts at even-handed management of the liquor system and his general bloody-mindedness became strong assets. During the legislative session of 1905, which began six weeks after he became premier and for which he had low expectations, he introduced relatively minor tweaks to the licensing law. But in 1906, after having a year to investigate further the state of liquor in the province, and having settled into their new roles, Whitney and Hanna presented a bill with substantial changes to the liquor law. The subsequent debates demonstrated that, in contrast to the charges often levelled at the previous government, Whitney was not interested in currying favour with either the Wets or the Drys. His expectation that liquor laws should not cater to the views of "liquor men or the people who call themselves the temperance men," an imperative when selecting license commissioners, became manifest in the amendments of 1906.[67]

On 20 March 1906, Hanna stood to introduce An Act to Amend the Liquor License Laws, legislation intended to address what the government saw as significant deficiencies in the provincial licensing regime. It made notable changes. License fees were boosted significantly (see Table 11.1); municipal councils could increase the fee beyond the statutory amount but had to submit such an increase for the approval of the electors.[68] Brewery ownership or other financial involvement in tavern operations (often called the "tied house system") was to end. Liquor licenses for steamships and trains, which had been eliminated under the Liberals, were to be reinstated. Bartenders were required to take out a license to be able to work in a tavern, and only licensed bartenders were to be employed in licensed hotel beverage rooms. All bartenders had to be over twenty-one years of age. Hotels would be allowed to sell liquor on Sundays but only to registered guests with their meals. New requirements for inspectors were intended to avoid licensees being repeatedly charged with first offences rather than second and third offences, which had higher fines and could include incarceration. The legislation also altered the local option process. It compelled a municipal council to hold a local option

Table 11.1 Minimum license fees for taverns (categorized by population)

	Cities			Towns/villages		
1886	Over 20,000	Under 20,000		Town	Village	
	$250	$200		$150	$80	
1906	Over 100,000	30–100,000	10–30,000	5–10,000	2–5,000	Under 2,000
	$1,200	$700	$500	$450	$350	$250

Sources: An Act Respecting the Sale of Fermented or Spirituous Liquors, *Consolidated Statutes of Ontario* (1886), Cap. 194, Sec 41; An Act to Amend the Liquor License Laws, *Statutes of Ontario* (1906), Cap 47 Sec 10.

Note: The statute passed in 1886 added a premium to the law of 1876. Municipalities could increase the law to a specified maximum. So in some municipalities taverns might have been paying more already.

vote upon receipt of a petition from 25 percent of the electors; however, such a vote required three-fifths of votes cast to be in favour of the measure before local option would be enacted. It also required three-fifths of votes to rescind local option. Local option votes could be taken only every two years.[69]

Initial reaction was mixed but suggested that Hanna and Whitney had succeeded in walking a fine line between temperance and liquor interests. Several newspapers reported that temperance advocates were pleased with the law given the increase in license fees, the requirement that councils submit a bylaw upon receipt of a petition of 25 percent of the electors, and the elimination of tied houses (considered to be inducements to sell more beer).[70] In contrast, liquor men were less enthusiastic. Hotel keepers criticized the extensive rise in license fees, and brewers and licensees alike argued that the tied house arrangement was necessary in a business that relied heavily on credit.[71] Quickly, however, criticism became more ossified. The *London Advertiser*, a Liberal newspaper with strong temperance leanings, was unimpressed, observing that there were "some praiseworthy features" in the bill but not enough to satisfy temperance people. Even the increase in license fees was considered to be a "retrograde" move since, the editor argued, it would give municipalities a greater financial stake in the continuation of a liquor licensing system and decrease enthusiasm for local option.[72] Upon reading the legislation, S.D. Chown said that the law "does not reach the point the temperance people had a right to expect," but he admitted that he was unsure how to "characterize" the bill. "For instance, it strikes a body blow at the brewers of Toronto" by eliminating tied houses, "and it strikes the temperance people in a vital spot" by allowing local option to be considered only every two years.[73] The reinstatement of licenses on steamships was similarly criticized as a backward step that would create boozy chaos on the waterways of the province.[74]

Both Wets and Drys focused their criticism on specific issues. Temperance advocates quickly zeroed in on the changes to the local option act, especially the three-fifths vote, seeing it as un-British and contrary to the principle of majority rule. Moreover, by requiring two years between local option votes, the law reduced opportunities for Drys to achieve local option since the previous law did not stipulate how often temperance advocates could launch a local option campaign. The two-year clause also made it possible for a vote rescinding the law to take place more frequently since the previous law had permitted a repeal vote only every three years. Drys were deeply concerned about the prospect of drinking on steamships, presenting images of party boats full of drunks plying the peaceful waters of Ontario. Liquor interests were also unhappy. Hotel keepers were concerned yet again about the lack of compensation in the event that hotels would be shut down (either by a commission rejecting the renewal of a license or by a successful local option campaign), but their main concern was the direct impact of increased license fees. When C. Berkley Powell of Ottawa warned Whitney that the law was "raising a perfect storm amongst the licensed victuallers, and does not please the temperance people," Whitney was nonplussed.[75] He observed that "one of the proofs that we are not far wrong about this is that it does not suit either the license holders or the temperance people," and he admitted that "we are not trying to please either of them, we are trying to steer a straight course" that would appeal "to all good citizens and men of common sense."[76]

Whitney and Hanna, along with sympathetic newspapers, quickly dismissed many of these complaints. Referring to the "three-fifths clause" on local option votes, Hanna noted in the legislature that many temperance supporters, including George Ross when he was premier, had agreed that more than a simple majority would be needed for a prohibition measure to be enforceable, pointing especially to the referendum in 1902. In the legislature, Ross contended that local option was different from full prohibition.[77] Whitney fielded many letters from concerned temperance advocates who claimed that they had trusted that he would fulfill his promises. Along with complaining about the three-fifths clause, some deployed unique math to argue that making local option more difficult to pass would break Whitney's promise to reduce the number of licenses, suggesting that fewer local option successes would cause the number of licenses to increase. Whitney had little patience for such complaints. S.B. Wilson, general secretary of the YMCA in Brantford, complained to the premier that a vote carried by anything more than a majority "seems to be utterly foreign to the usage of [the] Canadian government."[78] Whitney replied that requiring three-fifths majority was fair to business owners, who would see more stability because they would not be constantly threatened with closure, and that since a three-fifths result would be required to rescind local option, such a measure would remain in force longer, again ensuring stability. T.S. Edwards from Whitney's riding contended that requiring a three-fifths majority vote to rescind local option seemed to contradict Whitney's justification for the clause. If a repeal vote failed because a majority below 60 percent opposed local option, the measure would remain in place, but by Whitney's own logic it would be unenforceable. Edwards explained that "temperance people want simple justice – British fair play – and believe that the vote of every man entitled to the franchise should have equal weight."[79] In a detailed reply, Whitney noted that he was legislating not for the liquor men or "the people who call themselves the temperance men" but for the people as a whole. He also countered the "un-British" argument by noting that

> people who ought to know better talk about our proposition being un[-]British, whereas the facts are that in every attempt in Great Britain within the last dozen years at any rate, to deal with anything of a similar nature with reference to the liquor traffic, a larger vote than a majority has been required, and I may be allowed to express my astonishment that statements exactly the opposite of the truth in this respect are made right and left by individuals.[80]

Whitney concluded by reminding Edwards that the 25 percent petition compelling municipalities to hold a local option vote was an advantage to the temperance movement. Previously, councils could use any range of tactics to delay or refuse to hold a vote. To another angry correspondent, Whitney made a plea for balance, arguing that "an individual or Government having, say, five things to do, all of which are equal value in a public sense, and who do four things right, ought not to receive condemnation simply because they fail in the fifth."[81] The standard of fairness had to go both ways.

Despite such opposition, Whitney remained steadfast. He found that similar requirements for local option votes were used in Australia and

New Zealand, adding to his argument that requiring a 60 percent majority was within the scope of "British fair play." He told Hanna, who had begun to waffle on the three-fifths clause, that it would remain in the bill. Not only were there good legal precedents for it from other British jurisdictions, but the clause also had good support across the province (including a surprisingly positive article in the journal *The Presbyterian*). "Our position," he argued, "is unassailable," and almost as an afterthought he noted that changing its position at that point would make the government look weak.[82] It did heed, however, other complaints. The steamship issue had considerable opposition, and almost immediately the government backed down. Two days after the bill was introduced, Hanna offered the unconvincing explanation that the government had never intended to pass such legislation; it had simply included the clause "for the purpose of having the matter discussed and settled definitely."[83] It was dropped in committee, where the government also returned to three years the period that a local option law would be in force before it could be voted on again. It also removed a contentious clause that would have given the provincial government veto rights over the decisions of license commissioners.

Whitney's government was even less receptive to complaints from hoteliers than to entreaties from temperance advocates. On 4 April, hundreds of liquor men descended on Toronto in what by most accounts was an impressive show of force.[84] They argued that the removal of the tied house system was unfair because it placed them on an uneven footing with other types of business. They reproduced the argument favouring some form of compensation when licensees were cut off. They wanted the repeal of local option to be by a majority vote in places where it had been passed by a majority vote (granted in the final version of the law). And they were especially concerned about the increase in fees and the increase in penalties. By all accounts, Whitney and Hanna rebuffed their requests; they suggested that there might be minor modifications but nothing more. The *Ottawa Citizen* reported that, contrary to F.S. Spence's charge that the government was "desirous of catering to the liquor men," Hanna explained that he "did not expect to please the extremists in any party."[85] Neither the clauses about tied houses nor the increases in license fees were changed, although a new fee category was created, and the bartender license requirements were loosened so that an unlicensed bartender could work under extenuating circumstances.[86] Whitney and Hanna justified the increase in fees not only as a high license measure that would make hotel keepers improve their premises but also as a way of allowing the government to benefit from what, in some jurisdictions, was a remarkably lucrative liquor business. When introducing the bill, Hanna read a list of the profits that had been derived from the sales of hotels in Toronto. He argued that such high profitability meant both that hotel keepers could afford an increase in license fees and that higher license fees would bring more revenue into the province and its municipalities. Looking beyond the province for comparisons, Hanna argued that whereas the license in Ontario "paid only 30 odd cents per head of population," in other cities the value was much higher. Boston received $2.42 per head, Buffalo $3.19, Montreal $1.40, and Quebec City $1.26.[87] Moreover, a tweak of the law that allowed 50 percent of the fees to go to municipalities was framed as giving a direct benefit to a community's coffers.[88]

Frustrated hotel keepers reacted through veiled threats that had an uncertain impact. Across the province, hotel associations concluded that in all likelihood they would have to raise their rates to compensate for increased fees. The president of the provincial hotel men's association said that "increased hotel rates are bound to come as a result of the new license rates."[89] Ottawa's Licensed Victuallers Association planned at least to increase the costs of beer and whiskey from five cents to ten cents and from ten cents to fifteen cents, respectively.[90] The *Ottawa Citizen* called this threat "to soak the public for thousands of dollars because the government puts the license fee up a few hundred dollars" "rather childish." It also observed that such an increase would be "an excellent temperance measure."[91] Nevertheless, licensees in London and Toronto made similar threats.[92]

The hotel keepers' concerns added to a growing discussion about the place of the hotel in the social fabric of the province. Hotel keepers and their supporters began to push back against what often seemed to be a simplistic characterization of the purpose of a licensed hotel in a community. The *Canadian Wine and Spirit Journal and Brewers' Review* criticized Hanna's imperative that license holders must "keep hotel," calling it a "delightfully wide and indefinite phrase covering with a single blanket every license from the palatial 'King Edward' in Toronto to the roadside tavern on the concession lines running into Punkville."[93] It criticized the definition of a hotel based upon the number of rooms, "for over half the licensed houses in Ontario could not secure a single transient lodger in a year owing to their location." Moreover, some hotels in cities might not need horse stabling, wagon sheds, or sleeping accommodations but play an essential role providing restaurant facilities. The *Journal and Review* concluded that "every license should meet the requirements of its locality whether for bar, dining room, stable, or lodging, and the particular feature in demand should dominate that establishment."[94] Other critics argued that the demand to "keep hotel" was unfair in places such as Toronto where the "rights" of drinkers were being violated. As the Board of License Commissioners in Toronto investigated the hotel facilities there (many of which came up short), James Haverson, the long-time solicitor for the Licensed Victuallers Association, argued that focusing only on sleeping accommodations "leaves no provision whatever for the wants of the drinking public in Toronto."[95] Such arguments, essentially advocating for the rights of people who drank, were rarely uttered in entreaties to the previous government. Haverson likely was emboldened by an administration run by Conservatives, considered to be less supportive of temperance than the Liberals.[96] However well argued, these were still the mutterings of people with a vested interest in a generally unfettered hotel business. It was up to other voices to argue for a reconsideration of the role of the hotel in the community.

These voices came from a business community that was concerned about the loss of good hotel accommodation in local option districts. Since profits from liquor sales supported, and often sustained, the operations of many hotels that otherwise could not have survived, the loss of a liquor license could kill a hotel business. As a result, hotels in some local option areas closed when their licenses were eliminated. As noted in earlier chapters, this problem had been alluded to repeatedly in the 1880s and 1890s, with some community leaders arguing that, without hotels, farmers had no place to house their horses and wagons on market days, resulting in a decline in business for the community in general. Temperance adherents were generally dismissive, arguing that a decent temperance hotel could do the work of a licensed hotel. Yet, as reported soon after the implementation of the Crooks Act, some "temperance hotels" sold liquor illegally, so they were "temperate" only in their unlicensed status, not in their immoderate sales of surreptitious booze. By the time the Royal Commission on the Liquor Traffic was taking evidence, there was less suspicion of temperance hotels being covers for illegal drinking, but most witnesses agreed that a hotel could not remain in business without a bar.[97]

In 1906, a new cohort added its voice to concerns about the effects of local option on the availability of hotel accommodations. In early March, representatives of commercial travellers in London and Toronto met with Hanna and several other members of cabinet to request that the license act require local option municipalities to provide suitable hotel accommodations for travellers and that these places be inspected. The *Mail and Empire* called the requests "radical reforms."[98] In a subsequent letter to Whitney, the president of the Travellers' Club of London, C.W. McGuire, explained the problem faced in local communities by commercial travellers across the province. He insisted that this was not an issue of commercial travellers who needed bar facilities; rather, "accommodation for board, lodging, sanitary conveniences, &c has been taken away from the travelers, with no responsibility upon either the government or [the] municipality to supply it." McGuire noted that license officials inspected licensed premises, attending not only to the sale of liquor but also to "accommodation necessary for the travelling public both as to meals, rooms, sanitation, security for property, board and lodgings for horses &c." But these officials claimed they had no mandate to inspect, let alone license, places in dry communities. As a result, most hotels had closed down, and those that remained were often inadequate for travellers' needs. He asked the government to amend the license act to require any municipality that passed local option to provide some form of adequate accommodation as an alternative to the licensed hotel.[99]

The request of commercial travellers captured the attention of the media. Here was a group of respectable individuals whose work was considered essential to the smooth operation of the economy but who were disadvantaged by the consequences of local option. They presented a complication to the easy binary of "temperance men" versus "liquor men," suggesting that there was collateral damage in the battle between Wets and Drys that could have significant consequences for the province. In an open letter to the leadership of the Dominion Alliance, McGuire offered to pay for a representative of "any temperance association" to accompany a commercial traveller for one week or for half of the expenses for representatives from six organizations to go into six different regions.[100] There is no indication that the alliance took him up on this offer.

Most striking about the commercial travellers' dilemma was that they were arguing not about the necessity of a bar but about the importance of a hotel in the community. Repeatedly, the justification for having hotels licensed was derived from the idea that the hotel was a "home away from home" for the "travelling public," and, just as one could have a drink at home, so too one should be able to get a drink in a hotel. McGuire's entreaty set aside the issue of the bar and focused specifically on the needs of the travelling public. It was a compelling argument. The *Globe*, resistant to many wet perspectives, engaged in an extensive editorial supporting the idea that proper accommodations were necessary, but it drew the line at the requirement for liquor: "A clear-cut and properly expressed distinction should be drawn between hotel keeping and liquor selling, and if these two functions are authorized to be undertaken by one person he should be licensed separately for each."[101] As the *London Free Press* explained it, commercial travellers "are unconcerned about the bar; they are not troubled about the extra pay." Their concern was about smaller communities "where, the license being withdrawn, the public house is closed, the driving shed boarded up, and the pump chained."[102] Some temperance supporters saw merit in these arguments. The Methodist *Christian Guardian* argued that temperance people in local option areas should "see that the wants of the travelling public are provided for."[103] A few commentators challenged the commercial travellers' entreaties. The *Newmarket Era* seems to have missed that McGuire's plea was for the government to license hotels in local option areas. Its editor, clearly not a fan of these travelling salesmen, argued that "it is not the duty of local municipalities to provide accommodation for persons who do not contribute to the municipal treasury, especially a class of people who do not produce anything."[104] Nevertheless, when Hanna was asked if the liquor bill would be amended to provide for such inspection, he said no.[105] Two years later he capitulated, and the license law amendment of 1908 included a provision creating the category of "inspected hotel" and requiring all such licensed hotels to have most of the same facilities (except for a bar) that could be found in hotels outside local option areas.[106]

The amendments of 1906 had a powerful impact on the licensing system. Concerns among temperance advocates that the three-fifths clause would affect the progress of local prohibition were confirmed in the results of local option votes in 1907. Although forty-seven communities saw a majority of votes support local option, in only forty-one were three-fifths of the votes cast for prohibition. Nevertheless, with forty-one communities having 60 percent of electors support local option, one could argue that in fact Whitney's goal to have a more enforceable license law was being achieved.[107] The following year, out of seventy local option contests, twenty-eight met the three-fifths requirement, twenty polled a majority in favour but below 60 percent, and in twenty-two a majority was against the law. The *Globe* noted that "Mr. Whitney's three-fifths clause has been the salvation of bars."[108] Drys continued to press for change, attempting to insert numerous amendments during various readings of other liquor license bills, but never saw the three-fifths clause reversed before prohibition, and every year temperance leaders and sympathetic newspapers would lament how many licenses were "saved" by the three-fifths clause.

This water-glass-half-empty perspective of temperance advocates persisted despite evidence that another aspect of the changes in 1906 meant that local option was becoming increasingly familiar across Ontario and more stable. Since the law compelled municipalities to hold a referendum on the petition of 25 percent of electors, more local option votes were held since municipal councils could not legally refuse to hold a referendum. Indeed, the law triggered a vote even without any action by council.[109] Moreover, since the law also required a majority of 60 percent for a vote to repeal local option, once local option laws passed they were rarely rescinded. The effect of the law can be seen in Table 11.2 and Figure 11.3. From 1905, the license act report included a list of communities (towns, villages, and townships) in which local option was in effect the previous year. In 1904, thirty-one municipalities were under local option; the next year an additional twenty went dry. In the first year after the new regulations, fifty-one municipalities rejected liquor, and one community, the town of Sault Ste. Marie, repealed local option. For the next decade, few communities repealed it, and the number of total local option communities grew from that base of 20 to 319 in 1914. There is some evidence that this was the result of often vigorous campaigns. For example, in 1910, temperance organizations mounted a concerted effort to implement local option, resulting in seventy-six new dry communities, although three communities repealed the law. The changes are remarkable, and the ability of temperance organizations to succeed in achieving local option likely was related directly to the amendment of 1906. It is difficult, however, to say this with complete confidence for several reasons. First, these local option vote numbers are extracted from the annual reports of the License Branch, but consolidated records of local option contests prior to 1905 are not available in an easily comparable format.[110] Second, local option votes prior to 1905 were held at different times across the province, so data would be inconsistent at best. Third, given the complaints by temperance supporters that prior to 1905 some municipal councils simply refused to hold a vote notwithstanding a petition in its favour, any data available from the pre-1905 period likely would not provide a clear representation of temperance activity.

Table 11.2 Local option votes, 1904–14

Year	1904	1905	1906–7	1907	1908	1909	1910	1911	1912	1913	1914
Net increase	31	20	51	40	26	19	73	17	19	23	13
Previous year		31	51	102	142	168	187	260	277	296	319

Source: Reports of the Liquor License Branch, in *Sessional Papers of the Legislature of Ontario* (1905–15).

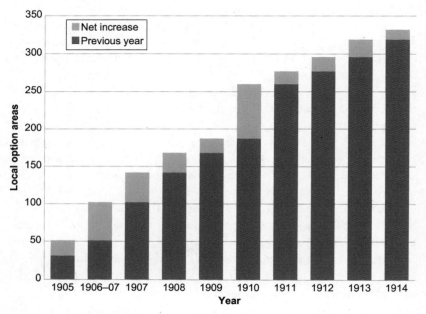

Figure 11.3 Increase in local option areas, 1905–14
Source: Reports of the Liquor License Branch, in *Sessional Papers of the Legislature of Ontario* (1905–15).

More significant than the effects of changes to the local option process were the effects on the license system of the tied house prohibition, especially as it operated in Toronto. Many observers, not only temperance supporters, viewed tied houses as problematic because the system bound the owner of a licensed premises to the economic interests of a brewer. Often under such arrangements, a brewery would either own or financially support the hotel business, and licensees were required to sell the brewery's products. Along with offending the ideal of free-market economics, the "tie" was seen to encourage higher beer sales to increase the brewery's profits. In the United Kingdom, the relationship between breweries and vendors had been a perpetually problematic issue, but by the beginning of the twentieth century brewery ownership of pubs was nearly ubiquitous.[111] Moreover, some saw this as creating stability in the pub business because brewers could carry the heavier costs of running or renovating a pub given that larger brewers had a better chance of carrying mortgages and loans than did individual pub managers. In many parts of Ontario, the tied house was not as prevalent as in Great Britain. However, Toronto, yet again, was a notable and notorious exception.

By the 1900s, many hotels in Toronto had become highly valuable investments. The number of licenses had been capped at 150 by municipal ordinance in 1887, even though the per capita limit established in the Crooks Act would have permitted over 200 licensed premises.[112] Yet the city was growing rapidly. In 1871, the population was 59,000; in 1881, it had increased by more than 50 percent to 96,196; by 1891, it had nearly doubled, at 181,215; and by 1901, it was 238,040.[113] The limit on hotel licenses remained firm at 150 even though, according to the Crooks Act's population-based allotment, it could have nearly 400 licensed taverns. As a result, when a hotel was sold, it could net $10,000 or more. Some commentators contended this meant that the license itself was worth thousands of dollars since the price of a hotel's building and chattels was not nearly equal to the selling prices of licensed hotels. This created a process of hotel speculation in which individuals would buy a licensed hotel, make minor modifications to it, and turn it over for a significant profit. It was this situation that led Hanna to increase the license fee in the amendment of 1906, especially in cities over 100,000 in population (which at the time applied only to Toronto). Even this increase did not capture the remarkable profit in the city's hotel business.

In such a lucrative market, the tie between brewers and hotel proprietors was a logical result. With such high selling prices, many entrepreneurs sought financial support for their hotels. Brewers were happy to comply by fronting them mortgages or providing other loans. The elimination of the tied house ended the ease with which such arrangements were made, but it did not end the high cost of buying a hotel business, and of course the increased fee meant that operating a hotel was even costlier. As a result, many brewers and hoteliers developed new, and not clearly legal, means of financing. This shadowy system faced the glaring light of scrutiny in 1907 after the Toronto Board of License Commissioners asked the government to investigate potential attempts at bribery and political influence peddling in the hotel and liquor businesses of the province. The subsequent commission lifted the shades covering many of these business arrangements, revealed a range of problems with the operation of the license system in Toronto, and described influence peddling, economic relationships, personal connections, and active gaming of the system that challenged the integrity of most people involved with licensing in Toronto and possibly the whole province. It also resulted in recommendations for systemic change that, if implemented, would fundamentally alter the licensing system in the province.

The Starr Commission and the Future of Licensing in Ontario

The investigation was sparked by an apparent case of attempted bribery. In the evening of 30 July 1906, Chair of the Toronto Board of License Commissioners Dr. R.J. Wilson returned home from Muskoka to find a cheque for $1,000 on his desk. It was from J.F. Hynes, a man whom Wilson did not know. Concerned that it was a bribe, Wilson asked his solicitor, John Ferguson, to investigate. Hynes, a hotel owner and purported "hotel speculator," told Ferguson that he was applying for the transfer of a lease on the Clarendon Hotel and that the current occupant wanted $1,000 to vacate it. Hynes then explained that he was "advised that he should send you this check ... pending the settlement." On the surface, it was simply an innocent and awkward misreading of the licensing process.[114] Nevertheless, Wilson remained wary of Hynes's motives, even though the license board granted the transfer in September. It soon became apparent that the cheque had nothing to do with the Clarendon Hotel. Chief License Inspector W.L. Purvis explained that Hynes had an "arrangement" with brewer James Cosgrave and Dr. Beattie Nesbitt. The latter was a notorious Conservative "heeler" who had recently resigned as MLA for Toronto North to take a partisan appointment as registrar for West Toronto (he was the target of the cartoon about patronage in Figure 11.1). In November, Hynes's solicitor approached Wilson asking him whether Hynes would be able to get a license for another hotel. Still wary, Wilson demanded that Hynes meet with him to explain the cheque. The interview led Wilson to alert Provincial Secretary Hanna about the corruption and influence peddling that seemed to be rife in the hotel business of the city. Hanna began asking questions and had a provincial constable investigate the situation. By January, things had become so toxic that Hanna's office decided to cease issuing license transfers in the city until the concerns were addressed.

Thus began a long and convoluted exploration of the politics, economics, and shady dealings of the liquor business in Toronto. In a letter steeped in indignation at the shenanigans, Wilson informed Hanna that he had learned the identities of the "culprit or culprits" working with Hynes. "If you will send for Dr. Beattie Nesbitt and Jim or John Cosgrave brother of Larry Cosgrave, they will be able to give you the whole story of their conspiracy[.] [M]ake them tell the truth and make them take the consequences of their low down attempt to as I believe corrupt a public official."[115] Only an hour later he followed up with a second letter, providing the context for such "low down" activities:

> Ever since I insisted on the rigid enforcement of the law regarding the sale to or serving of guests during prohibited hours – and the strict observance of the rule and law as to tied houses – I have incurred the ill will of certain persons invested in the liquor business. This ill will ... has developed into the most malice I have had to meet and am prepared to meet as a necessary incident of my office. I am anxious to have either in public or private as you deem best the most thorough and searching investigation made by your dept of any official act of [the] Board since I assumed office.[116]

Hanna replied that he had the utmost confidence in Wilson. In the next few days, the government initiated a commission of inquiry into the whole business.

The commission was struck on 18 February 1907, with Conservative barrister J.R.L. Starr as the sole commissioner and Frank Hodgins as the commission's council. The scope of the inquiry was threefold: to inquire into irregularities related to the transfer of liquor licenses in Toronto, any violation of the tied house clause of the license act, and "any failure to carry out or enforce the provisions of the Liquor License Act."[117] It was a broad mandate to examine the actions of companies, licensees, and government officials. The Liberal press was especially eager to jump into what would certainly be revelations of partisanship, patronage, bribery, and influence peddling that would belie Whitney's claims of balanced, unbiased, and even-handed administration of the liquor laws. Indeed, even the Conservative *Toronto World* recognized the threat to the premier's reputation for "rugged honesty that will not tolerate for a moment the merest suggestion of underhand influence" and called on Whitney to allow the commission to do a thorough job: "Without fear and without favor the whole truth must be brought out and if there are wrongdoers they must be named and punished."[118] The paper was satisfied when

Whitney told one of its reporters that the commission "would not please him if it did not probe as deep as the probe could reach."[119] Accordingly, the investigation quickly looked far beyond the unexpected cheque left on Wilson's desk in July.

With a variety of witnesses providing different stories, the commission pulled on several narrative threads. Hearing that various brewers, political figures, and business investors were forming partnerships to buy or build hotels and attempting to use Conservative connections to influence the license board's decisions, Starr and Hodgins traced the often obscured but interconnected relationships in the Toronto license market. They learned that the profitability of a liquor license increased exponentially the selling price of a hotel; in one example, a hotel that had sold in 1898 for $8,000 was resold eight years later for $25,000, a "fabulous increase."[120] With such high costs, aspiring hotel owners often looked to brewers for financial support. Starr and Hodgins learned that when the 1906 law eliminated tied houses, brewers continued to support hoteliers with promissory notes and mortgages and that, despite (and some said because of) the tied house prohibition of 1906, the economic relationships were becoming more coercive. Previously, brewers had provided hoteliers with ten-year mortgages, but now they were providing mortgages with "pay on demand" clauses, meaning that brewers, unhappy with licensees, could demand full payment of mortgages with little warning. Although there was limited evidence that a brewer would demand that a hotel carry exclusively his "wet goods" (a euphemism for booze), there seemed to be an unstated agreement that this would be the case.

The brewery arrangements were egregious, but the politics of the licensing system revealed an ecology of exploitation for personal gain. James Haverson, a solicitor for the liquor industry, explained how politics continued to affect licensing. He argued that liquor commissioners faced intense pressure by Tories (such as Nesbitt) who thought that they should receive partisan favour.[121] Haverson told of a shady economy of "political solicitors" who used their connections with the party in power to build their businesses. They would claim, he said, to have political influence with the board, get friends to confirm this influence, and then convince aspiring licensees that they needed to retain the Tory solicitors if they hoped to get licenses. Starr and Hodgins noted that license board records showed repeated appearances of specific solicitors; Haverson confirmed that J.W. Burns was an especially notorious political solicitor under the current regime. He also noted that the same situation had existed under the Liberals. Others corroborated Haverson's statements. Liberal hotel keeper J. Lyndon admitted that when the Conservatives came to power, his own solicitor recommended that he retain a Tory to deal with licensing matters, although Lyndon did not do so and did not seem to have problems from Conservatives on the license board. Similarly, Percy Kerwin, secretary of the Toronto License-Holders' Association, explained that although people continued to insinuate that their political influence was essential for the licensing process to be successful, it was mostly self-serving bluster by those aspiring to make money from the change in government.[122] Kerwin argued that whereas previous license boards might have been partisan, the current board was not. Starr was learning that rumours, innuendo, and influence peddlers, combined with the tradition of partisan manipulation and clientelism, made many believe that the licensing system was rife with partisan machinations even when the board was acting appropriately.

Political influence was not the only way that hoteliers attempted to affect the decisions of the board: economics also came into play. Since commissioners were unpaid, they relied on income from other businesses. Starr and Hodgins looked at the financial interests of all three license commissioners in Toronto. Wilson was a practising physician who, to his credit, refused to treat any licensees or their families except the few who had been patients before he became a commissioner. Reuben Millichamp was a partner in a dry goods merchant company and on the board of a fire insurance company, but he also seemed to be untouched by the attempts of the liquor industry to influence him by patronizing his businesses.[123] There were significant concerns, however, about the business of the third commissioner, D.M. Defoe. He was an insurance agent and had several fire insurance accounts with breweries and hoteliers. The commission heard from other insurance agents who claimed that they had lost brewery and hotel insurance clients to Defoe after he became a commissioner.[124] In his final report, however, Starr wondered whether that was about Defoe seeking new clients or about the well-known tendency for members of the liquor industry to attempt to influence a board by patronizing commissioners' businesses.[125] Despite this suggestion of the corruptibility of the board, in his final report Starr noted that all decisions of the board had been unanimous, and he concluded that the board was "absolutely clean."[126]

Starr's investigation also revealed a liquor system that had been deeply dysfunctional until the Tories came to power and Whitney insisted on removing politics from licensing. Both Wilson and Millichamp explained how, when they began their tenure, they undertook an extensive investigation of several problematic hotels in the city. Millichamp explained that the board demanded improvements to hotels near the St. Lawrence Market because in many cases "no respectable Chinaman would live in such places, and in some of these there was not a room fit for a dog."[127] Joseph Flavelle, a prominent Toronto entrepreneur who had served briefly as the first chair of the board appointed by Whitney's administration, noted that when his board took over it immediately cancelled the licenses of the three hotels that had fewer rooms than the law required, and it gave any hotel that had substandard accommodations but enough rooms a grace period of three months to allow management to get the premises into shape. When asked how he defended the licensing of such poor premises, Flavelle said that this had been the case for some time and that he could not explain why inspectors had permitted the hotels to continue to operate.[128] Long-time inspector T.A. Hastings, who had retained his Liberal-appointed position after Whitney's government took over, could not offer much clarification.[129] Such witnesses implied that under the previous Liberal administration, many of these hotels were simply allowed to run with few improvements and no attention to the hotel side of the business. Such observations blended into a general criticism of the license board prior to 1905. Starr found that under the Liberal commissioners the licensing system was characterized by improper administration, no clear and consistent documentation, and little evidence that inspectors wrote regular reports on each hotel in the city. This was all in violation of the license act, and Starr concluded that under the new board such disorganization had been replaced by "a full and complete system of keeping track of the documents."[130]

The poor situation under Liberal administrations was exacerbated by the changes insisted on by the Tories. The directive from Hanna to "MAKE THEM KEEP HOTEL!" was repeatedly shown to have caused problems for Toronto's licensees. The demand for full hotel accommodations was much lower than the demand for licensed drinking spaces, yet all licensees needed to run proper hotels. As a result, several witnesses noted, hotels such as those near the St. Lawrence Market had become mere saloons with substandard rooms to meet the law's requirements. Haverson argued in favour of reinstating a saloon license because "the present system of calling everything hotels was absolutely dishonest." He repeated his assertion that people had a right to drink.[131] Moreover, several witnesses argued that the tied house system had at least kept the hotels respectable because brewers "would probably wish the house conducted in an orderly manner" and that removing the tie meant that hotel keepers had less incentive to keep things respectable and had less money with which to maintain their premises.[132] Pressed to comment on the assumption that tied houses resulted in brewers forcing licensees to push their own products, Millichamp did not see this as a significant problem since the brewer "would have to have the place properly conducted, and the license kept secure, in order to sell his beer."[133]

Nevertheless, the investigation was not simply a validation of the integrity of the Conservative administration and a condemnation of the Liberals. Several highly placed Conservatives were found to have attempted to influence the licensure and patronage appointments of Tory supporters. Beattie Nesbitt was not the last politician whose motives were suspect. Flavelle mentioned how Minister of Education Robert Pyne had urged the board to grant a license to a hotel keeper who had numerous violations of the license act on his record. Flavelle's entire Conservative-appointed board had resigned in disgust at the end of 1905 when Hastings, the chief inspector for Toronto and a Liberal appointee, had been removed ostensibly for refusing to grant a hotel to a problematic hotel keeper who had been a Tory.[134] A captain of the fire department and an active Conservative ward worker told stories of meetings with Hanna and others at the elite Albion Club at which the merits of applicants whom they believed not to be "good Conservatives" were discussed. Yet Starr decided that many of these claims were either not credible or not problematic. His decision not to call Pyne to the stand was criticized by the more virulent Liberal press. There was some discussion that Hanna, the well-liked and energetic provincial secretary who also oversaw the License Branch, should be investigated, but nothing came of it. Starr resisted calls to dig deeply into these actions, which suggests that the Conservative barrister was interested in keeping pressure off his political friends.

The hearings ended in March 1907, but instead of heeding requests to release his report quickly Starr undertook a further examination of the potential alternatives to the licensing system established by the Crooks Act over three decades earlier. In this work, he might have been encouraged by Hanna. In correspondence with Earl Grey, the advocate of public house trusts and by now the governor general of Canada, the provincial secretary demonstrated an openness to considering other systems of liquor distribution despite resistance from the premier, who rejected suggestions of any substantial changes. In a friendly series of letters, Grey encouraged Hanna to consider a public house trust or other Gothenburg-inspired alternative to Ontario's licensing system. Starr researched the licensing system in the United Kingdom and read the publications of

Joseph Rowntree and Arthur Sherwell on how the Gothenburg system had been modified to suit the conditions in Britain through organizations such as Earl Grey's Public House Trust.[135] He also investigated the South Carolina Dispensary. In his final report, he used these examples to suggest a new approach to liquor licensing in Ontario.

The report that Starr submitted to the government (and to the major newspapers) in September 1907 was an exhaustive analysis of over 1,000 transcript pages of testimony and recommendations on the best way to reduce many of the problems that Starr and Hodgins had uncovered. Starr argued that the inflated value of a hotel, which he calculated to average about $24,000 per license, meant that "every time the License Commissioners of the City of Toronto issue a license," they give the licensee "a present of $24,000."[136] The solution, he suggested, was for the province to recoup this value by taking 80 percent of the cost of a license transfer and leaving 20 percent of the price of the hotel in the hands of the licensee. Although he recognized that there would be opposition to this proposition, he argued that it would eliminate speculation.[137] Moreover, Starr observed that the license fee was inequitable: regardless of the amount of business done by a hotel, or the value of a hotel in terms of real estate, all licensees paid the same $1,200 per year. But beyond arguing for such changes to the existing licensing system, Starr presented a detailed and well-researched alternative to the Crooks Act, which, as far as his investigation had determined, seemed to be in desperate need of renovation.

Although the Starr Commission was established to examine the politics of licensing in Toronto, its report included recommendations that could alleviate the dysfunctions of the liquor system across the province. Starr dismissed the South Carolina Dispensary, noting that "the control of the liquor traffic by the State [was] a much worse evil than we have at present." Regarding the public house trust, he refused to support a system designed "to make the surroundings of the saloon agreeable and enticing." He did not think that it was a good idea to attempt to bring "respectable people into the saloon." Starr also saw little value to the province in the Gothenburg system since it did not apply to beer and wine, placing restrictions only on spirits. Thus, he explained, although the consumption of spirits had decreased in Sweden, beer and wine drinking had increased; Starr did not see how such a system would be helpful in Ontario. He did point out that there was nothing in the current law that prevented a group of investors from creating such a company since all that was necessary was for a Board of License Commissioners to grant all licenses in its region to one company.[138] Nevertheless, his assessments of these systems, notably his utter rejection of a government-run dispensary as the worst kind of evil, suggest a clear laissez-faire approach to liquor licensing.

The alternative that Starr encouraged built upon the possibility of an expanded professional bureaucracy as the best way to stave off the predations of the liquor industry. He argued that many of the problems of political influence, attempts to curry favour with a board by engaging in business with its commissioners, and numerous importunities on license commissioners by liquor men could be eliminated by centralizing the board in Toronto, paying commissioners well, and developing a network of inspectors to keep an eye on the licensees across the province. Starr recognized that there might be some objections to such a system, and that people might argue that a government should not "lay aside its responsibility for the administration of law by handing it over to a Commission," but he also noted that the government already did so in some cases (referencing the railway commission) and that "if there is any one instance where it might be helpful and justifiable it would be in the liquor traffic." He concluded by recommending "an independent, salaried Board of three to be appointed with large powers, to administer licenses in and throughout the Province of Ontario."[139] The vendors would remain independent, but they would be closely watched by an expanded administration. The liberal state would then manage liquor at a distance.

The implications of Starr's report were clear. Starr validated the approach to administering the license law that Whitney had advocated since before he was elected premier. Starr found that the corrupt, or at least inept, system that had existed before 1905 had resulted in substandard hotels being licensed for years. By pointing the finger at inspector Hastings, a Liberal appointee, for the conditions of some hotels, especially around the market, Starr gave strength to Whitney's decision to remove Hastings, which at the time had driven the members of Flavelle's license board to resign. Yet at the same time, Starr's report illustrated the persistence of partisan manoeuvring in general. Although Starr concluded that the ministers in Whitney's government were not inappropriately partisan and that the license commissioners were "clean," the numerous documented attempts to influence licensing at the ward level demonstrated that the clientelist system that Oliver Mowat harnessed to the government's administration in the 1870s was still strong, the integrity of the licensing system remained fragile, and it could be strengthened or undermined depending on the characters of board members and license officers. For example,

Chief Inspector Purvis had been publicly friendly with "political solicitor" James Burns, going to lunch with him and sometimes meeting with brewer James Cosgrave. This had allowed Burns to intimate to others that he had "pull" with the license board. Purvis was condemned not for being a bad inspector but for being naive about the how people might perceive his relationship with Burns.

The impact of Starr's report is less straightforward. Although the focus on the actions of several major players in the Conservative ranks led to calls for resignations, only Purvis quit; commissioner D.M. Defoe grumbled about the pressure that he faced, but both he and Minister of Education Robert Pyne weathered repeated criticisms in the Grit press and remained in their positions. Beattie Nesbitt, who arrogantly and unconvincingly dismissed charges that he had used his Tory connections for financial gain, rejected calls that he resign his patronage position of registrar for West Toronto. Although he stepped down in November, two months after Starr issued his damning report, it is unclear whether this was because of pressure from the report or because he was encouraged to run for office. Nesbitt remained popular among Conservatives, was considered to be tremendously influential, and in December 1907 was chosen as the "standard bearer" for the party in the upcoming mayoral election (he came in third behind another Tory, both of whom lost to Joseph Oliver, a Grit and teetotaller who took the mayoralty in a landslide).[140] This election led to further indirect repercussions of Starr's report. In 1908, a motion to reduce the number of liquor licenses in Toronto from a maximum of 150 to a maximum of 110 was presented soon after the newly elected city council met. One of the justifications for this law was that, as noted in the Starr Report, most of the hotels were used not for accommodation but merely for selling liquor and thus were not needed for the "travelling public." The council of the city's Board of Trade flatly rejected such arguments, noting that the current number of 150 had been set when the city was half the size that it was in 1905 and that a more appropriate approach would be (you guessed it) a referendum on the issue.[141] This suggestion was rejected, and when the bylaw was passed, all three commissioners (Wilson, Millichamp, and Defoe) resigned, saying that it was contrary to the wishes of the majority, a violation of the principles of true temperance, and that it would simply create more illegal drinking.[142]

Beyond effects on personnel, the Starr Report's impact on policy was generally minimal. The idea of recouping a percentage of the price of a hotel transfer was not implemented. In 1909, amendments to the law gave the License Branch veto power over some of the decisions of license commissioners, but it was far from the centralized board that Starr had recommended.[143] In 1911, the recognition of an uneven profitability of hotels led to the implementation of a 5 percent tax on profits from beer, cigars, and similar consumables, above a nominal daily amount, and a requirement that the receipts be submitted monthly to the government.[144] It is difficult to determine whether this had any effect on the rampant speculation and hyper-inflated value of hotel properties that Starr found to be tending toward corruption, but it did increase the bureaucracy of licensing in the province. Similarly, his suggestion of strengthening the provisions forbidding contracts with brewers and other manufacturers was not implemented, although this might have been because the clauses ending tied houses in the 1906 legislation were sufficient and just needed better enforcement.

***

The end of the thirty-two-year Liberal reign in Ontario saw more than just a replacement of one party by another; it ushered in, with James Whitney at the helm, a different approach to governing. As his biographer explains, Whitney was a unique politician for the time. Autocratic in tendency, "he kept his own counsel, seeking guidance only from a few close political friends." He "forced his personal honesty upon all his followers," which resulted "in a new standard of political morality for the province." And, though he used patronage, he did not use it in a vindictive way.[145] These qualities reflect how Whitney approached the liquor question, which, although a major issue for the temperance and liquor forces, was not his most pressing concern. He sought to bring adherence to regulations and honest management to the system, openly eschewing the impractical idea of prohibition in favour of tightening laws and enforcing them. Even in his approach to the Starr Commission, Whitney remained consistent, insisting that Starr dig as deeply as possible in order to reach the heart of the problem. He might have appreciated Starr's conclusion that the system needed an overhaul; what he did not welcome was Starr's argument that the Crooks Act needed to be replaced with a more tightly run centralized administration. That conclusion might indicate the influence of Hanna, who, in his correspondence with Earl Grey especially, indicated that he was more sympathetic to the temperance cause than his premier and more amenable to an overhaul of how liquor was managed in the province. Such debates reached into a shifting conception of the role of government in the liberal state. Whitney, insistent on a degree of regional autonomy and limited government action, rejected modifications that would involve more administration overseen by a junta of paid commissioners seated in Toronto and travelling the province to make decisions in regions about which they might have known little. As a lawyer from Dundas, this might have rankled Whitney, but as a Conservative it simply would have been too much government involvement in the lives of the people. Besides, to Whitney, whose election was prefaced by a scandal involving a violation of liquor laws in small-town eastern Ontario, the liquor question was simply not as big a deal as other people contended. It did not need such an overhaul, just better enforcement. Nevertheless, within a decade of the Starr Report, notwithstanding the premier's rejection of its precepts, the system would indeed see significant change, and government would reach into the very liberties that all sides had debated for decades, ostensibly to preserve the future of the liberal state itself.

12

Centralization, II: Beyond the Crooks Act, 1907–16

It might be tempting to begin this chapter with some grand observation about the "march to prohibition" in Ontario since, indeed, it ends with a discussion of how provincial prohibition came to pass. But that would distort the record, suggesting that the policy choices made in the decade after J.R.L. Starr issued his report were inexorably pointing to that single end. They were not. Indeed, in 1907, with an administration that viewed prohibition as unworkable and a premier who would have nothing to do with it, any potential change would see little more than a variation on the system in existence. Reform of the system was more likely than prohibition, and suggestions about how to deal with the liquor problem that would not lead to the unpopular and remarkably illiberal solution of prohibition were also under consideration. Starr's report, Lord Grey's influence, and examples of other variations following market-driven, moderationist principles became subject to concerted evaluations. That a decade later the province would ban the sale of all liquor was not predictable, notwithstanding the hopefulness of prohibitionists. A system of incremental restriction and expanding administration was a more realistic expectation despite the premier's initial rejection of that strategy. When prohibition did come, it was under the shadow of total war and what, for some, was an existential threat to the liberal state itself.[1]

***

After 1907, Starr's argument for a centralized, professional board garnered considerable attention but little traction in the province. James Whitney rejected suggestions for such a significant change, preferring to strengthen local license commissions and encourage them to enforce the law fairly. He saw this, combined with encouraging a growing network of detectives and inspectors, as being suitably effective to control the worst excesses and violations of the law.[2] In January 1908, Provincial Secretary William J. Hanna wrote to the premier advocating several changes to the law, notably the idea of "putting this whole Province under one commission of three ... [and the] Commissioners to be big men and well paid." He also noted that the idea was supported by the Ontario Liberals, members of temperance organizations, and Starr himself.[3] Apparently, Hanna knew that Whitney would be difficult to convince, so he attached to his letter a series of extracts from Whitney's own public statements about the liquor trade, attempting to convince his boss that such a change would be in keeping with the premier's own arguments about needing the moral leadership and intestinal fortitude to make big changes to the system. Whitney remained resolute. When the idea was floated in the press in 1911, he quashed discussion by saying that there was "no foundation" to the rumours even though Hanna had "intimated the possibility of legislation of this nature being introduced."[4]

    Hanna might well have been a subtle and persistent advocate of change in the operation of liquor licensing in the province. Although he did not have a receptive ear with the premier, he did have some influential support. As mentioned in the previous chapter, the provincial secretary engaged in friendly correspondence with Earl Grey, president of the Central Public House Trust association and by this time governor general of Canada. The relationship that they forged seems to have been more personal and intimate than that of simply a government official contacting the head of state. Grey reached out to Hanna at the start of the provincial secretary's tenure, encouraging him to consider a bill "which would secure the application of the principle of disinterested management," the achievement of which, Grey noted, "would be giving an example which will be followed eventually by other parts of the Empire."[5] Hanna proceeded to dig into the issue with some vigour. He informed Grey that "Mrs. Hanna has followed your plans from the outset," assuring the governor general that his wife "is in no sense a 'new woman' [but] ... an enthusiastic convert to your scheme as furnishing the most practical remedy for an evil that may be modified but cannot be wiped out." Hanna also noted that he would be unapologetically "prejudiced in its favor when we come to consider the whole question here."[6] Grey forwarded him books by Rowntree and Sherwell on the Gothenburg system and liquor control, which the governor general had also given to the new chair of the Toronto Board of License Commissioners, Joseph Flavelle; Hanna ordered copies of his own (he might well have passed these books on to Starr during the latter's research on alternatives to the Crooks Act).[7]

Hanna and Grey were united in their belief that something needed to be done about liquor consumption and that the solution offered by prohibitionists was hardly suitable. Together they reflected on the reasons that temperance people did not like the public house trust idea. Grey told Hanna that temperance people vilified state control, which he defined as using liquor funds to relieve taxation, since excess profits would go into public coffers, and that the alternative of the trust company would avoid "the great objection of the state handling the trade and making profits for the relief of taxation out of it."[8] Hanna concurred and noted that, in speaking to "a leading prohibitionist here," he had mentioned the public house trust system, but his suggestion "was denounced." He was frustrated, noting that "the prohibitionists are apparently disposed to treat as the worst enemy of their cause any remedy that will modify the evil without attempting prohibition, which is impossible."[9] Over the next few years, the governor general took occasional interest in the licensing situation in Ontario, suggesting at times opportunities to do a trial run of the trust system. Since the northern part of the province was opening up to development, Grey asked Hanna to consider introducing a trust system in Cobalt; although Hanna suggested that the towns of "Haileybury and New Liskeard ... offer a splendid opportunity for testing the virtues of the trust principle," it does not appear that he put this suggestion into action.[10] When, in 1911, he amended the license act to impose a 5 percent levy on the sale of drinks over a certain volume, he sent a copy to Grey. The governor general replied with another pamphlet on the trust principle and a dismissal of any such levy, which he considered high license. He recommended that Hanna consider an economic arrangement that would replace any form of high license with a "poundage upon the amount of alcoholic drinks consumed," thereby putting a specific price on overdrinking. At the same time, Grey commiserated with the provincial secretary about the stubbornness of temperance adherents who wanted nothing but a complete and unrealistic cessation of the drink trade:

> Of course the intemperate teetotaler [sic] who sees virtue not in temperance but only in abstinence, regards with horror the drinking of a glass of beer under any circumstances whatsoever. It would be irrational and

unreasonable to look for any approval from him for the Trust regulation of public houses; but to the great majority of level-headed, fair minded men, the principle of regulation which finds its expression in the Trust House of England must appear as a fair and sensible attempt to settle the drink problem.[11]

The trust system was not tried in Ontario, but this correspondence indicates that Hanna was concerned about the liquor question and aware that the licensing system in the province might need more significant changes, be they a public house trust or a centralized board overseeing the province's liquor network, than his boss might support. Such interest reappeared over the next few years.

Starr was not the only person in Ontario suggesting that the government take more direct control of liquor sales. In 1907, while Starr was mulling over the results of his investigation, Rev. S.D. Chown, a persistent and generally cordial correspondent with Hanna, explained that the recent province of Saskatchewan had accepted Chown's proposal to establish a centralized license commission.[12] Hanna was reluctant to comment and told Chown that he was gathering "what data I can on the subject."[13] Such data might have come in the form of analyses undertaken by Eudo Saunders, a barrister from Glengarry who had been appointed in 1903 by the Liberal government to replace the long-serving chief officer of the License Branch, Henry Totten (who survived the change in government of 1905).[14] In several reports, Saunders detailed the potential benefits of a centralized board. In a memo dated 7 September 1909, he outlined the main problems of the existing municipal licensing system, reflecting many of the abuses that Starr had found but in smaller jurisdictions throughout the province. Saunders explained that in many places commissioners were "men ... of business in the localities in which they reside, and their personal interests are often bound up with those of the license holders of the district and experience shows that this has a very bad effect." Yet such overlap between personal business and provincial licensing seemed to be unavoidable as the system currently existed. Many people told Saunders that since "they receive no salaries ... some of [the commissioners] seem to think it legitimate to use their positions ... for their own benefit." He noted that this even affected the enforcement of basic sanitary and safety rules for hotel operations. He recommended, instead, the

> abnegation of the present system, generally known as the Crooks Act, and the adoption in its stead of some system which will give to one body the

control of this whole subject. A Central Board ... say of five members of the right class drawn from different parts of the Province would be ample for the work, and would do it much more satisfactorily than it is done now.[15]

In a subsequent undated memo, Saunders noted that, even though many boards were run well, "experience shows that the system as a whole is absolutely bad."[16] Despite being appointed by the Liberals, Saunders admitted that many of the "evils" of the system had been worse before Whitney's government took over, but he repeated that a centralized system would be far more effective and efficient. He pointed out that under the current system, with a patchwork of local option municipalities throughout license districts, some inspectors were responsible for inspecting only one or two places, whereas others had to investigate many more. Under a centralized system, "twenty-five or thirty efficient local inspectors" would be enough to oversee the system, along with "the special staff which has done such effective work during the last two or three years," referring to detectives and special inspectors.[17]

It was a detailed, well-considered, and convincing argument from a former Crown attorney, but it did not sway the premier. Whitney remained steadfast in his rejection of the push toward centralization. Perhaps as a small-town lawyer from eastern Ontario, perpetually in the orbit of the larger centres of Ottawa, Montreal, and Kingston, not to mention Toronto, Whitney was wary of placing all authority in one central body. Or perhaps he respected local autonomy. More likely, though, Whitney saw the operation of the licensing system as it stood to be good enough. He held to his assertion that he was doing what was best for the province in retaining and strengthening the existing system; moreover, given all of the other changes that he had made in his first few years as premier, he likely did not see liquor licensing as an issue as dire as others on his docket. Whitney had seen his government's policies (not just on liquor) confirmed in the election of 1908, in which a weakened Liberal Party had been reduced from twenty-nine seats in 1905 to nineteen seats, and his party had increased its count from sixty-nine to eighty-six. This strong showing persisted in 1911 (eighty-three seats to twenty-two seats), but when the Liberals selected a new leader – prominent lawyer, Methodist, and temperance stalwart Newton Rowell – Whitney faced a new challenge from a party that had thrown its lot even more firmly in with the Dominion Alliance. His response was to present his success in strengthening the licensing system and facilitating local option as a much better form of liquor restriction (and one that Ontario could legislate constitutionally) than anything more radical.

Still, when Rowell announced that his party's platform included a pledge to "abolish the bar," Whitney had to respond to concerns that the Liberals were taking the initiative on temperance measures.[18] Rowell was not a sitting member of the legislature when he took over the leadership, but he won his seat in the heavily temperance-oriented riding of Oxford North (Mowat's old riding) in a by-election in 1912. During the session of 1912, Rowell introduced a multifaceted measure that would commit the legislature to "the immediate abolition of the bar," impose restrictions on the liquor traffic "to limit its operations and ... remedy its evils," and ensure that the law would be enforced by "officials in sympathy with law enforcement" and eliminate political influence.[19] It faced an immediate response from Whitney. The premier proposed an amendment to Rowell's motion that wiped out the opposition measures and replaced them with a motion that recognized the legislature's "duty ... to minimize as far as possible the evil effects of the drink habit by wise restrictions upon the traffic in intoxicating liquors." This motion also included assertions not only that it was ultra vires the province to make laws affecting manufacturing but also that "no good object would be served by simply diverting the habit from the bar to some other place."[20] It was fully consistent with Whitney's ideas about the importance of strict enforcement and the futility of any attempt at prohibition. It also affirmed the importance of banning treating. Moving even further from the spirit of Rowell's motion, another Conservative MLA proposed a subsequent amendment in which the legislature commended the government for its work in the "earnest and faithful administration of the Liquor License Laws." After extensive debate that continued into the next morning, the legislature overwhelmingly supported these changes.[21] Tellingly, Whitney's papers include an unsigned text of his amendment, which originally concluded with a section asserting that the best way to deal with liquor licenses was through a "commission having jurisdiction over the entire province." This section was struck out and not read in the legislature, suggesting that the motion was penned by someone sympathetic to the idea of a centralized board, but that Whitney continued to resist the significant change in the licensing system encouraged by Starr, Hanna, Chown, and Saunders.[22]

Whitney's addition of treating in the countermotion was an attempt to reiterate his government's interest in making pragmatic changes to the liquor licensing system rather than banning the barroom, which might not even have been intra vires the provincial government. As noted in

Chapter 10, many commentators, both diehard prohibitionists and moderates, recognized that treating could have a negative effect on the drinking culture of the community. The standard rationale was that someone who visited a tavern with friends would be expected to buy a round (treat them), just as they bought rounds for him.[23] This could lead to excessive drinking and a considerable hit to the pocketbook. The *Windsor Record* printed a reflection on treating by George Fitch, probably the American evangelical minister. He characterized it as

> the process of drinking a drink which you do not want in order to buy another man a drink which he probably doesn't want, and then drinking another drink which you want still less in order to give him the opportunity of paying you back before you can consider him a tight wad who would rather squander his money on hats for his wife than in a noble effort to drown his friends.[24]

Supporting Whitney's motion, the *St. Thomas Times* called treating "most absurd and pernicious in its consequences."[25] Yet finding an effective solution to the problem of treating was elusive. Whitney saw it as beyond the scope of what the provincial government should do. When in July 1905 he received a letter from Jennie Brander of Port Lambton asking him to do away "with the public bar and this dreadful treating for the sake of the poor weaklings who have no strength of mind to resist temptation," Whitney told her to speak to her local commissioners. He cautioned, however, that "the question of moral reform, to which you refer, is a very broad one and one which can never be determined or settled by the enactment of any laws."[26] Nine years later Whitney's inclusion of treating in his response to Rowell's banish-the-bar campaign was a recognition that perhaps it was time to change the situation, although it might have been a way of placating temperance forces to whom the promise of "banish the bar" appealed.

The anti-treating motion dogged Whitney for a year. Initially, it received mixed reviews. Some saw it as a reasonable approach to an intractable problem, whereas others argued that one could not eliminate treating without eliminating the bar.[27] The *Newmarket Era* was skeptical but suggested that eliminating treating could work if it was accompanied by a centralized liquor-vending system.[28] At least one dry commentator argued that by eliminating the treating system even local option would no longer be necessary.[29] Even Liberal newspapers such as the *Windsor Record*, which acknowledged that it supported Whitney's three-fifths clause, thought that Whitney fell short if he believed that his anti-treating amendment would be enough to deal with the problems that Drys saw in the liquor system.[30] Other writers, such as the editor of the *Canadian Courier* and an observer in the Detroit *Journal,* were skeptical of both policies. The *Courier* concluded that both leaders must be "joking," and the *Journal* editor suggested that neither had considered the loss of revenue and thus could not be taken seriously.[31] The editor of the *Kingsville Reporter* referred to "the treatless bar" and "the barless treat" as "very attractive playthings for the politicians" but not what temperance people wanted.[32] In any case, the province had a year to mull it over, since a week after the amended motion passed, Provincial Secretary Hanna presented minor amendments to the law that did not include anything to do with treating. Reportedly, the License Branch was investigating the best way to institute the policy. Responding to this delay, the *Globe* joked that Whitney "has become academic."[33] Privately, his secretary, Horace Wallis, contacted the research bureau at New York–based encyclopedia company Nelson and Sons to investigate how anti-treating laws had worked in various municipalities in the United States. A specific experiment in Tacoma, Washington, was futile, with few attempts to enforce the measure. The Nelson correspondent noted that the anti-treating bylaw was "practically a dead letter." He had heard of a few other places with such a law but was unaware that it was effective anywhere, and he opined that "the anti-treating law can be successfully enforced only where an entire state or province is affected by it."[34]

While the government investigated the practicalities of banning treating, Whitney had to contend with Rowell's banish-the-bar pledge, which was getting a lot of attention. As noted above, many argued that stopping treating was impossible as long as the bar remained. The Dominion Alliance reiterated its emphasis on banning the bar, ending treating, and banning drinking in clubs, an issue that persisted even after the Liberal government had implemented a licensing system for clubs selling booze in 1897, and it was especially problematic because private clubs could provide liquor to their members even in local option districts.[35] Nevertheless, correspondents told Whitney in confidence not to worry about Rowell's pledge. One argued that Whitney just needed to give Rowell "all of that kind of rope he wants and the sooner it will accomplish his finish as it did the Ross Government."[36] Such assurances seemed to be borne out when the Tories easily beat the Liberals in by-elections in North Waterloo and East Middlesex in October 1912.[37] The East Middlesex win was especially poignant since the "banish-the-bar" pledge had been considered a major issue there.[38] The *Windsor Record* called it more of a loss for Rowell than a victory for Whitney and noted that "abolition of the bar won't win for the simple reason that it isn't practical."[39] Reflecting on these victories, Whitney told a confidant that "Rowell has made a great blunder in taking up his 'banish the bar' policy and then failing to go out and fight for it."[40] Rowell, meanwhile, reasoned that the loss in East Middlesex should not be indicative of the weakness of his policies, and he accused the government of siding with the liquor interests in that campaign.[41]

By the time the legislative session began in 1913, much anticipation of the anti-treating law and rumours about what it would look like had stoked expectations. In the middle of 1912, several newspapers had reproduced detailed information about the anticipated law, stating that it would make a tavern keeper, or bartender, or buyer, or recipient of treating subject to fines of from $100 to $200.[42] Such details suggest that someone who knew what the government was planning had provided this information, but neither Whitney nor Hanna revealed publicly any details of the law, if they had even planned one. Thus, when the speech from the throne in February 1913 failed to mention treating, the opposition was disappointed but not surprised. When the legislature debated the speech, Huron Centre Liberal William Proudfoot (who had seconded Rowell's ban-the-bar motion the year earlier) introduced an amendment to the traditional motion that thanked the lieutenant governor for the speech by specifically referring to this omission. Proudfoot's amendment expressed disappointment that the government was not following through on its promise to enact anti-treating legislation.[43] One week later, Hanna amended Proudfoot's amendment so that it expressed confidence that the government "will, at the proper time, submit legislation ... which will place further restrictions upon the drink traffic and minimize the evils thereof," thereby expunging any mention of the anti-treating promise from the motion.[44] A few weeks later, when Rowell reintroduced his banish-the-bar motion, expanding it to capture the need both to eliminate treating and to end drinking in clubs (thereby fully mirroring the policy of the Dominion Alliance), the government again amended it in its own favour. Hanna's amendment affirmed that the legislature "recognizes the duty cast upon it to minimize, as far as possible, the evil effects of the drink habit by wise restrictions upon the traffic in intoxicating liquors." It went on to state that local option had been a success, and it asserted that banning liquor sales in bars while continuing it in shops would "increase the evils resulting from the traffic and habit."[45] It was an attempt to confirm the government's lack of interest in advancing any form of province-wide prohibition while reasserting its own achievements. The motion also again erased any commitment to anti-treating. The amendments to the liquor law that did pass that year made it illegal for tavern keepers to allow people to take liquor out of a tavern, but apart from a few other tweaks, no further changes were made.

The renewed interest in treating reveals a new feature in the legislation related to liquor under Whitney: drinkers' activities inside a barroom were becoming targets of regulation. Under the Crooks Act, the number of licensees and the costs of licenses, as well as the distribution of the licensed premises, were based upon population numbers and assessments of the best places and the best people to hold such a privilege. But the law left decisions about what constituted a well-run tavern and a suitable tavern keeper to the discretion of commissioners and inspectors. The government did not reach into licensed spaces apart from determining who could and could not be there. When it took office, Whitney's government began to attempt, in a general way, to consider the inner workings of a barroom. The bartenders' licenses in 1906 were intended to make sure that the right type of people were serving alcohol, suggesting a degree of control over the actions of bartenders, who faced a loss of career if they lost that license. The amendments of 1911 had included a prohibition on cashing cheques, a practice that temperance people had argued for decades enabled workers to take their pay directly to the bar and blow it all on booze. The promise to address treating was a further infiltration of the drinking space and, had it come to fruition, would have allowed the government to stay the hand of the drinker when he raised it to order a round. The *Hamilton Times* called it "a very drastic law ... which will aim to reach the hotel-keeper, the bar-tender, the man who is given the treat and the man who buys the treat."[46] It was a significant modification of the action of the liberal state since the measure would have limited the freedom of the individual to choose how to spend his or her money. Such illiberal ideas were rife in the language of temperance, with sentiments such as Jennie Brander's characterization of drinkers as "poor weaklings who have no strength of mind to resist temptation" typical of the justification for a violation of individual autonomy. Yet, by ignoring the anti-treating promise, Whitney demonstrated that such actions were merely political tactics to counter the pressures of the temperance movement and undermine the temperance bona fides of the Liberals. It certainly did not hurt the Conservatives, who, in the middle of 1914, won another confident victory, with the seat count hardly changed.

The Conservative government elected in 1914 had retained its authoritative majority, but it would soon face significant challenges. On 4 August,

Britain declared war on Germany, and Canada followed the mother country into battle. The initial optimistic promise to be home by Christmas was soon found to be an illusion, and the subsequent mobilization of the country and its industries resulted in significant economic, social, and cultural changes. Whitney did not live to see the effects of the war on his province. His health had been flagging for a while, especially after a suspected heart attack in New York in 1913 had forced him to reduce his activities. Although by the end of the summer he had reportedly begun to be back to his old self, he died suddenly on 25 September.[47] Hanna took over as temporary leader before Sault Ste. Marie MLA William Hearst, the minister of lands, forests, and mines and a temperance supporter, was selected as the new Conservative leader and premier.[48]

At the next session of the legislature, Hanna introduced a bill to realize his goal of centralizing the liquor system. The new legislation would create a five-person board to oversee the administration of licenses across the province. This Board of License Commissioners took over the work of the License Branch, distancing the issue of liquor licensing from the everyday politics in a government ministry and lifting the level of oversight from municipal to provincial offices. The provincial board would determine the sizes of license districts and travel around the province to hold hearings on licensing, altering the dates on which licenses would be issued to suit regional priorities. The work of this paid board was to be facilitated by paid inspectors and an expanding bureaucracy.[49] The legislation also required liquor shops to close at 7 p.m. and soldiers in uniform not to be sold liquor, but it left other regulations, such as the closing times for taverns, up to the board. The temperance forces in the Liberal opposition protested immediately. William Proudfoot introduced a motion that would turn the legislation into a prohibitionist measure. He noted that "in this hour of national crisis and financial strain," the legislation did nothing to lessen the power of the liquor traffic, which he described as "an internal enemy seriously impairing both the offensive and [the] defensive powers of the nation." Proudfoot therefore moved that the government replace its licensing legislation with a bill that would close all drinking places and make local option "county-wide," which would "wipe out any shops which may remain," effectively instituting prohibition across the province.[50] This motion was defeated, and when the legislature proceeded to third reading the opposition introduced a series of motions attempting to impose several of Proudfoot's parameters on the law. None was successful.[51] Although called an act to amend the license law, the Liquor License Act of 1915 effectively marked the end of the Crooks Act era.

This significant change was short lived, replaced by an even more radical change a year later. The intensification of the war and the realization that it would last much longer than originally believed gave the temperance movement a further argument to eliminate the liquor traffic. The Drys had always been focused on an idealistic future without booze in which sober citizens would be able to realize their full potential unburdened by the shackles of King Alcohol, but now they could tap into an even more pertinent and immediate fear that the liquor traffic would lead to the downfall of the country because it would weaken its soldiers, undermine its industry, and lead to defeat at the hands of The Hun. Ontario's prohibitionists had some powerful allies in expressing such views. David Lloyd George, minister of munitions for Great Britain, where decades earlier the liquor issue had divided along party lines, famously argued in 1915 that Britain was "fighting Germany, Austria and Drink, and so far as I can see the greatest of these three deadly foes is Drink."[52] Lloyd George, who became prime minister in 1916, was not a teetotaller, but his Liberal Party was allied with temperance, and he supported reducing if not eliminating the drink trade for the duration of the war.[53] Many temperance supporters tied the strength of the troops to the dryness of the camps, pushing to eliminate wet canteens in military compounds. Such efforts provided a push toward prohibition, and in several provinces plebiscites confirmed increased support for it. In 1916, faced with a petition of 825,000 signatures (which included 350,000 eligible voters), Premier Hearst did what Whitney had always contended was impractical and unenforceable. Hearst introduced legislation replacing the Liquor License Act of 1915, which still had that new-law smell, with the Ontario Temperance Act, banning the retail sale of liquor for all but medicinal, industrial, and sacramental purposes and giving the provincial Board of License Commissioners authority to manage the distribution of those few remaining legal forms of liquor.[54] In effect, he implemented the requests that prohibitionists had brought to the Ross government over a decade earlier: prohibition supported by government dispensaries. Eighteen months later the dominion's Union government introduced a series of orders in council banning the importation of intoxicating liquor (any liquor with more than 2.5 percent alcohol) and instituting a ban on the manufacture of and interprovincial trade in liquor to begin in April 1918. On 24 December 1917, the *Globe* declared that prohibition was in place.[55] These bans were to remain until one year after the end of the war.[56] By this time, all provinces had voted themselves dry except Quebec, but even there many municipalities were implementing local option.[57] With the dominion ban on the manufacture, importation, and interprovincial trade of liquor, even those few remaining wet jurisdictions would be, essentially, dry as well.[58]

***

When the Conservatives took office in Ontario in 1905, it was after over thirty-two years of Liberal governance and nearly three decades of the operation of the Crooks Act. A law that had been intended to address municipal interference in the lucrative licensing system had succeeded in diminishing the number of places to drink and making local option a functional possibility across the province. At the same time, it had created its own culture of patronage and opportunities for partisan advancement throughout Ontario, while in the government a tendency to strike a near-impossible balance between pleasing – or not overly displeasing – both Wets and Drys made subsequent policy changes incremental and limited. By the time George Ross became premier, this tendency to mollify but not satisfy had become so entrenched that even a temperance figurehead like Ross could not avoid a wishy-washy approach to the temperance cause that he had advocated for decades. James Whitney then provided a fundamental shift in the tone of the government with respect to liquor laws. Believing that his victory in 1905 was a credit to his leadership and clear statements about policies such as licensing, Whitney felt no need to cater to either the Wets or the Drys. Moreover, having limited patience for partisan overtures, he saw his role as making the existing liquor system work. For Whitney, the liberal state was guided by the rule of law and distanced from influence peddling, patronage, and personal enrichment. Moreover, he believed that it was a state in which a strong leader lays out his platform and is bound to implement it. In this work, he was aided by his provincial secretary, William Hanna. More amenable to temperance arguments, but also interested in the practical operation of the law, Hanna appears to have acted as a foil for Whitney's single-minded adherence to his three-part promise about liquor licensing. Although Whitney succeeded in reducing partisanism in the licensing system – it would have been nearly impossible to rid a system of all partisan activity when it depended on the independent actions of so many government appointees – he was generally not interested in more radical changes to the regulation of the liquor traffic. Consequently, the recommendations of the Starr Report were virtually ignored, and it was not until after Whitney's death that Hanna was able to implement a system that he had advocated as a viable alternative to the flawed legislation that many still called the Crooks Act. Gradual changes by the Liberals led to a radical change by the Conservatives, but that resulted in further gradual changes, tweaks, and modifications before the ultimate centralization of licensing administration in the province. The dreams of prohibitionists, however, needed the international catastrophe of the Great War to provide salient arguments about the dangers of the liquor traffic to the health and future of the people. Even that rationalization was controversial since the people whom many of the temperance folks hoped to protect, the soldiers, rarely supported such measures. The liberal state might have prevailed, but even a threat to its very existence could not assuage the complications of liquor.

Conclusion: Liquor, Liberalism, and the Legacy of the Crooks Act

By 1916, that newly minted Ontarian whom we met in that tavern in 1867, now long in tooth and tired, would be boring young men at the tavern bar about the remarkable changes in the business of booze. He would talk about how the rowdy drunkenness in his community became a little less raucous when Adam Crooks passed his liquor licensing law in 1876. Remember when you could go to the store and buy a bottle or get your bucket filled? That ended slowly; from the middle of the 1880s, fewer stores were allowed to sell liquor, and in the 1890s you were no longer able to buy liquor in any grocery stores. Remember the Scott Act years, when it seemed that you could not travel at all without finding that you were in a community with no legal booze? You needed to find a knowing local to tell you where drink could be had. Thankfully, that ended, but soon after, when you headed into big towns, there were no saloons at all, just hotels with bars, although many of them were really just saloons with shoddy rooms. A wary traveller had to know where to go for a decent sleep and a good meal. And don't get him started about those "taverns" around that big market in Toronto, or the decade of constant liquor plebiscites that went nowhere. Most of his audience would remember the change in government in 1905. Having lived under Liberal rule for much if not all of their lives, they might have been apprehensive about a new administration, or perhaps they would have celebrated the collapse of a tottering Liberal machine. They might remember the sensation created by Mr. Starr's investigation, reported in detail in the newspapers, and how his report seemed to uncover all sorts of unsavoury relationships between the brewers and the hotels. Still, they might not have understood the significance of the Whitney government's activities until Mr. Whitney died and things really changed. They knew that stories of drinking, drunkenness, and easy access to a tipple was under threat because the new premier, Mr. Hearst, a temperance man from up north, was about to impose prohibition. He and his listeners might not be so bothered; many of them had friends and relatives in the trenches, and besides, they all still knew they could get drink when they wanted.

Beyond noting changes in the place and the time in which public drinking occurred, the old Ontarian might have expressed his sense that drinking itself was different. In 1867, he might have toasted the creation of Canada with a whiskey distilled by Mr. Seagram or Messrs. Gooderham and Worts, but in 1916 he was more likely to be quaffing a beer brewed by Mr. O'Keefe, or Carling, or Labatt, or Cosgrave, or Dow, or their children. His impression would be accurate. Inland revenue records indicate a shift in the production of spirits and beer between Confederation and 1914. Whereas the volume of beer being brewed was increasing, spirits production remained relatively stable, even though the population had grown significantly. The shift to beer, especially lighter lagers, was something that many moderates had argued was a preferable form of "true temperance" than prohibition (Figure 13.1).[1] Whether this indicated a

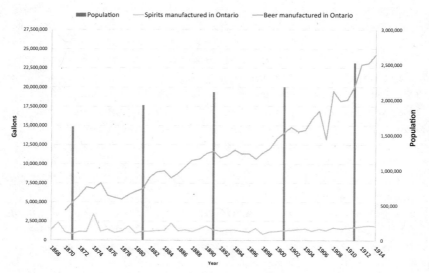

Figure 13.1 Change in liquor consumption in Ontario, 1868–1914
Source: Trade and Navigation Tables, in *Sessional Papers of the Parliament of Canada* (1867–1914).

general decline in individual consumption, however, was difficult to determine since Mowat's apparent success in restoring the right of the province to institute prohibition meant that local option communities were popping up all over the place. Although Whitney's strengthening of local option provisions had made it more difficult to pass local option, it also became more difficult to rescind those provisions. Could the growth of local option mean that more Ontarians were not drinking, so that those who remained "wet" were drinking the same or even more liquor? This is impossible to determine, so we must accept the correlation and avoid speculation of causation.

Changes in the location, hours, and extent of individual drinking might have been obvious to our old Ontarian, but perhaps less apparent was the transformation, over the first half century, of the place of the state in the lives of the people. Municipal licensing was highly subjective and individualized; councillors, reeves, aldermen, and other local leaders would run the show, hire the staff, determine who got the licenses, and maybe even take a cut. This took place despite the ideal in the nascent liberal state of the virtuous citizen, and especially responsible middle-class leadership, as engaged in civic governance that transcended individual interests.[2] Despite pre-Confederation laws that applied a few limits to licensing, and that many municipal councils seem to have ignored, decisions on from whom residents could buy liquor, where they could drink it, and when all this could take place were normally at the whim of municipal authorities. Inspectors tended to be marginal characters, less interested in enforcing the law than in making sure that licenses were issued on time and that fees were collected. By removing the licensing authority from municipalities, the Mowat government continued a process of centralizing aspects of governance, rationalizing the operations of the liberal state while still maintaining a degree of local autonomy.[3] Preserving local autonomy while reinforcing central authority, seemingly contradictory impulses, was also important to the ideal of liberalism.[4] Nevertheless, the work of the Boards of License Commissioners and inspectors removed some lucrative power from community leaders. The Crooks Act imposed, gradually and outside the view of most residents, more specific control on the liquor system in Ontario. The increased use of provincial inspectors or detectives further reinforced this central authority, demonstrating to the population as well as the local operatives the reach of the provincial government. Things became a little less casual, and the state was a little more present, however subversively, even subconsciously, in the act of drinking in public.

This examination of the development of Ontario's increasingly centralized liquor licensing system opens numerous windows of understanding of the operation of the liberal state in Ontario and to a lesser extent in Canada. The need to impose a specific form of order on the population, an interactive process of tweaking and modifying laws, and respecting local contexts but applying general principles, involved a process of standardizing local governance in the liberal state. In their early years in power, Mowat's Grits spent considerable energy analyzing and evaluating the operation of liquor laws in the municipalities. They tweaked laws to create stricter and more specific requirements for a municipal drinking environment that many considered to be out of control. The failure of these changes to effect standardization, combined with the intransigence of municipal politicians, the apparent nepotism and conflicts of interest at the local level, and the repeated demands for more action to deal with disorder caused by drunkenness, resulted in the centralization of licensing. Yet it was a centralization that still respected the need for municipal autonomy, and built as it was upon the province's long tradition of clientelism it could not be entirely objective in its operation (if any system run by humans ever could be). Boards of License Commissioners were to be composed of well-informed local elites, and inspectors were to be efficient local residents. Notwithstanding the tremendous opportunity for patronage, for rewarding party loyalists and building local power, the system also needed to be effective, lest the government's bold (and what Mowat called distasteful) efforts to impose a standardized and centralized form of liquor licensing on the province would fail.

Failure itself was distasteful for several reasons. The temperance movement, growing in volume and influence, sought prohibition, which was extreme and distasteful to many Ontarians. Not only would it mean that the hand of the state stayed the hand of the citizen, a remarkable imposition on the liberty of individuals, but also to impose prohibition would be to cripple a valuable industry that employed many workers and contributed significant funds to government coffers. Mowat, himself not a drinker but hardly a prohibitionist, manifested a central characteristic of leadership in a liberal state: he tried to balance the demands of very different sides of a highly contentious issue. Prohibition was anathema to the idea of liberalism, but so was the sort of disorder found by the investigations of the early 1870s and decried in the repeated entreaties by temperance people. The rational actor of the ideal liberal state could not be found in such disorder. Under the influence of alcohol, the liberal ideal of freedom to trade confounded the arguably more essential goal of the liberal state to nurture and encourage rational individuals whose sobriety (in temperament if not through temperance) would strengthen the state itself.

Here we see how different versions of liberalism could be manifested to justify a variety of government approaches to liquor. Representatives of the liquor industry manifested a classic liberalism, emphasizing equality in their insistence on fair treatment by the government and the law, individual freedom to pursue material desires as long as that freedom did not infringe the freedom of others, and the protection of property rights or, in the event of prohibition, reimbursement for the devaluation of property that had been engaged in a legal industry. Moderates relied on the straightforward assertion that the government did not have a role in managing the activities of individuals, but there was a place for encouraging moderation in and reasonable limitation on cultures of drink. They pointed to activities such as treating, which many agreed could be an infringement on the freedoms of others when someone bought them a drink because it encouraged them to repay the favour. Advocating the very illiberal activity of forbidding an individual to undertake an activity that did not seem to hurt others, the Drys increasingly represented a version of liberalism that Robert McDonald notes was "deliberately collectivist" while retaining adherence to the three main pillars of liberalism. Indeed, as McDonald reminds us, John Stuart Mill himself affirmed that individual liberty "had meaning 'only within the collective identity provided by local self-governing units.'"[5] In his study of voluntary associations in nineteenth-century Ontario, Darren Ferry argued that voluntary organizations, including temperance societies, "simultaneously buttressed the formation of collective liberal identities."[6] Such groups "often provided a bridge between the larger liberal project of state and market, and the collective identities of family, church, and neighbourhood," thereby representing the values of the community within a broader discourse of government action in the liberal state.[7] Liberalism could fit a variety of interests, and the three main pillars of liberalism, liberty, equality, and property, could be manifested for a variety of purposes when under the influence of liquor.

By establishing this new liquor licensing system, centralized but still respecting the importance of local self-governance, Oliver Mowat also ushered in an administration that could stand between politics and the people. The power of the tavern keeper was well known, and the decisions of government appointees to accept or reject license applications could and did appear to be symptoms of the ongoing partisan skirmishes in communities across the province. Although clientelism and patronage remained accepted, though often criticized, aspects of governance in the early part of the period under study, they were seen as increasingly problematic, especially in the issue of licensing, which affected so many people across the province.[8] In an attempt to undercut such criticisms, the Grits initially attempted to create bipartisan Boards of License Commissioners and published a table showing how many Grit and Tory tavern keepers received or lost their licenses. The former strategy of pluralism was abandoned, Mowat argued, because Tories on the boards tried to undermine the system that he and Crooks had built. It is more difficult to determine whether the latter approach continued or whether, as many opposition critics grumbled, the system was constructed to favour party loyalists or at least to silence opposition mutterings in the bars.[9]

Looking to the broader impact of liquor on the liberal state, we see that the passage of the Crooks Act was part of a more extensive transformation of the legal and political development of the country. The efforts to ascertain provincial and dominion responsibilities for liquor licensing placed liquor at the centre of several key disputes about constitutional jurisdiction. Although the provinces faced setbacks, by the end of the nineteenth century they had won the power to manage the liquor licensing system and the right to impose prohibition on sales but not manufacture, and the centralizing impulse at the dominion level, best represented by the failed McCarthy Act, was thwarted. For this reason, when prohibition did come to Canada, it came in the form of provincial legislation to forbid sales rather than the sort of national prohibition seen in the United States. The brief period during the Great War when the dominion government stopped the manufacture of recreational liquor was never as severe as the dreams of total suppression of the liquor traffic held by prohibitionists, and it was a temporary measure taken at a time of national crisis. It served, ultimately, to enrich some of the major distillers in Canada because the prohibition that appeared in the United States was indeed "total," however poorly realized it might seem to have been.[10]

This examination provides an important understanding of the idea of liberalism itself in the context of Ontario and, to a degree, throughout English Canada. Wets, Drys, and moderates all expressed an idea of British liberalism – British fair play, hard-won freedoms, Anglo-Saxon chauvinism toward "mercurial" francophone compatriots – but this liberalism was complex and contextual. The ideal of a government based upon the representative British parliamentary model was contrasted with the seemingly incessant need to garner the opinion of the people through plebiscites, a strategy that some critics saw as decidedly un-British, a manifestation of republican liberalism that Michel Ducharme argues had been rejected in the failure of the rebellions in 1837–38.[11] Yet plebiscites also reflected different notions of how the emerging liberal state should operate in a way that based its legitimacy upon the collective will. So the persistence of plebiscites can be interpreted as a government seeking to consult with a population that would be subject to the illiberal measure of prohibition; although let's be honest, they were also delaying tactics. Oliver Mowat, Wilfrid Laurier, and George Ross, three leaders who turned to plebiscites but rejected the majority vote, all understood liquor to be too complex an issue to be subjected to a simple plurality. Was this a manifestation of liberalism in which the citizen was sovereign but in which leaders did not see a convincing expression of support for prohibition to implement it or a throwback to what Elsbeth Heaman calls "Tory paternalism," in which the government implemented policies "designed to keep politics in the hands of the politicians"?[12] Whichever form of governance it represents, it was also good policy: all of them knew that it would require much more than 50 percent of the voters, arguably more than 50 percent of the population, to support prohibition before such an extreme measure could hope to be effective.

It is a further irony, then, that both a key instance of non-paternalism and the ultimate realization of prohibition in Ontario came at the hands of Tory governments. The McCarthy Act sought to give back to the municipalities a degree of autonomy from a paternalistic partisan appointment system. The Boards of License Commissioners under that legislation were drawn from two local office holders and only one government appointee. This frustrated local Tory operatives, who wanted to counter what they saw as Mowat's patronage-based liquor licensing system with their own version, but also respected the idea of municipal self-governance. Then, when prohibition was implemented across the province, it was by a Conservative government. Premier William Hearst, like Liberal George Ross before him, was a temperance advocate, but also like Ross he did not rush to implement prohibition upon entering the premier's office. It required both the national emergency of the Great War and the weight of public opinion to justify one of the most illiberal solutions to the liquor problem. However, the convergence of the start of the Great War, Whitney's death, Hanna's implementation of the centralized Board of License Commissioners, and Hearst's selection as premier makes it impossible for us to make any argument about the "inevitability" of prohibition, as if such metahistorical musings had any value.[13] Even this endpoint of the story illustrates a unique element of Canada's engagement with the liquor question. Although partisan interests were replete through the half century under examination here, the drink issue never clung to one party. Both the liquor trade and the temperance movement enjoyed bipartisan support, which meant that they could appeal to both parties and criticize any outcome no matter who was in power.

The story of the centralization of the liquor licensing process, as mundane as it might seem to those who do not indulge in alcohol and drug history, does offer some useful insights into the changing nature of the liberal state in late-Victorian and Edwardian Canada. First, the story illustrates the tensions among different aspects of liberalism and how opposing groups could still manifest the liberal ideal while disagreeing fundamentally about how it would look. Liberalism was fluid; it flowed into and took the shapes of different vessels. It could be a philosophy to elevate the vulnerable, a manifestation of collective rights against elites, or a system that protected the privileged. The ideal that it represented could both enrage and inspire. Second, the story of liquor legislation is a story of the tensions among all levels of government. Liquor flowed into and around the highest court in the land and the final arbiter of legal matters in the British Empire, and it complicated the Canadian Constitution. It is not an overstatement to say that decisions related to liquor fundamentally transformed the federal-provincial relationship and continue to do so. Third, the story illustrates the slow development of a bureaucracy that oversaw and evaluated the activities of residents across the province. This was not an intense surveillance network, a Foucaultian panopticon, and the surviving documentation of the License Branch is too limited to allow us to apply the concept of governmentality to its operation.[14] Many inspectors were too well known in their communities and possibly even complicit in law breaking, so there were many gaps in the field of visibility of the state. The employment of detectives, however unsavoury they were to many respectable citizens, did add to the state's capacity for uncovering deviation, but it too was limited by the initial tendency to underinvest in licensing apparatus. The fact that Whitney vocally endorsed the use of detectives, members of what was once seen as a disreputable profession, to strengthen the hand of the state illustrates the importance of centralized control of the liberties of individuals by the twentieth century.[15] Further illustrating the tendency to emphasize the importance of a smooth-running apparatus of state enforcement were the many jeremiads, expressed at the Royal Commission on the Liquor Traffic and in many reflections on the failures of local option, that temperance people were happy to vote for prohibition but less happy to help enforce it. Internalizing the imperative for the citizen to support the work of the state was a slow process.[16]

This growing state apparatus was also apparent in the remarkable documentation that the License Branch generated. Each inspector in the license districts was expected to produce a report on each tavern applying for a license; boards held meetings and kept minutes; inspectors who travelled throughout the province wrote more extensive reports about the places that they visited; and community members with various interests communicated frequently with the central office, a process that, as Henry Totten's reply to the editor of the *Brantford Expositor* illustrates, created such an amount of work that License Branch staff were empowered to respond without clearing every action with their boss, the politician in charge. The weight of such administration was not new, but the increased standardization of processes, such as found in the numerous appendices at the end of each amended license law, indicates a growing rationalization of the licensing process itself. This reiterates the authority of the liberal state by separating subjective interpretations and personal connections from the regulatory role of the state, underscoring the importance to the liberal state, indeed the liberal order, of rational processes and laws. Such was the nature of what Max Weber labelled the "ideal-typical" (or "ideal-type") bureaucracy, in which the rationalization of processes and the impersonalization of rules were fundamental to the fair operation of the modern state.[17] Under the liberal order, fairness, a fundamental component of justice, was a virtue. Another key element of the ideal typical bureaucracy that Weber discussed is the creation of a professional administration.[18] This can be seen in the Garrow Resolution, agreed to in 1897, which attempted to remove partisan politics from the civil service, in references to the British Parliament's depoliticizing of the civil service in the 1870s, and more directly in the careers of people like Henry Totten and especially Eudo Saunders, whose work spanned different political regimes. The fact that this principle of non-partisan civil service was not always observed does not negate the fact that the movement toward such an ideal can be seen in the operation of liquor licensing in the provincial administration. Indeed, Whitney's apparent need to explain how his replacement of Grit inspectors in 1905 with Tories did not violate that principle illustrates the growing importance among all parties of the non-partisan operation of government administration.

In his memoirs, Sir John Willison, editor of the *Globe* from 1890 to 1902, observed that the liquor question was not one that either the federal government or provincial governments wanted to own. "There has been no greater comedy in Canadian politics," he wrote, "than the manoeuvres between the federal and provincial authorities to evade responsibility for prohibitory legislation." Faced with pressure to deal with the liquor question, "generally the object was not to establish jurisdiction but to evade and confuse."[19] Liberal stalwart that he was, and one who had ongoing communication with Liberal leaders, Willison might not have been willing to acknowledge the tremendous partisan advantage that his party gained from controlling the liquor licensing system for thirty-two years. Indeed, even if politicians preferred to "evade" the liquor question, Mowat's dogged pursuit of provincial rights with respect to that question meant that the premier preferred to expand the province's authority over "distasteful" liquor policy rather than shuffle it onto a different level of government. Nevertheless, Willison's statement might shed some light on the occasional confusing aspects of the story that I have told. It might explain why Sir John A. Macdonald seemed to be uninterested in pursuing *Russell v. The Queen* to London.[20] It might also give some insight into George Ross's conversion from an ardent prohibitionist when a cabinet minister to a pragmatic legislator when the premier. The liquor issue could be intoxicating, or it could be toxic. The stories of license boards standing between the disgruntled local tavern keeper who lost his or her license and the politicians blamed for the loss of that livelihood illustrate the profound challenges that governments faced with the liquor issue. Politicians might have become drunk on the spoils of power, those offices that they could fill with partisan supporters, but they had to face sobering pressures from both Wets and Drys who inisisted that their perspective more adequately represented the ideals of the liberal state. When attempting to solve the liquor problem, then, governments had to negotiate complicated interpretations of freedom, equality, property rights, rationality, and the fair and just application of the law, all for the common good, whatever they saw that good to be.

The notion of common good as a principle upon which to base policy needs to be considered carefully. The recent growth of arguments about indulgences such as liquor, sugary drinks, and fatty foods manifest a philosophy that suggests the state has a role in directly affecting the choices of individual citizens, notwithstanding the fact that these choices are personal and have no real impact on others. Tobacco laws were strengthened based not on the argument that tobacco was bad for the smoker but on the one that second hand smoke was harmful to others. Yet "clean air" policy set a precedent for anti-drink, anti-fat, and anti-sugar arguments that violate the harm principle.[21] In a society that still holds liberty, equality, and property as standards against which policies should be assessed, this attack on individual autonomy has echoes of the illiberal righteousness of prohibitionists. It draws upon scanty evidence to attack a personal choice and makes people wish they would, as Mill put it, "mind their own business." But unlike the temperance agitators, this advice comes from agents of the state themselves, public health officials, who are advocating illiberal approaches to defend citizens of the liberal state. As this book has argued, from Confederation to the First World War, liquor in the liberal state demanded that leaders negotiate a narrow middle path between protecting individual and collective rights, lest the foundation upon which liberalism sits is itself undermined; as this final paragraph has illustrated, that narrow path is becoming increasingly difficult to find.

Appendix 1: Questions Sent by the Select Committee

Medical Practitioners

1. Does the use of intoxicating liquors, as a beverage, predispose to mental and physical disease ... or otherwise?
2. In respect of the fatal tendencies of disease, state the differences as between total abstainers and others. Have total abstainers an advantage?
3. In your opinion, can diseases be treated as efficiently without ... as with alcoholic remedies?
4. Is it the custom to prescribe alcoholic remedies in the treatment of disease; and if so, to what extent?

Clergy

1. State the extent of the evils of drunkenness.
2. Probable cause thereof.
3. Results of intemperance.
4. The best remedy therefor.
5. Has the number of places for the sale of intoxicating liquors in your county increased or diminished during the last three years?
6. Are the regular taverns as productive of injury to the community as the saloons, shops, recesses and other groggeries?
7. Is public opinion, in your judgment, prepared to support a Prohibitory Liquor Law?

8. Has your municipality made an effort to pass the Dunkin Act?
9. Was it successful?
10. If so, what has been the result?

Sheriffs, County Attorneys, Magistrates, and Chief Constables

1. Of those brought under your official notice for the past three years, how many were the victims of intemperance?
2. To what extent do your official records as well as your own observation[s] ... point to the use of intoxicating drinks as productive of crime?
3. What remedial measure would you suggest for the suppression of the use of intoxicating liquor as a beverage?
4. Has the number of places for the sale of intoxicating liquors in your county increased or diminished during the last three years?
5. Are the regular Taverns as productive of injury to the community as the Saloons, Shops, Recesses, and other Groggeries?
6. Is the public opinion, in your judgment, prepared to support a Prohibitory Liquor Law?
7. Has your Municipality made an effort to pass the Dunkin Act?
8. Was it successful?
9. If so, what has been the result?

Judges, Police and Stipendiary Magistrates, and Justices of the Peace

1. What proportion of the crimes tried under your jurisdiction ... can be traced to intemperance?
2. Do you consider licensing the sale of intoxicating drinks as a beverage ... productive of crime?
3. What remedial measures against intemperance will you kindly suggest as best calculated to arrest the evil?
4. Have the number of places for the sale of intoxicating liquors in your county increased or diminished during the last three years?
5. Are the regular Taverns as productive of injury to the community as the Saloons, Shops, Recesses, and other Groggeries?
6. Is public opinion, in your judgment, prepared to support a Prohibitory Liquor Law?

7. Has your Municipality made an effort to pass the Dunkin Act?
8. Was it successful?
9. If so, what has been the result?

Coroners

1. What proportion of cases brought under your notice as Coroner has been the result of intemperance?
2. What prompt, efficient, remedial measure against intemperance can you suggest?

Superintendents and Inspectors of Lunatic Asylums, Hospitals, and Poor Houses, Wardens of Penitentiaries, Inspectors of Gaols and Reformatories, Gaol Surgeons, and Overseers of Houses of Refuge

1. What proportion of those who have come under your charge have been the victims of intemperance?
2. How far do you consider the health of the intemperate to be affected by total abstinence from intoxicating drinks, suddenly enforced?
3. What remedial measures against intemperance do you suggest?

Brewers and Distillers

1. How long have you been engaged in the distilling or brewing business?
2. What amount of capital have you invested in fixtures in connection with your business?
3. What additional amount of capital have you [invested] in the business?
4. What quantity of grain do you distil annually?
5. Where is the grain produced?
6. What is the value thereof?
7. How many gallons of liquor do you produce annually?
8. What is the wholesale price per gallon?
9. Is your liquor consumed in the Province ... or exported; and if the latter, to what place?

Manufacturers, Merchants, and Contractors

1. What proportion of accidents can you trace to the use of intoxicating drinks, and what is the percentage of property destroyed annually from these causes alone, in connection with your business?
2. Have you any preference in favour of total abstainers as agents, clerks, foremen, and workmen?
3. In what respect do you consider the use of intoxicating liquor as a beverage in these classes productive of injury?

Railway Managers, Owners, and Masters of Vessels

1. What proportion of accidents can you trace to the use of intoxicating drinks, and what is the percentage of property destroyed annually from these causes alone, in your company or vessels?
2. As between total abstainers and those workmen who use liquors as a beverage, state their comparative efficiency and trustworthiness.

Insurance Companies

1. What difference, if any, do you make in regard to insurances on life ... as between total abstainers and those who use intoxicating liquors as a beverage?
2. Also on fire and marine insurances, what difference, if any, do you make in insuring a vessel sailed by a captain and crew who are total abstainers?
3. What proportion of your losses do you attribute to the use of intoxicating liquors?

Appendix 2: Liquor-Related Laws in Force in Ontario

Informal title	Formal title and sponsor	Scope	Years in operation
Dunkin Act	Temperance Act of 1864 (Christopher Dunkin)	Enabled local option votes in municipalities in Canada East and Canada West	1864–1984[a]
N/a	Tavern and Shop License Act of 1868 (n/a)	Replaced pre-Confederation Act Respecting the Provincial Duty on Tavern Keepers (repealed in 1868 in legislation that placed minimal restrictions on licensees)	1869–76
		Set minimal license fees, created basic enforcement measures, and reiterated municipal councils' authority to issue licenses	
Crooks Act	Liquor License Act, 1876 (Adam Crooks)	In name a broad amendment of the earlier Tavern and Shop License Act but fundamentally different from it	1876–1915
		Centralized oversight of the licensing system	
		Provincially appointed, unpaid licensing board and paid inspector for each license district	
		Set population-based limit on number of licenses in a district	
		Established baseline fee for licenses	
		After 1893 included local option provisions	

(Continued)

(Continued)

Informal title	Formal title and sponsor	Scope	Years in operation
Scott Act	Canada Temperance Act (Richard Scott)	Local option legislation for the entire country	1878–1984[a]
		Created a system for county- or city-level local option (other provinces had other political units)	
		Local option to be in force for minimum of three years	
McCarthy Act	Dominion Liquor Act (D'Alton McCarthy)	Licensing system for the whole country	1883–85
		Main components parallel to the Crooks Act: three-person Board of License Commissioners, paid appointed inspector, population-based license limits	
		Declared ultra vires the dominion government by the Judicial Committee in 1885	
N/a	Liquor License Act, 1915	Replaced Crooks Act unpaid, regional Boards of License Commissioners with a central, provincially appointed, paid board	1915–16
		Established detailed processes for granting and refusing licenses	
		Was replaced by the Ontario Temperance Act in 1916, which instituted prohibition across the province	

Note:

a Determining the date for the end of the Dunkin Act is tricky. The Scott Act deleted many of the Dunkin Act's provisions, but the 1864 law remained in force in municipalities in which it had been in operation when the Scott Act was passed. In the event that the Scott Act was passed and then repealed in a Dunkin Act municipality, the Dunkin Act provisions would be re-imposed in the relevant jurisdiction. The Scott Act was repealed in 1984, and this would ostensibly mark the date of the end of the Dunkin Act, too.

Notes

Introduction

1 Morris J. Fish, "The Effect of Alcohol on the Canadian Constitution ... Seriously," *McGill Law Journal* 57 (2011): 189–209.
2 John T. Saywell, *The Lawmakers: Judicial Power and the Shaping of Canadian Federalism* (Toronto: Osgoode Society, 2002), 36–38.
3 Saywell, *The Lawmakers*, especially 141. Saywell says this ideal of the Judicial Committee of the Privy Council's Lords having a legal background was not always achieved. See Saywell, *The Lawmakers*, 63–65.
4 E.A. Heaman argues that at the end of the century there was also a significant shift in the government's approach to taxation, which she contends was the main point of Confederation. E.A. Heaman, *Tax, Order and Good Government: A New Political History of Canada, 1867–1917* (Montreal and Kingston: McGill-Queen's University Press, 2017).
5 This was granted by the Province of Canada. See An Act Respecting the Municipal Institutions of Upper Canada, *Consolidated Statutes of Upper Canada* (1859), c. 54, specifically s. 246.
6 See Dan Malleck, *Try to Control Yourself: The Regulation of Public Drinking in Post-Prohibition Ontario 1927–44* (Vancouver: UBC Press, 2012).
7 B.J. Grant, *When Rum Was King: The Story of Prohibition in New Brunswick* (Fredericton: Fiddlehead Books, 1984); James Sturgis, "Beer under Pressure: The Origins of Prohibition in Canada," *Bulletin of Canadian Studies* 8 (1984): 83–100; Frank W. Anderson, *The Rum Runners: Dodging the Law during Prohibition* (Edmonton: Folklore Publishing, 2004); Gerald Hallowell, *Prohibition in Ontario: 1919–1923* (Ottawa: Ontario Historical Society, 1972).
8 And, to be sure, I began my academic career studying temperance, and being sympathetic to the organizational passion and progressive values of its adherents, though not to their disdain for a good drink.
9 Historian Margeurite Van Die has observed that the liberal ideals of these middle-class temperance adherents could also include some remarkably illiberal ideas about how to

improve the lives of others. Margeurite Van Die, "Protestants, the Liberal State, and the Practice of Politics: Revisiting R.J. Fleming and the 1890s Toronto Streetcar Controversy," *Journal of the Canadian Historical Association* 24 (2013): 93.
10 Christopher Armstrong and H.V. Nelles, *Monopoly's Moment: The Organization and Regulation of Canadian Utilities 1830–1930* (Philadelphia: Temple University Press, 1986).
11 John Stuart Mill, *On Liberty*, 3rd ed. (London: Longman, Green, Longman, Roberts and Green, 1866), 161.
12 Mill, *On Liberty*, 155.
13 Mill, *On Liberty*, 161.
14 Mill, *On Liberty*, 156.
15 The individual, of course, is fundamental to liberalism. See, for example, Ian McKay, "The Liberal Order Framework: A Prospectus for a Reconnaissance of Canadian History," *Canadian Historical Review* 81 (2000): 625; Michel Ducharme and Jean-François Constant, "Introduction: A Project of Rule Called Canada – The Liberal Order Framework and Historical Practice," in *Liberalism and Hegemony: Debating the Canadian Liberal Revolution*, ed. Jean-François Constant and Michel Ducharme (Toronto: University of Toronto Press, 2009), 7; and Bruce Curtis, "After 'Canada': Liberalism, Social Theory, and Historical Analysis," in *Liberalism and Hegemony: Debating the Canadian Liberal Revolution*, ed. Jean-François Constant and Michel Ducharme (Toronto: University of Toronto Press, 2009), 180.
16 McKay, "The Liberal Order Framework," 621.
17 McKay, "The Liberal Order Framework"; E.A. Heaman, *A Short History of the State in Canada* (Toronto: University of Toronto Press, 2015).
18 Michel Ducharme, *The Idea of Liberty in Canada during the Age of Atlantic Revolutions 1776–1839* (Montreal and Kingston: McGill-Queen's University Press, 2014); Philip Girard, "Liberty, Order, and Pluralism: The Canadian Experience," in *Exclusionary Empire: English Liberty Overseas 1600–1900*, ed. Jack P. Greene (Cambridge: Cambridge University Press, 2010), 160–90.
19 Girard, "Liberty, Order, and Pluralism," 161.
20 Ducharme, *The Idea of Liberty*, 5. Girard references Ducharme's liberties as "Classic" and "Modern."
21 Girard, "Liberty, Order, and Pluralism," 173–74, 181.
22 Girard, "Liberty, Order, and Pluralism," 174; Allan Greer, *The Patriots and the People: The Rebellion of 1837 in Rural Lower Canada* (Toronto: University of Toronto Press, 1993).
23 Catharine Anne Wilson, *Tenants in Time: Family Strategies, Land, and Liberalism in Upper Canada, 1799–1871* (Montreal and Kingston: McGill-Queen's University Press, 2009), Chapter 1. Her book spans the existence of Upper Canada, Canada West, and Ontario, but for the sake of simplicity I have used the last term.
24 Bruce Curtis, *True Government by Choice Men? Inspection, Education and State Formation in Canada West* (Toronto: University of Toronto Press, 1992), 20.
25 Robert Macdonald, "'Variants of Liberalism' and the Liberal Order Framework in British Columbia," in *Liberalism and Hegemony: Debating the Canadian Liberal Revolution*, ed. Jean-François Constant and Michel Ducharme (Toronto: University of Toronto Press, 2009), 324.
26 Macdonald, "'Variants of Liberalism,'" especially 329.
27 Michèle Dagenais, "The Municipal Territory: A Product of the Liberal Order?," in *Liberalism and Hegemony: Debating the Canadian Liberal Revolution*, ed. Jean-François Constant and Michel Ducharme (Toronto: University of Toronto Press, 2009), 208.
28 Dagenais, "The Municipal Territory," 211.

29 Dagenais, "The Municipal Territory," 211.
30 Curtis, "After 'Canada.'"
31 Curtis, *True Government by Choice Men?*
32 Curtis, "After 'Canada,'" 181.
33 See Curtis, *True Government by Choice Men?*
34 Jarret Rudy, *The Freedom to Smoke: Tobacco Smoking and Identity* (Montreal and Kingston: McGill-Queen's University Press, 2005).
35 John Greenaway, *Drink and British Politics since 1830* (Basingstoke, UK: Palgrave Macmillan, 2003), 11.
36 James Nicholls, *The Politics of Alcohol: A History of the Drink Question in England* (Manchester: University of Manchester Press, 2009), 115.
37 Greenaway, *Drink and British Politics*; also see Nicholls, *The Politics of Alcohol*.
38 Greenaway, *Drink and British Politics*, 88–89.
39 Nicholls, *The Politics of Alcohol*; Annemarie McAllister, *Demon Drink? Temperance and the Working Class* (self-pub., 2014), Kindle; William Rorabaugh, *Alcoholic Republic: An American Tradition* (Oxford: Oxford University Press, 1979); Jack S. Blocker, Jr., *American Temperance Movements: Cycles of Reform* (Boston: Twayne, 1989); Ann-Marie E. Szymanski, *Pathways to Prohibition: Radicals, Moderates, and Social Movement Outcomes* (Durham, NC: Duke University Press, 2003); Jan Noel, *Canada Dry: Temperance Crusades before Confederation* (Toronto: University of Toronto Press, 1995); F.L. Barron, "The Genesis of Temperance in Ontario, 1828–1905" (PhD diss., University of Guelph, 1976); Craig Heron, *Booze: A Distilled History* (Toronto: Between the Lines, 2003).
40 Nicholls, *The Politics of Alcohol*, 80–95.
41 Nicholls, *The Politics of Alcohol*, 83–84; David Beckingham, *The Licensed City: Regulating Drink in Liverpool 1830–1920* (Liverpool: Liverpool University Press, 2017), 28–29.
42 Beckingham, *The Licensed City*, 28–29.
43 Beckingham, *The Licensed City*, 29; the population of Liverpool from Edwin Butterworth, "Liverpool," in *Statistical Sketch of the County Palatine of Lancaster* (London: Longman and Company, 1841), 52.
44 Nicholls, *The Politics of Alcohol*, 91–92.
45 Beckingham, *The Licensed City*, 29, 30.
46 *Statutes of the Province of Canada* (1855), c. 54, "Municipal Institutions," 583.
47 In 1860, the legislature of the Province of Canada did place a population-based limit on the number of taverns in a community. It was a generous 1 tavern for every 250 residents. See An Act to Diminish the Number of Licenses Issued for the Sale of Intoxicating Liquors by Retail, *Statutes of the Province of Canada* (1860), c. 53, 105–6.
48 On the depression of the 1870s, see Randall White, *Ontario, 1610–1985: A Political and Economic History* (Toronto: Dundurn Press, 1985); and Heaman, *Tax, Order and Good Government*.
49 See Malleck, *Try to Control Yourself*.
50 John Burnham, *Bad Habits: Drinking, Smoking, Taking Drugs, Gambling, Sexual Misbehavior and Swearing in American History* (New York: NYU Press, 1994).

CHAPTER 1: THE PLACE OF THE GOVERNMENT IN THE DRINKS OF THE PEOPLE

1 Julia Roberts, *In Mixed Company: Taverns and Public Life in Upper Canada* (Vancouver: UBC Press, 2009).

2   It is common lore that McGregor (or MacGregor) was the first settler, tavern keeper, and entrepreneur of London. There seems to be some uncertainty on the internet about the spelling of his name. See "MacGregor, Peter (1794–1846)," London Public Library, Ivey Family London Room Digital Collections, http://images.ourontario.ca/london/2972554/data; and Amanda Stratton, "Startup Grind Is Coming to London, Ontario!," https://www.startupgrind.com/blog/startup-grind-is-coming-to-london-ontario/.

3   In *In Mixed Company*, Roberts describes the multifaceted uses of the tavern in Ontario society, mostly in smaller communities but, likely owing to the paucity of sources, does not delve too deeply into the urban working-class tavern. The most well-known description of the multipurpose working-class tavern is drawn from the example in Peter DeLottinville, "Joe Beef of Montreal: Working-Class Culture and the Tavern 1869–1889," *Labour/Le travail*, 8/9 (1981–82): 9–40. There is no reason to believe that many of the activities that took place in this tavern were not also found in urban drinking spaces in Ontario, save, possibly, for the drunken bears.

4   An Act to Diminish the Number of Licenses Issued for the Sale of Intoxicating Liquors by Retail, *Statutes of the Province of Canada* (1860), c. 53, 105–6.

5   Roberts, *In Mixed Company*.

6   David Beckingham, *The Licensed City: Regulating Drink in Liverpool 1830–1920* (Liverpool: Liverpool University Press, 2017), 42.

7   Michèle Dagenais, "The Municipal Territory: A Product of the Liberal Order?," in *Liberalism and Hegemony: Debating the Canadian Liberal Revolution*, ed. Jean François Constant and Michel Ducharme (Toronto: University of Toronto Press, 2009), 201–20.

8   An Act to Diminish the Number of Licenses Issued for the Sale of Intoxicating Liquors by Retail, *Statutes of the Province of Canada* (1860), c. 53, 105–6.

9   An Act Respecting Tavern and Shop Licenses, *Statutes of Ontario* (1868–69), 32 Vict., c. 32.

10 See E.A. Heaman, *Tax, Order and Good Government: A New Political History of Canada, 1867–1917* (Montreal and Kingston: McGill-Queen's University Press, 2017).

11 Randall White, *Ontario 1610–1985: A Political and Economic History* (Toronto: Dundurn Press, 1985), 132.

12 An Act Respecting Tavern and Shop Licenses, *Statutes of Ontario* (1868–69), 32 Vict., c. 32, s. 6(4).

13 Literature on the early nineteenth century is vast; Canadian accounts are much less robust. See Jan Noel, *Canada Dry: Temperance Crusades before Confederation* (Toronto: University of Toronto Press, 1995); F.L. Barron, "The Genesis of Temperance in Ontario, 1828–1905" (PhD diss., University of Guelph, 1976); Glenn J. Lockwood, "Temperance in Upper Canada as Ethnic Subterfuge," in *Drink in Canada: Historical Essays*, ed. Cheryl Warsh (Montreal and Kingston: McGill-Queen's University Press, 1993), 43–69; and James Sturgis, "Beer under Pressure: The Origins of Prohibition in Canada," *Bulletin of Canadian Studies* 8 (1984): 81–100.

14 See Noel, *Canada Dry*.

15 John Burnham, *Bad Habits: Drinking, Smoking, Taking Drugs, Gambling, Sexual Misbehavior and Swearing in American History* (New York: NYU Press, 1994).

16 On the concept of status anxiety and the temperance movement, see Joseph R. Gusfield, *Symbolic Crusade: Status Politics and the American Temperance Movement*, 2nd ed. (Urbana: University of Illinois Press, 1986).

17 An Act to Amend the Laws in Force Respecting the Sale of Intoxicating Liquors and the Issue of Licenses Therefor, and Otherwise for Repression of Abuses Resulting from

Such Sale, *Statutes of the Province of Canada* (1864), 27 and 28 Vict., c. 18. On top of the Dunkin Act, many city charters in Quebec specifically assigned rights to enact local prohibition to city councils.
18 On the United Kingdom, see James Nicholls, *The Politics of Alcohol: A History of the Drink Question in England* (Manchester: University of Manchester Press, 2009); and John Greenaway, *Drink and British Politics since 1830* (Basingstoke, UK: Palgrave Macmillan, 2003).
19 My initial count said eighty-nine.
20 Introduced by Dr. John Clarke.
21 The first was introduced by Conservative MLA Herbert S. MacDonald (spelled McDonald in *Journals*); see Ontario, Legislative Assembly, *Journals of the Legislative Assembly*, 2nd Leg, 2nd Sess, Vol 6 (21 January 1873), 42. The second was introduced by Mr. Farewell. Neither passed.
22 Bill No. 3, introduced by Grit MLA James Bethune. See Ontario, Legislative Assembly, *Journals of the Legislative Assembly*, 2nd Leg, 2nd Sess, Vol 6 (13 January 1873), 21. This was discussed on 3 February 1874 and printed in the *Globe* [Toronto], 4 February 1874. The description of this measure is found in a speech by Mr. Pardee, quoted in "Legislature of Ontario," *Globe* [Toronto], 26 February 1873.
23 Ontario, Legislative Assembly, *Journals of the Legislative Assembly*, 2nd Leg, 2nd Sess, Vol 6 (17 February 1873), 133.
24 Quoted in "Legislature of Ontario," *Globe* [Toronto], 26 February 1873.
25 John Crowley and William M. White, *Drunkard's Refuge: The Lessons of the New York State Inebriate Asylum* (Amherst: University of Massachusetts Press, 2004), 21–23.
26 Quoted in "Legislature of Ontario," *Globe* [Toronto], 26 February 1873.
27 Quoted in "Legislature of Ontario," *Globe* [Toronto], 26 February 1873.
28 Quoted in "Legislature of Ontario," *Globe* [Toronto], 26 February 1873.
29 Paraphrased from "Legislature of Ontario," *Globe* [Toronto], 26 February 1873.
30 See Ontario, Legislative Assembly, *Journals of the Legislative Assembly*, 2nd Leg, 2nd Sess (5 February 1873), 99.
31 Quoted in "Legislature of Ontario," *Globe* [Toronto], 26 February 1873. For more on Clarke, see *Illustrated Historical Atlas of Norfolk County* (Toronto: H.R. Page, 1877), 102, reproduced on the Norfolk Genealogy website, http://www.nornet.on.ca/~jcardiff/transcripts/1877atlas/bios/index.html.
32 Numerous historians have examined the debates among physicians at this time. See Philip J. Pauly, "The Struggle for Ignorance about Alcohol: American Physiologists, Wilber Olin Atwater and the Woman's Christian Temperance Union," *Bulletin of the History of Medicine* 64 (1990): 366–92; Jonathan Zimmerman, "When the Doctors Disagree: Scientific Temperance and Scientific Authority, 1891–1906," *Journal of the History of Medicine and Allied Sciences* 48 (1993): 171–97; and Joanne Woiak, "A Medical Cromwell to Depose King Alcohol: Medical Scientists, Temperance Reformers, and the Alcohol Problem in Britain," in *Changing Face of Drink: Substance, Imagery, and Behaviour*, ed. Jack S. Blocker, Jr., and Cheryl K. Warsh (Ottawa: Les Publications Histoire Sociale/Social History, 1997), 237–70.
33 "Legislature of Ontario," *Globe* [Toronto], 11 March 1873.
34 These points were summarized in two articles in the Toronto *Globe* on 20 March 1873, "The Legislature" and "Legislature of Ontario," the latter giving more detail, but each having its specific angle. Information on traditional volumes is tricky. See Olive R. Jones, *Cylindrical English Wine and Beer Bottles, 1735–1850*, Studies in Archaeology, Architecture and History (Ottawa: National Historic Parks and Sites Branch Environment Canada, 1986), especially 110.

35 Some investigations included consideration of adulteration but found little evidence of it. However, there are apocryphal stories of country taverns watering down their whiskey. See Ramsay Cook, *The Regenerators: Social Criticism in Victorian Canada* (Toronto: University of Toronto Press, 1985), 27–28, an apocryphal story of a farmer shaking up a bottle of whiskey offered by Goldwyn Smith before pouring himself a dram. The reason was that whiskey in country taverns was usually diluted, and patrons needed to shake the bottle to get to the good stuff. (This is odd because whiskey is lighter than water and should sit at the top.) Subsequent investigations found little evidence of widespread adulteration. See the investigations in 1874 as part of the Crooks report: Ontario, Legislative Assembly, "Report Relative to the General Working of the Tavern and Shop Licenses Acts by the Honourable the Provincial Treasurer," *Sessional Papers*, No. 7 (1874), 4–13.
36 Quoted in "The Legislature," *Globe* [Toronto], 20 March 1873. I have seen no other references to something called "concert saloons."
37 Quoted in "Legislature of Ontario," *Globe* [Toronto], 20 March 1873.
38 These discussions are quoted in "Legislature of Ontario," *Globe* [Toronto], 20 March 1873.
39 "The Legislature," *Globe* [Toronto], 20 March 1873.
40 An Act to Amend the Acts Respecting Tavern and Shop Licenses, *Statutes of Ontario* (1873), c. 34, s. 8.
41 Quoted in "Legislature of Ontario," *Globe* [Toronto], 18 February 1873.
42 Ontario, Legislative Assembly, *Journals of the Legislative Assembly*, 2nd Leg, 2nd Sess, Vol 6 (17 February 1873), 133. Note that although the motion related to the Act of 1868, the law at issue received royal assent on 23 January 1869.
43 The temperance sympathies of some members could not be determined.
44 See Raisa B. Deber and Catherine L. Mah, eds., *Case Studies in Canadian Health Policy and Management*, 2nd ed. (Toronto: University of Toronto Press, 2014).
45 Nicholls, *The Politics of Alcohol;* Greenaway, *Drink and British Politics;* Beckingham, *The Licensed City.*
46 These were the standard images of the effects of drunkenness. For examples, see John Crowley, *Drunkard's Progress: Narratives of Addiction, Despair, and Recovery* (Baltimore: Johns Hopkins University Press, 1999); John Adam, *The Drunkard's Progress* (Edinburgh: Johnstone and Hunter, 1853); T.S. Arthur, *Ten Nights in a Barroom and What I Saw There* (Philadelphia: J.W. Bradley, 1854); and George Cruickshank, *The Bottle* (eight plates) (London: David Bogue, 1847). Thanks to Anne Marie McAllister for finding the publication information for Cruikshank.
47 Ontario, Legislative Assembly, "Report of the Select Committee on the Liquor Traffic" (hereafter "Report of Select Committee"), *Journals of the Legislative Assembly*, 2nd Leg, 3rd Sess, Vol 7 (1874), Appendix 2, "Class III" (responses of sheriffs, county attorneys, etc.), 32–44.
48 "Report of the Select Committee," response of J. Easton, n.p., 5.
49 "Report of the Select Committee," response of Daniel Clark, Princeton, 6.
50 "Report of the Select Committee," response of A. Groves, Fergus, 7.
51 "Report of the Select Committee," response of E. Hickman, Bolton, 14.
52 "Report of the Select Committee," response of William Morton, Wellesley, 14.
53 "Report of the Select Committee," response of Hamnet Hill, Ottawa, 5 (emphasis in original).
54 "Report of the Select Committee," response of A. Beamer, 19.
55 "Report of the Select Committee," response of William Burgess, East Tilbury, 19.
56 "Report of the Select Committee," assorted responses, 18–21.

Notes to pages 38–44

57 "Report of the Select Committee," response of P. Eugene Funcken, St. Agatha, 22.
58 "Report of the Select Committee," responses of J. Mclean Ballard (curate) and Henry Holland (rector), St. Catharines, 24.
59 "Report of the Select Committee," 60.
60 "Report of the Select Committee," 56.
61 "Report of the Select Committee," 2.
62 "Report of the Select Committee," 2.
63 An Act to Amend the Acts Respecting Tavern and Shop Licenses, *Statutes of Ontario* (1873), c. 34, s. 8.
64 "Liquor License in Toronto" [editorial], *Globe* [Toronto], 12 February 1874.
65 The method of appointing inspectors was not detailed either in the legislation or in the government records. However, given the partisan tendencies of governments in general, it is unlikely that these inspectors were hired through some non-partisan application process; see A. Margaret Evans, *Sir Oliver Mowat*, Ontario Historical Studies Series (Toronto: University of Toronto Press, 1992). Hence, they were interested in presenting the best face of the government's licensing initiative, but they were also interested in making sure that some kind of functional licensing system could be created.
66 Ontario, Legislative Assembly, "Report Relative to the General Working of the Tavern and Shop Licenses Acts by the Honourable the Provincial Treasurer," *Sessional Papers*, No. 7 (1874), 4–13 (hereafter License Report 1874a). Note that the legislature had two sessions in 1874, and instances of the second session will be identified with 1874b.
67 License Report 1874a, 4.
68 License Report 1874a, 3.
69 License Report 1874a, 15.
70 An Act Respecting Tavern and Shop Licenses, 23 Vict., c. 32, s. 6.
71 License Report 1874a, 17.
72 License Report 1874a, 12.
73 License Report 1874a, 16.
74 License Report 1874a, 8.
75 License Report 1874a, 18.
76 License Report 1874a, 17.
77 License Report 1874a, 12.
78 License Report 1874a, 11.
79 License Report 1874a, 9 (London), 7 (Hamilton).
80 License Report 1874a, 15.
81 License Report 1874a, 15.
82 License Report 1874a, 17.
83 License Report 1874a, 17.
84 License Report 1874a, 16.
85 License Report 1874a, 16.
86 License Report 1874a, 18. Forty rods is 220 yards, 660 feet, or a little over 201 metres. Here the term "saloon" is used as a euphemism for place of refreshment.
87 License Report 1874a, 16.
88 License Report 1874a, 18.
89 License Report 1874a, 19.
90 See Don Akenson, *The Orangeman: The Life and Times of Ogle Gowan* (Toronto: Lorimer, 1986); and Hereward Senior, "Gowan, Ogle Robert," in *Dictionary of Canadian Biography*,

vol. 10 (Toronto: University of Toronto; Laval: Université Laval, 2003–), http://www.biographi.ca/en/bio/gowan_ogle_robert_10E.html. On Gowan's reputation among Liberals, see Luke Sharp, "Mr. Ogle R. Gowan and the Licenses" [letter to the editor], *Globe* [Toronto], 27 February 1874; and "The License Law and Its Enforcement" [editorial], *Globe* [Toronto], 9 May 1874.
91 "More 'Accomodation' [sic] Demanded," *Grip*, 5 September 1874.
92 License Report 1874a, 19.

Chapter 2: Centralization, I: The Crooks Act

1 "In the Legislature," *Daily Mail* [Toronto], 26 February 1874.
2 See Ontario, Legislative Assembly, "Report Respecting Tavern and Shop Licenses for the Year 1874," *Sessional Papers*, No. 4 (1874), 3.
3 Act to Amend and Consolidate the Law for the Sale of Fermented or Spirituous Liquors, *Statutes of Ontario* (1874), c. 32, s. 9.
4 Act to Amend and Consolidate the Law for the Sale of Fermented or Spirituous Liquors, *Statutes of Ontario* (1874), c. 32, s. 20.
5 "A Bill for the Consolidation and Amendment of the Liquor Laws" [editorial], *Globe* [Toronto], 10 February 1874.
6 Quoted in "In the Legislature," *Daily Mail* [Toronto], 26 February 1874.
7 Quoted in "Legislature of Ontario," *Globe* [Toronto], 26 February 1874.
8 Quoted in "In the Legislature," *Daily Mail* [Toronto], 26 February 1874.
9 "A Bill for the Consolidation and Amendment of the Liquor Laws" [editorial], *Globe* [Toronto], 10 February 1874.
10 "The Temperance Movement" [editorial], *Daily Mail* [Toronto], 2 March 1874.
11 "The License Law and Its Enforcement" [editorial], *Globe* [Toronto], 9 May 1874.
12 A Son of Temperance, "Temperance and the Liquor Traffic" [letter to the editor], *Daily Mail* [Toronto], 26 February 1874.
13 "Licensing of Shops and Taverns," *Globe* [Toronto], 5 December 1874.
14 "Prohibitory Liquor Law," *Globe* [Toronto], 17 March 1875.
15 Temperance, "The Dunkin Bill – No Prohibition" [letter to the editor], *Globe* [Toronto], 19 March 1875 (emphasis in original).
16 James Gray, "Prohibition" [letter to the editor], *Globe* [Toronto], 8 April 1875. This view was supported by J. Thomson, who argued that Toronto's police commissioners were unwilling to have officers clash with the population over the issue of liquor laws. J. Thomson, "The Liquor Traffic" [letter to the editor], *Globe* [Toronto], 25 May 1875.
17 J.B. Aylsworth, "Temperance and Prohibition" [letter to the editor], *Globe* [Toronto], 12 April 1875.
18 J.A. McClung, "Prohibition" [letter to the editor], *Globe* [Toronto], 13 April 1875.
19 John T. Saywell, *The Lawmakers: Judicial Power and the Shaping of Canadian Federalism* (Toronto: Osgoode Society, 2002), 36–37.
20 See David Gutzke, *Protecting the Pub: Brewers and Publicans against Temperance* (London: Royal Historical Society, 1989); John Greenaway, *Drink and British Politics since 1830* (Basingstoke, UK: Palgrave Macmillan, 2003); and James Nicholls, *The Politics of Alcohol: A History of the Drink Question in England* (Manchester: University of Manchester Press, 2009).
21 *Oxford English Dictionary*, s.v. "victualler," https://www.lexico.com/definition/victualler?locale=en.

22 Biographies of Smith and O'Keefe can be found in *Dictionary of Canadian Biography*. Dawson's details are from Geo. Maclean Rose, ed., *A Cyclopaedia of Canadian Biography Being Chiefly Men of the Time* (Toronto: Rose Publishing, 1886), 184. The Bodega Wine Company might have been an importer, claimed to cater to the elite tastes of the time, and had tasting rooms in Ottawa. See the ad for "Ottawa's Big Firms," *Ottawa Journal*, 21 September 1887. Close is listed in Rose, *Cyclopaedia*, 84. Copeland is more difficult to identify since his name was often spelled Copland, but his brewery, W. Cop[e]land's East Toronto Brewery, appears in various brewing paraphernalia and references in newspapers.

23 The Toronto *Globe* identified this group as the Licensed Victuallers Association of Western Ontario, and the Toronto *Daily Mail* identified them as the Licensed Victuallers Association of Canada. It is not clear which associations they represented, but Smith was the president of the Licensed Victuallers Association of Ontario when it was founded in 1874, and Dawson was its secretary. See *Bylaws of the Licensed Victuallers Association of Ontario* (Toronto: Ontario Workman Office, 1874).

24 Quoted in "The Liquor Traffic: The Views of the Licensed Victuallers," *Globe* [Toronto], 7 January 1876.

25 Quoted in "Licensed Victuallers – Interview with the Attorney General – Their Opinion on the License Laws – How the Trade Would Promote Temperance," *Daily Mail* [Toronto], 7 January 1876.

26 Quoted in "The Liquor Traffic: The Views of the Licensed Victuallers," *Globe* [Toronto], 7 January 1876.

27 For a discussion of policy learning in the drink issue, see John Greenaway, "Policy Learning and the Drink Question in Britain 1850–1950," *Political Studies* 96 (1998): 903–18.

28 See Stormont Grit James Bethune, speaking in the legislature, as paraphrased in "In the Legislature," *Daily Mail* [Toronto], 1 February 1876. On the disqualification of anyone who sold liquor from sitting on a municipal council, see An Act Respecting Municipal Institutions in the Province of Ontario," *Statutes of Ontario* (1873), c. 48, s. 75.

29 Canadian, "The Temperance Question" [letter to the editor], *Daily Mail* [Toronto], 11 January 1876.

30 Licensed Victualler, "The Liquor Traffic" [letter to the editor], *Globe* [Toronto], 12 January 1876.

31 Traveller, "Liquor License" [letter to the editor], *Globe* [Toronto], 31 January 1876.

32 Quoted in "Ontario Legislature," *Globe* [Toronto], 1 February 1876.

33 Quoted in "In the Legislature," *Daily Mail* [Toronto], 1 February 1876.

34 "Ontario Legislature," *Globe* [Toronto], 21 January 1876.

35 "The New License Act" [editorial], *Globe* [Toronto], 1 February 1876.

36 "Reduction of Liquor Licenses and a Certain Consequence" [editorial], *Daily Mail* [Toronto], 24 December 1875.

37 "The Temperance Question" [editorial], *Daily Mail* [Toronto], 6 January 1876.

38 "Legislature of Ontario," *Globe* [Toronto], 4 February 1873.

39 "Licensed Victuallers," *Daily Mail* [Toronto], 7 January 1876.

40 A licensed victualler, "The Liquor Bill" [open letter to the government], *Daily Mail* [Toronto], 25 January 1876.

41 John Cosgrave, "The License Bill" [open letter to Crooks], *Daily Mail* [Toronto], 2 February 1876.

42 Cosgrave, "The License Bill."

43 "Complaints of the Unlicensed," *Grip*, 27 May 1876.

44 Quoted in "Ontario Legislature: First Session," *Globe* [Toronto], 21 January 1876.
45 "The New License Act," *Globe* [Toronto], 1 February 1876.
46 Quoted in "Legislature of Ontario," *Globe* [Toronto], 20 March 1873; "In the Legislature," *Daily Mail* [Toronto], 26 February 1874.
47 Quoted in "Licensed Victuallers," *Daily Mail* [Toronto], 7 January 1876.
48 "The New License Law" [editorial], *Globe* [Toronto], 27 January 1876.
49 Quoted in "Ontario Legislature," *Globe* [Toronto], 1 February 1876.
50 "Current Events" [editorial], *Canadian Monthly Review,* February 1876, 163.
51 "The Policy of Centralisation" [editorial], *Daily Mail* [Toronto], 26 January 1876.
52 "Current Events," *Canadian Monthly Review,* February 1876, 163.
53 "The Liquor Bill," *Leader* [Toronto], 21 January 1876; "More Arbitrariness," *Leader* [Toronto], 27 January 1876.
54 Quoted in "Ontario Assembly," *Daily Mail* [Toronto], 21 January 1876. MacDougall's political affiliation was Independent-Liberal but on this issue he was highly critical of the government.
55 Quoted in "Ontario Legislature," *Globe* [Toronto], 1 February 1876.
56 Quoted in "In the Legislature," *Daily Mail* [Toronto], 1 February 1876.
57 Cosgrave, "The License Bill."
58 "The Policy of Centralisation" [editorial], *Daily Mail* [Toronto], 26 January 1876.
59 "Ontario Legislature," *Globe* [Toronto], 21 January 1876.
60 "Ontario Legislature," *Globe* [Toronto], 3 Feb 1876.
61 "Ontario Legislature," *Globe* [Toronto], 1 Feb 1876.
62 "The New License Law," *Globe* [Toronto], 23 February 1876.
63 Craig Heron, "Thomas Phillips Thompson," in *The Canadian Encyclopedia,* edited 4 March 2015, https://www.thecanadianencyclopedia.ca/en/article/thomas-phillips-thompson.
64 "Jimuel Biggs, DB," *Daily Mail* [Toronto], 26 February 1876.
65 "The New Liquor Law," *Daily Mail* [Toronto], 21 January 1876.

CHAPTER 3: POWER AND INFLUENCE IN THE NEW SYSTEM

1 Michèle Dagenais, "The Municipal Territory: A Product of the Liberal Order?," in *Liberalism and Hegemony: Debating the Canadian Liberal Revolution,* ed. Jean François Constant and Michel Ducharme (Toronto: University of Toronto Press, 2009), 207.
2 Mowat quoted in "Ontario Legislature," *Globe* [Toronto], 21 January 1876; "The New License Law" [editorial], *Globe* [Toronto], 27 January 1876.
3 S.J.R. Noel, *Patron, Client, Broker: Ontario Society and Politics* (Toronto: University of Toronto Press, 1990); 76.
4 Patronage might have been more formalized and expected than clientelism, but it was no less reciprocal. Examining the relationships between a Toronto politician and his constituents in early twentieth-century Ontario, Alan Gordon has argued that, far from a top-down relationship, patronage is better described as "an intricate and somewhat reciprocal set of social relations." Alan Gordon, "Patronage, Etiquette, and the Science of Connection: Edmund Bristol and Political Management, 1911–21," *Canadian Historical Review* 80 (1999): 4.
5 Noel, *Patron, Client, Broker,* 238–39.
6 Noel, *Patron, Client, Broker,* especially 283; A. Margaret Evans, *Sir Oliver Mowat,* Ontario Historical Studies Series (Toronto: University of Toronto Press, 1992), 108–9.

7   These practices, deployed on both sides, could range from facilitating partisan discussion to rewarding electors who voted the right way by providing free liquor. Such tactics might have eased after the reforms to the elections in 1875 that eliminated the testimonial vote and replaced it with a secret ballot. See Evans, *Sir Oliver Mowat*, 94–96.
8   Sir John Willison, *Reminiscences, Political and Personal* (Toronto: McClelland and Stewart, 1919), 93.
9   Noel, *Patron, Client, Broker*, 283.
10 Quoted in "Ontario Legislature," *Globe* [Toronto], 21 January 1876.
11 "The Liquor Traffic" [editorial], *Globe* [Toronto], 26 January 1876. Caution was important. The *Toronto Leader* was sure that this was an attempt to seize municipal rights and hijack the temperance cause for the good of the party. "The Liquor Bill" [editorial], *Toronto Leader*, 21 January 1876.
12 Noel, *Patron, Client, Broker*, 286.
13 Evans, *Sir Oliver Mowat*, 109.
14 Noel, *Patron, Client, Broker*, 241.
15 Bruce Curtis, "After 'Canada': Liberalism, Social Theory, and Historical Analysis," in *Liberalism and Hegemony: Debating the Canadian Liberal Revolution*, ed. Jean François Constant and Michel Ducharme (Toronto: University of Toronto Press, 2009), 178.
16 Ontario, Legislative Assembly, "Report Relative to the General Working of the Tavern and Shop Licenses Acts," *Sessional Papers*, No. 7 (1874), 8–9.
17 W.A. Gill to Adam Crooks, 3 February 1876, RG 8–31, B223998, "City of London" folder, License Branch Correspondence, Archives of Ontario (hereafter LBC/AO).
18 Alex Abbot, Clerk of Board of Police Commissioners, resolution made 4 February 1876, "City of London" folder, LBC/AO.
19 W.R. Parker, Pastor of Dundas Street Methodist Church, to Crooks, 7 February 1876, "City of London" folder, LBC/AO.
20 John Gemley, Minister of St. Paul's Church, to Crooks, 8 February 1876, "City of London" folder, LBC/AO.
21 Benjamin Cronyn to Adam Crooks, 15 February 1876, "City of London" folder, LBC/AO.
22 D.C. Macdonald to T.B. Pardee, 10 February 1876, "City of London" folder, LBC/AO.
23 Undated petition, "City of London" folder, LBC/AO.
24 "The License Officers" [editorial], *Daily Mail* [Toronto], 14 March 1876.
25 Untitled article, *Daily Mail* [Toronto], 16 March 1876.
26 "The License Officers" [editorial], *Daily Mail* [Toronto], 14 March 1876.
27 D.J. O'Donoghue to S.C. Wood, 16 February 1876, "Ottawa" folder, LBC/AO.
28 E.J.J. Stevenson to Adam Crooks, 7 February 1876, "Lanark" folder, LBC/AO.
29 J. Maconchy to Hon. M. Mcmaster, 28 January 1876, "Simcoe" folder, LBC/AO.
30 [Name obscured] Lount to Adam Crooks, 11 February 1876, "Simcoe" folder, LBC/AO.
31 John Howell to Adam Crooks, 3 March 1876, "Misc. Letters" folder, LBC/AO.
32 Rev. C.V. Pettit to Adam Crooks, 3 March 1876, "Carleton" folder, LBC/AO.
33 Sylvester Neelon to Adam Crooks, 22 March 1876, "Lincoln" folder, LBC/AO.
34 Sylvester Neelon to Adam Crooks, 22 March 1876, "Lincoln" folder, LBC/AO.
35 See untitled editorial, *Canadian Law Journal* 12 (1876): 157–58.
36 John Worgan (or Morgan) to Oliver Mowat, 3 February 1876, "Carleton" folder, LBC/AO.
37 D. Eccles to T.B. Pardee, 26 February 1876, "Middlesex North and West" folder, LBC/AO.
38 A.H. Sorely to Adam Crooks, 10 March 1876, "Misc. Letters" folder, LBC/AO.

39 Angus McKay to Adam Crooks, 22 February 1876, "Simcoe" folder, LBC/AO.
40 William McRae to Adam Crooks, February 1876, "Kingston" folder, LBC/AO.
41 P.C. McGregor to Adam Crooks, 10 February 1876, "Lanark" folder, LBC/AO.
42 E.J.J. Stevenson to Adam Crooks, 7 February 1876, "Lanark" folder, LBC/AO.
43 Lodge of Good Templars to Adam Crooks, 17 January 1876, "Durham" folder, LBC/AO.
44 Gideon Striker to Adam Crooks, 28 February 1876, "Prince Edward" folder, LBC/AO.
45 John Tierney to Adam Crooks, 23 February 1876, "Carleton" folder, LBC/AO.
46 W.D. Lyon to Adam Crooks, 3 March 1876, "Halton" folder, LBC/AO.
47 Archibald Bishop to S.C. Wood, 21 February 1876; Sinclair to S.C. Wood, n.d., "Huron" folder, LBC/AO.
48 Isaac B. Aylesworth to Adam Crooks, February 1876, "Simcoe" folder, LBC/AO.
49 D.L. Cruikshank to Sylvester Neelon, 25 February 1876, "Lincoln" folder, LBC/AO.
50 G.W. Monk to S.C. Wood, 8 February 1876, "Carleton County" folder, LBC/AO.
51 James Brady to Adam Crooks, 3 February 1876, "Oxford South" folder, LBC/AO.
52 James Moscow to Adam Crooks, 17 February 1876, and W.S. King to Adam Crooks, 17 February 1876, "Oxford South" folder, LBC/AO.
53 See Evans, *Sir Oliver Mowat*, 106–7.
54 J.W. McLaughlin (President of the Darlington Reform Association) to Crooks, 6 March 1876, "Durham" folder, LBC/AO.
55 D.J. O'Donoghue to S.C. Wood, 16 February 1876, "City of Ottawa" folder, LBC/AO.
56 Anonymous to Adam Crooks, 7 March 1876, "City of Ottawa" folder, LBC/AO. O'Donoghue recommended Xavier Groule, James Cunningham, and William Kehoe, but when the commission was announced James Warnock was in Kehoe's stead. Since recommended commissioners could refuse the position, we cannot be certain that Crooks offered it to the three men whom O'Donoghue recommended or whether he chose Warnock instead of Kehoe.
57 George Watson to Crooks, 28 March 1876, "Simcoe" folder, LBC/AO.
58 William McInnes (or Innes) to Adam Crooks, 2 March 1876, "West Hastings," misc. files, LBC/AO.
59 William Hargraft to Provincial Secretary, 23 February 1876, "Northumberland" folder, LBC/AO.
60 Cecil Mortimer, Commissioner, to S.C. Wood, 7 February 1876, "Northumberland" folder, LBC/AO. Mortimer was concerned enough to send a duplicate letter to Timothy Pardee, a popular minister in Mowat's cabinet who held the influential post of commissioner of Crown lands.
61 Thomas Clarke to Adam Crooks, 2 February 1876, "Northumberland" folder, LBC/AO; David B. Netherby to Adam Crooks, 26 February 1876, "Northumberland" folder, LBC/AO.
62 John Hartman Clark to Adam Crooks, 25 February 1876, "Northumberland" folder, LBC/AO.
63 C. Ian Kyer, "Gooderham, William George," in *Dictionary of Canadian Biography*, vol. 16 (Toronto: University of Toronto; Laval: Université Laval, 2003), http://www.biographi.ca/en/bio/gooderham_william_george_16E.html.
64 William Alger to Adam Crooks, 29 February 1876, "Northumberland" folder, LBC/AO.
65 Ontario, Legislative Assembly, "License Report," *Sessional Papers,* No. 42 (1877), 1–2 (hereafter License Report 1877).
66 "The License Law" [editorial], *Daily Mail* [Toronto], 2 May 1876.

67 "The License Law" [editorial], *Daily Mail* [Toronto], 2 May 1876.
68 "The Liquor Law" [editorial], *Daily Mail* [Toronto], 8 May 1876.
69 Temperance, "The License Law" [letter to the editor], *Globe* [Toronto], 5 May 1876.
70 "Tavern-Keeping" [editorial], *Globe* [Toronto], 8 May 1876.
71 "The New License Law" [editorial], *Globe* [Toronto], 5 May 1876.
72 "The New License Law" [editorial], *Globe* [Toronto], 5 May 1876.
73 John Bengough, "Complaints of the Unlicensed," *Grip,* 27 May 1876.
74 "The Unlicensed Milesian," *Grip,* 6 May 1876.
75 This was an observation of Sir John Willison, editor of the *Globe* from 1890 to 1902, whose autobiography provides a broad assessment of the governance of several leaders and devotes many pages to Mowat's use of patronage. See Willison, *Reminiscences,* especially 92–94; Noel, *Patron, Client, Broker,* Chapter 16, especially 295; and Evans, *Sir Oliver Mowat,* 109, who lists Mowat's general guidelines on deploying patronage in a way that did not sully the reputation of the government.
76 Adam Crooks, "Instructions to Board of License Commissioners" [form letter], 20 March 1876, "Departmental Form Letters," LBC/AO.
77 License Report 1877, response from South Simcoe, 68.
78 License Report 1877, response from Cornwall, 43.
79 License Report 1877, response from Elgin, 46.
80 License Report 1877, response from Welland, 70.
81 License Report 1877, response from Northumberland East, 60.
82 License Report 1877, response from York West, 74.
83 License Report 1877, response from Huron West, 53.
84 License Report 1877, response from Elgin, 45.
85 License Report 1877, response from Dundas, 44.
86 License Report 1877, response from Russell, 66–67.
87 License Report 1877, response from Ottawa, 63.
88 License Report 1877, response from West Peterborough, 64–65.
89 License Report 1877, response from Elgin, 46.
90 "Notes from London," *Globe* [Toronto], 21 June 1876.
91 License Report 1877, response from Toronto, 69.
92 "City News," *Globe* [Toronto], 11 May 1876.
93 "City News," *Globe* [Toronto], 31 May 1876.
94 "City News," *Globe* [Toronto], 10 June 1876.
95 "Act to Amend the Law Respecting the Sale of Fermented or Spirituous Liquors," *Statutes of Ontario* (1874), c. 26, s. 56.
96 License Report 1877, response from West Hastings, 51.
97 License Report 1877, response from Huron South, 52; response from West Hastings, 51.
98 Most commissioners reported the existence of dubious "temperance hotels" in their reports.
99 License Report 1877, response from Wellington Centre, 71.
100 License Report 1877, response from Dufferin, 45.
101 License Report 1877, response from Halton, 50.
102 License Report 1877, response from Prince Edward County, 65.
103 License Report 1877, response from Huron East, 52.
104 License Report 1877, response from London, 57.
105 License Report 1877, response from Dufferin, 45.

106 See, for example, the complaint from the commissioners, License Report 1877, response from London, 56–57.
107 License Report 1877, response from Durham East, 42.
108 License Report 1877, response from Grey South, 49.
109 License Report 1877, response from North York, 73–74.
110 License Report 1877, response from Toronto, 68–69.
111 License Report 1877, response from Lanark South, 55–56.
112 License Report 1877, response from Glengarry, 47–48.
113 License Report 1877, response from North York, 73.
114 License Report 1877, response from West Hastings, 51.
115 License Report 1877, report of S.C. Wood, 2.
116 License Report 1877, Schedule F, report of Totten, 32.
117 License Report 1877, Schedule F, report of Totten, 32.
118 License Report 1877, Schedule F, report of Totten, 33.
119 License Report 1877, Schedule F, report of Totten, 34.
120 License Report 1877, Schedule F, report of Totten, 34.
121 License Report 1877, Schedule F, report of Totten, 35.
122 Ontario, Legislative Assembly, "License Report," *Sessional Papers,* No. 11 (1881) (hereafter License Report 1881), response from South Huron, 85.
123 License Report 1881, response from East Huron, 82.
124 License Report 1881, response from East Northumberland, 78.
125 License Report 1881, response from North Leeds and Grenville, 70.
126 License Report 1881, response from Kingston, 66.
127 License Report 1881, response from Toronto, 59.
128 License Report 1881, response from Kingston, 66.
129 License Report 1881, response from South Huron, 84.
130 License Report 1881, response from East York, 79.
131 License Report 1881, response from East York, 80.
132 License Report 1881, response from North Grey, 76.
133 License Report 1881, response from Addington, 61.
134 License Report 1881, response from South Essex, 81.
135 License Report 1881, response from South Grey, 89.
136 License Report 1881, response from West Wellington, 79.
137 License Report 1881, response from South Ontario, 84.
138 License Report 1881, response from North Perth, 62.
139 License Report 1881, response from South Grey, 89.
140 License Report 1881, response from East Middlesex, 71.
141 License Report 1881, response from East Peterborough, 87.
142 License Report 1881, response from East Durham, 90.
143 License Report 1881, response from East Huron, 82.
144 License Report 1881, response from North York, 106.

CHAPTER 4: POLITICS, LAW, AND THE LICENSE BRANCH

1 "The New License Law" [editorial], *Globe* [Toronto], 9 February 1876.
2 Bruce Curtis, "After 'Canada': Liberalism, Social Theory, and Historical Analysis," in *Liberalism and Hegemony: Debating the Canadian Liberal Revolution,* ed. Jean François

Constant and Michel Ducharme (Toronto: University of Toronto Press, 2009), 176–200; Michèle Dagenais, "The Municipal Territory: A Product of the Liberal Order?," in *Liberalism and Hegemony: Debating the Canadian Liberal Revolution*, ed. Jean François Constant and Michel Ducharme (Toronto: University of Toronto Press, 2009), 201–21; also see Bruce Curtis, *True Government by Choice Men? Inspection, Education and State Formation in Canada West* (Toronto: University of Toronto Press, 1992).

3 Mowat always kept a few Tory commissioners on board according to S.J.R. Noel, *Patron, Client, Broker: Ontario Society and Politics* (Toronto: University of Toronto Press, 1990), 282.
4 "Ontario Legislature," *Empire* [Toronto], 4 May 1893.
5 Sir John Willison, *Reminiscences, Political and Personal* (Toronto: McClelland and Stewart, 1919), 93.
6 Noel, *Patron, Client, Broker*, 283.
7 Apparently, the board was upset that Dilly was telling people what was being discussed in the private board meetings.
8 John Orchard, James Morin, and James Henderson to A.S. Hardy, 13 April 1880, RG 8-14-0-103, Provincial Secretary fonds, Archives of Ontario.
9 For the membership of Boards of License Commissioners and inspectors, see *Ontario Gazette*. Normally, announcements of License Branch appointments were made between February and May each year.
10 Petition sent to License Branch from ratepayers of Petrolia, 13 September 1882. In Ontario, Legislative Assembly, "Return to an Order Passed by the Legislative Assembly on the 29th Day of February 1884 for a Return of all Correspondence between the Executive of the Lambton Prohibitory Association and the Provincial Secretary...," *Sessional Papers*, No. 90 (1884) (unprinted) (hereafter Sessional Paper 90 (1884)). Unprinted sessional papers are held at the Archives of Ontario in RG 49-19 (hereafter RG 49-19/AO). They often have very long titles that I'm abbreviating for the sake of all involved.
11 Ontario's population grew 30 percent between 1871 and 1891, whereas Petrolia's population grew 64 percent in that time period. The population in Ontario was 1,620,851 (1871); 1,923,228 (1881); and 2,114,321 (1891). See Census of Ontario, 1871, 1881, 1891, vol. 1 in each series.
12 Arthur Hardy to Boosey, 29 November 1882, Sessional Paper 90 (1884), RG 49-19/AO.
13 Henry Totten to R.C. Palmer, Inspector, 29 November 1882, Sessional Paper 90 (1884), RG 49-19/AO.
14 R.C. Palmer to Henry Totten, 30 November 1882, Sessional Paper 90 (1884), RG 49-19/AO.
15 An Act Respecting Private Detectives, *Statutes of Ontario* (1909), cap 83. Even when licensing was created, the law placed few constraints upon a detective's work.
16 "London," *Daily Mail* [Toronto], 23 August 1876.
17 "Editorial Notes," *Northern Advance* [Barrie], 22 November 1877.
18 "A Denial," *London Advertiser*, 19 August 1876.
19 Bryce and Mills, "The Case of Constable Allen" [letter to the editor], *London Advertiser*, 23 August 1876. They did not sign their full names.
20 I recount this story in *When Good Drugs Go Bad: Opium, Medicine, and the Origins of Canada's Drug Laws* (Vancouver: UBC Press, 2015), 53–54.
21 "Evidence of the Royal Commission on the Liquor Traffic, Ontario" (hereafter RCLT), *Sessional Papers of the Dominion of Canada*, vol. 15, No. 21 (1894), evidence of Thomas Dexter, 13714a. (The final number represents the question number.)

22 RCLT, evidence of Thomas Dexter, 13691a.
23 RCLT, evidence of David Dumble, 1582a.
24 RCLT, evidence of John McKenzie, 2406a.
25 Evidence of A.G. Hodge to the McCarthy Committee, 20 April 1883, in "Report of the Special Committee Appointed to Consider the Subject of the Unrestrained Sale of Intoxicating Liquors and the Regulation of the Granting of Shop, Saloon, and Tavern Licenses," in House of Commons, *Journals*, 5th Leg, 1st Sess, No 17 (1883), Appendix 5.
26 RCLT, evidence of George Cochrane, 1406.
27 Henry Totten to Walter Cowan, Inspector, 25 September 1903. In Ontario, Legislative Assembly, "Return to an Order of the House That There Be Laid before the House Copies of all Complaints Received by the License Department against W S Cowan, Formerly Inspector of Licenses for South Wellington ...," *Sessional Papers*, No. 69 (1904) (unprinted), RG 49-19/AO.
28 RCLT, evidence of Francis Bell, 4050.
29 RCLT, evidence of Walter Cowan, 8193.
30 "The Reward for Party Service," *Globe* [Toronto], 2 April 1905.
31 "Greer, Detective," RG 8–5, Provincial Secretary's Correspondence, Archives of Ontario.
32 H.M. Deroche to N.I. Cartwright, 29 February 1876, "Lennox" folder, LBC/AO; N.I. Cartwright to Adam Crooks, 1 March 1876, "Lennox" folder, LBC/AO.
33 William A. Hogle to N.I. Cartwright, 16 January [1877], "Lennox" folder, LBC/AO.
34 T.W. Casey to S.G. Wood, 24 January 1877, "Lennox" folder, LBC/AO.
35 See notes of the meeting held 16 February 1877, "Lennox" folder, LBC/AO.
36 Wood was secretary and registrar from July 1875 to March 1877.
37 S.C. Wood to "Gentlemen," 21 February 1877 [onion skin copy], "Lennox" folder, LBC/AO.
38 Circular return for Lennox County, "Lennox" folder, LBC/AO. Despite such success, by the early 1880s Hogle was no longer an inspector, although the reason is difficult to determine.
39 RCLT, evidence of John Murton, 2782.
40 RCLT, evidence of Alexander Bartlett, 4784.
41 RCLT, evidence of William McKay, 4389.
42 Hardy became treasurer after Wood, in 1877.
43 A.J. Conover to A.S. Hardy, 24 May 1882. In Ontario, Legislative Assembly, "Return of Copies of Correspondence and Documents between the Provincial Secretary and the License Commissioners or License Inspector of East Huron in Reference to the Granting of a Hotel License to One Conover in the Village of Blue Vale," *Sessional Papers*, No. 25 (1884) (unprinted), RG 49-19/AO (hereafter Sessional Paper 25 (1884)).
44 T. Farrow to A.S. Hardy, 23 May 1882, in Sessional Paper 25 (1884).
45 William Ross and others, petition to Provincial Secretary A.S. Hardy [transcribed], April 1882, in Sessional Paper 25 (1884).
46 A.S. Hardy to A.J. Conover, 30 May 1882, in Sessional Paper 25 (1884).
47 Donald Scott, Inspector, to A.S. Hardy, 1 June 1882, in Sessional Paper 25 (1884).
48 Originally, this was s. 9(16), but by 1887 it had become s. 11(14).
49 George Pike to Provincial Secretary, 17 February 1892, in Ontario, Legislative Assembly, "Return to an Order of the House of the Third Day of May, 1893, for a Return of Copies of All Correspondence between the License Inspector of North Brant, or Other Parties, and the License Department ...," *Sessional Papers*, No. 77 (1893) (unprinted), RG 49-19/AO (hereafter Sessional Paper 77 (1893)).

50 J.E. Waterous to A.S. Hardy, 31 March 1892, in Sessional Paper 77 (1893).
51 A.S. Hardy to J.E. Waterous, 21 April 1892, in Sessional Paper 77 (1893).
52 Joseph Hartley to A.S. Hardy, 20 April 1892, in Sessional Paper 77 (1893).
53 A.S. Hardy to Joseph Hartley, 22 April 1892, in Sessional Paper 77 (1893).
54 Henry Totten to T.H. Preston, 13 May 1892, in Sessional Paper 77 (1893).
55 John Green to Oliver Mowat, 27 November 1876, "Cardwell" folder, LBC/AO.
56 Richard Stedman to [Provincial Secretary], 24 December 1876, "Cardwell" folder, LBC/AO.
57 See *Ontario Gazette* 10, no. 7 (17 February 1877): 177.
58 His first name was not identified in the court filings, but Pizer appeared in the census of 1891 as a hotelier. See Manuscript Census, District 63, Subdistrict No. 2 (Essex Centre), 11 (documents available from Library and Archives Canada "ancestor" search). In the 1901 census, his name was expanded to Wm. His family had moved to Amherstburg, but he still kept a hotel in Essex Centre.
59 "*Pizer v. Fraser et al.*," in *The Ontario Reports: Containing Reports of Cases Decided in the High Court of Justice for Ontario*, vol. 18, ed. James F. Smith (Toronto: Rowsell and Hutchison, 1889), 635.
60 "*Pizer v. Fraser et al.*," in *The Ontario Reports*, judgment of Street, 642. A brief summary of the case is also found in James Frederick Smith and Frank John Joseph, *A Digest of the Reported Cases Determined in the Superior Courts of Ontario* (Toronto: Rowsell and Hutchison, 1892), 1053–54. It is not clear whether this was a decision that the commissioners preferred, although they had been recorded as saying that, except for the petition itself, they had no reason to refuse the license.
61 There are no records of this case in the government archives; all details come from the court filing and decision in *The Ontario Reports*.
62 J.H. Leitch to License Inspector (postscript by N. Mills), 29 June 1889, in Ontario, Legislative Assembly, "Return to an Order of the House of the Twelfth Day of March, 1890, of a Copy of the Judgment Pronounced by the Honourable Mr. Justice Robertson, in an Action in the High Court of Justice, wherein John J. Gosnell is Plaintiff and Isaac Swarthout and Others Are Defendants, and Copies of All Correspondence …," *Sessional Papers*, No. 73 (1890), 7 (hereafter Sessional Paper 73 (1890)).
63 "Agin [sic] the Scott Act," *Globe* [Toronto], 5 April 1889.
64 The time between the vote and the gazetting was intended to allow for appeals.
65 Henry Totten, memo to Provincial Secretary re *Gosnell v. Swarthout et al.*, 21 February 1890, in Sessional Paper 73 (1890), 17–18.
66 *Gosnell v. Swarthout et al.*, judgment of Justice Robertson, 13 January 1890, Sessional Paper 73 (1890), 5–7.
67 Henry Totten, memo to Provincial Secretary re *Gosnell v. Swarthout et al.*, 21 February 1890, Sessional Paper 73 (1890), 18.

Chapter 5: How Drinking Affects the Constitution, 1864–83

1 Dara Lithwick, "A *pas de deux:* The Division of Federal and Provincial Legislative Powers in Sections 91 and 92 of the *Constitution Act 1867*," in *In Brief*, 2015–128E (Ottawa: Library of Parliament, 2015). John T. Saywell, *The Lawmakers: Judicial Power and the Shaping of Canadian Federalism* (Toronto: Osgoode Society, 2002), discusses the complications in detail. See, of course, An Act for the Union of Canada, Nova Scotia, and New

Brunswick, and the Government Thereof; and for Purposes Connected Therewith, 30 & 31 Vict. (UK), c. 3 (commonly known as the British North America Act or BNA Act).
2 Saywell, *The Lawmakers*, 36–37.
3 Canada Temperance Act, *Statutes of the Province of Ontario* (1864), 27 & 28 Vict., c. 18, s. 12(3).
4 Canada Temperance Act, *Statutes of the Province of Ontario* (1864), 27 & 28 Vict., c. 18, s. 12(4).
5 Canada Temperance Act, *Statutes of the Province of Ontario* (1864), 27 & 28 Vict., c. 18, s. 13.
6 This viewpoint was especially articulated in numerous editorials of the *Globe* and the *Canadian Monthly Review*.
7 "Communications – The Dunkin Act," *Globe* [Toronto], 15 May 1878.
8 Canada Temperance Act, *Statutes of the Province of Ontario* (1864), 27 & 28 Vict., c. 18, ss. 14–35.
9 Ontario, Legislative Assembly, "Report of the Hon. The Provincial Secretary on the Working of the Tavern and Shop Licenses Act for the Year 1878," *Sessional Papers*, No. 11 (1879), 7–8. Subsequent references to these reports will use the common title "License Report" with date appended.
10 James Cameron, "Temperance Legislation or Our New License Bill," *Canadian Christian Monthly*, April 1876, 164–65.
11 "The Dunkin Act" [editorial], *Globe* [Toronto], 27 November 1876.
12 "Vox Populi," *British American Presbyterian*, 3 August 1877, 4.
13 Graeme Decarie, "Temperance Movement in Canada," 23 July 2013, updated by Janice Tibbetts and Andrew McIntosh and last edited 13 November 2020, in *The Canadian Encyclopedia*, https://www.thecanadianencyclopedia.ca/en/article/temperance-movement.
14 Jack S. Blocker, Jr., *American Temperance Movements: Cycles of Reform* (Boston: Twayne, 1989); Jack S. Blocker, *"Give to the Winds Thy Fears": The Women's Temperance Crusade 1873–1874* (Westport, CT: Greenwood Press, 1985).
15 See S.G.E. McKee, *Jubilee History of the Ontario Woman's Christian Temperance Union 1877–1927* (Toronto: C.A. Goodfellow and Son, 1927); Sharon Anne Cook, *Through Sunshine and Shadow: The Woman's Christian Temperance Union, Evangelicalism, and Reform in Ontario, 1874–1930* (Montreal and Kingston: McGill-Queen's University Press, 1995); Graeme Decarie, "The Prohibition Movement in Ontario: 1894–1916" (PhD diss., Queen's University, 1972); Brian Paul Trainor, "Towards a Genealogy of Temperance: Identity, Belief and Drink in Victorian Ontario" (MA thesis, Queen's University, 1993); and Dan Malleck, "Priorities of Development in Four Local Woman's Christian Temperance Unions in Ontario 1877–1895," in *The Changing Face of Drink: Substance, Imagery, Behaviour*, ed. Jack S. Blocker, Jr., and Cheryl Krasnick Warsh (Ottawa: Les Publications Histoire Sociale/Social History, 1997), 189–208.
16 Ontario, Legislative Assembly, "License Report," *Sessional Papers*, No. 11 (1881) (hereafter License Report 1881), Schedule F, for license districts where the Dunkin Act had been repealed in 1878–79. See License Report 1879, 7, for the thirteen counties where it had passed since 1876.
17 "The Dunkin Bill," *British American Presbyterian*, 24 August 1877, 4.
18 "The Dunkin Act in Brant," *Globe* [Toronto], 16 March 1878.
19 "Re *Mace v. County of Frontenac*," *Canada Law Journal* 14 (January 1878): 17.
20 "Re *Regina v. Prettie*," *Canada Law Journal* 14 (April 1878): 118. See also "Queen's Bench," *Globe* [Toronto], 16 March 1878. There is a Prettie mentioned in the Common Law Chambers records in "Legal Intelligence," *Globe* [Toronto], 7 September 1877, heard by Justice Wilson.

21 "The Dunkin Act – Test Case – No Decision," *Globe* [Toronto], 15 May 1878.
22 "Liquor Prosecutions," *Globe* [Toronto], 16 May 1878.
23 See, for example, "Queen's Bench in Banco – Hilary Term," *Canada Law Journal* 14 (1878): 118–19. The case was thrown out because the charge had been laid under the Dunkin Act for "keeping liquor without license," but the Dunkin Act did not deal with licenses. The court noted that it should have been "for keeping liquor at all." The précis of the case noted that "the conflict of jurisdiction between the Dominion and Local Legislatures under the power to regulate trade and commerce on the one side and the right to impose police regulations on the other [was] considered and discussed."
24 See An Act to Amend the Acts Respecting the Sale of Fermented or Spirituous Liquors," *Statutes of Ontario* (1877), c. 18, s. 30.
25 On the passage of the Dunkin Act, see T.A. Crowley, "Creighton, Letitia," in *Dictionary of Canadian Biography*, vol. 12 (Toronto: University of Toronto; Laval: Université Laval, 2003), http://www.biographi.ca/en/bio/creighton_letitia_12E.html.
26 Quoted in *Report of the Women's International Temperance Convention Held at Philadelphia, June 12, 1876* [pamphlet] (Toronto: WCTU, 1876), available on Early Canadiana Online, http://eco.canadiana.ca/view/oocihm.51039, and part of the CIHM microfiche series, 51039.
27 In the 1881 provincial license report, the inspector for Prince Edward County details the "confusion" at the end of the Dunkin Act in the county. See License Report 1881, response from Prince Edward County, 109. Not to worry, Prince Edward County retained its weirdness in other ways.
28 House of Commons, *Journals*, 3rd Leg, 4th Sess, No 9 (23 February 1877), 61.
29 House of Commons, *Journals*, 3rd Leg, 4th Sess, No 9 (16 March 1877), 140.
30 *Senate Debates*, 3rd Parl, 5th Sess (15 March 1878), 162 (Hon. Richard Scott).
31 *Senate Debates* (15 March 1878), 161–63 (Hon. Richard Scott).
32 *Senate Debates* (28 March 1878), 357 (Hon. Robert Dickey).
33 *Senate Debates* (28 March 1878), 358 (Hon. Robert Dickey).
34 *Senate Debates* (28 March 1878), 359 (Hon. Richard Scott).
35 Saywell, *The Lawmakers*.
36 Eugene O'Keefe to John A. Macdonald [telegram], 8 April 1878, MG 26 A, Sir John A Macdonald Papers, Library and Archives Canada (hereafter Macdonald Papers), Reel C-1714, 160250. The reels for the Sir John A Macdonald Papers are available (as of the date of writing) in the Heritage collection at Canadiana.ca.
37 Scott mentioned the role of the Dominion Alliance when he presented the bill on 28 March 1878, and its role in framing the article was clearly acknowledged during the Senate debates. See *Senate Debates* (28 March 1878), 79; *Senate Debates*, 3rd Parl, 5th Sess (4 April 1878), 465.
38 *Senate Debates*, 4th Parl, 1st Sess (5 May 1879), 451 (Hon. George Alexander).
39 Senate, *Journals*, 4th Leg, 2nd Sess, No 14 (5 May 1880), 261–62. Discussion of this motion was pushed back until 12 May. However, the Senate session ended on 7 May, so senators who supported the amendment knew that they were giving it the hoist.
40 James H. Killey to John A. Macdonald, 9 February 1881, Macdonald Papers, Reel C-1751, 173639–40.
41 Eugene O'Keefe to John A. Macdonald [telegram], 14 March 1881, Macdonald Papers, Reel C-1751, 174181.

42 Thomas Davies to John A. Macdonald [telegram], 14 March 1881, Macdonald Papers, Reel C-1751, 174189–90.
43 Henry Cronmiller to John A. Macdonald, 14 March 1881, Macdonald Papers, Reel C-1751, 174187–88.
44 James H. Killey to John A. Macdonald, 11 March 1881, Macdonald Papers, Reel C-1751, 174119–20.
45 George Jackson to John A. Macdonald, 12 May 1881, Macdonald Papers, Reel C-1752, 175133–34.
46 Eugene O'Keefe to John A. Macdonald, 17 March 1881, Macdonald Papers, Reel C-1752, 174296–97.
47 Eugene O'Keefe to John A. Macdonald, 17 March 1881, Macdonald Papers, Reel C-1752, 174296–97.
48 Eugene O'Keefe to John A. Macdonald, 1 December 1880, Macdonald Papers, Reel C-1750, 172697–99.
49 "The Liquor Bill" [editorial], *Leader* [Toronto], 21 January 1876.
50 Eugene O'Keefe to John A. Macdonald, 1 December 1880, Macdonald Papers, Reel C-1750, 172697–99.
51 Frank Smith to S.L. Tilley, 28 December 1881, copy sent to John A. Macdonald, Macdonald Papers, Reel C-1679, 120650–53.
52 Frank Smith to S.L. Tilley, 28 December 1881, copy sent to John A. Macdonald, Macdonald Papers, Reel C-1679, 120650–53.
53 See "Latest from New Brunswick," *Globe* [Toronto], 1 November 1878. The Supreme Court ruling mistakenly listed the date that the Scott Act came into force in Fredericton as 1 May 1878, an impossibility since the law had not yet received royal assent on that day. See *City of Fredericton v. The Queen*, (1880), 3 SCR 505.
54 An Act Respecting the Traffic in Intoxicating Liquors, 41 Vic., c. 16, preamble.
55 *City of Fredericton v. The Queen*, (1880), 3 SCR 505, 526.
56 Committee of the Privy Council to John A. Macdonald, 26 October 1881, Macdonald Papers, Reel C-1699, 142571–81; Joseph Gibson, Ingersoll, to John A. Macdonald, 1 October 1881, Macdonald Papers, Reel C-1753, 175779–81; and J.F. Brown, Vice-President of the Dominion Alliance, to John A. Macdonald, 12 October 1881, Macdonald Papers, Reel C-1753, 176016–19. See also Saywell, *The Lawmakers*, 87.
57 Saywell, *The Lawmakers*, 87–93.
58 The British North America Act (1867), 30 & 31 Vic., c. 3, s. 92(13).
59 Saywell, *The Lawmakers*, 29.
60 "Tory: Sir John at Yorkville," *Globe* [Toronto], 2 June 1882.
61 S.J.R. Noel, *Patron, Client, Broker: Ontario Society and Politics* (Toronto: University of Toronto Press, 1990).
62 *House of Commons Debates*, 5th Leg, 1st Sess, Vol 13 (16 March 1883), 245 (Hon. Edward Blake).
63 "Report of the Special Committee Appointed to Consider the Subject of the Unrestrained Sale of Intoxicating Liquors and the Regulation of the Granting of Shop, Saloon, and Tavern Licenses" (hereafter McCarthy Committee Report), in House of Commons *Journals*, 5th Leg, 1st Sess (1883), Appendix 5, 34.
64 See Philip Girard, "Liberty, Order, and Pluralism: The Canadian Experience," in *Exclusionary Empire: English Liberty Overseas 1600–1900*, ed. Jack P. Greene (Cambridge: Cambridge University Press, 2010), 183.
65 McCarthy Committee Report, 34–35.

66 McCarthy Committee Report, 41.
67 McCarthy Committee Report, 42.
68 McCarthy Committee Report, 46.
69 McCarthy Committee Report, 47.
70 Draft bill, in McCarthy Committee Report, 1.
71 The original bill reportedly allowed this upon petition of one-half of the electors.
72 Draft bill, in McCarthy Committee Report, s. 65, 14. The Crooks Act did not ban liquor sales overnight except on weekends, but municipalities could pass their own bylaws making such restrictions.
73 An Act Respecting the Sale of Intoxicating Liquors, and the Issue of Licenses Therefor, in *Acts of the Parliament of the Dominion of Canada*, vol. 1 (Ottawa: Queen's Printer, 1883), c. 30, s. 47.
74 As noted in Chapter 2, summer licenses were added in amendments to the Crooks Act in 1877.
75 The proposed legislation was included in the McCarthy Committee Report.
76 *House of Commons Debates*, 5th Leg, 1st Sess, Vol 14 (21 May 1883), 1347 (Georges Auguste Gigault).
77 *House of Commons Debates*, 5th Leg, 1st Sess, Vol 14 (21 May 1883), 1351 (D'Alton McCarthy).
78 W.R. Davis to John A. Macdonald, 27 January 1883, Macdonald Papers, Reel C-1760, 185756–57.
79 Eugene O'Keefe to John A. Macdonald, 29 January 1883, Macdonald Papers, Reel C-1760, 185788–89.
80 Eugene O'Keefe to John A. Macdonald, 2 February 1883, Macdonald Papers, Reel C-1760, 185912–13.
81 Thomas Elliott to John A. Macdonald, 16 March 1883, Macdonald Papers, Reel C-1760, 186941–42.

CHAPTER 6: MCCARTHY AND CROOKS ENTER A TAVERN, 1883–85

1 Eugene O'Keefe to John A. Macdonald, 28 March 1883, MG 26 A, Sir John A. Macdonald Papers Library and Archives Canada (hereafter Macdonald Papers), Reel C-1761, 188159.
2 Resolution of the Independent Order of Good Templars, 14 December 1883, Macdonald Papers, Reel C-1764, 191512.
3 See "Dominion License Act Null and Void," *Globe* [Toronto], 7 January 1884; and "The Smart Boy Takes a Tumble," illustration on the first page of *Grip*, 2 May 1885.
4 "Judgement of the Lords of the Judicial Committee of the Privy Council on the Appeal of *Hodge v. The Queen*" (hereafter Hodge Decision), 1–3, available on the Bailii website, http://www.bailii.org/uk/cases/UKPC/1883/1883_59.html.
5 Hodge Decision, 10.
6 John T. Saywell, *The Lawmakers: Judicial Power and the Shaping of Canadian Federalism* (Toronto: Osgoode Society, 2002).
7 Repeated in "Sir John and the Privy Council," *Globe* [Toronto], 15 January 1884.
8 John A. Macdonald to Eugene O'Keefe, 23 March 1883, Macdonald Papers, Letterbook 22 (Reel C-34), 92–94. Macdonald's letterbooks are listed by volume and page number within each volume, and several letterbooks are on each microfilm reel.

9 Act to Amend the Municipal Law, *Statutes of Ontario* (1879), c. 31, s. 2.
10 "What Will He Do with It?," *Globe* [Toronto], 4 January 1884.
11 "Queen v. Hodge" [editorial], *Daily Mail* [Toronto], 1 January 1884.
12 J.B. Robinson, Lieutenant Governor, Ontario, to Honourable Secretary of State, Ottawa, 19 January 1884, in Canada, Parliament, "Return to an Address of the House of Commons, Dated 3rd March, 1884 For Copies of All Correspondence between the Government and Any of the Local Governments of the Provinces, Respecting the Liquor License Act of 1883," *Sessional Papers*, No. 30f (1884), 144 (hereafter Sessional Papers 30f (1884)). The letter was penned by Mowat in his capacity as Attorney generally but following protocols, it was forwarded by the Lieutenant Governor.
13 J.B. Robinson, Lieutenant Governor, Ontario, to Honourable Secretary of State, Ottawa, 16 February 1884, in Sessional Papers 30f (1884), 144.
14 The request was made on 3 March 1884; see House of Commons, *Journals*, 5th Leg, 2nd Sess (3 March 1884), 181. The paper was presented to the House on 18 April 1884, immediately before Parliament was prorogued.
15 Gerald Friesen, "Norquay, John," in *Dictionary of Canadian Biography*, vol. 11 (Toronto: University of Toronto; Laval: Université Laval, 2003–), http://www.biographi.ca/en/bio/norquay_john_11E.html.
16 John Norquay to Alexander Campbell, Minister of Justice, 30 January 1884, in Sessional Papers 30f (1884), 145.
17 "License Confusion" [editorial], *Globe* [Toronto], 1 March 1884.
18 "The License Controversy," *Globe* [Toronto], 21 April 1884.
19 These parliamentary machinations were likely arranged in advance. On 13 March 1884, Houde wrote to Macdonald noting that the prime minister had asked him not to make his motion that day. The fact that he moved it five days later, despite his concern that a delay would make him look bad, indicates that the motion and amendment were preplanned. See Frédéric Houde to John A. Macdonald, 13 March 1884, Macdonald Papers, Reel C-1765, 193453.
20 House of Commons, *Journals*, 5th Leg, 2nd Sess (18 March 1884), 251.
21 House of Commons, *Journals*, 5th Leg, 2nd Sess (18–19 March 1884), 251–52.
22 "The License Conflict – The Attorney General of Quebec to Ignore the McCarthy Act," *Globe* [Toronto], 6 March 1884; "The License Conflict," *Globe* [Toronto], 10 March 1884; "License Troubles" [editorial], *Whig* [Kingston], 3 April 1884; "Opposition to the McCarthy Act," *Examiner* [Barrie], 20 March 1884.
23 As lighthearted as this statement might appear, I include it because when prohibition ended and the Ontario government again licensed hotels for drinking purposes, the hotel keepers were required to register the personal booze that they kept and to specify where they would drink it. See Dan Malleck, *Try to Control Yourself: The Regulation of Public Drinking in Post-Prohibition Ontario, 1927–1944* (Vancouver: UBC Press, 2012).
24 "Canadian – St. John – Infringement of Municipal Rights," *Globe* [Toronto], 19 February 1884.
25 G.E. Foster to John A. Macdonald, 15 March 1884, enclosing letters from A.L. Belyea, license commissioner for York County, NB, dated 15 March 1884 and 11 March 1884, Macdonald Papers, Reel C-1520, 38143–51.
26 W.B. Ives to John A. Macdonald, 26 March 1884, Macdonald Papers, Reel C-1520, 38176–79.
27 "License Troubles," *Whig* [Kingston], 3 April 1884.

28 "The License Conflict," *Globe* [Toronto], 29 February 1884.
29 "Dominion License Act," *Globe* [Toronto], 25 March 1884.
30 "Quebec and the McCarthy Act," *Globe* [Toronto], 11 January 1884.
31 Act to Amend the Municipal Law, *Statutes of Ontario* (1879), c. 31, s. 2.
32 "The Dominion License Act," *Whig* [Kingston], 21 February 1884.
33 "Did Not Take Their Seats," *Whig* [Kingston], 25 February 1884. See also "The Board," *Whig* [Kingston], 21 February 1884, on the dilemma facing the warden of Frontenac.
34 "Pertinent Points," *Whig* [Kingston], 13 February 1884.
35 Untitled article, *Whig* [Kingston], 28 February 1884; "Mayors, Wardens, and the McCarthy Act," *Globe* [Toronto], 27 February 1884.
36 I am assuming here that most tavern keepers were not lawyers. I am not sure which occupation was more lucrative, appealing, or powerful.
37 Robert Henry to John A. Macdonald, 5 April 1884 (note in file says 5 May), Macdonald Papers, Reel C-1766, 194534–36.
38 Eugene O'Keefe to John A. Macdonald, 31 January 1884, Macdonald Papers, Reel C-1765, 192615–17.
39 Patrick Kelly to John A. Macdonald, 22 February 1884, Macdonald Papers, Reel C-1765, 193077–78.
40 John Harvey to John A. Macdonald, 17 March 1884, Macdonald Papers, Reel C-1765, 38152–55.
41 I.J. McCaul to anonymous tavern keeper in South Norfolk, 5 April 1884, sent to John Costigan, Secretary of State, from R.T. Livingstone, 14 April 1884, Macdonald Papers, Reel C-1766, 38192–95.
42 Untitled article, *Whig* [Kingston], 26 February 1884.
43 J.B. Lennox to John A. Macdonald, 7 June 1884, Macdonald Papers, Reel C-1766, 195299–195302.
44 "Licenses on the Island" [editorial], *Globe* [Toronto], 17 April 1884.
45 "Another License Outrage" [letter to the editor], *Globe* [Toronto], 19 April 1884. The Italian problem may have been a reference to a riot in St. Thomas, Ontario, on 11 April 1884 between a group of Irish and Italian labourers. See "Irish and Italians," *Globe* [Toronto], 12 April 1884.
46 On the organization of the Trades Benevolent Association, see "Licensed Victuallers," *Globe* [Toronto], 16 December 1881.
47 "They'll Take Out Both," *Whig* [Kingston], 1 March 1884.
48 "Ontario Legislature," *Globe* [Toronto], 5 March 1884.
49 "The License Debate" [editorial], *Globe* [Toronto], 5 March 1884.
50 "Ontario Assembly Notes," *Globe* [Toronto], 5 March 1884.
51 "Backbone at Last," *Examiner* [Barrie], 6 March 1884.
52 "License Increase," *Whig* [Kingston], 14 April 1884; "Refusing the Licenses," *Whig* [Kingston], 23 April 1884; "Taking Provincial Licenses Only" [on Belleville], *Whig* [Kingston], 24 April 1884.
53 *House of Commons Debates*, 5th Parl, 2nd Sess, Vol 16 (10 April 1884), 1476–77 (Sir John A. Macdonald).
54 *House of Commons Debates*, 5th Parl, 2nd Sess, Vol 16 (15 April 1884), 1595 (Hon. D'Alton McCarthy).
55 *House of Commons Debates*, 5th Parl, 2nd Sess, Vol 16 (17 April 1884), 1638 (Sir John A. Macdonald).

56 "Dominion License Law Emasculated," *Globe* [Toronto], 24 April 1884.
57 "Dominion License Law Emasculated," *Globe* [Toronto], 24 April 1884.
58 "License Question – The Last Tinkering which the Bill Received," *Whig* [Kingston], 16 April 1884.
59 Untitled editorial, *Whig* [Kingston], 21 April 1884.
60 Untitled editorial, *Examiner* [Barrie], 24 April 1884.
61 John A. Macdonald to Alexander Campbell, 26 April 1884, Macdonald Papers, Letterbook 22 (Reel C-34), 381–82. (The LAC database says 25 April, but the letterbook shows 26 April).
62 "The Grit Bulldozing Act," *Daily Mail* [Toronto], 1 May 1884.
63 "Disallowance Again," *Daily Mail* [Toronto], 1 May 1884.
64 "Despotic Disallowance," *Globe* [Toronto], 3 May 1884; "Another Invasion of Provincial Rights," *Globe* [Toronto], 2 May 1884.
65 "License Law Vetoed," *Whig* [Kingston], 1 May 1884.

CHAPTER 7: ATTEMPTING TO WATER DOWN THE SCOTT ACT, 1884–92

1 "Licensed Victuallers," *Globe* [Toronto], 19 December 1883.
2 John Seaton to John A. Macdonald, 27 March 1885, MG 26 A, Sir John A. Macdonald Papers, Library and Archives Canada (hereafter Macdonald Papers), Reel C-1770, 200208–9.
3 A. MacCormack to John A. Macdonald, 27 April 1885, Macdonald Papers, Reel C-1771, 200879–81.
4 The Royal Commission on the Liquor Traffic examined in detail the fate of the Scott Act in Canada. See Canada, Parliament, "Report of the Royal Commission on the Liquor Traffic in Canada, with Full Index to the Report and to the Evidence," *Sessional Papers*, Vol. 11, No. 21 (1895) (hereafter RCLT report). It found that the Scott Act had been in force in the entire province of Prince Edward Island by 1881 (RCLT report, 116); in thirteen of eighteen counties in Nova Scotia (RCLT report, Appendix 60, 768); in New Brunswick, nine of fifteen counties adopted it, as had the city of Fredericton (RCLT report, 88).
5 George Orton to John A. Macdonald, 26 May 1886, Macdonald Papers, Reel C-1776, 208007–10.
6 Thomas Davies to John A. Macdonald, 14 January 1884, Macdonald Papers, Reel C-1769, 198394.
7 Eugene O'Keefe to John A. Macdonald, 11 March 1885, Macdonald Papers, Reel C-1770, 199841–43.
8 Eugene O'Keefe to John A. Macdonald, 13 May 1885, Macdonald Papers, Reel C-1771, 201159–62.
9 Thomas Macdonald to John A. Macdonald, 2 March 1886, Macdonald Papers, Reel C-1770, 199629–30.
10 Elizabeth Temple to John A. Macdonald, 11 May 1885, Macdonald Papers, Reel C-1771, 201137–40.
11 J. Calcutt to John A. Macdonald, 12 January 1885, Macdonald Papers, Reel C-1769, 198360.
12 Alex Turner to John A. Macdonald, 6 June 1885, Macdonald Papers, Reel C-1772, 201666–68.

13 Thomas Conant to John A. Macdonald, 14 May 1885, Macdonald Papers, Reel C-1771, 201172–74.
14 John A. Macdonald to J.R. Dundas, 26 May 1885, Macdonald Papers, Letterbook 23 (Reel C-34), 171.
15 Billa Flint to John A. Macdonald, 22 November 1886, Macdonald Papers, Reel C-1779, 212093.
16 On 30 March 1885, not halfway through the session, the clerk of the House of Commons reported that 939 petitions (with 76,501 signatures) requesting no change to the Scott Act and for the House to pass prohibition legislation had been presented to date (House of Commons, *Journals,* 5th Leg, 3rd Sess (30 March 1885), 255). No similar request was made to calculate the petitions supporting changes to the act that would reduce its stringency, but a rough count finds 194 petitions supporting Wet amendments, most coming near the end of the session when Senate amendments were contemplated in the House. If you wish to count the petitions, they were presented at the beginning of each sitting. They are listed in the index (House of Commons, *Journals,* 5th Leg, 3rd Sess, lxviii–lxix). The Senate received 783 petitions from temperance supporters and 80 from supporters of the liquor trade (Senate of Canada, *Journals,* 5th Leg, 3rd Sess (1885), calculated from index listing of petitions, xxvi–xxxi).
17 *House of Commons Debates,* 5th Parl, 3rd Sess, Vol 17 (25 February 1885), 235 (D'Alton McCarthy).
18 *House of Commons Debates,* 5th Parl, 3rd Sess, Vol 17 (25 February 1885), 236 (Hugo Kranz); House of Commons, *Journals,* 5th Leg, 3rd Sess (26 February 1885), 134.
19 Many of these changes regarded the provisions for enforcement and dealt with the variation in operation of courts across the country, although they would also allow physicians to dispense however much liquor as medicine that they thought was necessary. *House of Commons Debates,* 5th Parl, 3rd Sess, Vol 17 (10 March 1885), 448.
20 *House of Commons Debates,* 5th Parl, 3rd Sess, Vol 17 (26 March 1885), 743.
21 Townshend proposed a bill on 5 March 1885, but the records do not indicate its contents. *House of Commons Debates,* 5th Parl, 3rd Sess, Vol 17 (5 March 1885), 362. However, during third reading of Jamieson's bill, Townshend proposed an amendment to this effect, and it is likely that this was the essence of his bill. The same thing happened with the bill presented by Bourbeau on 18 March 1885, which he later tried to have incorporated into the legislation.
22 Jamieson amended a motion to continue debate on the Factory Act to turn the motion into one of debating second reading of his bill. When he introduced the amendment, he noted that Mr. Bergin, the MP shepherding the Factory Act through the legislature, should not be upset because he had used the same tactic to get his legislation to second reading.
23 House of Commons, *Journals,* 5th Leg, 3rd Sess (13 April 1885), 297–98.
24 John A. Macdonald to J.R. Dundas, 26 May 1885, Macdonald Papers, Letterbook 23 (Reel C-34), 171.
25 Spectator, "Scalping the Scott Act" [letter to the editor], *Globe* [Toronto], 30 May 1885.
26 *Senate Debates,* 5th Leg, 3rd Sess (6 May 1885), 877 (Hon William Almon).
27 Senate of Canada, *Journals,* 5th Leg, 3rd Sess (7 May 1885), 295.
28 Calculated from the lists in Senate of Canada, *Journals,* 5th Leg, 3rd Sess (26 and 29 May 1885), 320–21, 326.
29 *Senate Debates,* 5th Leg, 3rd Sess (27 May 1885), 1011–12; "Notes from the Capital," *Globe* [Toronto], 28 May 1885.

30 Billa Flint to John A. Macdonald, 14 May 1885, Macdonald Papers, Reel C-1771, 201182-86.
31 "Notes and Comments," *Globe* [Toronto], 11 May 1885.
32 "Notes and Comments," *Globe* [Toronto], 22 May 1885.
33 J.R. Dundas to John A. Macdonald, 22 May 1885, Macdonald Papers, Reel C-1771, 201361-62.
34 Thomas Dight to John A. Macdonald, 16 June 1885, Macdonald Papers, Reel C-1772, 201852-53.
35 William Campbell to John A. Macdonald, 16 July 1885, Macdonald Papers, Reel C-1772, 202376-80.
36 John Seaton to John A. Macdonald, 27 March 1885, Macdonald Papers, Reel C-1770, 200208-9.
37 "Rate Payer" to John A. Macdonald, 22 April 1885, Macdonald Papers, Reel C-1771, 200758-61.
38 A Friend to John A. Macdonald, 10 February 1885, Macdonald Papers, Reel C-1770, 199097-100.
39 Eugene O'Keefe to John A. Macdonald, 13 May 1885, Macdonald Papers, Reel C-1771, 201159-62.
40 Eugene O'Keefe to John A. Macdonald, 2 June 1885, Macdonald Papers, Reel C-1772, 201569-71.
41 John A. Macdonald to Eugene O'Keefe, 4 June 1885, Macdonald Papers, Letterbook 23 (Reel C-34), 176.
42 House of Commons, *Journals*, 6th Leg, 3rd Sess (13 February 1889), 49; House of Commons, *Journals*, 6th Leg, 3rd Sess (21-22 February 1889), 78-81.
43 House of Commons, *Journals*, 7th Leg, 1st Sess (24 June 1891), 251.
44 House of Commons *Journals*, 7th Leg, 1st Sess (24 June 1891), 252.

Chapter 8: Plebiscites as Tools for Change? 1883–94

1 "Report of the Special Committee Appointed to Consider the Subject of the Unrestrained Sale of Intoxicating Liquors and the Regulation of the Granting of Shop, Saloon, and Tavern Licenses," in *Journals of the House of Commons of Canada* (1883), Appendix No. 5, 34.
2 John Orchard, James Morin, and James Henderson to A.S. Hardy, 13 April 1880, RG 8-14-0-103, Provincial Secretary fonds, Archives of Ontario.
3 "New License Act," *Daily Mail* [Toronto], 26 February 1884.
4 Liquor License Act, 1884, *Statutes of Ontario* (1884), c. 34, 105.
5 "Canadian/London," *Globe* [Toronto], 27 February 1884.
6 "City and Suburban," *Globe* [Toronto], 23 January 1883.
7 Quoted in "Grocers' Licenses," *Globe* [Toronto], 17 February 1883.
8 Thanks to Jennifer Wallis for a copy of this pamphlet. I do not have evidence that it was read by Canadian temperance supporters; I mention it here as an illustration of the work done against grocery store licenses in the United Kingdom.
9 "The Grocer's License," *Church of England Temperance Chronicle* 12, no. 7 (1884): 103.
10 "Grocers' Licenses," *Canada Citizen and Temperance Record*, 11 January 1884, 325.
11 "Intemperance among Women," *Canada Citizen and Temperance Record*, 11 January 1884, 325. This article was first published in the *Hamilton Spectator*.

12 "Drink and Crime in 1882," *Canada Citizen and Temperance Record,* 11 January 1884, 325–26.
13 "Grocers' Licenses," *Globe* [Toronto], 23 January 1884.
14 Quoted in "The Temperance Cause," *Daily Mail* [Toronto], 5 February 1884.
15 Barbara Welter, "Cult of True Womanhood: 1820–1860," *American Quarterly* 18 (1966): 151–74. For an excellent discussion of how the cult of true womanhood was complicated by the realities of women who wanted to drink, see Cheryl Krasnick Warsh, "'Oh Lord Pour a Cordial in Her Wounded Heart': The Drinking Woman in Victorian and Edwardian Canada," in *Drink in Canada: Historical Essays,* edited by Cheryl Krasnick Warsh (Montreal and Kingston: McGill-Queen's University Press, 1993): 70–91.
16 Quoted in "The Temperance Cause," *Daily Mail* [Toronto], 5 February 1884.
17 "Grocers' Licenses and the Council," *Globe* [Toronto], 6 February 1884.
18 "Grocers' Licenses and the Council" [editorial], *Globe* [Toronto], 6 February 1884.
19 Quoted in "Grocers' Liquor Licenses," *Daily Mail* [Toronto], 13 February 1884.
20 "Grocers' Licenses" [editorial], *Globe* [Toronto], 13 February 1884.
21 Russell G. Hann, "Fahey, James A.," in *Dictionary of Canadian Biography,* vol. 11 (Toronto: University of Toronto; Laval: Université Laval, 2003–), http://www.biographi.ca/en/bio/fahey_james_a_11E.html.
22 "Grocers' Liquor Licenses," *Daily Mail* [Toronto], 13 February 1884.
23 Jaffray and Ryan, "Grocers' Licenses" [letter to the editor], *Globe* [Toronto], 14 February 1884.
24 W.J. McCormick, "Grocers' Licenses" [letter to the editor], *Daily Mail* [Toronto], 15 February 1884.
25 T.H. George, "Grocers' Licenses" [letter to the editor], *Daily Mail* [Toronto], 19 February 1884.
26 William Kyle, untitled letter to the editor, *Daily Mail* [Toronto], 19 February 1884.
27 Quoted in "Grocers' Liquor Licenses," *Daily Mail* [Toronto], 15 February 1884.
28 "Grocers' Liquor Licenses," *Daily Mail* [Toronto], 15 February 1884.
29 YMCA Secretary's letter was included in a column entitled "What the People Say," *Daily Mail* [Toronto], 22 February 1884.
30 George S. Michie, "An Answer to 'A YMCA Secretary,'" *Daily Mail* [Toronto], 23 February 1884.
31 "Grocers' Licenses" [editorial], *Globe* [Toronto], 14 February 1884.
32 James Knowles, Jr., "Licensed Grocers" [letter to the editor], *Daily Mail* [Toronto], 22 February 1884.
33 J. McLean Ballard, untitled letter to the editor, *Daily Mail* [Toronto], 22 February 1884.
34 Adapted from "Groceries and Liquors: Circular Issued by Advocates for Their Separate Sale," *Globe* [Toronto], 21 February 1884.
35 "City Council," *Globe* [Toronto], 5 February 1884; "Groceries and Liquor," *Globe* [Toronto], 26 February 1884.
36 See Ontario, Legislative Assembly, *Journals of the Legislative Assembly,* 5th Leg, 1st Sess (13 February 1884), 61; An Act to Improve the Liquor License Laws, *Statutes of Ontario* 1884, c. 34.
37 An Act Respecting Liquor Licenses, *Statutes of Ontario* (1886), c. 39, s. 18.
38 "Police Magistrates in Scott Act Counties" [letter to the editor], *Globe* [Toronto], 5 February 1886.
39 "The Liquor Laws," *Globe* [Toronto], 5 February 1886.

40 Quoted in "The Liquor Laws," *Globe* [Toronto], 5 February 1886.
41 A. Margaret Evans, *Sir Oliver Mowat*, Ontario Historical Studies Series (Toronto: University of Toronto Press, 1992), 298–300.
42 "At the Mercy of the Liquor Traffic" [editorial], *Globe* [Toronto], 9 May 1890.
43 An Act to Improve the Liquor Laws, *Statutes of Ontario* (1890), c. 56, s. 18.
44 An Act to Improve the Liquor Laws, *Statutes of Ontario* (1890), c. 56, s. 18.
45 John T. Saywell, *The Lawmakers: Judicial Power and the Shaping of Canadian Federalism* (Toronto: Osgoode Society, 2002), 95.
46 On the New Party, see Evans, *Sir Oliver Mowat*, especially 262–67.
47 "Mr. Mowat's Temperance Legislation" [editorial], *Globe* [Toronto], 22 April 1890.
48 "At the Mercy of the Liquor Traffic" [editorial], *Globe* [Toronto], 9 May 1890.
49 Evans, *Sir Oliver Mowat*, 265.
50 The judgment was rendered on 22 April 1891, and nearly immediately Liberal members Absalom Allan and Angus McKay requested that the details be submitted to the legislature. See Ontario, Legislative Assembly, *Journals of the Legislative Assembly*, 7th Leg, 1st Sess, Vol 24 (29 April 1891), 156; Ontario, Legislative Assembly, "Return to an Order of the House of the 29th April 1891 for Copies of the Judgements of Chief Justice Galt Quashing the Local Option Liquor By-Laws Adopted by the Municipalities of Oakland, South Norwich and London West under the Authority of Section 18 of Cap 56 of the Statutes of Ontario 1890," *Sessional Papers*, No. 65 (1891).
51 An Act Respecting Local Option in the Matter of Liquor Selling, *Statutes of Ontario* (1891), c. 46, s. 2.
52 See "Local Option: Hon. Oliver Mowat Once More Sustained in the Courts," *Globe* [Toronto], 24 September 1891; "Mowat Wins," *Whig* [Kingston], 24 September 1891. A similar judgment had been made in the Quebec Court of Appeal earlier in 1891. See "Local Option," *Globe* [Toronto], 2 April 1891.
53 "Local Option: Hon. Oliver Mowat Once More Sustained in the Courts," *Globe* [Toronto], 24 September 1891.
54 Ontario, Legislative Assembly, *Journals of the Legislative Assembly*, 7th Leg, 3rd Sess, Vol 24 (6 April 1893), 11.
55 "A Warm Gathering," *Daily Mail* [Toronto], 11 April 1893.
56 "A Difference of Opinion," *Empire* [Toronto], 11 April 1893.
57 "A Warm Gathering," *Daily Mail* [Toronto], 11 April 1893.
58 On Buchanan, see "Memorable Manitobans: William Wallace Buchanan (1855–1915)," Manitoba Historical Society, http://www.mhs.mb.ca/docs/people/buchanan_ww.shtml.
59 "A Warm Gathering," *Daily Mail* [Toronto], 11 April 1893.
60 "A Difference of Opinion," *Empire* [Toronto], 11 April 1893.
61 "The Prohibition Cause: Two Shades of Opinion in Conflict," *Globe* [Toronto], 11 April 1893.
62 "A Warm Gathering," *Daily Mail* [Toronto], 11 April 1893. McKendry was noted as being from Picton in a subsequent meeting.
63 "A Difference of Opinion," *Empire* [Toronto], 11 April 1893.
64 "A Warm Gathering," *Daily Mail* [Toronto], 11 April 1893; "A Difference of Opinion," *Empire* [Toronto], 11 April 1893; "The Prohibition Cause: Two Shades of Opinion in Conflict," *Globe* [Toronto], 11 April 1893. Although the *Daily Mail* had declared itself independent in the 1880s, its politics tended to support the political views of Conservatives.
65 John J. Maclaren, "The Temperance Cause" [letter to the editor], *Daily Mail* [Toronto], 17 April 1893.

66 F.S. Spence, "The Prohibition Convention" [letter to the editor], *Daily Mail* [Toronto], 17 April 1893.
67 J.B. Brooks, "The Prohibition Rally" [letter to the editor], *Daily Mail* [Toronto], 19 April 1893.
68 "For Prohibition," *Daily Mail* [Toronto], 21 April 1893. This is a slight distortion. According to the report of the Royal Commission on the Liquor Traffic, after Charlottetown repealed the Scott Act in 1891, "there was a practically unregulated free trade in liquor in the city," but this description applied only to Charlottetown, not to the entire province. Canada, Parliament, "Report of the Royal Commission on the Liquor Traffic in Canada, with Full Index to the Report and to the Evidence," *Sessional Papers*, No. 21 (1895), 95.
69 Quoted in "For Prohibition," *Daily Mail* [Toronto], 21 April 1893.
70 "Mr. Marter's Bill Approved," *Globe* [Toronto], 21 April 1893.
71 "A Difference of Opinion," *Empire* [Toronto], 11 April 1893.
72 "For Prohibition," *Daily Mail* [Toronto], 21 April 1893.
73 Quoted in "Liquor Traffic Scorched," *Daily Mail* [Toronto], 24 April 1893.
74 "Temperance Legislation" [editorial], *Daily Mail* [Toronto], 22 April 1893.
75 "At the Legislature" [editorial], *Empire* [Toronto], 3 May 1893.
76 Ontario, Legislative Assembly, *Journals of the Legislative Assembly*, 7th Leg, 3rd Sess, Vol 24 (1 May 1893), 93.
77 Ontario, Legislative Assembly, *Journals of the Legislative Assembly*, 7th Leg, 3rd Sess, Vol 24 (2 May 1893), 96–97.
78 "At the Legislature" [editorial], *Empire* [Toronto], 4 May 1893.
79 "The Prohibition Question" [editorial], *Daily Mail* [Toronto], 2 May 1893.
80 "The Prohibition Plebiscite," *Journal* [Ottawa], 29 December 1893.
81 "A Victory for Prohibition" [editorial], *Globe* [Toronto], 2 January 1894.
82 For the full text of Watson's decision, see *The Attorney General for Ontario v. The Attorney General for the Dominion of Canada (Canada)*, [1896] UKPC 20, 9 May 1896, http://www.bailii.org/uk/cases/UKPC/1896/1896_20.html.
83 John T. Saywell, *The Lawmakers: Judicial Power and the Shaping of Canadian Federalism* (Toronto: Osgoode Society, 2002), 141–42.

CHAPTER 9: TALKING AND BLOCKING NATIONAL PROHIBITION, 1891–99

1 Canada, Parliament, "Royal Commission on the Liquor Traffic. Minutes of Evidence Taken in the Province of Ontario" (hereafter RCLT), *Sessional Papers*, Vol. 15, No. 21 (1895), evidence of James Hay, 3751a. (The final number represents the question number.) The commission's evidence was published as Sessional Paper No. 21 but in six volumes (11 to 16). Volume 11 contained the index and the two reports, and subsequent volumes contained evidence from Nova Scotia, New Brunswick, and Prince Edward Island (Volume 12); Quebec (Volume 13); Manitoba, North-west Territories, and British Columbia (Volume 14); Ontario (and a return trip to Montreal) (Volume 15); and the United States (Volume 16). Note that this ordering of the volumes does not match exactly the order of the commission's sessions, since it held its sittings as commissioners' schedules permitted and visited the US at different times during their travels.
2 RCLT, evidence of James Hay, 3754a.
3 RCLT, evidence of George Roach, 3601a.
4 RCLT, evidence of George Inglis, 9356a.

5   RCLT, evidence of William J. Thomas, 12934a.
6   RCLT, evidence of Robert Reid, 5951a.
7   Commercial travellers were roughly the equivalent of a "travelling salesman." They travelled across a region bringing samples of products to retailers and taking orders for more. Their focus was on drumming up retail trade orders, not individual sales to private homes.
8   RCLT, evidence of D.H. Williams, 6919a.
9   RCLT, evidence of William Bowman, 6330a.
10 RCLT, evidence of Joseph Jamieson, 8030a, 8037a. A brief biography of Jamieson can be found in "Jamieson, His Hon. Joseph KC," in *Who's Who and Why: A Biographical Dictionary of Men and Women of Canada and Newfoundland* (Ottawa: International Press, 1914), 5: 895.
11 RCLT, evidence of William Richardson, 622a.
12 RCLT, evidence of Richardson, 625a.
13 RCLT, evidence of Eudo Saunders, 5289a. His bona fides are discussed on 5226a–5233a. Saunders became the head of the License Branch in 1902.
14 RCLT, evidence of Emmanuel Essery, 5740a.
15 RCLT, evidence of Arthur Mulholland, 9034a.
16 RCLT, asked by Joseph McLeod during evidence of William Richardson, 629a.
17 RCLT, evidence of Archdale Wilson, 3125a.
18 RCLT, evidence of Archdale Wilson, 3131a.
19 RCLT, evidence of J.C. Farthing, 4240a.
20 RCLT, evidence of J.C. Farthing, 4256a–59a.
21 There are contrasting characterizations of Smith's politics. Elizabeth Wallace entitled her biography of Smith *Goldwyn Smith, Victorian Liberal* (Toronto: University of Toronto Press, 1957), whereas S.J.R. Noel, *Patron, Client, Broker: Ontario Society and Politics* (Toronto: University of Toronto Press, 1990), 291, referred to Smith as the most prominent voice of a "conservative intelligentsia." In this case, it is safe to see Smith as a classical liberal, interested in individual freedom and limited government. He certainly had little time for Mowat's party.
22 RCLT, evidence of Goldwyn Smith, 13752a.
23 RCLT, evidence of Goldwyn Smith, 13757a.
24 RCLT, evidence of Goldwyn Smith's letter to the *Globe*, reproduced in RCLT, Appendix 5, 1388.
25 RCLT, vol. 5, Appendix 5.
26 RCLT, evidence of Goldwyn Smith, 13782a.
27 RCLT, evidence of Goldwyn Smith, 13769a.
28 RCLT, evidence of Goldwyn Smith, 13810a.
29 RCLT, evidence of Stinson Bradley, 3427a–29a.
30 RCLT, evidence of William Grey, 4546a.
31 RCLT, evidence of Henry G. Lackner, 7008a.
32 RCLT, evidence of Robert Philips, 308a.
33 RCLT, evidence of John Motz, 7610 1/2a.
34 RCLT, evidence of James McLaughlin, 8727a.
35 RCLT, evidence of Franklin H. Walker, 5345a.
36 RCLT, evidence of G.T. Labatt, 658a.
37 RCLT, evidence of Lawrence Cosgrave, 15255a.
38 RCLT, evidence of W.L. Cummer, 2910a.

39 Matthew J. Bellamy, *Brewed in the North: A History of Labatt's* (Montreal and Kingston: McGill-Queen's University Press, 2019), 74–91.
40 RCLT, evidence of George Gooderham, 15092a.
41 RCLT, evidence of Joseph Fife, 1458a.
42 RCLT, evidence of Joseph Fife, 1515a.
43 RCLT, evidence of James Hay, 3778a.
44 RCLT, evidence of Francis Ball, 4035a–36a.
45 RCLT, evidence of Francis Ball, 4052a.
46 RCLT, evidence of Francis Ball, 4055a.
47 RCLT, evidence of Charles Pearce, 8993a–95a. Also see "The Dunkin Act in Grey: Disgraceful Assault on License Inspector," *Globe* [Toronto], 3 November 1877. Pearce shot a man in the leg.
48 Canada, Parliament, "Report of the Royal Commission on the Liquor Traffic in Canada, with Full Index to the Report and to the Evidence," *Sessional Papers*, Vol. 11, No. 21 (1895), 481 (hereafter RCLT Report).
49 RCLT Report, 487. There was one caveat. After the commission had gathered its evidence, F.S. Spence sent information about the prohibition on Pitcairn Island, on which the *Bounty* mutineers were stranded.
50 RCLT Report, 492.
51 RCLT Report, 672.
52 RCLT Report, 672–73.
53 RCLT Report, 688.
54 RCLT Report, 691.
55 My apologies to Ann-Marie Szymanski for stealing her book title *Pathways to Prohibition*, which had nothing to do with Canada or Laurier.
56 "In North Perth," *Globe* [Toronto], 10 June 1896.
57 Sir John Willison, *Reminiscences, Political and Personal* (Toronto: McClelland and Stewart, 1919), 95.
58 "At the Capital – Prohibition Delegates Wait on the Government," *Globe* [Toronto], 4 September 1896. Numerous city charters passed prior to Confederation had given municipal councils the power to enact local option notwithstanding the parameters of the Dunkin Act.
59 "On the Plebiscite – The Premier's Reply to the Licensed Victuallers," *Ottawa Citizen*, 14 May 1897; "Vote on Prohibition – Deputation of Liquor Men before the Government," *Globe* [Toronto], 14 May 1897.
60 W.A. Mackay, "Prohibition" [letter to the editor], *Globe* [Toronto], 4 September 1896.
61 Untitled article, *The Commercial* [Winnipeg], 7 September 1896.
62 Walter Street to Wilfrid Laurier, 14 April 1897, MG 26G, Sir Wilfrid Laurier Papers, Library and Archives Canada (hereafter Laurier Papers), Reel C-748, 13923–24.
63 Quoted in "At the Capital," *Globe* [Toronto], 31 March 1897.
64 A. Philip Brace, Uxbridge District of Methodist Church, to Wilfrid Laurier, 3 June 1898, Laurier Papers, Reel C-757, 23897.
65 J.C. O'Neil, "The Plebiscite Voters," *Globe* [Toronto], 10 October 1896.
66 William Houston to Wilfrid Laurier, 19 December 1896, Laurier Papers, Reel C-745, 9895–9900.
67 W.E. Norton to Wilfrid Laurier, 14 April 1897, Laurier Papers, Reel C-748, 13902–5.
68 Quoted in "In North Perth – Mr. Laurier Speaks at Stratford and Listowel," *Globe* [Toronto], 10 June 1896.

69 Laurier's Liberals won a significant majority of seats but lost the popular vote by nearly 30,000. Data calculated from Elections Canada's dataset, https://open.canada.ca/data/en/dataset/ea8f2c37-90b6-4fee-857e-984d3060184e.
70 Presbyter, "Anti-Plebiscite" [letter to the editor], *Globe* [Toronto], 12 June 1897.
71 Edward Williams to Wilfrid Laurier, 26 March 1897, Laurier Papers, Reel C-748, 13431–32.
72 Charles McLelland to Wilfrid Laurier, 2 August 1898, Laurier Papers, Reel C-758, 25527–30.
73 "A Word of Caution" [editorial], *London Free Press*, 24 September 1898.
74 Willison, *Reminiscences*, 94.
75 "Party and Prohibition," *Ottawa Journal*, 26 August 1898.
76 "The *Globe* on Prohibition," *Evening News* [Toronto], 11 December 1897.
77 "Four Telling Letters from Principal Grant … Some Substantial Reasons for Voting 'No,'" *London Free Press*, 17 September 1898.
78 Eugene O'Keefe to Wilfrid Laurier, 9 September 1898, Laurier Papers, Reel C-759, 26295–96.
79 J.H. Carson to Wilfrid Laurier, 8 May 1897, Laurier Papers, Reel C-749, 14339–40.
80 "On the Plebiscite – The Premier's Reply to the Licensed Victuallers," *Ottawa Citizen*, 14 May 1897; "Vote on Prohibition – Deputation of Liquor Men before the Government," *Globe* [Toronto], 14 May 1897.
81 F.S. Spence, "Direct Taxation" [letter to the editor], *Globe* [Toronto], 22 May 1897.
82 Frank Spence to Wilfrid Laurier, 18 May 1897, Laurier Papers, Reel C-749, 14845–48.
83 P.L. Richardson to Wilfrid Laurier, 19 May 1897, Laurier Papers, Reel C-749, 14912–13.
84 William Kettlewell to Wilfrid Laurier, 20 May 1897, Laurier Papers, Reel C-749, 15061.
85 "Prohibition and the National Revenue" [editorial], *Ottawa Journal*, 22 May 1897.
86 J.S. Ross, "Taxes and Liquor" [letter to the editor], *Globe* [Toronto], 5 June 1897.
87 Excise, "Taxes and Liquor" [letter to the editor], *Globe* [Toronto], 3 July 1897.
88 Cymric, "Prohibition and Revenue" [letter to the editor], *Globe* [Toronto], 9 June 1897.
89 "The Ballot on Prohibition," *Ottawa Citizen*, 19 January 1898.
90 Sydney Fisher to Wilfrid Laurier, 12 April 1898, Laurier Papers, Reel C-756, 22434–35.
91 Frank Spence to Wilfrid Laurier, 28 April 1898, Laurier Papers, Reel C-756, 22859–60.
92 W.E. Saunders to Wilfrid Laurier, 30 August 1898, Laurier Papers, Reel C-759, 26090–91.
93 A.J. Armstrong, Grand Scribe of the Grand Division of the Sons of Temperance of New Brunswick, to Wilfrid Laurier, 18 May 1898, Laurier Papers, Reel C-757, 23433.
94 "Prospects for the Plebiscite," *Evening News* [Toronto], 8 September 1898.
95 The Casual Observer, "Observations," *Toronto Star*, 20 August 1898.
96 "The Situation" [editorial], *Monetary Times, Trade Review and Insurance Chronicle*, 23 September 1898, 399.
97 "Apathy of the People," *Toronto Star*, 29 September 1898.
98 Canada, Parliament, "Report on the Prohibition Plebiscite Held on the 29th Day of September 1898 in the Dominion of Canada by Samuel E. St. O. Chapleau, Clerk of the Crown in Chancery for Canada," *Sessional Papers*, No. 20 (1899), x.
99 Such views were especially prominent in evidence presented at the Royal Commission.
100 "Cannot Ask Prohibition," *Toronto Star*, 30 September 1898.
101 "They Want Legislation," *Globe* [Toronto], 5 October 1898; "Demand for Legislation," *Toronto Star*, 5 October 1898; "The Outcome," *Ottawa Citizen*, 5 October 1898.
102 "At the Capital – The Prohibitionists Present Their Case," *Globe* [Toronto], 4 November 1898.

103 James McMullen to Wilfrid Laurier, 7 November 1898, Laurier Papers, Reel C-760, 27845–46.
104 See, for example, A. Sinclair to Wilfrid Laurier, 9 November 1898, Laurier Papers, Reel C-760, 27926–28.
105 J.R. Dougall to Wilfrid Laurier, 28 November 1898, Laurier Papers, Reel C-761, 28378–407.
106 James Henry Frank, Jr., to Wilfrid Laurier, 28 January 1899, Laurier Papers, Reel C-762, 3000; Jane and John McLeod to Wilfrid Laurier, 31 January 1899, Laurier Papers, Reel C-762, 30134; James Stevens to Wilfrid Laurier, 2 February 1899, Laurier Papers, Reel C-762, 30189; F. Richardson to Wilfrid Laurier, 2 February 1899, Laurier Papers, Reel C-762, 30190; Russel Wright to Wilfrid Laurier, 7 February 1899, Laurier Papers, Reel C-763, 30328.
107 "Prohibition Refused: Answer of Sir Wilfrid to the Request of the Dominion Alliance," *Globe* [Toronto], 10 March 1899.
108 Mrs. M.A. Colby to Wilfrid Laurier, 15 February 1897, Laurier Papers, Reel C-747, 12082–85.
109 William Frissell, "Plebiscite on Prohibition" [letter to the editor], *Globe* [Toronto], 25 December 1897.
110 "The Coming Plebiscite," *Globe* [Toronto], 3 August 1898.
111 Dominion Alliance, "Final Circular in Prohibition's Behalf," *Toronto Star*, 13 September 1898.
112 Untitled item, *Northern Messenger*, 30 September 1898, 3.
113 F.S. Spence, "The Case for Prohibition," *Globe* [Toronto], 28 September 1898.
114 Quoted in "At the Capital," *Globe* [Toronto], 1 April 1897.
115 C.E. Toye, "Prohibition and Enforcement" [letter to the editor], *Globe* [Toronto], 1 May 1897.
116 Walter Street to Wilfrid Laurier, 10 October 1898, Laurier Papers, Reel C-760, 27093–94.
117 "The Reasons against Prohibition," *London Free Press*, 17 September 1898.
118 "On 'Total Abstinence' and 'Teetotalism'" [editorial], *London Free Press*, 17 September 1898.
119 J. Kennedy, "Says Prohibition Is Right," *London Free Press*, 23 September 1898.
120 F.S. Spence, "The Case for Prohibition," *Globe* [Toronto], 28 September 1898.
121 John Stuart Mill, *On Liberty*, 3rd ed. (London: Longman, Green, Longman, Roberts and Green, 1864), 145–46.
122 "Dr. Grant on Prohibition" [editorial], *Globe* [Toronto], 9 December 1897.
123 "Liquor Traffic Again Condemned," *Evening News* [Toronto], 22 September 1898.
124 "The Liberty Question," *Northern Messenger*, 30 September 1898.
125 Wakefield Hardgrave, "In Support of Dr. Grant's Position," letter on page titled "The Plebiscite on Prohibition – Prohibitionists Deal with Many of the Arguments of Principal Grant," *Globe* [Toronto], 8 January 1898.
126 James Haverson, "No Coercion," *Globe* [Toronto], 15 January 1898.
127 The Casual Observer, "Observations," *Toronto Star*, 20 August 1898.
128 "About the Quebec Vote," *Toronto Star*, 3 November 1898.
129 Frank Spence, "Analysis of the Vote" [letter to the editor], *Globe* [Toronto], 15 October 1898.
130 Rev. Dr. A. Carman, "The Prohibition Vote" [letter to the editor], *Globe* [Toronto], 12 November 1898.
131 "Prohibition Refused," *Evening News* [Toronto], 10 March 1899.

132 Wilfrid Laurier to C.R. Morrow, 13 March 1899, Laurier Papers, Reel C-763, 31193. (Whereas Macdonald's replies were recorded in separate letterbooks, Laurier's replies were often included in the archives file immediately after the letter to which he was replying.)
133 Wilfrid Laurier to A.C. Courtice, 27 March 1899, Laurier Papers, Reel C-764, 31704–8.
134 Wilfrid Laurier to J.R. Dougall, 19 November 1898, Laurier Papers, Reel C-761, 28400–7.
135 Ed McCaulay to Wilfrid Laurier, 14 November 1898, Laurier Papers, Reel C-761, 28070–78.
136 A Mother, "The Liquor Evil" [letter to the editor], *Globe* [Toronto], 18 December 1897.
137 "The Prohibition Plebiscite," *Northwest Review,* 20 September 1898.
138 James Douglas to Wilfrid Laurier, n.d., received 12 October 1898, Laurier Papers, Reel C-760, 27145–46.
139 James Spencer to Wilfrid Laurier, 9 February 1898, Laurier Papers, Reel C-754, 20476–77.
140 "The Coming Plebiscite," *Globe* [Toronto], 3 August 1898.
141 "Dives" [editorial], *Toronto Star,* 22 September 1898.
142 John A. Cooper, "Editorial Comment," *Canadian Magazine,* October 1898, 540.
143 Spectator, "The Vote on Prohibition" [letter to the editor], *Globe* [Toronto], 26 November 1899.
144 Quoted by Robert Macdonald, "'Variants of Liberalism' and the Liberal Order Framework in British Columbia," in *Liberalism and Hegemony: Debating the Canadian Liberal Revolution,* ed. Jean-François Constant and Michel Ducharme (Toronto: University of Toronto Press, 2009), 329–30.

Chapter 10: Dodging Decisions at the End of the Liberals' Era, 1894–1905

1 The Privy Council confirmed that the province could prohibit sales "if it were shown that the manufacture was carried on under such circumstances and conditions as to make its prohibition a merely local matter in the province." *The Attorney General for Ontario v. The Attorney General for the Dominion of Canada (Canada)* [1896] UKPC 20 (9 May 1896), 21.
2 Sharon Anne Cook, *Through Sunshine and Shadow: The Woman's Christian Temperance Union, Evangelicalism, and Reform in Ontario, 1874–1930* (Montreal and Kingston: McGill-Queen's University Press, 1995); Graeme Decarie, "The Prohibition Movement in Ontario: 1894–1916" (PhD diss., Queen's University, 1972); Brian Paul Trainor, "Towards a Genealogy of Temperance: Identity, Belief and Drink in Victorian Ontario" (MA thesis, Queen's University, 1993).
3 David G. Burley, "Hardy, Arthur Sturgis," in *Dictionary of Canadian Biography,* vol. 13 (Toronto: University of Toronto; Laval: Université Laval, 2003–), http://www.biographi.ca/en/bio/hardy_arthur_sturgis_13E.html.
4 See "Prohibitionists Not Satisfied," *Ottawa Journal,* 27 February 1897.
5 As quoted in Burley, "Hardy, Arthur Sturgis."
6 See Dan Malleck, "Medicinal Purposes: Pharmacists, Professionalism, and Liquor Laws in Victorian Ontario," in *Pleasure and Panic: New Essays on the History of Alcohol and Drugs,* ed. Dan Malleck and Cheryl Krasnick Warsh (Vancouver: UBC Press, 2022).
7 "Amendments to the License Act," *Evening News* [Toronto], 26 February 1897.
8 "Liquor Law Is Denounced," *Evening News* [Toronto], 3 March 1897.
9 "Liquor Law Is Denounced," *Evening News* [Toronto], 3 March 1897.
10 "The Premier Wouldn't Give In," *Evening News* [Toronto], 12 March 1897.

11 "A Cold Douse for Temperance People," *Ottawa Journal*, 12 March 1897.
12 Untitled editorial, *London Free Press*, 13 March 1897.
13 "Liquor Men Heard," *Globe* [Toronto], 18 March 1897; "Was Very Guarded," *Ottawa Journal*, 18 March 1897.
14 "The Liquor Interest," *London Free Press*, 19 March 1897.
15 "Brewers and Maltsters," *London Free Press*, 24 March 1897.
16 "The License Bill Amended," *Evening News* [Toronto], 26 March 1897; "License Act Changed," *Globe* [Toronto], 26 March 1897; "Further Restrictions," *Ottawa Journal*, 26 March 1897. For details of the Methodist meeting, see "The Liquor Traffic – Discussion with Premier Hardy by Leading Methodists," *Ottawa Citizen*, 26 March 1897.
17 "A Temperance Victory," *Evening News* [Toronto], 29 March 1897.
18 "An Atom of Temperance," *Evening News* [Toronto], 27 February 1897.
19 "The Proposed License Bill," *Ottawa Citizen*, 4 March 1897.
20 Eye Witness, "License Amendments" [letter to the editor], *Globe* [Toronto], 17 March 1897.
21 On Thornley, see Dan Malleck, "Priorities of Development in Four Local Woman's Christian Temperance Unions in Ontario 1877–1895," in *The Changing Face of Drink: Substance, Imagery, Behaviour*, ed. Jack S. Blocker, Jr., and Cheryl Krasnick Warsh (Ottawa: Les Publications Histoire Sociale/Social History, 1997), 189–208; and S.G.E. McKee, *Jubilee History of the Ontario Woman's Christian Temperance Union 1877–1927* (Toronto: C.A. Goodfellow and Son, 1927).
22 "Intemperate Language" [editorial], *London Free Press*, 9 March 1897.
23 "Intemperate Conduct," *Evening News* [Toronto], 12 March 1897.
24 "Cold Douse for Temperance People," *Ottawa Journal*, 12 March 1897.
25 Quoted in "The Premier and the Prohibitionists," *Globe* [Toronto], 12 March 1897.
26 "The Premier Was Hissed," *London Free Press*, 12 March 1897.
27 "Liquor Men Heard," *Globe* [Toronto], 18 March 1897.
28 On Dow and the Maine Law, see Jack S. Blocker, Jr., *American Temperance Movements: Cycles of Reform* (Boston: Twayne, 1898), 30–34, 54–58.
29 See, for example, "How Prohibition Works Out" [editorial], *London Free Press*, 23 March 1906.
30 "License Act Changed," *Globe* [Toronto], 26 March 1897.
31 G.W. Ross, *Getting into Parliament and After* (Toronto: William Briggs, 1913), 217–18.
32 "The Prohibition Bill," *Commercial* [Winnipeg], 9 June 1900, 127.
33 Jim Blanchard, "Roblin, Sir Rodmond Palen," in *Dictionary of Canadian Biography*, vol. 16 (Toronto: University of Toronto; Laval: Université Laval, 2003–), http://www.biographi.ca/en/bio/roblin_rodmond_palen_16E.html.
34 *The Attorney General for the Province of Manitoba v. The Manitoba License Holders Association (Canada)*, [1901] UKPC 52 (22 November 1901).
35 Sources on Roblin include H.R. Ross, *Thirty-Five Years in the Limelight: Sir Rodmond P. Roblin and His Times* (Winnipeg: Farmer's Advocate, 1936); and W.L. Morton, *Manitoba: A History*, 2nd ed. (Toronto: University of Toronto Press, 1967).
36 Quoted in "Referendum Will Stand," *Globe* [Toronto], 27 February 1902.
37 "The Premier to the Alliance," *Ottawa Journal*, 27 February 1902.
38 "Prohibition Question," *Ottawa Citizen*, 3 January 1902; "The Situation," *Monetary Times Etc.*, 10 January 1902, 879.

39 In his memoirs, Ross misremembers the decision to use this funky math. He says that the referendum sought approval from a majority of the electors. Ross, *Getting into Parliament*, 218.
40 Quoted in "Referendum Will Stand," *Globe* [Toronto], 27 February 1902.
41 "A Provincial Convention," *Ottawa Journal*, 14 February 1902.
42 "Ross' Breach of Faith," *Ottawa Citizen*, 18 February 1902.
43 "Ross' Breach of Faith," *Ottawa Citizen*, 18 February 1902.
44 "Ross' Breach of Faith," *Ottawa Citizen*, 18 February 1902.
45 "Templars and Hon. Mr. Ross," *Ottawa Journal*, 19 February 1902.
46 "Ross Referendum," *Ottawa Citizen*, 25 February 1902.
47 "Referendum Accepted," *Globe* [Toronto], 26 February 1902.
48 "Hon. G.W. Ross' Subterfuge," *Ottawa Citizen*, 29 January 1902.
49 "Ross Not Honorable," *Ottawa Citizen*, 22 January 1902.
50 Quoted in "Extricating Ross" [editorial], *Ottawa Citizen*, 15 February 1902.
51 Quoted in "Referendum Will Stand," *Globe* [Toronto], 27 February 1902.
52 "Two Policies on the Drink Evil," *Globe* [Toronto], 6 March 1902.
53 "Mr. Whitney on the Referendum" [editorial], *Ottawa Citizen*, 7 March 1902.
54 Information from Graeme Decarie, "Spence, Francis Stephens," in *Dictionary of Canadian Biography*, vol. 14 (Toronto: University of Toronto; Laval: Université Laval, 2003–), http://www.biographi.ca/en/bio/spence_francis_stephens_14E.html.
55 Dr. J.J. Maclaren, quoted in "Referendum Accepted," *Globe* [Toronto], 26 February 1902.
56 "Bringing in the Liquor Act," *Globe* [Toronto], 13 February 1902; "Premier Ross's Prohibition Bill," *Globe* [Toronto], 13 February 1902.
57 Edwin A. Pratt, *The Licensing Question: Disinterested Management in Norway, a Reply to the Report of the Commission Appointed by the Scottish Temperance Legislation Board to Inquire into the Liquor Licensing Laws of Norway* (London: P.S. King and Son, 1907).
58 James Hill Welborn, "Dispensing the Progressive State: Benjamin Tillman's South Carolina State Dispensary," *The Social History of Alcohol and Drugs: An Interdisciplinary Journal* 27 (2013): 82–101; Benjamin Tillman, "Our Whiskey Rebellion," *North American Review* 158 (1894): 513–19; G. Thomann, *South Carolina Liquor Dispensary* (New York: United States Brewers Association, 1905).
59 See "South Carolina Dispensary Law Unconstitutional," *Harvard Law Review* 10 (1897): 441–42.
60 "The Prohibition Bill" [editorial], *Globe* [Toronto], 6 February 1902. I have been unable to find the original *Westminster* issue.
61 "Want a Tab Kept on the Druggists," *Toronto Star*, 5 February 1902; "Government Control," *Globe* [Toronto], 5 February 1902.
62 "Want a Tab Kept on the Druggists," *Toronto Star*, 5 February 1902; "Government Control," *Globe* [Toronto], 5 February 1902.
63 Mark Kuhlberg, *In the Power of the Government: The Rise and Fall of Newsprint in Ontario, 1894–1932* (Toronto: University of Toronto Press, 2015); Christopher Armstrong and H.V. Nelles, *Monopoly's Moment: The Organization and Regulation of Canadian Utilities 1830–1930* (Philadelphia: Temple University Press 1986).
64 Charles Richardson, "The Public and Prohibition" [letter to the editor], *Globe* [Toronto], 8 February 1902.
65 Medicus, "The Public and Prohibition" [letter to the editor], *Globe* [Toronto], 8 February 1902.

66 M. Rainey, "The Public and Prohibition" [letter to the editor], *Globe* [Toronto], 8 February 1902.
67 Maggie Brady, *Teaching "Proper" Drinking? Clubs and Pubs in Indigenous Australia* (Canberra: ANU Press, 2017), 41. On the Gothenburg system in Britain, see David Gutzke, *Pubs and Progressives: Reinventing the Public House in England, 1896–1960* (DeKalb: Northern Illinois University Press, 2005).
68 "Earl Grey Tells of the Hotel Trust," *Toronto Star,* 3 March 1902.
69 Quoted in "Earl Grey Tells of the Hotel Trust," *Toronto Star,* 3 March 1902.
70 G.M. Grant, "A Hopeless Crusade" [letter to the editor], *Globe* [Toronto], 12 February 1902.
71 G.M. Grant, "Regulating Liquor Sale" [letter to the editor], *Globe* [Toronto], 21 February 1902.
72 G.M. Grant, "The Company System" [letter to the editor], *Globe* [Toronto], 1 March 1902.
73 G.G. Huxtable, "For and against Prohibition" [letter to the editor], *Globe* [Toronto], 8 March 1902.
74 W.C. Good, "For and against Prohibition" [letter to the editor], *Globe* [Toronto], 8 March 1902.
75 "Ross' Henchmen at Convention – Another Report," *Ottawa Citizen,* 25 February 1902.
76 "The Gothenburg System," *Camp Fire* 6, no. 11 (1900): 1.
77 "The Gothenburg System," *Camp Fire* 6, no. 12 (1900): 4.
78 "Government Ownership," *Camp Fire* 8, no. 1 (1901): 1.
79 "In Dalecarlia," *Methodist Magazine and Review,* December 1902, 520.
80 "The Liquor Bill," *Globe* [Toronto], 21 March 1902. Rowell's use of the term "government control" is somewhat confusing. In the article on "Government Ownership," *Camp Fire* 8, no. 1 (1901): 1, Spence suggested that some people mislabelled "government ownership" as "government control" but that indeed government control was the system currently in place, with the government controlling the issuing of licenses. Nevertheless, the context of Rowell's statement suggests that Rowell was referring in fact to some form of government ownership of the apparatus of liquor distribution and the increased restriction on liquor sales and drunkenness that would possibly result.
81 This is described in Charles W. Humphries, *Honest Enough to Be Bold: The Life and Times of Sir James Pliny Whitney,* Ontario Historical Series (Toronto: University of Toronto Press, 1985). Ross and the other Conservative candidate in Ottawa did not prevail.
82 "That Scotch at Napanee," *Globe* [Toronto], 4 January 1905; "An Incident Not an Issue" [editorial], *Globe* [Toronto], 7 January 1905.

Chapter 11: Drinking in Whitney's Conservative Liberal State, 1905–07

1 Jeffrey Simpson, *Spoils of Power: The Politics of Patronage* (Toronto: HarperCollins Canada, 1988), 226.
2 Charles W. Humphries, *Honest Enough to Be Bold: The Life and Times of Sir James Pliny Whitney,* Ontario Historical Series (Toronto: University of Toronto Press, 1985).
3 Humphries, *Honest Enough,* 175.
4 Salaries for inspectors are difficult to determine. In records from the early period, inspectors' salaries were recommended to be anywhere between $150 (what inspectors in Lanark County were estimated to have received before the Crooks Act) and $1,200 (what a correspondent recommended Ottawa inspectors receive). There was also the opportunity for

well-performing inspectors to get a bonus based upon his prosecution record. See License Branch Correspondence, Archives of Ontario, RG 8-31, various files.
5 "Welcome to Whitney" [comic], *Telegram* [Toronto], 8 February 1905.
6 "There's No Place Like Home" [comic], *Telegram* [Toronto], 16 February 1905.
7 "Civil Servants Are Safe" [editorial], *Telegram* [Toronto], 11 February 1905; also see "Keep the Spoilsmen at Bay," *Telegram* [Toronto], 3 April 1905.
8 "Promises and Practices," *Record* [Windsor], 4 April 1905.
9 See John Greenaway, "Parliamentary Reform and Civil Service Reform: A Nineteenth-Century Debate Reassessed," *Parliamentary History* 4 (1985): 157–69.
10 "Public Service and the Spoils System," *Toronto World*, 6 April 1905.
11 James Whitney to Judge W. C. Mahaffy, 7 July 1905, F 5-1, "Correspondence of Sir James Whitney," Sir James Whitney Fonds, Archives of Ontario (hereafter Whitney letters), container b273263.
12 Humphries, *Honest Enough*, 248.
13 Bernard McAllister to James Whitney, 28 August 1905, Whitney Letters, container b273263.
14 James Whitney to James York, 3 June 1905, Whitney Letters, container b273263.
15 James Whitney to H.H. Ross, 27 March 1905, Whitney Letters, container b273262.
16 Humphries, *Honest Enough*, 248.
17 James Whitney to A.L. McIntyre, 22 June 1905, Whitney Letters, container b273261.
18 A.E. Donovan to James Whitney, 15 February 1905, Whitney Letters, container b273261.
19 James Whitney to A.E. Donovan, 16 February 1905, Whitney Letters, container b27326. Donovan won a by-election in Brockville in 1907 when Liberal MLA G.P. Graham was appointed the minister of railways and canals in Laurier's dominion government.
20 Ontario, Legislative Assembly, *Journals of the Legislative Assembly*, 8th Leg, 3rd Sess, Vol 30 (17 March 1897), 73.
21 "In the Legislature: Civil Servants in Political Contests – Mr. Garrow's Resolution," *Globe* [Toronto], 18 March 1897. By discouraging partisan activities by civil servants, the Garrow Resolution also, by the transitive property, sought to remove partisan influence from the staffing of government offices.
22 James Whitney to W. Gibbons, 13 July 1905, Whitney Letters, container b273263.
23 W.D. Hogg to James Whitney, 3 February 1905, Whitney Letters, container b273261.
24 James Whitney to Joseph Goodwin, 17 February 1905, Whitney Letters, container b273261.
25 R. Lawrence to James Whitney, 3 April 1905, Whitney Letters, container b273262.
26 Mrs. J.H. McKnight to James Whitney, 8 March 1905, Whitney Letters, container b273262.
27 James Whitney to Mrs. J.H. McKnight, 10 March 1905, Whitney Letters, container b273262.
28 "The License Commission" [editorial], *Telegram* [Toronto], 13 February 1905.
29 "Those License Boards" [editorial], *Toronto Star*, 18 March 1905.
30 "Those License Boards" [editorial], *Toronto Star*, 18 March 1905.
31 Staffing changes can be tracked in the Public Accounts records submitted annually to the sessional papers of the legislature. In 1903, Eudo Saunders replaced Henry Totten and remained in the position long after Whitney gained power. Although a few positions seem to have changed hands in 1905, notably that of the chief inspector, it is difficult to determine whether this was because of partisan appointments or simply the movement of low-level staff into other positions.
32 "The License Inspectors" [editorial], *Toronto Star*, 4 April 1905.

33 "Weed Out the Unworthy" [editorial], *World* [Toronto], 4 April 1905.
34 "The Patronage Committee," *Telegram* [Toronto], 4 April 1905.
35 Circular reproduced in Ontario, Legislative Assembly, "Return made by the House on the 11th day of May, 1905, that there be laid before this House a Return of (1), Copies of all correspondence, documents, memoranda, instructions and circulars, in connection with the appointment of License Commissioners and Inspectors for the present year, or in connection with their administration of their offices. (2), The names of all License Inspectors who were dismissed, or have resigned during the present year and the reason for their dismissals, or resignations, with the names of those appointed in their places," *Sessional Papers*, No. 52 (1906), RG 49-19, Unprinted sessional papers, Archives of Ontario (hereafter Sessional Paper 52 (1906)).
36 "The Spoils Doctrine in the License Department?," *Toronto Star*, 29 March 1905.
37 "Development of New Ontario" [and other issues in the legislature], *Globe* [Toronto], 30 March 1905.
38 "No Partisanship," *Globe* [Toronto], 6 April 1905; circular reproduced in Sessional Paper 52 (1906).
39 James Whitney to Charles Patton, 14 March 1905, Whitney Letters, container b273262.
40 James Whitney to T.S. Edwards, 10 March 1905, Whitney Letters, container b273262.
41 S.D. Chown, "Dr. Chown to Temperance People" [letter to the editor], *Globe* [Toronto], 31 March 1905.
42 "Notes and Comments," *Globe* [Toronto], 3 April 1905.
43 "The Spoils System" [editorial], *Toronto Star*, 3 April 1905. The *Star* might have been referring to the Garrow Resolution made on 17 March 1897. See note 21 on page 364.
44 James Leitch to James Whitney, 17 April 1905, Whitney Letters, container b273262.
45 A. Johntson [sic] to James Whitney, 6 March 1905, Whitney Letters, container b273262.
46 "Wielding the Axe," *Globe* [Toronto], 24 April 1905; "How Inspectors Are Cut Off," *Globe* [Toronto], 2 May 1905. The list of inspectors was provided in Sessional Paper 52 (1906). The only inspector not replaced was Gaspard Pacaud, whose Windsor and North Essex district was split. He became the inspector for Windsor.
47 "Off with Their Heads: Lincoln Tories Fight over the Spoils of Office," *Globe* [Toronto], 23 March 1905.
48 "Trouble in Essex?," *Globe* [Toronto], 31 March 1905; "Dr. Anderson Is Obdurate," *Windsor Record*, 4 April 1905.
49 See the annual reports of the License Branch, which listed inspectors' names and addresses. Both Smyth and King stayed at their posts well after 1905.
50 "Business-Like Methods," *Ottawa Citizen*, 17 April 1905.
51 "York County and Suburbs – West York Licenses Given," *Toronto World*, 20 April 1905.
52 "York County and Suburbs – Endorsed License Board," *Toronto World*, 17 May 1905.
53 "19 Licenses Are Cut Off by Peel County's Board," *Toronto World*, 24 April 1905.
54 "Over Half the Hotels Go in Peel County," *Telegram* [Toronto], 24 April 1905.
55 "Will Strictly Enforce the Letter of the Law," *Ottawa Journal*, 18 April 1905; "To Enforce Liquor Law on Non-Partisan Basis," *Ottawa Citizen*, 18 April 1905. Also see "South Ontario Licenses," *Toronto World*, 25 April 1905; and "Plain Talk for Licensees," *Telegram* [Toronto], 26 April 1905.
56 "Work of Commissioners Please[s] Moral Reformers," *Toronto World*, 27 April 1905.
57 "License Inspector Kicks Open Osborne Hotel Bar," *Toronto World*, 8 May 1905.
58 "Good Outlook in Toronto" [editorial], *Toronto Star*, 29 April 1905.

59 "Liquor Law in Port Hope," *Globe* [Toronto], 17 May 1905.
60 "Mighty Is the Pull," *Windsor Record,* 24 April 1905.
61 "New Government's Methods," *Toronto Star,* 25 April 1905.
62 M. Bailey to James Whitney, 11 January 1906, Whitney Letters, container b273264.
63 S.D. Chown to James Whitney, 15 May 1905, Whitney Letters, container b273262.
64 Jennie Brander to James Whitney, 6 July 1905, Whitney Letters, container b273263.
65 O.D. Casselman to James Whitney, 4 September 1905, Whitney Letters, container b273263.
66 James Whitney to O.D. Casselman, 5 September 1905, Whitney Letters, container b273263.
67 Whitney to T.S. Edwards, 7 April 1906, Whitney Letters, container b273265.
68 License fees varied across the province since municipalities were allowed to charge additional fees to a legislated maximum.
69 See "New Liquor License Act for Stricter Enforcement," *Ottawa Journal,* 21 March 1906, for details.
70 "Criticize the Liquor Act but Approve It in the Main," *Toronto World,* 24 March 1906; "Temperance People in Accord with Bill," *Ottawa Journal,* 21 March 1906; "For Stringent Liquor Law," *Ottawa Citizen,* 20 March 1906.
71 Quoted in several newspapers.
72 "The New License Bill" [editorial], *London Advertiser,* 21 March 1906.
73 "Dr. Chown on License Bill," *London Advertiser,* 22 March 1906.
74 "The Vessel License Evil," *Globe* [Toronto], 22 March 1906.
75 C. Berkley Powell to James Whitney, 31 March 1906, Whitney Letters, container b273265.
76 James Whitney to C. Berkley Powell, 2 April 1906, Whitney Letters, container b273265.
77 "Exciting Scene Startles House," *Globe* [Toronto], 30 March 1906.
78 S B Wilson to James Whitney, 26 March 1906, Whitney Letters, container b273265.
79 T.S. Edwards to James Whitney, 6 April 1906, Whitney Letters, container b273265.
80 James Whitney to T.S. Edwards, 7 April 1906, Whitney Letters, container b273265.
81 James Whitney to Rev. Richard Corrigan, 12 April 1906, Whitney Letters, container b273265.
82 James Whitney to William Hanna, 3 April 1906, Whitney Letters, container b273265.
83 "No Steamship Licenses," *Globe* [Toronto], 23 March 1906.
84 Estimates of the number ranged from 300 to over 1,000. See "1000 License Holders to Wait on Government," *Toronto World,* 4 April 1906; "Refusal of Hanna for the Hotelmen," *London Free Press,* 5 April 1906 (estimated 1,000); "Govt Stands by New License Bill," *London Advertiser,* 5 April 1906 (estimated 300); "No Concessions to Hotelkeepers," *Mail and Empire* [Toronto], 5 April 1906 (estimated 350); "Liquor Men State Case," *Ottawa Journal,* 5 April 1906 (estimated 800). Discrepancies do not appear to have broken along party lines.
85 "Hotel Men Interview the Ontario Cabinet," *Ottawa Citizen,* 4 April 1906.
86 See "Cabinet Tinker with Liquor Act," *London Advertiser,* 21 April 1906.
87 "New Liquor License Act for Stricter Enforcement," *Ottawa Journal,* 21 March 1906; "Hanna Boosts the Liquor Licenses: Radical Amendments to Present Act," *London Advertiser,* 21 March 1906.
88 Some disputed this claim, arguing that the limited ability of a municipal government to increase fees itself without a bylaw passed by the electors meant that the proportion of fees would remain essentially the same. "The New License Act," Lindsay *Weekly Post* [reproducing an editorial from Listowel *Banner*], 20 April 1906.

89 Quoted in "Hanna's Measure Sends Rates Up," *London Advertiser*, 3 April 1906.
90 "Will Raise Price of Drinks," *Ottawa Citizen*, 3 April 1906.
91 Untitled editorial, *Ottawa Citizen*, 4 April 1906.
92 "Whiskey Goes Up," *London Free Press*, 30 April 1906; "Higher Prices for Liquor," *Ottawa Journal*, 30 April 1906.
93 Reproduced in "Keeping a Hotel," *Northern Advance* [Barrie], 1 March 1906. As far as I can tell, there is/was no Punkville, Ontario, although there is a Punkydoodles Corners between St. Mary's and Stratford. People keep stealing the sign.
94 "Keeping a Hotel," *Northern Advance* [Barrie], 1 March 1906.
95 "Must Have the Saloon," *Telegraph* [Toronto], 29 April 1905.
96 The Toronto *Telegraph* noted that hotel keepers in that city had been surprised by the vigour with which the government had enforced the license act, suggesting that they expected a looser system from a sympathetic government. "Liquor Men Will Meet," *Telegraph* [Toronto], 29 April 1905.
97 See Canada, Parliament, "Royal Commission on the Liquor Traffic. Minutes of Evidence Taken in the Province of Ontario," *Sessional Papers*, Vol. 15, No. 21 (1895), notably testimony of Samuel Heakes (10107a and 10108a) and John M Dillon (6554a). William Orr (10330a and 10331a) indicates that two temperance hotels were successful in Toronto, which seemed to the commissioners to be a rather small number for such a big city.
98 "Inspection of Hostelries," *Mail and Empire* [Toronto], 3 March 1906.
99 C.W. McGuire to James Whitney, 7 March 1906, Whitney Letters, container b273265. The argument of McGuire's inspector contact was not correct. The Crooks Act did require inspectors to follow upon on complaints of liquor sales in unlicensed premises, but this statement suggests that they did not do so on a regular basis, if at all.
100 "Want the Temperance People to Know State of Affairs," *London Advertiser*, 12 March 1906.
101 "Liquor Law Enforcement," *Globe* [Toronto], 5 March 1906.
102 "The Travelers' Disability," *London Free Press*, 13 March 1906.
103 Reproduced in "Local Option and the Travelling Public," *Liberal* [Richmond Hill], 29 March 1906.
104 Untitled editorial, *Newmarket Era*, 9 March 1906.
105 "New Liquor Act Was under Fire," *London Advertiser*, 4 April 1906.
106 Act to Amend the Liquor License Act, *Statutes of the Province of Ontario* (1909), c. 82, s. 35.
107 "Many Places Vote for Local Option," *Globe* [Toronto], 8 January 1907.
108 "Notes and Comments," *Globe* [Toronto], 8 January 1908.
109 Hanna explained this in a letter to S.D. Chown, 27 October 1909, RG 8–5, Provincial Secretary Correspondence, Archives of Ontario, container B226450.
110 It might be possible to gather such records from newspaper reports of local option contests since temperance-friendly papers tended to report on such votes. The problem here is that prior to 1906 local option votes were not held on a set date across the province, so there is a high likelihood that not all votes would be published in major newspapers.
111 See Paul Jennings, *The Local: A History of the English Pub* (Cheltenham: History Press, 2007).
112 "The Number of Taverns," *Globe* [Toronto], 30 January 1883. The number of taverns and shops was capped in 1887 by a bylaw sponsored by R.J. Fleming. See "The Fleming By-law Passed: The Drink Traffic Must Be Reduced," *Globe* [Toronto], 15 February 1887. See also

Marguerite Van Die, "Protestants, the Liberal State, and the Practice of Politics: Revisiting R.J. Fleming and the 1890s Toronto Streetcar Controversy," *Journal of the Canadian Historical Association* 24 (2014): 96.

113 See Canada, Census Office, *Fourth Census of Canada 1901*, Vol 1: Population, "Table V: Population of Cities and Towns having over 5,000 inhabitants in 1901, compared with 1871-81-91," 22.

114 "The License Inquiry Was Opened Today. Witnesses Thought the Check a Bribe," *Toronto Star*, 18 February 1907.

115 R.J. Wilson to William Hanna, 24 January 1907 (first letter), RG 8–5, "Wilson" file, Provincial Secretary Correspondence, Archives of Ontario.

116 R.J. Wilson to William Hanna, 24 January 1907 (second letter), RG 8–5, "Wilson" file, Provincial Secretary Correspondence, Archives of Ontario.

117 As reported in Ontario, Legislative Assembly, "Ordered That There Be Laid before This House the Report of Mr. Starr, Who Was Appointed a Commissioner to Enquire into Certain Matters Relating to Liquor Licenses in the City of Toronto, Has Not Been Printed for Public Distribution, the Original Report Be Laid upon the Table of the House," *Sessional Papers*, No. 63 (1909) (unprinted), RG 49-19, Unprinted Sessional Papers, Archives of Ontario (hereafter Starr Report), 1.

118 "Make It Thoro," *Toronto World*, 13 February 1907.

119 "Varying Views as to Licenses," *Toronto World*, 23 February 1907.

120 Starr Report, 8.

121 "Party Politics and the License System," *Toronto Star*, 22 February 1907.

122 "Partyism Plus Law Basis of Influence," *Toronto Star*, 2 March 1907.

123 "Toronto Rails' Good Showing," *Toronto Star*, 6 February 1907, lists R. Millichamp as appointed a director of the Anglo-American Fire Insurance Company.

124 "Insurance Men Tell of Competition with Defoe," *Toronto Star*, 1 March 1907.

125 Starr Report, 32–34.

126 "Central License Board in Toronto to Control All Ontario Licenses," *Toronto Star*, 9 September 1907; Starr Report, 47.

127 "Kickers May Be Summoned," *Toronto Star*, 22 February 1907.

128 Starr Report, 28.

129 As Starr noted, Hastings "excused" but "could not explain" the poor conditions of these hotels. Starr Report, 29.

130 Starr Report, 29–31.

131 "Party Politics and the License System," *Toronto Star*, 22 February 1907.

132 "Kickers May Be Summoned," *Toronto Star*, 22 February 1907.

133 "Party Politics and the License System," *Toronto Star*, 22 February 1907.

134 "Premier Approves the Dismissals," *Globe* [Toronto], 29 November 1905; James Whitney to Charles Magee, 4 December 1905, Whitney Letters, container b273264.

135 Joseph Rowntree and Arthur Sherwell, *British "Gothenburg" Experiments and Public-House Trusts* (London: Hodder and Stoughton, 1901); Joseph Rowntree and Arthur Sherwell, *Public Control of the Liquor Traffic: Being a Review of the Scandinavian Experiments in the Light of Recent Experience* (London: Grant Richards, 1903). Rowntree and Sherwell also penned *The Temperance Problem and Social Reform* (London: Hodder and Stoughton, 1899), which had gone through multiple editions by the time Starr wrote his report.

136 Starr Report, 10.

137 Starr Report, 11.

138 Starr Report, 54.
139 Starr Report, 55.
140 "Oliver Is Toronto's Mayor," *Globe* [Toronto], 2 January 1908.
141 "They Want No Reduction," *Globe* [Toronto], 24 January 1908.
142 R.J. Wilson, Reuben Millichamp, and D.M. Defoe to William Hanna, 18 February 1908, "Wilson" file, Provincial Secretary Correspondence, Archives of Ontario.
143 An Act to Amend the Liquor License Act, *Statutes of Ontario* (1909), c. 82, ss. 7 and 15.
144 An Act to Amend the Liquor License Act, *Statutes of Ontario* (1911), c. 64, s. 1.
145 Humphries, *Honest Enough,* 430–31.

Chapter 12: Centralization, II: Beyond the Crooks Act, 1907–16

1 It is not possible here to dissect the potential future of the world had the Great War ended differently (even if I were qualified to do so). My point is that the "War to end all wars" appeared to many to be a war for civilization itself, which was probably a slight misreading of the tea leaves.
2 See Charles W. Humphries, *Honest Enough to Be Bold: The Life and Times of Sir James Pliny Whitney,* Ontario Historical Series (Toronto: University of Toronto Press, 1985).
3 William Hanna to James Whitney, 4 January 1908, F 5-1, "Correspondence of Sir James Whitney," Sir James Whitney Fonds, Archives of Ontario (hereafter Whitney letters), container b273870. The letter is dated 1907, but the information in it situates it clearly after the Starr Report.
4 "Tories Fight Shy of License Board," *Globe* [Toronto], 8 November 1911.
5 Earl Grey to William Hanna, 30 April 1905, RG 8-5, "Earl Grey" file, Provincial Secretary Correspondence, Archives of Ontario (Hereafter PSC/AO).
6 William Hanna to Earl Grey, 5 May 1905, RG 8-5, "Earl Grey" file, PSC/AO.
7 William Hanna to Earl Grey, 9 May 1905, RG 8-5, "Earl Grey" file, PSC/AO.
8 Earl Grey to William Hanna, 15 May 1905, RG 8-5, "Earl Grey" file, PSC/AO.
9 William Hanna to Earl Grey, 22 May 1905, RG 8-5, "Earl Grey" file, PSC/AO.
10 Earl Grey to William Hanna, 4 June 1906; William Hanna to Earl Grey, 7 June 1906, RG 8-5, "Earl Grey" file, PSC/AO.
11 Earl Grey to William Hanna, 21 June 1911, RG 8-5, "Earl Grey" file, PSC/AO.
12 S.D. Chown to William Hanna, 17 April 1907, RG 8-5, "S.D. Chown" file, PSC/AO.
13 William Hanna to S.D. Chown, 19 April 1907, "S.D. Chown" file, PSC/AO.
14 Saunders was appointed when Totten resigned, apparently because of the illness of his wife. See the obituary for Totten, *Windsor Star,* 10 February 1906; and "Canadian News in Brief," *Buffalo Evening News,* 2 October 1903. Saunders had also given evidence to the Royal Commission on the Liquor Traffic in 1893 when he was a Crown attorney in Windsor.
15 Eudo Saunders, memo to the license branch, 7 September 1909, RG 8-5, "Saunders" file, PSC/AO.
16 Eudo Saunders, undated memo to the license branch, RG 8-5, "Saunders" file, PSC/AO.
17 Eudo Saunders, "The Administration of the Liquor License Laws of Ontario," undated memo to the license branch, RG 8-5, "Saunders" file, PSC/AO.
18 "Policy of Liberals Is Banish the Bar," *Windsor Evening Record,* 27 March 1912; "Abolish the Bar" [editorial], *Windsor Evening Record,* 27 March 1912; "Banish the Bar," *Newmarket Era,* 29 March 1912.

19 Ontario, Legislative Assembly, *Journals of the Legislative Assembly*, 13th Leg, 1st Sess (3 April 1912), 266–67.
20 Ontario, Legislative Assembly, *Journals of the Legislative Assembly*, 13th Leg, 1st Sess (3–4 April 1912), 266–70.
21 Ontario, Legislative Assembly, *Journals of the Legislative Assembly* 13th Leg, 1st Sess (3–4 April 1912), 266–70.
22 See clipping and motion in Whitney Letters, container b273279. The clipping is a reprint of an editorial from the *Brockville Times* dated 4 April 1912.
23 The gendered pronoun is necessary since this was believed to be a troubling aspect of male drinking culture.
24 George Fitch, "The Treating Habit," *Windsor Record*, 20 September 1912.
25 "Striking at the Root," *St. Thomas Times*, reprinted in *Windsor Record*, 6 April 1912.
26 Jennie Brander to James Whitney, 6 July 1905, Whitney Letters, container b273263; James Whitney to Jennie Brander, 10 July 1905, Whitney Letters, container b273263.
27 The *Windsor Record* reproduced many editorials from newspapers across the province, both Liberal and Conservative, supporting and opposing the issue. Those in favour included "Striking at the Root," *St. Thomas Times*, reprinted in *Windsor Record*, 6 April 1912; and "The Treating Custom," *Mail and Empire* [Toronto], reprinted in *Windsor Record*, 6 April 1912. The *Windsor Record* itself was opposed to the measure, as it noted in "A Political Trimmer" [editorial], 5 April 1912; also see "Hard Thing to Abolish," *Hamilton Herald*, reprinted in *Windsor Record*, 8 April 1912; "Not Practical," *Hamilton Herald*, reprinted in *Windsor Record*, 10 April 1912; and "As to Treating," *Ottawa Free Press*, reprinted in *Windsor Record*, 10 April 1912.
28 "Of the Two Policies – Which?," *Newmarket Era*, 12 April 1912.
29 "Local Option Meeting," *Whitby Gazette and Chronicle*, 11 April 1912.
30 "A Political Trimmer" [editorial], *Windsor Record*, 5 April 1912.
31 "Reflections by the Editor," *Canadian Courier* 11, no. 20 (1912): 12; "Bars and Revenue Therefrom," *Journal* [Detroit], reproduced in *Windsor Record*, 17 April 1912.
32 Untitled editorial, *Kingsville Reporter*, 2 May 1912.
33 "Sir James Becomes Academic," *Globe* [Toronto], 10 April 1912.
34 M.C.R., Nelson and Sons, to Horace Wallis, 15 July 1912, Whitney Letters, container b273279.
35 "A Straight Temperance Issue" [editorial], *Globe* [Toronto], 22 February 1913; "Club Licenses Stay in 'Dry' Districts," *Windsor Record*, 11 April 1913.
36 M. Ringrose to James Whitney, 27 March 1912, Whitney Letters, container b273279.
37 "Ald Mills Elected in North Waterloo," *Globe* [Toronto], 29 October 1912; "The Bar Must Go, Says Mr. Rowell," *Globe* [Toronto], 29 October 1912.
38 "Abolition of the Bar the Clear-Cut Issue," *Globe* [Toronto], 23 October 1912.
39 "Black Eye for Rowell," *Windsor Record*, 30 October 1912.
40 James Whitney to George W. Neely, 9 October 1912, Whitney Papers, container b273260.
41 "The Bar Must Go, Says Mr. Rowell," *Globe* [Toronto], 29 October 1912.
42 "Anti Treating Law Is Strict," *Newmarket Era*, 7 June 1912; "Anti-Treating Law," *Hamilton Times*, reprinted in *Windsor Record*, 30 May 1912.
43 Ontario, Legislative Assembly, *Journals of the Legislative Assembly*, 13th Leg, 2nd Sess, Vol 47 (13 February 1913), 31
44 Ontario, Legislative Assembly, *Journals of the Legislative Assembly*, 13th Leg, 2nd Sess, Vol 47 (18 February 1913), 51.

45 Ontario, Legislative Assembly, *Journals of the Legislative Assembly*, 13th Leg, 2nd Sess, Vol 47 (5 March 1913), 109–10.
46 "Anti-Treating Law," *Hamilton Times*, reprinted in *Windsor Record*, 30 May 1912.
47 Humphries, *Honest Enough*, 418.
48 B.D. Tennyson, "The Succession of William H. Hearst to the Ontario Premiership – September 1914," *Ontario History* 56 (1964): 185–89.
49 An Act to Improve the Administration of the Liquor License Laws, *Statutes of Ontario* (1915), c. 39.
50 Proudfoot reportedly said "county-wide," but he might have said "country-wide" since often, then as now, Ontarians equate their province with the entire country. Ontario, Legislative Assembly, *Journals of the Legislative Assembly*, 14th Leg, 1st Sess, Vol 49 (30 March 1915), 213.
51 It was really an amazing attempt at last-minute interference. Ontario, Legislative Assembly, *Journals of the Legislative Assembly*, 14th Leg, 1st Sess, Vol 49 (1 April 1915), 246–57.
52 The *Daily Telegraph* paraphrased him. "Mr. Lloyd George and the Lure of Drink," *Daily Telegraph* [London, UK], 30 March 1915; see also "Drink Worst Foe of Great Britain," *Globe* [Toronto], 30 March 1915.
53 Lloyd George was not successful. The Central Control Board (Liquor) instituted some controls and took over the pub business in some cities, but prohibition was hardly contemplated. See James Nicholls, *The Politics of Alcohol: A History of the Drink Question in England* (Manchester: University of Manchester Press, 2009); and Robert Duncan, *Pubs and Patriots: The Drink Crisis in Britain during World War One* (Liverpool: University of Liverpool Press, 2013).
54 B.D. Tennyson, "Sir William Hearst and the Ontario Temperance Act," *Ontario History* 55 (1963): 233–45.
55 "Prohibition for the Dominion," *Globe* [Toronto], 24 December 1917.
56 Craig Heron, *Booze: A Distilled History* (Toronto: Between the Lines Press, 2003), 180; "Prohibition in Canada," *Globe* [Toronto], 12 March 1918; "Nation-Wide Prohibition," *Globe* [Toronto], 13 March 1918.
57 Quebec's government introduced a version of prohibition in 1919, but it was watered down before it could be implemented and in the end resulted only in a ban on spirits. Even that ban only lasted until 1921. See Heron, *Booze*, 272.
58 "Prohibition for the Dominion," *Globe* [Toronto], 24 December 1917.

Conclusion

1 The data come from the annual Trade and Navigation data provided in Canada, Parliament, *Sessional Papers* (various volumes and pages). I used manufacturing output as a proxy for consumption. Although liquor flowed into and out of Ontario, I have used this strategy because of two interesting phenomena in the data. First, the reports from which the data have been expertly extracted, mostly by research assistant and trainee historian extraordinaire Kaitlyn Carter, stopped indicating specific imports by province in 1901. Second, when I graphed the production numbers against the numbers of importation and production, minus exports, the two sets of data graphed almost exactly on top of each other. I therefore surmise that the next fourteen years of data would follow a similar pattern. So production becomes a reasonable proxy for consumption.
2 Bruce Curtis, "After 'Canada': Liberalism, Social Theory, and Historical Analysis," in *Liberalism and Hegemony: Debating the Canadian Liberal Revolution*, ed. Jean-François Constant and Michel Ducharme (Toronto: University of Toronto Press, 2009), 178.

3 Michèle Dagenais, "The Municipal Territory: A Product of the Liberal Order?," in *Liberalism and Hegemony: Debating the Canadian Liberal Revolution,* ed. Jean François Constant and Michel Ducharme (Toronto: University of Toronto Press, 2009); Curtis, "After 'Canada,'" 176–200; Bruce Curtis, *True Government by Choice Men? Inspection, Education and State Formation in Canada West* (Toronto: University of Toronto Press, 1992).
4 Dagenais, "The Municipal Territory"; Robert McDonald, "'Variants of Liberalism' and the Liberal Order Framework in British Columbia," in *Liberalism and Hegemony: Debating the Canadian Liberal Revolution,* ed. Jean François Constant and Michel Ducharme (Toronto: University of Toronto Press, 2009), 329.
5 McDonald, "'Variants of Liberalism,'" 329.
6 Darren Ferry, *Uniting in Measures of Common Good: The Construction of Liberal Identities in Central Canada 1830–1900* (Montreal and Kingston: McGill-Queen's University Press, 2008), 7.
7 Ferry, *Uniting in Measures of Common Good,* 15.
8 A. Margaret Evans, *Sir Oliver Mowat,* Ontario Historical Studies Series (Toronto: University of Toronto Press, 1992), 109.
9 Noel says that Mowat continued to keep a small number of Conservatives on license boards across the province. See S.J.R. Noel, *Patron, Client, Broker: Ontario Society and Politics* (Toronto: University of Toronto Press, 1990).
10 On US prohibition, see Daniel Okrent, *Last Call: The Rise and Fall of Prohibition* (New York: Scribner, 2010); and William J. Rorabaugh, *Prohibition: A Concise History* (New York: Oxford University Press, 2018). For a discussion of the impact of prohibition on the distillers and brewers of Canada, see Dan Malleck, "Bronfman Family," in *Alcohol and Temperance in Modern History: A Global Encyclopedia,* ed. Jack S. Blocker, Jr., David M. Fahey, and Ian R. Tyrrell (Santa Barbara, CA: ABC-Clio Press, 2003), 116–17; Malleck, "Seagram," in *Alcohol and Temperance in Modern History,* 554–55; and Matthew Bellamy, *Brewed in the North: A History of Labatt's* (Montreal and Kingston: McGill-Queen's University Press, 2019).
11 See Michel Ducharme, *The Idea of Liberty in Canada during the Age of Atlantic Revolutions 1776–1839* (Montreal and Kingston: McGill-Queen's University Press, 2014).
12 E.A. Heaman, *Tax, Order and Good Government: A New Political History of Canada, 1867–1917* (Montreal and Kingston: McGill-Queen's University Press, 2017), 135.
13 Although it is true that Prince Edward Island instituted prohibition in 1901, all other provincial prohibitory regimes (except in Quebec) were wartime measures.
14 The loss of these sources breaks my heart.
15 The use of detectives in the enforcement operations of the state could be an important history that extends well beyond the confines of liquor licensing.
16 As I describe elsewhere, in post-prohibition Ontario, temperance associations dedicated much of their time to ratting out intransigent license holders. See Dan Malleck, *Try to Control Yourself: The Regulation of Public Drinking in Post-Prohibition Ontario 1927–44* (Vancouver: UBC Press, 2012).
17 Max Weber, *Economy and Society: An Outline of Interpretive Sociology,* ed. Guenter Roth and Claus Wittich (Los Angeles: University of California Press, 1978), 2: 956–1006.
18 Weber, *Economy and Society,* 2: 959–63.
19 Sir John Willison, *Reminiscences, Political and Personal* (Toronto: McClelland and Stewart, 1919), 93.

20 John T. Saywell, *The Lawmakers: Judicial Power and the Shaping of Canadian Federalism* (Toronto: Osgoode Society, 2002), 87.
21 Full disclosure: I do not like tobacco smoking. It is a filthy habit and makes you stink and it may have even killed my father. But if you do it on your own, have at 'er. What I like even less is self-righteous people who feel it is their right to shame and ostracize and tell people what they should do with their own bodies. It is a strange liberalism that defends some forms of bodily autonomy while condemning others.

Index

Note: Page numbers with (f) refer to figures and those with (t) refer to tables.

Abbott, John, 211
An Act Respecting Tavern and Shop Licenses (1868). *See* Tavern and Shop License Act (1868)
An Act Respecting the Provincial Duty on Tavern Keepers, 325
An Act Respecting the Sale of Intoxicating Liquors, and the Issue of Licenses Therefor (1883). *See* McCarthy Act (1883–85)
An Act to Amend and Consolidate the Law for the Sale of Fermented or Spirituous Liquors (1874), 5, 31–33, 46–54. *See also* Tavern and Shop License Act (1868)
An Act to Amend the Acts Respecting Tavern and Shop Licenses (1873). *See* Tavern and Shop License Act, administration
An Act to Amend the Law Respecting the Sale of Fermented or Spirituous Liquors (1876). *See* Crooks Act (1876–1915)
An Act to Amend the Laws in Force Respecting the Sale of Intoxicating Liquors and the Issue of Licenses Therefor, and Otherwise for Repression of Abuses Resulting from Such Sale (1864). *See* Dunkin Act (1864)
An Act to Amend the Liquor License Laws (1906). *See* Liquor License Amendment Act (1906)
An Act to Diminish the Number of Licenses Issued for the Sale of Intoxicating Liquors by Retail (1860), 23, 24, 329n47
An Act to Enable the Electors of the Province to Pronounce upon the Desirability of Prohibiting the Importation, Manufacture, and Sale as a Beverage of Intoxicating Liquors (1893), 192–95
An Act to Improve the Liquor Laws (1890), 186
An Act to Prohibit the Sale of Intoxicating Liquors as a Beverage in Ontario (1868), 29–30
Addington County, 90, 93, 160(f)
Alberta: dominion plebiscite (1898), 221–22, 222(t)
alcohol. *See* beer and wine; liquor and alcoholic beverages
alcohol industry. *See* breweries; liquor industry

375

Index

Alexander, George, 125–26
Allen, Charles, 100–1
alliance. *See* Dominion Alliance for the Total Suppression of the Liquor Traffic
Almon, William, 126–27, 167–69
alternative liquor control. *See* liquor interests, disinterested management systems
Anglicans, 38, 252
Assiniboia, District of: dominion plebiscite (1898), 221–22, 222(t)
asylum, inebriate, 26–30, 39, 45, 323. *See also* health care and alcohol
Atlantic provinces: Scott Act, 159, 350n4. *See also* New Brunswick; Nova Scotia; Prince Edward Island
Attorney General for Ontario v. Attorney General for the Dominion of Canada (1896), 195, 355n82, 360n1
Attorney General for the Province of Manitoba v. The Manitoba License Holders Association (1901), 244, 361n34

Ball, Francis, 207–8
barf, temperance, 38
Barrie, 100, 153–54, 155, 174
bartenders' licenses, 272, 276, 303, 304
Beckingham, David, 13, 22–23
Beer Act [Beerhouse Act] (UK, 1830), 13–14, 25
beer and wine: adulterated drinks, 87; "beer and wine" licenses, xii, 206(f)n; cider, 126, 162, 164, 166–70, 220; consumption (1867–1914), 310–11, 310(f); dominion plebiscite question (1898), 220–21; Dunkin Act, 38; Gothenburg system exclusion of, 290; moderates, 37, 162, 202, 203, 310–11; as partial prohibition, 164; Scott Act, 145, 161–62, 164, 206–7, 206(f); Scott Act failed amendments (1885), 166–70; shift from alcohol to beer, 94–95, 206–7, 206(f), 310–11, 310(f); wineries, 51, 158, 335n22. *See also* breweries; licensed victuallers' associations; liquor and alcoholic beverages
Bell, Francis, 102
Bellamy, Matthew, 206–7
Belleville, 41, 76, 91, 161, 163

Bengough, John W., 58–59, 78, 80–81, 143
Bethune, James, 32, 33, 331n22, 335n28
beverages. *See* beer and wine; liquor and alcoholic beverages
Blake, Edward (Liberal Premier of Ontario, 1871–72), 26, 132, 139
BNA Act (British North America Act) (1867): about, 4–5, 117–18; absence of specific municipal powers, 23; continuation of pre-Confederation laws, 122; division of powers, 4–5, 117–18; dominion/provincial power struggles, 140; impact of jurisdictional uncertainties (1883–85), 157; liberal state, 10, 157, 316–17; municipal powers, 5; overlapping jurisdictions, 4–5, 117–18, 131, 140; provincial powers over municipalities, 23, 187; rationality and order, 10
BNA Act, jurisdictional uncertainties (1883–85): about, 141, 134–46, 156–57, 314; boards of commissioners, 143–46, 149–50, 155; competing requirements, boards, and fees, 148–55, 158; Crooks amendment (1884) on provincial jurisdiction, 153–54; disinformation campaigns, 151–52; fees and fines, 143–46, 148, 151–56, 158; *Hodge* (1883), 141–48, 144(f), 150, 175; hotels, taverns, and saloons, 150–51; JCPC decisions, 130–31; legacy of, 156–57; McCarthy Act ultra vires (1885), 144(f), 143–45, 155; newspapers on, 145–50, 156; partisanship, 150–51; policing powers, 142, 143, 146; provincial resistance to McCarthy Act, 146–50; refusal to rescind McCarthy Act, 145, 146
BNA Act, licensing powers of provinces, s. 92(9): about, 4–5, 117–18; Clarke's bill (1873), 30; *Fredericton* (1880), 129–31; JCPC decisions, 130–31, 195, 234; Marter's bill on retail sales (1893), 195, 234, 360n1; provincial revenues, 117–18; for retail sales, 234; *Russell* (1880), 130–31, 142–43; subordinate to dominion power over trade and commerce, 130–31, 195, 234
BNA Act, peace, order, and good government (preamble of s. 91):

Index

dominion licensing laws for orderly society, 117–18; JCPC decision in *Russell*, 130–31, 142–43, 159, 318; liberal state, 8; McCarthy Act, 135, 140
BNA Act, property and civil rights powers of provinces, s. 92(13), 117–18, 131
BNA Act, trade and commerce powers of dominion, s. 91(2): about, 4–5, 117–18; Clarke's bill (1873), 30; freedom and liberty, 312–13; JCPC decisions, 130–31, 195, 234; manufacture and importation of liquor, 234; Marter's bill on retail sales (1893), 195, 234, 360n1; McCarthy Act, 140; overlapping jurisdictions, 131; prohibition as restriction on trade, 30; property rights, 131; provincial licensing powers subordinate to, 130–31, 140, 195, 234
boards of commissioners. *See* Crooks Act, boards of commissioners; McCarthy Act, boards of commissioners
Bodega Wine Co., 51, 335n22
Boultbee, Alfred, 32–33, 126, 128
Bourbeau, Désiré, 164, 166
Bourniot, John, 249
Bowell, Mackenzie, 211
Bowmanville, 174
Brady, Maggie, 252
Brampton, 261, 270
Brander, Jennie, 271, 301, 304
Brant County, 106–8, 121–22, 160(f), 235
Brantford, 106–8, 123, 140, 150, 168, 219, 235, 275, 317
Brantford Expositor, 108–9, 317
breweries: committee questionnaire (1873), 323–24; Dunkin Act communities, 118–19; license act (1906), 272, 273; licenses, 4, 50–51; licensing under BNA Act, 4, 118; manufacturing (1867–1914), 310–11, 310(f); manufacturing (1873–90), 206–7, 206(f); prominent brewers, 36, 51, 58, 125, 126, 169, 206, 217, 284, 292, 310, 335n22; property rights, 12; Scott Act, 145, 161–62, 166–70, 206–7, 206(f); *Severn* (1878), 118, 125, 130–31; Starr commission, 286; terminology, xiii; tied houses, 272, 273, 276, 282–86, 288–89,

293. *See also* beer and wine; licensed victuallers' associations; liquor industry; Wets
Briggs, Jimuel (pseudonym), 62–63, 65, 66
Britain. *See* United Kingdom
British Columbia: dominion plebiscite (1898), 221–22, 222(t); petitions on licenses, 134; Scott Act, 159
British North America Act. *See* BNA Act (British North America Act) (1867)
Brockville, 198, 200, 205, 263
Brooks, J.B., 190
Brown, George, 48–50, 56, 59–60, 65, 78, 96, 120
Bruce County, 160(f), 184
Buchanan, William W., 189
Burgess, William, 38
Burnham, John, 16–17
Burns, James W., 286, 292

Cameron, James, 119–20
Cameron, John (editor), 147, 178
Cameron, John Hillyard (politician), 85–86
Cameron, Malcolm, 146, 166
Cameron, Matthew, 28, 47, 55–56, 61
Camp Fire, 253–54, 363n80
Campbell, Alexander, 155
Canada, Constitution. *See* BNA Act (British North America Act) (1867)
Canada, courts. *See* Judicial Committee of the Privy Council (JCPC); Supreme Court of Canada (SCC)
Canada, dominion governments, 4. *See also* Laurier, Wilfrid (Liberal Prime Minister, 1896–1911); Macdonald, John A. (Conservative Prime Minister, 1867–73, 1878–91); Mackenzie, Alexander (Liberal Prime Minister, 1873–78)
Canada, liquor question. *See* beer and wine; breweries; Drys; liquor and alcoholic beverages; liquor industry; moderates; prohibition; Wets
Canada, local option laws. *See* Dunkin Act, local option; local option; Scott Act (1878–1984)

Canada, Ontario political parties. *See* political parties, Ontario

Canada Citizen and Temperance Record, 175–76, 187

Canada Courier, 302

Canada Temperance Act (1864). *See* Dunkin Act (1864)

Canada Temperance Act (1878) (CTA). *See* Scott Act (1878–1984)

Canadian Monthly Review, 60, 61, 344*n*6

Le Canadien (newspaper), 149

cannabis laws, 16–17

capitalism. *See* economy and liquor industry

Capron, John, 71

Carleton County, 70–71, 74, 160(f)

Carling, John, 24, 310

Carman, A., 229

cartoons, 78–81, 79(f), 143, 144(f), 258–61, 259(f), 260(f)

Catholics, 72, 76, 81, 232

children and youth: drinking age, 186; girls' drunkenness, 178; prohibition impacts, 205; shops and exposure to liquor, 53, 174, 177, 181

Chown, S.D., 248, 268, 271, 273–74, 298, 300

Christian Guardian, 230, 280

Christians: Anglicans, 38, 252; Catholics, 72, 76, 81, 232; as commissioners, 76; committee questionnaire for clergy (1873), 35–38, 321; evangelicals, 7–8, 25, 26; Methodists, 26, 214, 218, 230, 239–40, 254, 268, 280, 299; J.S. Mill on, 7–8; Presbyterians, 120–21, 216–17, 240, 245, 250, 276; prohibitionist arguments, 7–8

cider, 126, 162, 164, 166–70, 220. *See also* beer and wine

cities. *See* municipal governments

Clarke, Edward F., 198

Clarke, John, 29–30, 32, 34, 40, 47–49, 117, 331*n*31

Clarke, W., 210

clientelism: about, 64–68; Crooks Act, 103–5; license act (1868), 24; temperance hotels, 87. *See also* patronage, partisanism, and clientelism

Close, Patrick G., 51, 335*n*22

closing times: Crooks Act, 82, 87, 92, 94, 133; Crooks Act amendment (1897), 236, 237, 238, 239–40; license act (1868), 31, 52–53; Sundays, 133, 136, 199, 201, 270, 272

clubs, private (unlicensed), 237, 239, 302, 303

Cochrane, George, 101–2

Coleman, Dilly, 98

collectivism and liberalism, 10–11, 233, 313, 315, 316, 319

commissioners. *See* Crooks Act, boards of commissioners; McCarthy Act, boards of commissioners

commissions, parliamentary, 194. *See also* Royal Commission on the Liquor Traffic (RCLT) (1892–95)

committee review of license act (1868). *See* Tavern and Shop License Act, committee review (1873–74)

Confederation: jurisdictional precedents, 187; liquor licensing act (1868) before, 325; municipal and provincial powers, 15, 22. *See also* BNA Act (British North America Act) (1867); municipal governments, pre-Confederation; Tavern and Shop License Act (1868); *and entries beginning with* Canada

Conover, A.S., 105–6, 111

Conservative Party, Canada: leaders after Macdonald, 211; patronage, 131–32, 139–40, 150. *See also* Macdonald, John A. (Conservative Prime Minister, 1867–73, 1878–91)

Conservative Party, Ontario: appointments under Crooks Act, 98, 341*n*3; license cancellations under Crooks Act, 78–79, 79(f), 80(t); liquor question, 317–18; political spectrum, 26; temperance forces, 124. *See also* Whitney, James (Conservative Premier of Ontario, 1905–14)

constitutional powers. *See* BNA Act (British North America Act) (1867)

Copeland, William, 51, 335*n*22

Cornwall, Clement, 124

Cosgrave, James, 284–85, 292

Cosgrave, John, 58, 61–62, 206, 285
Cosgrave, Lawrence, 206, 285
Courtice, A.C., 230, 246
courts. *See* Judicial Committee of the Privy Council (JCPC); Supreme Court of Canada (SCC)
Cowan, Walter, 102
Cronmiller, Henry, 126
Cronyn, Benjamin, 69
Crooks, Adam, 31–32, 46–47, 78–79, 79(f)
Crooks report (1873–74). *See* Tavern and Shop License Act, committee review (1873–74)
Crooks Act (1876–1915): about, 15–16, 54–55, 88–91, 94–95, 307–8, 311; constitutionality, 95, 142, 156–57, 186–88; cultural impacts, 88–89, 91–95; debates, 55–56, 59, 61–62; dominion attempt to disallow fees, 155–56; fair application of law, 106–9; *Hodge* (1883), 142, 175; liquor industry forces, 57–58, 75, 81, 92, 195–96; liquor question, 67, 112–13; local/central power shifts, 54–55, 59–62, 96–97, 105–9, 112–13, 139–40, 156–57, 311; McCarthy Act comparison, 134–38, 136(t)–137(t), 326; McCarthy Act's impacts, 156–57, 173–74, 186; moderate forces, 172; newspapers on, 55–56, 60–61, 78; partisanism, 98, 112–13, 134, 150, 158; private clubs (unlicensed), 237, 239, 302, 303; public notices, 173; RCLT review, 198–201, 207, 209–11; records, xii, 82, 97, 317; regional variations, 82–83, 97; replaced by Liquor License Act (1915), 15, 305, 306–8, 326; temperance forces, 73–75, 80, 94–95, 104–5, 156, 172, 186, 236–37; treating system, 91, 201, 300–4; years in operation (1876–1915), 325. *See also* BNA Act, jurisdictional uncertainties (1883–85); Crooks Act, liberal state; License Branch
Crooks Act, administration of licensing system: about, 59–68, 91, 94–95, 311, 325; balance of interests, 65–68, 75–77, 96–98, 105–9, 112–13, 341n3; clientelism, 65–68; evaluation (1877–1880), 82–83,

87–95, 97; ideal system, 65, 68, 72–73; License Branch, 15–16, 292–93; local/central power shifts, 59–62, 68, 70, 80, 96–97, 105–9, 112–13, 139–40, 156–57, 311; newspapers on, 60–62; partisanism, 98, 133–34, 158, 264–71, 313–14, 341n3; patronage, 60–73, 92, 96–97, 133, 136, 138, 139–40, 258, 261–71, 287–88, 313–14; public reception, 59–60; regional variations, 82–83, 97; temperance forces, 73–75, 80, 94–95, 104–5. *See also* License Branch; patronage, partisanism, and clientelism
Crooks Act, amendments and bills: about, 172–74, 195–96; amendments (1877), 83, 134; amendment (1884), 106–7, 110–13, 173; amendment (1890, 1897), 186–88, 236–40, 354n50; amendment (1906), 272–84, 304; amendment (1908, 1909), 280, 292–93; amendment (1911, 1913, 1915), 304–8, 326; anti-treating motion, 300–4; bartenders' licenses, 272, 276, 303, 304; cheque cashing, 304; drinking age, 186; Gibson's bill, 186–88; grocers' licenses, 174–84; JCPC decision on provincial prohibition powers, 195–96; local option, 186–88, 354n50; Marter's bill on retail sales (1893), 188–95, 234, 360n1; McCarthy Act's impacts, 156–57, 173–74, 186; newspapers on, 186, 188, 192–94; plebiscite on prohibition (1894), 193–96, 215, 315; provincial prohibition powers, 188; public input on licenses, 106–7, 110–13, 156, 173–74, 186; ships and trains, 186; summer licenses (1877), 134, 138; tavern fees (1906), 272–74, 273(t), 283; tied houses, 272, 273, 276, 282–86, 288–89, 293. *See also* Crooks Act, local option under 1906 amendment; License Amendment Act (1897); Liquor License Amendment Act (1906); Liquor License Amendment Act (1906), local option
Crooks Act, boards of commissioners: about, 15–16, 54, 94–95, 311, 314, 325; amendment (1915), 305–8, 326; appointed by province, 54, 96–98,

136(t), 325; balance of interests, 65–68, 75–77, 96–98, 105–9, 112–13, 341*n*3; benefits, 59; cancellation of earlier licenses, 78–79, 79(f), 80(t), 83–84, 88–89, 92–93, 101, 314; central board (1915), 305, 306–8, 326; centralized oversight by ridings, 15–16, 54–55, 59–62, 82–83, 325–26; closed meetings, 137(t); closing times, 82, 87, 92, 94, 133; court actions against, 85, 110–12; duties, 56, 82–83, 106–7; enforcement, 103; evaluation (1877–80), 82–83, 87–95, 97; fair application of law, 106–9, 111–12; ideal commissioner, 65, 68, 73–76; issuance of licenses, 56, 136(t); jurisdictional uncertainties (1883–85), 143–46, 149–50, 155–57; lack of transparency, 133, 137(t), 173; members, 54, 136(t), 325; partisanism, 98, 133–34, 264–71, 341*n*3; patronage, 96–97; regional variations, 82–83, 97, 112; resistance to, 84–86, 105–9; unpaid, 15, 54, 59, 109, 265, 287, 298–99, 325, 326

Crooks Act, enforcement: about, 207–9, 311; closing times, 82, 87, 92, 94, 133; detectives, 100–3, 207–9, 316; of Dunkin Act, 89–90, 93–95, 119–20, 184; evaluation (1877–80), 87–95; evidence, 73, 87, 90, 93, 99–100, 101, 105, 208; informants, 102, 207–8; intimidation of witnesses, 207–9; investigations, 73, 82, 86–87; liberal state, 103, 196; lodging standards, 269–71; magistrates, 84–85, 208; penalties, 134; police, 47, 85, 101, 334*n*16; private clubs (unlicensed), 237, 239, 302, 303; resistance to, 84–86; temperance hotels, 86–87, 278–80; unlicensed premises, 86–87; Whitney's views, 258. *See also* Crooks Act, boards of commissioners; Crooks Act, inspectors

Crooks Act, fees and fines: about, 55, 325; amendment (1906), 272–74, 273(t); dominion attempt to disallow fees (1884), 155–56; financing of enforcement, 89, 119; grocers' licenses, 183–84; jurisdictional uncertainties (1883–85), 143–46, 148, 151–57, 158; license fund, 137(t); minimum fees set by provinces, 55; municipal powers, 55; public reception, 58–59; tavern license fees (1886–1906), 272–74, 273(t), 277, 283; Whitney's views, 258

Crooks Act, inspectors: about, 15–16, 54, 94–95, 258, 311; appointed by province, 15, 54, 68–73, 76–77, 96, 97–98, 134, 136(t), 268–69, 325; balance of interests, 65–68, 75–77, 96–98, 112–13, 341*n*3; competence, 46, 71–73, 77, 98, 102, 103–5, 110, 173; detectives, 100–3; Dunkin Act enforcement, 90, 93–95, 119, 184; duties, 73, 82, 268; enforcement, 90–91, 101–3, 311; evaluation (1880), 88–89, 91–95, 97; ideal inspector, 65, 71–75, 96, 268–69; informants, 105; investigations, 73, 82, 86–87; liberal state, 72–73, 103, 311; municipal powers, 73; partisanism, 98, 103, 264–66, 268–69; patronage, 60–71, 76, 96–97, 258, 268–71; public awareness, 78; salaries, 363*n*4; temperance advocates, 73–74, 80, 104–5; visibility, 101–2; Whitney's views, 258, 261; work load, 98–99

Crooks Act, liberal state: about, 57, 91, 94–97, 196, 233, 311; balance of autonomy and control, 46, 97–98; efficient governance, 65, 81–82, 91, 112–13; fair application of law, 103, 106–9, 112–13, 180–83, 196; free markets, 57; grocers' licenses, 180–83; individual rights, 57; jurisdictional uncertainties (1883–85), 157; limited government, 55–56, 172, 196, 293–94; plebiscites, 194; property rights, 55, 57, 175, 196; rationality, 103, 311. *See also* liberalism and the state

Crooks Act, local option: about, 93–95, 186–88, 325; amendments, 186–88; constitutionality, 186–88; Dunkin Act enforcement, 90, 93–95, 119, 184; Marter's bill on retail sales (1893), 188–95, 234, 360*n*1; not permitted, 137(t); private clubs (unlicensed), 237, 239, 302, 303; temperance hotels, 86–87, 278–80

Crooks Act, local option under 1906 amendment: about, 272–73, 280–84; increase in votes and areas (1904–14), 281–82, 282(f), 282(t); petitions, 273, 275; temperance hotels, 278–80; three-fifths majority, 273–76, 280–81; vote timing, 273–74, 276

Crooks Act, population-based licenses: about, 54–55, 77–78, 325; balance of interests, 81; calculation of number of licenses, 136(t), 138; cancellation of earlier licenses, 78–79, 79(f), 80(t), 83–84, 88–89, 92–93; impacts on businesses, 57–58; jurisdictional uncertainties (1883–85), 153; license fund, 89; liquor industry, 81; monopolies, 55, 57; municipal powers, 54–55, 60, 92; newspapers on, 78–79; summer licenses, 83; temperance advocates, 80; Toronto, 283, 292

Crooks Act, shops: about, 92, 138, 174–84, 195; amendment (1915), 305–6, 326; amendments, 172–74, 183–84; cancellation of earlier licenses, 78–79, 79(f), 80(t), 83–84, 88–89, 92–93, 101; enforcement, 183–84; grocers' licenses, 174–84, 195; liberal state, 175, 179, 180–83; McCarthy Act, 134–35, 138, 174; municipal powers, 92, 137(t), 138, 174, 183; newspapers on, 176–83; secret drinking, 172, 176–79, 183; separation of goods and liquor, 92, 134, 174, 183–84; Wets vs Drys, 174–84, 195; women, 174–80, 182–83. *See also* shops

Crooks Act, taverns: about, 94–95; cancellation of earlier licenses, 78–79, 79(f), 80(t), 83–84, 88–89, 92–93, 101; evaluation (1877–1880), 87–95; jurisdictional uncertainties (1883–85), 148, 153, 156–57; license fees (1886–1906), 272–74, 273(t), 277, 283; lodgings, 137(t), 148, 153, 269–71, 277–80; political culture, 59; public notices, 82–83, 173; reasons for contesting licenses, 173–74; reduction in number, 78; stables required (6), 137(t). *See also* taverns

CTA (Canada Temperance Act). *See* Scott Act (1878–1984)

Cummer, W.L., 206
Currie, James G., 30, 62
Curtis, Bruce, 9–10, 11, 67, 96

Dagenais, Michèle, 10–11, 23, 64, 96
Daily Mail (Toronto newspaper): Conservative paper, 354*n*64; Crooks Act, 55, 57–58, 61–62, 69–70, 78; grocers' licenses, 179–81; on Hardy, 235; jurisdictional confusion (1883–85), 146, 156; license act amendments (1873–74), 48–49; Marter's bill, 188–89, 192; on patronage, 69–70, 78; provincial plebiscite on prohibition (1894), 193; satire (J. Briggs), 62–63, 65, 66
Daily News (Toronto newspaper), 239–40
Davies, Thomas, 126, 161
Davis, E.J., 190
Davis, W.R., 139–40
Dawson, George D., 51–52, 335*n*22
Dawson, John, 71
Defoe, D.M., 287, 292
democracy: liquor question, 3–4; plebiscites, 194, 249, 315; property rights, 9–10; referendums, 244–45, 249. *See also* elections; liberalism and the state; plebiscites; referendums
Desjardins, Alphonse, 154–55
detectives: Crooks Act, 100–3, 207–9, 311, 316; Dunkin Act, 235; entrapment, 100–1; liberal state, 103; license act (1906), 102–3; Totten on, 99–101; witnesses in court, 207–9
Dexter, Thomas, 101
Dickey, Robert, 124, 129
disinterested management. *See* liquor interests, disinterested management systems
dispensary system, 231–32, 249–50, 291, 306
distillers. *See* licensed victuallers' associations; liquor industry
division of powers. *See* BNA Act (British North America Act) (1867)
doctors. *See* health care and alcohol
dominion. *See* entries beginning with Canada
Dominion Alliance for the Total

Suppression of the Liquor Traffic: about, 120; amendment act (1906), 279–80; appeal of *Russell* to JCPC, 130; Crooks Act amendment, 186; disinterested liquor management, 253; dominion plebiscite (1898), 188–90, 213, 217–18, 223–25; grocers' licenses, 175; Jamieson's amendment to Scott Act, 351*nn*21–22; Laurier's refusal of prohibition bill, 223–24, 231; local option, 186; Marter's bill, 188–90; McCarthy committee, 133–34; members, 120, 124, 243; referendum (1902), 246–49, 253; Rowell's banish-the-bar pledge, 299–303; Scott Act, 124–25, 130, 166, 167, 169–70, 185, 186, 345*n*37; treating system, 302; WCTU allies, 235; Whitney's moderation, 299–300

Dominion Liquor Act (1883), federal. *See* McCarthy Act (1883–85)

dominion plebiscite (1898). *See* plebiscite, dominion prohibition (1898)

Donovan, A.E., 262–63, 364*n*19

Dougall, J.R., 230–31

Douglas, James, 232

druggists. *See* health care and alcohol

drunkenness: about, 11–12, 233; Canada as temperate society, 203; children, 178; committee questionnaire (1873), 35–38, 321–24; criminality, 56, 232; Crooks Act's impacts, 94–95; cultures of drink, 15, 309–10; Dunkin Act's impacts, 200–1; Gothenburg system, 253–54; images of effects, 332*n*46; immorality, 25; liquor question, 3–4, 28–30; medical vs moral issue, 28–30, 331*n*32; and number of licenses, 56; sales to people injured by drunkenness, 49; threat to liberal order, 8, 11–12, 176, 242, 312–13; women, 174–80. *See also* health care and alcohol

Drys: about, xiii, 6–7, 233, 314–15; binary arguments, 6–7, 36–37, 227; bipartisan support, 315–16; collectivist values, 313; extremism, 7–8, 12, 128–29; ideal of a moral society, 6–7; ideal of total suppression, xiii; liberal state, 6–7, 233, 314–15; J.S. Mill on, 7–8; political spectrum, 26; pragmatism, 6–7; RCLT reports, 209–11; righteousness, 6–7; terminology, xiii; as threat to liberal order, 8, 12, 312–13. *See also* liberalism and the state; prohibition; temperance movement

Ducharme, Michel, 9–10, 315, 328*n*20

Dufferin County, 87, 109–10, 160(f)

Dundas, J.R., 166, 168

Dundas County, 84, 160(f), 267, 271, 294

Dunkin, Christopher, 25–26

Dunkin Act (1864): about, 16, 25–26, 50, 118–19, 325; appeals, 121; constitutionality, 118, 122–24, 345*n*23, 345*n*27; vs Crooks Act, 122–23, 345*n*23; drunkenness, 119, 200–1; flaws, 89–91, 119–21; implementation, 89–90, 123, 186; lack of public support, 89–91, 121; legal challenges, 121–22; liberal state, 200–1; newspapers on, 49–50; Ontario, 26; pre-Confederation law, 16; *Prettie* (1877), 122; Quebec, 26, 123, 325, 330*n*17; RCLT review, 200–1, 205; Scott Act as replacement, 16, 123–26; temperance advocates, 89–90, 120–21, 123; Totten's report (1877), 89–91, 119, 123; years in operation (1864–1984), 325, 326n

Dunkin Act, local option: about, 16, 25–26, 89–91; ban on sale of small quantities, 118; criminality, 93–94, 207–9; detectives, 235; enforcement under Crooks Act, 89–90, 93–95, 119–21, 184, 207–9; implementation, 186; medicinal alcohol, 50; penalties, 119–20; sales by brewers and distillers, 118; sales in large quantities, 50, 124; sales to people injured by drunkenness, 49; Totten's report (1877), 89–91, 119, 123; transport of alcohol, 50

Dunkin Act, local option bylaws: about, 118, 121–23, 325; bylaws on liquor quantities, 118, 325; petitions for bylaws, 118; rescinded bylaws, 121; voting, 90, 118, 121–24; wording, 119

Durham County, 73, 75–76, 87–88, 94, 127, 160(f)

Index   383

economy and liquor industry: damage by prohibition, 159–62, 212; government ownership, 250–51; groceries as threat, 127; laissez-faire approach, 10, 13, 28, 250, 254, 291; liberal free market, 10, 57; monopolies, 55, 57, 231; property rights, 10, 57, 131; Scott Act's impact, 159–62; supply and demand, 56–57. *See also* breweries; liquor industry; property and liberalism

Edwards, T.S., 267, 275

elections: secret ballot (1875), 121, 123, 337n7; taverns and political culture, 337n7; women's vote, 193. *See also* local option; plebiscites; referendums

Elgin County, 83, 84–85, 160(f)

Empire (Toronto newspaper), 189, 192–93, 279

England. *See* United Kingdom

equality and liberalism: about, 3–4, 10, 233, 313; fairness and justice, 10, 110–11, 129, 157, 180–81, 204, 317; fairness in liquor trade, 177, 181; impact of jurisdictional uncertainties, 157; legal system, 10; liberal state, 10; liquor interests, 178–79; liquor question, 3–4; taxation, 218–19. *See also* liberalism and the state

Essery, Emmanuel, 200

Essex County, 93, 110, 160(f), 205, 269, 343n58, 365n46

evangelicals. *See* Christians

Evans, Margaret, 67, 75, 187, 339n75

Evening News (Toronto newspaper), 216–17, 221, 224, 229–30, 240, 242

Fahey, James, 179–81

fairness and justice, 10, 110–11, 129, 157, 180–81, 204, 317. *See also* equality and liberalism; liberalism and the state

Farewell, Abraham, 29, 30, 33–34, 39, 331n21

females. *See* women

Ferry, Darren, 313

First World War. *See* Great War

Fisher, Sydney, 220

Fitch, George, 301

Flavelle, Joseph, 288–89, 291, 297

Fleming, James, 147

Flint, Billa, 167

Foster, George E., 133–34, 170

Foucault, Michel, 40

Fredericton v. the Queen (1880), 129–31, 142

freedom, liberty, and liberalism: about, 3–4, 9–10, 226–27, 313; Britishness, 226–28; equality and liberty, 10; freedom by prohibition, 7, 12, 95, 127–28, 226–27; freedom of choice, 3, 7, 9, 12, 95, 128, 210, 318–19, 373n21; ideal citizen, 11, 65; impact of jurisdictional uncertainties, 157; individual sovereignty, 9; vs injury to others, 227; liberal state, 7, 12, 28, 95, 127–28; liquor industry arguments, 95; liquor question, 3–4, 7, 127–28; local option, 170–71; J.S. Mill on, 7–8, 226–27; modern liberty, 9–10; property, 7, 9–10, 131; rational actors, 312–13; representative democracy, 10; republican liberty, 9; trade and commerce, 312–13; treating system, 304, 313. *See also* liberalism and the state; property and liberalism

French Canadians: British liberalism, 314; as commissioners, 76; dominion plebiscite (1898), 228–29. *See also* Quebec

Frontenac County, 122, 151, 160(f)

Galt, Thomas, 187–88

Garrow, James T., 263

Garrow Resolution, 263–64, 268, 317, 365n43

gender and drinking spaces, 21. *See also* women

Gibson, John M., 186

Gigault, Georges, 139, 164, 198

Girard, Philip, 9, 328n20

Glengarry County, 160(f)

Globe (Toronto newspaper): commercial travellers, 280; Crooks Act, 55–56, 60, 62, 78, 98, 186; dominion plebiscite (1898), 214–18, 227, 229; Dunkin Act, 49–50, 119–20, 122; grocers' licenses, 176–78, 180–82; jurisdictional uncertainties (1883–85), 145–46, 147, 149, 152, 153, 156; license act amendments (1873–74), 48–49; liquor question,

317–18; local option, 187; Marter's bill, 192; moderate views, 80, 216; patronage, 268; prohibition act (1916), 306; RCLT review, 203; referendum (1902), 247, 250; treating system, 302; women's secret drinking, 176, 178–79

The Good Templar, 187, 189

Good Templars, 73, 120, 141, 189–90, 218–19

Gooderham, George, 207

Gothenburg system, 231–32, 249–54, 289–90, 296–97. *See also* liquor interests, disinterested management systems

governments: liberal order framework, 8–14, 312–13. *See also* Canada, dominion governments; liberalism and the state; municipal governments; provincial governments

Gowan, Ogle R., 44, 46, 333*n*90

Grange, John, 29, 32, 59–60

Grant, George M., 216–17, 225, 227, 228, 252–53

Great Britain. *See* United Kingdom

Great War: prohibition act (1916), 15, 306–8, 314

Greenaway, John, 12

Grenville County, 92, 160(f)

Grey, Earl, 251–52, 289–90, 293, 295–98

Grey County, 88, 93–94, 160(f), 161

Grip (satirical magazine), 44, 58, 63, 78, 79(f), 80–81, 143, 144(f)

Grits. *See* Reform Party, Ontario

grocers' licenses. *See* Crooks Act; shops; licensed victuallers' associations; liquor industry; shops

groggeries, 52, 55, 88–89, 127, 129

Guelph, 102, 199, 253

Haig, James, 77

Haldimand County, 160(f)

Halton County, 74, 87, 159, 160(f), 185

Hamilton: dominion plebiscite (1898), 216, 218; enforcement, 101, 105, 269–70; RCLT review, 201; Scott Act, 162; shops, 42–43; temperance advocates, 105, 121

Hamilton Herald, 216

Hamilton Spectator, 247, 265, 352*n*11

Hanna, William: about, 296–98, 307–8; amendment (1906), 272–80, 283–85, 288–89; amendments (1912, 1913, 1915), 302–3, 305–6; for centralized system, 300, 305, 307–8, 315, 326; disinterested liquor management, 296–98; Grey's relationship, 293, 296–98; moderate, 272, 307; partisanism, 266–71; secretary for License Branch, 289, 296; secretary to Whitney, 266–67, 289, 293, 296, 307; Starr commission, 285; temporary Conservative leader, 305. *See also* Liquor License Amendment Act (1906)

Harcourt, Richard, 108–9, 236–37, 238–39, 243

Hardgrave, Wakefield, 228

Hardy, Arthur Sturgis: career, 235; Crown lands commissioner, 107, 235; License Branch secretary, 91, 98–99, 105–9, 150, 153, 185, 235; personal qualities, 235, 237–39. *See also* License Branch

Hardy, Arthur Sturgis (Liberal Premier of Ontario, 1896–99): about, 234–43; Crooks Act amendment (1897), 236–40; deputations to, 236–39; liquor industry forces, 237–39, 242; Mowat's support, 239; newspapers on, 237–42; partisanism, 235; party loyalty, 241; promises of prohibition, 234–36, 239–40; G. Ross's relationship, 235–36; temperance forces, 236–40

Hardy, Russel, 40–43

Hargraft, William, 76–77

harm principle, 318–19

Hartley, Joseph, 107–8

Harvey, John, 151

Hastings, T.A., 288, 291, 368*n*129

Hastings County, 41, 76, 86, 88, 91, 160(f), 161, 163

Haverson, James, 228, 278, 286–89

Hay, James, 198–99, 207

health care and alcohol: committee questionnaire (1873), 35–37, 321–24; inebriate asylum, 26–30, 39, 45, 323; medical vs moral issue, 28–30, 331*n*32; medicinal alcohol, 50, 100–1, 166–67, 236, 306; pharmacists, 100–1, 236, 250;

physicians' prescriptions, 236; scholarship on, 331*n*32. *See also* drunkenness
Heaman, Elsbeth, 315
Hearst, William (Conservative Premier of Ontario, 1914–19), 305–6, 310, 315
Henderson, James, 98, 173
Henderson, Robert, 69–70
Hickman, E., 37
Hickson, Joseph, 198, 209–10
Higgins, Benjamin, 68–70, 72
Hodge, A.G., 101, 133–34, 173
Hodge, Archibald, 141–42
Hodge v. The Queen (1883), 141–48, 144(f), 150, 175
Hodgins, Frank, 285–87, 290
Hogg, W.D., 263–64
Hogle, William, 103–5, 342*n*38
hospitals. *See* health care and alcohol
hotels and lodging: corruption, 283–85; Crooks Act, 137(t), 148, 153, 269–71, 277–80; inspected hotels, 280; McCarthy Act, 135, 137(t), 148, 153; taverns, 22; temperance hotels, 86–87, 278–80; Toronto, 277–80, 283–85, 288–90, 292–93, 367*nn*96–97
Houde, Frédéric, 147, 348*n*19
Houston, William, 214–15
Humphries, Charles W., 257, 261, 262
Huron County, 74, 84, 86–87, 91–92, 94, 105–6, 111, 160(f)
Hynes, J.F., 284–85

Independent Order of Good Templars, 141
Indigenous peoples, xiii, 107
individualism as liberal ideal: about, 11, 233; freedom of choice, 3, 7, 9, 128, 210, 318–19, 373*n*21; ideal citizen, 11; rights, 57; self-control, 128; sovereignty, 9. *See also* freedom, liberty, and liberalism; rationality as liberal ideal
inebriate asylum, 26–30, 39, 45, 323. *See also* drunkenness; health care and alcohol
inspectors. *See* Crooks Act, inspectors; Scott Act, local option; Tavern and Shop License Act, administration

insurance industry: committee questionnaire (1873), 35–36, 324
intoxicating substances, 16–17. *See* beer and wine; liquor and alcoholic beverages
Italians, 152, 349*n*45
Ives, William Bullock, 164

Jamieson, Joseph, 164–66, 169–70, 199–200, 351*nn*21–22, 356*n*10
journals. *See* newspapers and journals
Judicial Committee of the Privy Council (JCPC): about, 4; dominion power over manufacture or importation, 195, 234; legal expertise of lords, 327*n*3; limited application of decisions, 142; Manitoba prohibition (1900), 244; Marter's bill on retail sales (1896), 195, 234, 360*n*1; McCarthy Act ultra vires (1885), 155; partial prohibition, 244; pre-Confederation precedents, 187; provincial power over retail sales, 195, 234; Scott Act constitutionality, 130; symmetrical federalism, 195
Judicial Committee of the Privy Council, decisions: *A.G. for Manitoba v. Manitoba License Holders Association* (1901), 244, 361*n*34; *A.G. for Ontario v. A.G. for Canada* (1896), 195, 234, 355*n*82, 360*n*1; *Hodge* (1883), 141–48, 144(f), 150, 175; *Russell* (1882), 130–32, 142–43, 159, 318
justice and fairness, 129, 157, 180–81, 204, 317. *See also* equality and liberalism; liberalism and the state

Kavanagh, Joseph, 134–35
Kent County, 111–12, 160(f)
Kerwin, Percy, 287
Kettlewell, William, 190, 191, 218
Killey, James, 127
Kingston, 42, 72, 91, 92, 148–49, 152–56, 158, 269
Kyle, William, 180

Labatt, G.T., 205–6
lager. *See* beer and wine
Lambton County, 98–99, 160(f)

Index

Lanark County, 70, 72, 88, 160(f), 363*n*4
land. *See* property and liberalism
Langevin, Hector, 147
Lauder, Abraham, 28–29, 32, 61
Laurier, Wilfrid (Liberal Prime Minister, 1896–1911): archives, 360*n*132; credibility of government, 215, 358*n*69; disinterested liquor management, 231–32; election (1896), 211; liberal values, 230–31; liquor question, 215, 233; plebiscite on prohibition (1898), 211–15, 222–24, 222(t), 229–31, 315; refusal of prohibition bill, 223–24, 229–31, 233. *See also* liquor interests, disinterested management systems; plebiscite, dominion prohibition (1898)
Leader (Toronto newspaper), 61, 63, 128, 337*n*11
Leeds County, 91, 160(f)
legal system: committee questionnaire (1873), 35–39, 322–23; due process, 263; equality as liberal ideal, 10; Garrow Resolution and equity in law, 263–64, 268, 317, 365*n*43; ideal of objective enforcement, 103, 106–8; liberal rationality, 10. *See also* liberalism and the state; rationality as liberal ideal
Leitch, James, 111–12, 268
Lennox County, 32, 82, 90, 103–6, 109, 160(f), 269, 342*n*38
Liberal Party, Canada. *See* Laurier, Wilfrid (Liberal Prime Minister, 1896–1911); Mackenzie, Alexander (Liberal Prime Minister, 1873–78)
Liberal Party, Ontario: liquor question, 317–18; patronage, 131–32, 136, 139–40, 307–8; political spectrum, 26. *See also* Hardy, Arthur Sturgis (Liberal Premier of Ontario, 1896–99); Mowat, Oliver (Liberal Premier of Ontario, 1872–96); Ross, George William (Liberal Premier of Ontario, 1899–1905)
Liberal Temperance Union (LTU), 202
liberalism and the state: about, 3–4, 7–12, 67, 196, 233, 311–13, 316–19; administrative systems, 67–68; American influences, 13; Britishness, 13, 227–28; classical vs radical, 10; and collectivism, 10–11, 233, 313, 315, 316, 318–19; common good, 318–19; freedom of the market, 128; Garrow Resolution and equity under law, 263–64, 268, 317, 365*n*43; harm principle, 201, 203, 318–19; ideal official, 65; impact of jurisdictional uncertainties, 157; individual choice, 3, 7, 9, 57, 128, 210, 318–19, 373*n*21; liquor question, 3–4, 195–96, 317–19; local autonomy, 311–12; McKay's liberal order, 8–11; J.S. Mill on, 7–8, 10, 12, 201, 226–27, 313, 319; orderly society, 11, 242, 312–13; parliamentary commissions, 194; patronage networks, 66–71, 263; plebiscites, 194; provincial plebiscite on prohibition (1894), 194–96, 315; rationality, 10, 317; scholarship on, 8–14; self-government, 10–11; standardization of governance, 312, 317; tensions within, 316–17; voluntary organizations, 313. *See also* equality and liberalism; freedom, liberty, and liberalism; property and liberalism; rationality as liberal ideal
liberty. *See* freedom, liberty, and liberalism; liberalism and the state
License Amendment Act (1873). *See* Tavern and Shop License Act, administration
License Amendment Act (1897): about, 236–40; closing times, 236, 237, 238, 239–40; deputations on, 236–38; drinking age, 236, 237, 239; as Harcourt's amendment, 236–37, 243; liberal state, 238; liquor industry forces, 237–39; local options, 237, 239; medicinal alcohol, 236; Mowat's support, 239; newspapers on, 237–38, 239–40; petitions on licenses, 236, 237, 239; population-based licenses, 236, 237–38; saloons, 236, 237, 238; temperance forces, 236–40
License Amendment Act (1906). *See* Liquor License Amendment Act (1906)
License Branch: about, 15–16, 64–65, 81–82, 317; balance of interests, 65–68, 96–98, 105–9; establishment of, 64–65;

evaluation (1877–80), 82–83, 87–95; fair application of law, 106–9; guidelines for officers, 82; ideal system, 65, 96; investigations of municipalities (1873–74), 40–45, 54, 68; liberal state, 97, 317; local/central power shifts, 54–55, 59–62, 96–97, 105–9, 112–13, 139–40; local/central relationships, 64–65, 81–82; non-partisan civil service, 317; records, xii, 82, 97, 317; shift to centralized system (1915), 305, 306–8, 326; veto over commissioners' decisions, 292–93

License Branch, secretaries and treasurers, 15–16, 64–65, 98, 108. *See also* Hanna, William; Hardy, Arthur Sturgis; Totten, Henry; Wood, S.C.

license commissioners. *See* Crooks Act, boards of commissioners; McCarthy Act, boards of commissioners

Licensed Victuallers Association of Ontario: about, 51–54, 335*n*23; amendment act (1906), 277–78; vs Crooks Act, 57–58, 85–86, 92; deputations to Mowat (1873–74), 51–54, 57–58, 60; liberal state, 53, 57–58, 228; members, 51, 53, 335*n*23; moderation, 53; property rights, 58; vs Scott Act, 129. *See also* liquor industry

licensed victuallers' associations: about, 51–55; Licensed Grocers' Association (Toronto), 179; Ontario Trades Benevolent Association, 101, 133–35, 152. *See also* Licensed Victuallers Association of Ontario; liquor industry; Wets

light beverages. *See* beer and wine

Lincoln County, 71, 74, 98, 160(f), 173

Liquor Act (1902): delegations on, 250; disinterested liquor management, 249–52; newspapers on, 247–48, 250–54; parliamentary debates, 247–48, 249; Whitney's view, 258. *See also* liquor interests, disinterested management systems; referendum, Ontario (1902)

liquor and alcoholic beverages: adulterated drinks, 32, 87, 209, 250, 332*n*35; Canada as temperate society, 203; consumption (1867–1914), 310–11, 310(f), 371*n*1; medicinal alcohol, 50, 236. *See also* beer and wine; breweries; liquor industry

liquor and state regulation: about, 4, 8–14; cultures of drink, 15, 309–10; liberal legality and constitutionality, 10, 156–57; liberal order framework, 8–14, 312–13; local vs central control, 11, 60–62; J.S. Mill on, 7–8; public support, 90–91, 105, 222, 316–17. *See also* Canada, dominion governments; Judicial Committee of the Privy Council (JCPC); liberalism and the state; municipal governments; provincial governments; Supreme Court of Canada (SCC)

liquor industry: about, 310–11, 310(f), 371*n*1; vs agitators, 128–29; bipartisan support, 315–16; committee questionnaire (1873), 35–36, 39, 323–24; compensation for losses under prohibition, 128–29, 162, 204, 212, 220, 313; Conservatives, 78; distribution systems, 231; early years, 24; economic benefits, 209; vs extremism, 128–29; government revenues, 29; in Great War, 15, 306–8, 314; for grocers' licenses, 178–79; impact of jurisdictional uncertainties, 157; as inspectors, 75; liberal state, 196; liberal values, 242, 313; lobbying, 51–55; manufacturing (1867–1914), 310–11, 310(f); manufacturing (1873–90), 205–7, 206(f); private clubs (unlicensed), 237, 239, 302, 303; production increase (1867–1914), 371*n*1; provincial licensing, 4; RCLT reports, 209–10; revenues in dry communities, 198; Scott Act impacts, 159–60, 198; taverns, 24; terminology, xiii. *See also* beer and wine; breweries; licensed victuallers' associations; liquor and alcoholic beverages; liquor and state regulation; Wets

liquor interests, disinterested management systems: about, 231–33, 249–54; British public house trust, 251–52, 254, 289–90, 297–98, 371*n*53; dispensary system, 231–32, 249–50, 291; Gothenburg system, 231–32, 249–54, 289–90, 296–97;

government ownership, 250–51, 253–54; Grant's non-profit joint-stock company, 252–53; Hanna's support for, 296–98; liberal state, 250–51; newspapers on, 250–54; Starr Commission review, 289–91; taxation, 249, 253

Liquor License Act (1876). *See* Crooks Act (1876–1915)

Liquor License Act (1915): provisions, 15, 305–6, 326; replaced by Ontario Temperance Act (1916), 306, 326

Liquor License Amendment Act (1906): about, 272–84; bartenders' licenses, 272, 276, 303, 304; corruption, 283–85; enforcement, 280, 282; fees and fines, 276–77, 283; hotels, 274, 277–80, 282–84, 292–93; hours, 272; newspapers on, 273; ships and trains, 272, 274, 276; tavern license fees (1886–1906), 272–74, 273(t), 277, 283; temperance hotels, 277–80; tied houses, 272, 273, 276, 282–86, 288–89, 293; Whitney's moderate approach, 272–75. *See also* Crooks Act (1876–1915)

Liquor License Amendment Act (1906), local option: about, 272–73, 280–84; commercial travellers, 277–80; hotels, 278–80; increases (1904–14), 281–82, 282(f), 282(t); petitions, 273, 275; temperance hotels, 278–80; three-fifths majority, 273–76, 280–81; vote timing, 273–74, 276. *See also* Crooks Act, local option; Crooks Act, local option under 1906 amendment

Lloyd George, David, 306, 371*n*53

local option: about, 16, 25–26, 159, 311; arguments against, 50; enforcement, 207–9, 222; historical background, 25–26; liberal state, 170–71; Marter's bill on retail sales (1893), 188–95, 234, 360*n*1; McCarthy Act, 138–40; under Mowat, 311; municipal elections, 16, 325; pre-prohibition (1916), 306–8; private clubs (unlicensed), 237, 239, 302, 303; public support, 90–91, 169–71, 185, 215, 222, 316–17; RCLT review, 198–201, 204–9, 206(f); Scott Act (1882, 1890), 159, 170–71, 186–88;

temperance hotels, 86–87, 278–80; under Whitney, 311. *See also* Crooks Act, local option; Dunkin Act, local option; Liquor License Amendment Act (1906), local option; Scott Act, local option

lodging. *See* hotels and lodging

London: closing times, 238; commercial travellers, 277–80; detectives, 100–1; dominion plebiscite (1898), 216, 220, 226; Dunkin Act, 121; enforcement, 85, 207–8; first settler, 21, 330*n*2; grocers' licenses, 174; jurisdictional uncertainties (1883–85), 152; license inspectors, 68–70, 72; liquor on fairgrounds, 152; newspapers, 100–1, 216, 217; patronage, 68–70, 72; police, 85; RCLT review, 199–200; report by inspectors (1874), 68; shops, 42–43; taverns, 21; temperance hotels, 87; temperance movement, 121, 241, 273

London Advertiser, 100–1, 273

London Free Press, 216–17, 226, 237, 238–39, 241, 242, 280

Macdonald, Hugh John (Conservative Premier of Manitoba, 1900), 244

Macdonald, John A. (Conservative Prime Minister, 1867–73, 1878–91): about, 16; archives, 360*n*132; centralist, 131; vs Crooks Act, 131–32; death (1891), 210–11; dominion-provincial relations, 16; elections (1882, 1891), 127, 143, 210–11; jurisdictional uncertainties (1883–85), 141, 150–51, 156–57, 516–17; liberal state, 127–28, 156–57; liquor industry forces, 24, 126–28, 158–59; liquor question, 125–27, 140, 170–71, 233, 317–18; Mowat's relationship with, 26, 131–32, 136, 143, 146–47, 155; parliamentary process, 165–68; partisanism, 158; patronage, 131–32, 136, 138, 139; RCLT establishment, 170, 189, 198, 211; *Russell*, 142–43, 318; Scott Act, 125–28, 130–31, 156, 158–59, 162–63, 168–69; temperance forces, 127, 162–64. *See also* McCarthy Act (1883–85); Scott Act (1878–1984)

Macdonald, John Sandfield (Premier of Ontario, 1867–71), 23, 24, 26–27. *See also* Tavern and Shop License Act (1868)
Macdonald, Robert, 10
Macdonald, Thomas, 161
MacDougall, George, 61, 336*n*54
Mackenzie, Alexander (Liberal Prime Minister, 1873–78): election loss (1878), 125; local option system, 16; Scott Act (1878), 16, 123, 125. *See also* Scott Act (1878–1984)
Maclaren, J.J., 190, 213, 222
Macpherson, Thomas, 226
Mail and Empire (Toronto newspaper), 279
Maine, partial prohibition, 243–44
maltsters. *See* breweries
Manitoba: dominion plebiscite (1898), 221–22, 222(t); Dunkin Act proponents, 123; jurisdictional uncertainties (1883–85), 146, 148; McCarthy Act opponents, 146, 148; prohibition act (1900), 244; referendums on prohibition, 244; temperance advocates, 123
manufacturing of liquor. *See* liquor industry
Maritimes. *See* Atlantic provinces
Marter, George F., 188–95, 234, 360*n*1
Marter's bill on retail sales (1893), 188–95, 234, 360*n*1
Martin, William, 40, 42, 43
McAllister, Bernard, 261
McCall, Simpson, 47, 60
McCarthy, D'Alton, 133, 154–55, 164, 326(t)
McCarthy Act (1883–85): about, 132–40, 136(t)–137(t), 156–58, 314, 326; amendments (1884), 147, 154–55, 348*n*19; application to provinces, 137n; cartoons, 143, 144(f); constitutionality, 135, 140–41, 143, 144(f), 156–57; Crooks Act comparison, 134–38, 136(t)–137(t), 326; debates, 139, 147; declared ultra vires (1885), 143, 326; draft bill, 133, 135–39, 347*nn*71–72; *Hodge* (1883), 141–48, 144(f), 150, 175; impact on Crooks Act, 156–57, 173–74, 186; jurisdictional uncertainties (1883–85), 141, 143–46, 148–58; liberal state, 157; licensing system, 135, 136(t)–137(t), 326; liquor industry, 133, 158; local option, 138–40, 156; McCarthy's committee, 101, 132–35, 152, 173; newspapers on, 143–47, 144(f); partisanism, 150, 158; patronage, 133, 136, 138, 139–40; temperance forces, 156; years in operation (1883–85), 326. *See also* BNA Act, jurisdictional uncertainties (1883–85)
McCarthy Act, administration of licensing system: about, 135–40, 136(t)–137(t); amendment suspending penal clauses, 154–55; character of potential licensees, 135; closing times, 133, 136; enforcement, 135, 137(t), 154–55; fees and fines, 136, 137(t), 137n, 143–46, 148, 151–57, 158; inspectors, 135–38, 136(t)–137(t), 326; jurisdictional uncertainties (1883–85), 141, 143–46, 148–58; local option, 135, 136, 137(t), 138–39, 156; local/central power shifts, 139–40, 156–57; petitions for/against licenses, 136–39, 137(t); population-based licenses, 134–35, 138, 153, 326; public approval requirements, 137(t), 138; public notices, 136, 137(t), 173; reasons to reject licenses, 136; regional variation, 137n, 138; shops, 134–35, 137(t), 138; transparency, 133, 137(t), 173
McCarthy Act, boards of commissioners: about, 135–36, 136(t)–137(t); Crooks Act comparison, 135–36, 136(t)–137(t), 315, 326; jurisdictional uncertainties (1883–85), 141, 143–46, 149–50, 156–57; members, 135–36, 136(t)–137(t), 138, 143–46, 149–50, 173, 326; transparency, 133, 137(t), 173
McCarthy Act, hotels, taverns, and saloons: about, 136(t)–137(t); jurisdictional uncertainties (1883–85), 141, 150–51, 153, 156–57; lodgings, 135, 137(t), 148, 153; petitions from voters, 136–39, 137(t); public notices, 136, 173; summer licenses, 83, 134, 138
McDonald, Herbert S., 198, 201, 204, 331*n*21

McDonald, Robert, 313
McGuire, C.W., 279–80, 367n99
McKay, Angus, 72, 354n50
McKay, Ian, 8–11
McKay, William, 105, 191, 246–47, 253
McKendry, John, 190, 354n62
McLeod, Joseph, 198, 200–4, 209–11
McMillan, Donald, 166–67
McMullen, James, 223
media. *See* newspapers and journals
medical care. *See* health care and alcohol
Meredith, William, 150, 153–54, 187
Methodists, 26, 214, 218, 230, 239–40, 254, 268, 280, 299
Michie, George S., 181–82
Middlesex County, 71, 94, 160(f), 199, 302–3
Mill, John Stuart: about, 7–8; collective identity, 10, 313; freedom of choice, 7–8, 319; harm principle, 201, 227; public policy following public opinion, 12; on religious extremism, 7–8; state role, 7–8, 226
Millichamp, Reuben, 287–89, 292, 368n123
ministers. *See* Christians
moderates: about, xiii, 127–28, 314–15; beer and wine, 162, 310–11, 310(f), 371n1; bipartisan support, 315–16; as commissioners, 74–75; Crooks Act, 172; disinterested liquor management, 249–56; vs extremism, 127–28; as inspectors, 74–75; liberal value of fairness and justice, 180–81; liberal values, 233, 314–15; liquor industry forces, 51–54; political spectrum, 26; protection of freedom, 127–28; RCLT testimony, 202–4; Scott Act, 127–28, 162; G. Smith's views, 202–4, 208, 210, 332n35, 356n21; in temperance movement, 25; terminology, xiii; Whitney's views, 272–75, 295–96. *See also* Drys; liberalism and the state; liquor interests, disinterested management systems; Wets
Monetary Times, 221, 224
Montgomery's Tavern, 21

Montreal: dominion plebiscite (1898), 213, 218, 223, 225, 226, 231; drunkenness, 178; licenses, 60, 149, 277. *See also* Quebec
Morin, James, 98, 173
Mortimer, Cecil, 77, 338n60
Mowat, Oliver (Liberal Premier of Ontario, 1872–96): about, 26–27; appointment as Senator, 234; cartoons, 143, 144(f); credibility of government, 241; debates, 27–30; election (1872, 1875, 1883), 49, 66, 140; election (1891, 1894), 186–88, 241; *Hodge* (1883), 142, 175; liberal state, 45, 46, 194, 196; liquor industry forces, 51–54, 55; liquor issue's importance, 140, 187, 191–92, 195–96; liquor question, 26, 67, 112–13, 140, 187–88, 195–96, 317–18; J.A. Macdonald's relationship with, 26, 131–32, 136, 143, 146–47, 155; party loyalty, 241; resignation (1896), 234; temperance forces, 26–27, 34–40, 185–88, 235; views on partisanism, 98, 341n3. *See also* Crooks Act (1876–1915); Tavern and Shop License Act, committee review (1873–74)
Mowat, Oliver, government: about, 15–16, 26–27, 313–14; balance of interests, 65–68, 75–76, 96–98, 112–13, 312, 341n3; clientelism, 65–68, 103–5; constitutional issues (1890s), 187–88, 191; inebriate asylum, 26–30, 39, 45, 323; jurisdictional uncertainties (1883–85), 141–43, 146–47, 156–57; License Branch's investigations of municipalities (1873–74), 40–45, 54, 68; liquor industry forces, 57–58, 60; liquor industry revenue, 29; local option, 186–88; Marter's bill on retail sales (1893), 188–95, 234, 360n1; partisanism, 313–14, 372n9; patronage, 33, 60–71, 96–97, 131–32, 136, 138, 139–40, 158, 185, 257, 258, 291, 339n75; petitions on liquor laws, 26–27; promises of prohibition, 191–92, 195–96, 234–35, 241; provincial plebiscite on prohibition (1894), 193–96, 215, 315; provincial

powers over prohibition, 191–92; *Russell*, 142–43. *See also* Crooks Act (1876–1915)
Mulholland, Arthur, 200
Municipal Act: council members as license officers, 145, 149–50; local option, 186–87; tavern owners as council members, 54
municipal governments: about, 4–5, 15, 45, 64–65, 311; balance of interests, 76; at Confederation, 15; corruption, 22; enforcement, 22, 85; *Hodge* (1883), 175; impact of Crooks Act, 15–16; liberal state, 10–11, 22; License Branch's investigations (1873-74), 40–45, 54, 68; licensing authority, 22–23; liquor industry forces, 24; liquor question, 3–4; local autonomy, 23, 311–12; local option, 25–26, 186–88; local order, 312–13; local/central power shifts under Crooks Act, 92, 96–97, 105–9, 311; population-based licenses, 22, 24, 92; property protection, 10–11; provincial powers under BNA Act, 5, 23, 175, 187; revenues, 24, 92, 366n68, 366n88
municipal governments, local option. *See* Crooks Act, local option; Dunkin Act, local option; Liquor License Amendment Act (1906), local option; local option; Scott Act, local option
municipal governments, pre-Confederation: about, 14–15, 22–23; jurisdictional precedents, 187; laws, 5, 14, 21–23; liberal ideals, 22–23; licensing authority, 5, 14, 22–24; local option, 16, 25–26; political culture, 14; power shift to provincial and dominion government, 15; provincial powers, 22; Tavern and Shop License Act (1868), 23; taverns, 21–23. *See also* Dunkin Act, local option

Neelon, Sylvester, 71
Nesbitt, Beattie, 258, 259(f), 284–86, 289, 292
New Brunswick: dominion plebiscite (1898), 220, 221–22, 222(t); *Fredericton* (1880), 129–31; jurisdictional uncertainties (1883–85), 148; local option, 129–31, 350n4; McCarthy Act opponents, 148; petitions on license applications, 138; Scott Act, 129–31, 148, 159, 350n4
New Party, 187, 354n46
newspapers and journals: cartoons, 78–81, 79(f), 143, 144(f), 258–61, 259(f), 260(f); pre-Confederation newspapers, 14; satire (J. Briggs), 62–63, 65, 66; in taverns, 21, 24, 32, 63. *See also specific publications*
Nicholls, James, 12, 13
Noel, S.J.R., 65–67, 98, 132, 341n3, 356n21, 372n9
Norfolk County, 160(f)
Norquay, John (Premier of Manitoba, 1878–87), 146–47
Northern Advance (newspaper), 100, 231
Northern Messenger (newspaper), 225, 227–28
Northumberland County, 76, 78, 83, 92, 119, 160(f), 168–69, 338n60
Norton, W.E., 214–15
Norway, Gothenburg system, 249, 252–54
Nova Scotia: Crooks Act support, 148–49; dominion plebiscite (1898), 221–22, 222(t); jurisdictional uncertainties (1883–85), 148–49; McCarthy Act opponents, 148; petitions on license applications, 134, 138; Scott Act, 159, 350n4

O'Donoghue, D.J., 70, 76, 338n56
O'Keefe, Eugene: dominion plebiscite (1898), 217; jurisdictional uncertainties (1883–85), 141, 143, 148, 151; letters to/from J.A. Macdonald, 24, 125, 128, 141, 143, 168–69, 240; Licensed Victuallers Association lobbying, 51–52; on McCarthy Act, 140, 141; Scott Act, 125–29, 161, 168–69
Oliver, Joseph, 292
On Liberty. See Mill, John Stuart
Ontario: dominion plebiscite (1898), 221–22, 222(t); liquor question, 3–4;

map of Scott Act implementation, 160(f); population, 283, 341*n*11; pre-Confederation, 22–24. *See also* liberalism and the state; provincial governments; Toronto
Ontario, liquor laws: overview of provisions, 325–26. *See also* Crooks Act (1876–1915); Dunkin Act (1864); Liquor License Act (1915); McCarthy Act (1883–85); Ontario Temperance Act (1916); Scott Act (1878–1984); Tavern and Shop License Act (1868)
Ontario, premiers. *See* Hardy, Arthur Sturgis (Liberal Premier of Ontario, 1896–99); Macdonald, John Sandfield (Premier of Ontario, 1867–71); Mowat, Oliver (Liberal Premier of Ontario, 1872–96); Ross, George William (Liberal Premier of Ontario, 1899–1905); Whitney, James (Conservative Premier of Ontario, 1905–14)
Ontario County, 94, 160(f), 184
Ontario Temperance Act (1916): about, 5–6, 15, 306–8, 326; cultures of drink, 15, 309–10; Great War, 15, 306–8, 314; as illiberal solution, 315; post-prohibition period, 5, 348*n*23, 372*n*16; pre-prohibition period, 295–97, 305–8; provincial regimes, 371*n*57, 372*n*13; provisions, 306–7, 326; as wartime measure, 15, 305–6, 372*n*13
Ontario Trades Benevolent Association, 101, 133–35, 152. *See also* licensed victuallers' associations
Orangeville, 174
Orchard, John, 98, 173
orderly society and liberalism, 7–14, 242, 312–13. *See also* rationality as liberal ideal
O'Reilly, John, 70
Orton, George, 159
Ottawa: commissioners, 76, 150, 338*n*56; inspectors, 70, 85, 363*n*4
Ottawa Citizen, 219–20, 240, 247–48, 253, 269, 276–77
Ottawa Journal, 193–94, 216, 218–19, 228–29, 237–38, 242, 255
Ouimet, Joseph, 147

Owen Sound, 120, 199, 200–1, 205, 208
Oxford County, 71, 75, 160(f), 300

Palmer, R.C., 99–100, 101
Pardee, Timothy B., 69, 331*n*22, 338*n*60
patronage, partisanism, and clientelism: about, 60–71, 312–14, 336*n*4; centralization of liquor licensing, 59–63; clientelism, 65–68, 103–5, 336*n*4; Crooks Act, 68–73, 92, 96–97, 103–5, 136, 158, 313–14; Garrow Resolution, 263–64, 268, 317, 365*n*43; under J.A. Macdonald, 131–32, 136; McCarthy Act, 138, 158; under Mowat, 60–71, 131–32, 136, 291, 313–14, 333*n*65, 339*n*75; partisanism under Mowat, 98, 133–34, 150–51, 158, 264–71, 313–14, 341*n*3, 343*n*3; partisanism under Whitney, 258, 261–71, 286, 365*n*46; patronage, 69–72, 336*n*4; vs professionalism, 261, 263–64, 291–92; Starr Commission, 287–89, 291–92; temperance hotels, 87; under Whitney, 257–71, 259(f), 260(f), 287–88, 291–93. *See also* Crooks Act, administration of licensing system
Patrons of Industry, 185
Patteson, Thomas, 48, 57, 69–70, 78
Pearce, Charles, 208
Peel County, 147, 160(f), 270
Perth County, 94, 160(f)
Peterborough County, 85, 94, 101–2, 160(f), 207
Peters, Robert, 40, 43
Petrolia, 42, 98–99, 341*nn*10–11
Pettit, C.V., 70–71
physicians and pharmacists. *See* health care and alcohol
Pizer v. Fraser et al., 110–13, 343*n*58, 343*n*60
plebiscites: collective will, 315; critiques of, 249; liberal state, 194, 220, 244, 249, 315; as political strategy, 211, 315; vs representative democracy, 194, 249, 315. *See also* referendums
plebiscite, dominion prohibition (1898): about, 197, 210–24, 222(t), 233, 315; appeal to Britishness, 227–28; delegations to Laurier, 212–13;

economic damage of prohibition, 212, 217–18, 220; election results, 221–24, 222(t); Laurier's refusal of prohibition bill, 222–24, 229–31, 233; liberal state, 218–20, 224–31; majority of electors vs votes, 212–14, 221–24, 315; newspapers on, 215–17, 221, 223–31, 252; political strategies, 211–12, 215–17, 223–24, 229–31; public interest in, 220–21; tax question proposal, 217–20; voters, 214–15, 219, 241; wording of question, 212–13, 220

plebiscites, Ontario: grocers' licenses (Toronto), 177–78; Marter's bill on retail sales (1893), 188–95, 234, 360*n*1; plebiscite on prohibition (1894), 193–96, 215, 315

political parties, Ontario: about, 26; Garrow Resolution, 263–64, 268, 317, 365*n*43; New Party, 187, 354*n*46; party loyalty, 240–41; Patrons of Industry, 185. *See also* Conservative Party, Ontario; Liberal Party, Ontario; patronage, partisanism, and clientelism; Reform Party, Ontario

Power, Lawrence, 166–67

power relations: impact of jurisdictional uncertainties, 156–57; inspectors and communities, 258; local/central power shifts, 54–55, 59–62, 68, 96–97, 105–9, 139–40, 156–57, 311; power-knowledge nexus, 40

pre-Confederation municipalities. *See* municipal governments, pre-Confederation

Presbyterians, 120–21, 216–17, 240, 245, 250, 276

press. *See* newspapers and journals

Preston, T.H., 108–9

Prettie, Regina v. (1877), 122, 344*n*20

priests. *See* Christians

Prince Edward County, 73–74, 87, 89–90, 123, 160(f), 345*n*27

Prince Edward Island: dominion plebiscite (1898), 221–22, 222(t); liberal ideals of property and liberty, 9–10; petitions on license applications, 138; prohibition (1901), 372*n*13; Scott Act,

138, 159, 190–91, 350*n*4, 355*n*68

private clubs (unlicensed), 237, 239, 302, 303

problematic drinking. *See* drunkenness

prohibition: about, 5–7, 40, 186–87, 209–10, 312–13; bipartisan support, 315–16; Clarke's bill (1873), 29–30; constitutionality of provincial bills, 30; cultures of drink, 15, 309–10; license act committee's bias (1873–74), 34–40; liquor question, 3–6; local option, 186–87; Maine experiment, 243–44; Marter's bill on retail sales (1893), 188–95, 234, 360*n*1; partial prohibition, 164, 190, 243–45; provincial plebiscite (1894), 193–96, 215, 315; public readiness for, 49, 169–70, 196, 231, 274; RCLT mandate, 170, 209–11; Rowell's banish-the-bar pledge, 300–3; sales vs manufacture, 188–89; terminology, xiii. *See also* Royal Commission on the Liquor Traffic (RCLT) (1892–95)

prohibition alternatives. *See* liquor interests, disinterested management systems

prohibition laws. *See* Crooks Act, local option; Dunkin Act, local option; Liquor License Amendment Act (1906), local option; local option; Ontario Temperance Act (1916); Scott Act, local option

prohibition opponents. *See* breweries; liquor industry; moderates; Wets

prohibition plebiscites. *See* plebiscite, dominion prohibition (1898); plebiscites, Ontario

prohibition supporters. *See* Drys; moderates; temperance movement

property and liberalism: about, 3–4, 7, 9–10, 131, 204, 233, 313; colonial lands, 9–10; compensation for losses under prohibition, 128–29, 162, 204, 212, 220, 313; freedom and liberty, 7, 9–10, 131; grocers' licenses, 175, 182–83; jurisdictional uncertainties, 131, 157; liquor licenses, 57–58; liquor question, 3–4, 7, 131, 313; local option, 170–71; modern liberty, 9–10; state role, 7, 10.

See also BNA Act, property and civil rights powers of provinces, s. 92(13); freedom, liberty, and liberalism; liberalism and the state

Proudfoot, William, 303, 305, 371*n*50

provincial governments: at Confederation, 15, 22; liquor question, 3–4, 317–19; local order, 312–13; Marter's bill on retail sales (1893), 188–95, 234, 360*n*1; overlapping powers with dominion government, 4; power over municipal governments, 10–11; power to pass prohibitory bylaws, 188; pre-Confederation, 22; prohibition status (1917), 306–7; reassertion of rights during jurisdictional uncertainties (1883–85), 148–49, 156–57, 314. *See also* BNA Act, licensing powers of provinces, s. 92(9); *and specific provinces*

Purvis, W.L., 284, 292

Pyne, Robert, 289, 292

Quebec: anti-prohibition, 212, 223–24, 228–30; dominion plebiscite (1898), 212, 213, 218, 221–24, 222(t), 223, 225, 226, 228–30, 231; drunkenness, 178; Dunkin Act, 26, 325, 330*n*17; jurisdictional uncertainties (1883–85), 147, 149; Laurier's refusal of prohibition bill, 223–24, 229–31; liberal ideals of property and liberty, 9–10; licenses, 60, 149, 277; local option, 212, 223, 306, 330*n*17; McCarthy Act opposition, 147, 149; nationalism, 228–29; prohibition, 306, 371*n*57; Scott Act, 166; seigneurial system, 9–10, 315, 328*n*20; shops, 32; temperance movement, 223, 228–29. *See also* Montreal

questionnaires on license act, 34–40, 35(t), 321–24. *See also* Tavern and Shop License Act, committee review (1873–74)

railways and ships, 186, 272, 274, 276, 324

rationality as liberal ideal: about, 10–12, 233, 312–13; drunkenness as threat, 8, 11–12, 242, 312–13; Drys as threat, 7–8, 12, 312–13; vs extremism, 12, 128–29; groggeries as threat, 127; ideal actor, 8, 11; legal system, 10; liberal order framework, 8–14; McKay's liberal order, 8–11; J.S. Mill on, 8; objective enforcement, 103; orderly society, 7–14, 242, 312–13; rational actors, 8, 11–12, 312–13; rational processes, 317; vs religious extremism, 7–8. *See also* liberalism and the state

RCLT. *See* Royal Commission on the Liquor Traffic (RCLT) (1892–95)

Reaume, J.O., 258, 260(f)

referendums: critiques of, 244–45, 249; Manitoba (1902), 244; as political strategy, 211, 245, 249. *See also* plebiscites

referendum, Ontario (1902): about, 244–48, 255; democratic validity, 244–45, 249; disinterested liquor management, 249–54; newspapers on, 250–54; Ross on majority vote, 272

Reform Party, Ontario: about, 26; appointments under Crooks Act, 98; asylum bill, 29; license cancellations under Crooks Act, 78–79, 79(f), 80(t); newspapers, 156; temperance cause, 26, 73

Regina v. Prettie (1877), 122, 344*n*20

religion. *See* Christians

Renfrew County, 160(f)

Richardson, Charles, 251

Richardson, P.L., 218

Richardson, William, 200–1

Roberts, Julia, 21, 330*n*3

Robertson, J.A., 222–23

Robinson, C. Blackett, 120–21

Roblin, Rodmond, 244

Roman Catholics, 72, 76, 81, 232

Ross, George William (Liberal Premier of Ontario, 1899–1905): about, 243–48, 255–56, 307; elections (1902, 1905), 245–48, 255–56; Liquor Act (1902), 247–49; liquor question, 317–18; newspapers on, 247–48; partial prohibition, 243–45; patronage, 258–61, 259(f), 260(f), 266, 287–88, 291; plebiscite on prohibition (1894), 192–95, 315; promises of prohibition, 234–35, 243–44, 255, 307; referendum (1902),

244–49, 274, 362n39; scandals, 255, 294; temperance forces, 243–44, 255–56
Ross, J.P., 255
Ross, J.S., 219
Rowell, Newton, 263n80, 299–303
Royal Commission on the Liquor Traffic (RCLT) (1892–95): about, 170, 197–211; beer and wine, 199, 201, 202–3; criminality, 207–9; Crooks Act review, 198–201, 207, 209–10; Dunkin Act review, 200–1, 205, 207–8; economic damage of prohibition, 39, 211, 212, 218; liberal state, 194, 200–4, 209–10, 233; licensing vs local option, 198–201, 204–9, 206(f), 215; liquor sales increases, 205–7, 206(f), 209; Maine's partial prohibition, 243–44; mandate and procedures, 170, 198; manufacturing and licenses (1873–90), 205–7, 206(f); members, 198, 200, 209–11; as political strategy, 189, 194, 198; reports, 209–11; Scott Act review, 198–200, 202–10, 206(f), 350n4; G. Smith's views, 202–4, 208, 210, 332n35, 356n21; temperance hotels, 278; temperance members, 200, 209, 211; treating, 201
Royal Templars, 189, 190, 218–19, 246
Rudy, Jarret, 11–12
Russell County, 84–85, 160(f)
Russell v. The Queen (1882), 130–32, 142–43, 159, 318
Ryan, Peter, 174–75
Rykert, John C., 29, 30, 33

saloons. *See* Crooks Act, taverns; McCarthy Act, hotels, taverns, and saloons; taverns
Saskatchewan: centralized license commission, 298; dominion plebiscite (1898), 221–22, 222(t)
satire. *See* newspapers and journals
Saunders, Eudo, 200, 298–300, 317, 356n13, 364n31, 369n14
Saunders, W.E., 220
Saywell, John, 4, 125, 130, 131, 195, 327n3
Scott, Richard, 16, 123–24, 166
Scott Act (1878–1984): about, 16, 158–59, 170–71, 326; Atlantic provinces, 159, 355n68; beer and wine, 145, 162, 167–70; constitutionality, 124–25, 129–31, 145, 159; debates, 123–26; economic and personal impacts, 159–62; flaws, 159–61, 171, 184–85, 198–99, 203–7, 233, 245; *Fredericton* (1880), 129–31; implementation, 159–61, 160(f), 169, 171, 184–86, 205–7, 206(f); liberal state, 127, 128, 129, 162, 170–71, 200, 203; liquor industry forces, 125–29, 159–61, 168–69; manufacturing and licenses (1873–90), 205–7, 206(f); moderate advocates, 126, 127–28, 162, 167–68; newspapers on, 167–68; as partial prohibition, 164, 243, 245; as political strategy, 124; RCLT review, 170, 198–200, 202–10, 206(f), 350n4; regional variations, 184–85; replacement for Dunkin Act, 16, 123–24; *Russell* (1880), 130–31, 159; temperance forces, 123–27, 156, 159, 162–64, 167–69, 185–86. *See also* Macdonald, John A. (Conservative Prime Minister, 1867–73, 1878–91)
Scott Act, amendments (1878–92): about, 163–71; Almon's bills (1881, 1885), 126–27, 167–69; amendment bills (1879–81), 125–27; amendment bills (1885–87), 162–69; amendments (1888–92), 169–70; beer and wine, 166–70; Bourbeau's bill, 166–67; Jamieson's bill, 164–66, 169–70, 351nn21–22; McCarthy's bill, 164, 169; parliamentary process, 165–68
Scott Act, local option: about, 16, 159–61, 160(f), 170–71, 326; boards of commissioners, 184–85; city or county level, 159, 326; criminality, 207–9; distribution of liquor, 164, 207, 231; elections, 126, 162–63, 164, 169–70; enforcement, 184–85, 198, 200, 203, 207–9; fines as fees, 198; implementation, 159–61, 160(f), 169, 171, 184–86, 205–7, 206(f); increased liquor sales, 198, 205–7, 206(f), 209; inspectors, 184–85; liquor industry, 124, 159–62, 198; map, 160(f); medicinal alcohol, 164, 166–67; minimum years in force, 326; partisanship, 158, 184; repeal process, 169–70

Seaton, John, 168
Severn v. The Queen (1878), 118, 125, 130–31
ships and trains, 35–36, 186, 272, 274, 276, 324
shops: detectives, 100–1; *Hodge* (1883), 175; liberal state, 180–83; license act (1868), 23–24, 31–32, 39–40, 42–43, 47–49, 52, 53; License Branch's investigations (1873–74), 42–44; liquor amounts, 31–32, 42–43; liquor industry forces, 51–54; McCarthy Act, 134–35, 137(t), 138; municipal bylaws, 92, 175; secret drinking, 47–48, 172, 176–79, 183; separation of goods and liquor, 39, 92, 134–35, 174, 183–84; temperance forces, 175–78, 182; Toronto, 43–44, 92, 134, 174–83; women, 53, 174–80, 182–83. *See also* Crooks Act, shops; licensed victuallers' associations; Tavern and Shop License Act (1868)
Simcoe County, 72, 74, 76, 82, 160(f), 205
Sleeman, George, 206
Smith, Frank, 51–53, 60, 129, 335nn22–23
Smith, Goldwyn, 202–4, 208, 210, 332n35, 356n21
Smith, James F., 343n60
Smith, William, 40–41, 43
social class, 25, 127, 180, 215, 330n3
Sons of Temperance, 74, 120, 190, 220
South Carolina Dispensary, 231–32, 249–50, 290. *See also* liquor interests, disinterested management systems
Spence, Frank: alliance officer, 175, 188–89, 225–26, 246; amendment act (1906), 276; *Camp Fire* editor, 253–54, 363n80; dominion plebiscite (1898), 217–18, 220, 225–27, 229; on government ownership, 363n80; Marter's bill on retail sales, 188–91; RCLT submission, 357n49
spirits. *See* liquor and alcoholic beverages
St. Catharines, 38, 219, 269
Stafford, Henry, 70, 72
Starr, J.R.L., 285, 289–90, 300
Starr Commission. *See* Toronto, Starr Commission (1907)
state. *See* liberalism and the state
Stedman, Richard, 110

Stevenson, E.J.J., 70, 72
Stormont County, 160(f)
Street, Walter, 213, 226
Striker, Gideon, 73–74
summer licenses, 83, 134, 138
Sunday liquor trade, 133, 136, 199, 201, 270, 272. *See also* closing times
Supreme Court of Canada (SCC): brewers' licensing by dominion, 4, 51, 125, 130–32; division of powers, 4, 118, 125; licensing by dominion, 118; Marter's bill on retail sales (1893), 195, 234, 360n1; McCarthy Act ultra vires (1884), 155; pre-Confederation precedents, 187; Scott Act, 129–31
Supreme Court of Canada, decisions: *Fredericton* (1880), 129–31; *Prettie* (1877), 122, 344n20; *Russell* (1882), 130–32, 142, 159, 318; *Severn* (1878), 118, 125, 130–31
Sweden, Gothenburg system, 249, 252–54, 290

Tait, Joseph, 192
taverns: about, 21–24, 88–89, 330n3; evaluation (1877–80), 88–89; groggeries, 52, 55, 88–89, 127, 129; impact of Crooks Act, 60–61; lodging and stables, 22–23; multipurpose public places, 21, 330n3; municipal licensing authority, 22–23; newspapers, 21, 24, 32, 63; political culture, 24, 60–63; population-based licenses, 22, 24; pre- and post-Confederation, 21–23; temperance hotels, 86–87, 278–80; tied houses, 272, 273, 276, 282–86, 288–89, 293; transportation networks, 21–22. *See also* Crooks Act, taverns; McCarthy Act, hotels, taverns, and saloons; Tavern and Shop License Act (1868)
Tavern and Shop License Act (1868): about, 5, 45, 325; constitutionality, 47, 51; court actions, 50–51; debates, 32–33, 47, 59–60; increase in drunkenness, 25, 33; liberal state, 23, 45, 47–48; liquor industry forces, 47–48, 50–54; liquor question, 33; local option, 186–87; municipal powers, 23, 325; newspapers

on, 47–50; patronage, 24, 33, 42, 333*n*65; public reception, 47–50; replaced pre-Confederation Act, 325; temperance forces, 25, 47–51; years in operation (1869–76), 325. *See also* Tavern and Shop License Act, committee review (1873–74)

Tavern and Shop License Act, administration: about, 23–24, 45, 325; adulterated drinks, 332*n*35; amendment (1869), 23, 24–25, 26; amendments (1873–74), 5, 31–33, 46–54; bylaws on licenses, 24–25, 41–42, 47; closing times, 31, 52–53; enforcement, 23, 31, 41–42, 47–48, 52, 54, 69, 325; fees and fines, 23, 47, 52, 325; inspectors, 24, 31–33, 40–45, 52; License Branch investigations (1873–74), 40–45, 54, 68; local revenue from licenses, 24–25; lodging requirements, 23; municipal licensing authority, 325; provincial inspectors, 40–45; saloons (no lodging), 23, 39–40, 43; shops, 23–24, 31–32, 39–40, 42–43, 47–49, 52, 53; taverns, 23–24; types of drinking spaces, 23–24; unlicensed premises, 52–53. *See also* Tavern and Shop License Act, committee review (1873–74)

Tavern and Shop License Act, committee review (1873–74): about, 27, 33–40, 45–46; mandate, 33–34; prohibitionist bias, 34–40; questionnaires, 34–40, 35(t), 321–24; recommendations, 39–40, 46

taxation: disinterested liquor management, 249, 253; equality as liberal ideal, 218–19; modern liberalism, 10; prohibition's impact, 217

Telegram (Toronto newspaper), xii, 258–61, 259(f), 260(f), 265–66, 270

Temperance Act (1864). *See* Dunkin Act (1864)

Temperance Act (1916). *See* Ontario Temperance Act (1916)

temperance hotels, 86–87, 278–80

temperance movement: about, xiii, 6, 25, 312–13; binary arguments, 6–7, 36–38, 227; criminality, 175; Dunkin Act support, 120; evangelicals, 25, 26; extremism, 7–8, 48, 128–29, 179–80, 241–42, 297–98; vs grocers' licenses, 174–78; historical background, 13, 25; idealism vs pragmatism, 6–7; inebriate asylum, 26–30, 39, 45, 323; liberal state, 179, 181, 182–83, 233; license act committee's bias (1873–74), 34–40; local option laws, 25–26; moderates in, 25; partial prohibition, 164, 243–44; party loyalty, 241, 315–16; retail sales vs total suppression, 188–89; social class, 180, 215; support for licensing regime, 105–7; terminology, xiii; women, 175–80, 235, 353*n*15. *See also* Drys; local option; moderates; plebiscite, dominion prohibition (1898); plebiscites, Ontario; prohibition; temperance societies

temperance societies: about, 120–21; Good Templars, 73, 120, 141, 189–90, 218–19; liberal values, 313; Royal Templars, 189, 190, 218–19, 246; Sons of Temperance, 74, 120, 190, 220; WCTU, 120–21, 123, 229, 235, 241, 254. *See also* Dominion Alliance for the Total Suppression of the Liquor Traffic

The Templar, 189, 218–19

Thomas, William J., 199

Thompson, John, 195, 211

Thompson, Thomas Phillips (Jimuel Briggs), 62–63, 65, 66

Thornley, May, 229, 241–42, 361*n*21

tied houses, 272, 273, 276, 282–86, 288–89, 293

tobacco, 11–12, 16

Tories. *See* Conservative Party, Canada; Conservative Party, Ontario

Toronto: commercial travellers, 277–80; commissioners, 287–88, 291–92; corruption, 284–85; Crooks Act, 88, 174–75, 283–87, 367*n*96; detectives, 102–3; Dunkin Act, 124; enforcement, 43–44, 52, 54, 85, 102–3, 269–70, 334*n*16; hotels, 277–80, 283–85, 288–90, 292–93, 367*nn*96–97; jurisdictional uncertainties (1883–85), 152, 174–75; liberal state, 175; local option failures, 161, 177; partisanship, 43–44, 283–87,

291–92; patronage, 265–66, 268, 271, 287–89, 291–92; petitions, 174–76; plebiscite on grocers' licenses, 177–78; population, 283; secret drinking, 176–79, 183; shops and grocers' licenses, 43–44, 92, 134, 174–83; temperance forces, 49, 174–80, 367*n*97; tied houses, 282–86, 288–89, 293; Totten's report (1874), 43–44, 54; women, 175–80, 182–83. *See also* Globe (Toronto newspaper); Toronto, Starr Commission (1907)

Toronto, Starr Commission (1907): about, 284–96; for centralized board, 291–96, 298, 300; disinterested liquor management, 289–91; patronage and partisanism, 285–89, 291–92; report, 290–96, 307; tied houses, 272, 273, 285–86, 288–89, 293

Toronto Star (newspaper), 221–23, 225, 228, 250, 252, 265–66, 268, 270–71

Toronto World (newspaper), 261, 266, 270, 285–86

Totten, Henry: on Crooks Act (1877), 89–91; on detectives, 99–100, 101; on Dunkin Act, 89–91, 119, 123; on licensing powers, 111–12; non-partisan civil service, 317, 364*n*31; on petitions to deny licenses, 106–7; reports on liquor laws, 95; resignation, 364*n*31, 369*n*14; on secrecy of procedures, 108–9; on Toronto, 43–44, 89. *See also* License Branch

towns. *See* municipal governments

trade, liquor. *See* liquor industry

trade and commerce. *See* BNA Act, trade and commerce powers of dominion, s. 91(2)

Trades Benevolent Association, 101, 133–35, 152

transportation networks: commercial travellers, 277–80; committee questionnaire (1873), 35–36, 324; ships and trains, 35–36, 186, 272, 274, 276, 324; taverns, 21–22. *See also* hotels and lodging

treating system: anti-treating motion, 300–4, 370*n*27; under Crooks Act, 91, 94, 250–51; liberal state, 242, 304, 313; newspapers on, 301–3, 370*n*27; as problematic, 232–33, 242, 250–51, 300–1; RCLT review, 201

United Kingdom: about, 12, 13–14, 227–29; Beer Act (1830), 13–14, 25; breweries and vendors, 13–14, 22, 283; depoliticizing of civil service, 317; disinterested liquor management, 251–52; Gothenburg system, 252–53, 289–90; Great War, 306; grocers' licenses, 175–78, 182; inns, 14, 22; liberalism, 12–14, 226–28; licensed victuallers' associations, 51; majority votes, 275; J.S. Mill on, 7–8, 12, 227–28; political spectrum, 12, 13–14, 26; public house trust, 251–52, 254, 289–90, 297–98, 371*n*53; referendums and plebiscites, 194, 249, 275; temperance movement, 12, 120, 175–76, 306, 371*n*53; women, 175–78. *See also* Grey, Earl; Judicial Committee of the Privy Council (JCPC)

United States: about, 12–13; anti-treating laws, 302; asylums, 28; disinterested liquor management, 231, 249–50, 252, 290; J.S. Mill on, 7–8; plebiscites, 194; prohibition, 13, 203, 243–44, 314; South Carolina Dispensary, 231, 249–50, 290; temperance movement, 13, 120–21, 123

Urquhart, Thomas, 252

Victoria County, 160(f)

victuallers, 51. *See also* licensed victuallers' associations

Vidal, Alexander, 124–26, 129, 133–34, 166–67

villages. *See* municipal governments

voting. *See* elections

Walker, Franklin, 205

Waterloo County, 38, 42, 160(f), 302

Watson, E.P., 40, 43

Watson, William, 195, 355*n*82

WCTU (Woman's Christian Temperance Union), 120–21, 123, 229, 235, 241, 254

Weber, Max, 317
Welland County, 83, 126–27, 160(f), 173
Wellington County, 86–87, 93–94, 160(f)
Wentworth County, 160(f)
Wets: about, xiii, 7, 233, 314–15; bipartisan support, 315–16; for grocers' licenses, 179–81; liberal state, xiii, 7–8, 181, 233, 314–15; political spectrum, 26; RCLT reports, 209–10; terminology, xiii. *See also* breweries; liberalism and the state; liquor industry; moderates
Whig (Kingston newspaper), 148–49, 151, 153, 154–56
Whitney, James (Conservative Premier of Ontario, 1905–14): about, 16, 255–58, 293–94, 307–8; anti-treating motion, 300–4; by-elections (1912), 302–3; cartoons, 258–61, 259(f), 260(f); vs centralized system, 298–301, 305; death, 305, 315; elections (1902, 1905), 248, 255–56, 261, 299; elections (1908, 1911, 1914), 299, 304; for enforcement, 102–3, 258, 294, 296, 300, 307, 316; Garrow Resolution, 263–64, 268, 317, 365n43; for high license fees, 258, 272–74, 273(t); liberal state, 254, 258, 263, 293–95, 304, 307; moderate, 272–75, 293–96, 307; newspapers on, 258–61, 259(f), 260(f), 261, 265–66; as opposition leader, 240, 246; partisanism, 258, 261–71, 286, 307, 365n46; patronage, 257–71, 259(f), 260(f), 287–88, 291–93; personal qualities, 257, 272, 293; professionalism, 261, 263–67, 291–92; vs prohibition, 247–48, 254–56, 258, 295, 300, 303–4; Starr recommendations, 291–96. *See also* Hanna, William; Liquor License Amendment Act (1906); Toronto, Starr Commission (1907)
Williams, Edward, 215–16
Willison, John, 66–67, 98, 211, 216, 317–18, 339n75
Wilson, Catharine Anne, 9, 328n23
Wilson, R.J., 284–85, 287–88, 292
Windsor, 105, 194, 200, 365n46, 369n14, 370n27
Windsor Record (newspaper), 261, 269, 271, 301–3, 370n27
wineries, 51, 158, 335n22. *See also* beer and wine
Woman's Christian Temperance Union (WCTU), 120–21, 123, 229, 235, 241, 254
women: cult of true womanhood, 177, 353n15; drunkenness, 174–80; secret drinking, 176–79, 183; shops and liquor, 53, 174–80, 182–83; temperance movement, 120–21, 123, 235; voters on plebiscite (1894), 193; WCTU, 120–21, 123, 229, 235, 241, 254
Wood, Edmund Burke, 28
Wood, S.C., 56, 60, 77, 78–79, 89, 104, 106, 342n36, 342n37
Woodstock, 105, 191, 198–99, 201, 204–5, 207–8
World War I. *See* Great War

York, James, 261–62
York County, 83–84, 88, 93, 95, 160(f), 269–70
Yorkville, 63, 122, 131, 141–43
Youmans, Letitia, 120–21, 123
Young, James, 168
youth. *See* children and youth

Printed and bound in Canada by Friesens
Set in in Garamond by Apex CoVantage, LLC
Copy editor: Dallas Harrison
Proofreader: Kristy Lynn Hankewitz
Indexer: Judy Dunlop
Cover designer: Michel Vrana
Cover image: Library and Archives Canada, 1977-015 NPC, box 3604, item 3193884